The
WATCHERS

Books by Raymond E. Fowler

UFOs: Interplanetary Visitors
The Andreasson Affair
Casebook of a UFO Investigator
The Melchizedek Connection [A Novel]
The Andreasson Affair, Phase Two

The
WATCHERS

The Secret Design Behind UFO Abduction

Raymond E. Fowler

FOREWORD BY WHITLEY STRIEBER
(AUTHOR OF *COMMUNION*)

BANTAM BOOKS
NEW YORK • TORONTO • LONDON • SYDNEY • AUCKLAND

THE WATCHERS
A Bantam Book / July 1990

Library of Congress Cataloging-in-Publication Data
Fowler, Raymond E., 1933–
  The watchers : the secret design behind UFO abduction / Raymond E.
Fowler ; foreword by Whitley Strieber.
    p.   cm.
  Includes bibliographical references.
  ISBN 0-553-05782-0
  1. Unidentified flying objects—Sightings and encounters.
2. Luca, Betty A. (Betty Andreasson), 1937–   .   I. Title.
TL789.3.F683   1990
001.9'42—dc20   90–140
                                                                              CIP

PRINTED IN THE UNITED STATES OF AMERICA

DH   0 9 8 7 6 5 4 3 2 1

D e d i c a t i o n

With love I dedicate this book to my husband, Bob Luca. I can trust in his constant support no matter how strange, how bizarre, the recovered reality of my UFO experiences appear to be. Bob is always there for me.

Thank you, honey, for being you.

Betty Luca

Contents

Foreword ix
Acknowledgments xiv
Introduction xv
Prologue xvii

Chapter One   Recapitulation 1
Chapter Two   The Face 16
Chapter Three   Alien Housecall 35
Chapter Four   Secret Rendezvous 57
Chapter Five   Scientific Miracles 69
Chapter Six   Visit to the Nursery 86
Chapter Seven   Return from Oz 110
Chapter Eight   Portents of Tragedy 126
Chapter Nine   UFOs and OBEs 141
Chapter Ten   *The Watchers* 192
Chapter Eleven   Anatomy of a Phenomenon 221
Chapter Twelve   Branded 240
Chapter Thirteen The Family Closet 272
Chapter Fourteen Rekindled Memories 286
Chapter Fifteen   Forbidden Fruit 300
Chapter Sixteen   The Message 327
Epilogue   Final Comments 351
Appendix A   Chronological Summary of
                    Known Encounters 358

Appendix B   The Latent Encounter Experience 364
Appendix C   A Letter to Betty 371

Selected Bibliography 375
Index 379

Photographs 217

Foreword

BY WHITLEY STRIEBER

This is certainly one of the most remarkable books ever written about the enigmatic experience that has been variously described as alien abduction or, more simply, the visitor experience.

Raymond Fowler has been a UFO investigator for twenty-five years. He is the recipient of the 1986 award for Outstanding Work in the UFO Field from the Mutual UFO Network. He has been working with Betty Andreasson Luca, the subject of this book, for eleven years.

During this time Ray has maintained the highest standards of research and reporting. Unlike too many UFO investigators, who systematically distort the reports of witnesses to fit an easily believed but only partially accurate model of the experience, Ray has had the courage to recount Betty's testimony without any censorship. He has not edited her narrative on behalf of false credibility.

The result is a book that accurately reflects the actual strangeness of this amazing phenomenon. As such, it will undoubtedly draw criticism from investigators eager to sell the public and the scientific community on the notion that more or less understandable aliens are here doing things that we can to a degree comprehend.

In *The Watchers* Ray Fowler offers a truly innovative and

startling theory about the possible hidden purpose of the visitors. It is one that I sense is in the direction of the truth. Certainly it is supported not only by Betty's testimony but also by the reports of other witnesses and—more importantly—by the overall structure of what has so far been ascertained from those reports.

It is far more compelling, far stranger, and much more subtle than the popular scenario of alien abduction that is becoming a sort of orthodoxy among UFO investigators. But it also fits more of the probable facts than that or any other scenario. If one grants that the visitors are real and in the end a part of the physical universe, then Ray Fowler may have come very close to discovering what they are doing.

From the beginning Ray has allowed Betty to lead him. Instead of rejecting the stranger aspects of her experience and hypnotizing—in effect, brainwashing—her into believing that she has been a victim of the typical abduction scenario, he has *listened* to her with an open mind.

And so we have the delicious and astonishing mystery that is *The Watchers,* probably the most accurately described case of apparent alien encounter that has ever been published. Instead of damaging the case for the presence of a nonhuman intelligence among us, it paradoxically strengthens it.

If aliens are actually here, we can expect them to be extremely strange—quite literally stranger than anything we can possibly imagine. Betty's testimony certainly suggests this.

It would be easy to dismiss her narrative as the product of a wildly overheated imagination. But there are enormous problems with this facile response.

First, Betty's initial experience began in the evening when she and everybody else in her family were wide awake. Her father was the first to see the beings who arrived at the Andreasson home. He watched them walk past the kitchen window and enter the house—by passing right through a closed door as if it was made of air! Thus the high-level strangeness began not with Betty but with one of the other witnesses.

During an early hypnosis session Betty repeated some words in an unknown language. She was apparently hearing them inside her head as she spoke, almost as if she was listening to a radio. For some years these words went untranslated until researcher Leonard Keane discovered that they were Gaelic. Why "aliens" would be speaking Gaelic simply added another mystery to the tangle. It is appropriate that this fantastic discovery also emerged from Betty

Andreasson's testimony. The translation itself argues in favor of an origin outside of Betty's mind. "Children of the northern peoples, you wander in impenetrable darkness. Your mother mourns." Even if she knew Gaelic, which she does not, or had picked it up as a result of the mysterious psychological process known as xenoglossy, surely the translation of her words would have been somehow comprehensible, a hidden message, a trenchant prediction, a warning—something that was somehow relevant to Betty's own concerns and life experience.

Instead the message is full of unknown implications and suggestions that subtly support the testimony of other witnesses. My own experience, as I have mentioned in both *Communion* and *Transformation,* seems to involve an immensely powerful female figure. Certainly it is full of symbolic imagery that relates to ancient feminine dieties and feminine mythology. And here, hidden in Betty's recollections is another mysterious reference to a powerful female presence: "your mother mourns."

All of these things lead to an obvious conclusion: nobody—least of all mentally rigid UFO investigators—has as yet understood the origin of the visitors.

Beyond the presence of witnesses in the initial phases of her experience and the almost inexplicable nature of some of Betty's testimony there is a second issue, which is the matter of imagination itself. As a professional writer, I am very familiar with the workings of the human imagination. If Betty has imagined what she has reported she has more than a strong imagination, she has an imagination of historic importance—certainly one of the strongest imaginations that has ever emerged from the human species.

I would argue that much of her strangest testimony simply cannot have been imagined because it does not come in any way from the background of human experience. Instead, her observations appear to be rich memories of another world, a world so fundamentally different from our own that it bears almost no relationship to it at all. And yet there is deep sense to it. It has, if you will, semantic coherence.

But whose semantics? Certainly not ours. This approaches the third reason that I feel that Betty's experience is quite genuine. There is within it a hidden undertone of relationship to the experiences reported by other people who have confronted the visitors. It is not possible that these correspondences emerge out of imagination—not unless we have a group imagination—and even then it would be difficult to explain why subtle details would be consistent from experience to experience and gross descriptions would vary so much.

In the larger sense people's reports are almost infinitely varied. But practically all of them share subtle features, many of which have received only minimal publicity. A common report that has been widely publicized is that at least some of the visitors look like human neonates (fetuses) but with large, black eyes. Ray offers a reason for this that is at once remarkably strange and remarkably plausible.

People also report being physically levitated and often moving through walls or closed windows, but not in an out-of-body state. They report lapses of time and what seem to be other-worldly journeys. A little known fact is that they are often given white garments to wear and see other people in similar dress. Why a subtle detail like this would emerge from many different minds if it does not reflect a consistency based on real experience is very hard to know. Betty wore such a garment, as did I.

Another odd and hitherto unpublished fact is that people who have the visitor experience very often observe unmarked helicopters over their homes in the months and years afterward. Indeed, this bizarre outcome is surprisingly consistent. A fair number of these witnesses have photographed the helicopters, and they can usually be identified as unmarked versions of common types.

I once saw—in the presence of two other witnesses—two such helicopters flying low over a populated area with their rotors meshed together like eggbeaters! This was also observed from another part of the same town by another independent witness, who has had the visitor experience as well. Betty is among those who have photographed the helicopters that have buzzed her house.

People are frequently given disturbing information that appears to suggest catastrophe on a global scale. They also view events of a highly symbolized or mythological nature. Betty's testimony is the most richly symbolic that has ever been reported.

This combination of physical event and psychological content makes it seem as if the visitor experience is something that is external to the body and yet somehow internal to the mind *at the same time*!

It could be that this apparent paradox will be resolved when we better understand the human mind. It could also be that it is an intentional subterfuge, designed by somebody who is trying to keep what is essentially a public act secret.

Using techniques such as drugs, hypnosis, and intimidation it is surprisingly easy to cause profound distortions of human perception. During the Korean War Chinese experts could brainwash some G.I.s into believing that their Red Army interrogators were U.S. officers. But, because the underlying reality was that an interrogation was taking place, they could not brainwash them into believing, say, that they were not talking at all. So although the visitors can confuse us as to the origin of our experiences, they cannot altogether erase the fact that something is happening.

It is clear that one outcome of the visitor experience is distortion of perceptions. Beyond possible intentional distortion being imposed by the visitors themselves, there are also the distortions caused by fear, and—above all—our inability to clearly describe things and events that we do not understand. The mind strives to categorize experience, and when it cannot comprehend what it has observed, it tends to distort—especially if fear is present.

I suspect that Betty Andreasson Luca is unique in one critical and immensely valuable respect: she probably distorts less than almost any other witness who has come forward, myself included. And Ray Fowler is open-minded enough to take her reports at face value.

Why would she alone produce such rich and untainted reports from a world that has remained a confused mélange even for the few well-educated observers who have entered it? The reason, I feel, is her faith. She has a deep and exceptionally beautiful Christian faith. It is far more pure than the twisted remnant that passes for modern fundamentalism. Betty's faith is the real thing: kind, open, full of passionate love for Christ and His word. Her faith is such that I believe it sustains her even when her ego is drastically challenged. The result is that she is able to remember her experiences with almost the same accuracy that would be available to somebody who actually understood what was being observed and could see without fear.

Her faith is so deep that it does not need to impose itself on her experiences in order to survive. Betty's love of Christ and her belief in Him will survive *anything*, and she knows it. Thus she can see anything, do anything, go anywhere in full certainty that her faith will remain unshaken. She does not need to recast her experience in the terminology of her beliefs: her beliefs are too strong to require such support.

Thus she becomes the observer par excellence. Because of the invincibility of her faith, she can face anything—no matter how strange. And she can feel comfortable in reporting it correctly.

This is probably why her account is so surpassingly strange. And why Ray Fowler has been able to use it to approach what I suspect is the truth behind the whole visitor experience: That we are witness to something incredible and rare and grand. We are beginning to see behind the curtain of illusion that has for so long obscured our consciousness. Back in that dark place we are finding life and movement. Maybe we are seeing into God's very workshop. If so then his engineers appear to be engaged in a glorious creative act that has to do with us.

Or perhaps it is in that workshop what we are creating ourselves.

—Whitley Strieber

Acknowledgments

Anthony O. Constantino, Betty and Bob Luca, Fred Max, and David Webb for their direct participation in the preparation of certain segments of *The Watchers*.

Walter H. Andrus, Jr., Barry J. Greenwood, Richard M. Neal, Jr., M.D., Joseph Nyman, and Dr. Michael D. Swords for providing significant data.

Dr. Russell R. Camp, Professor of Biology, Gordon College, for his critique and helpful comments relating to biological aspects in this book.

Ann Druffel, John G. Fuller, Budd Hopkins, John Keel, D. Scott Rogo, Jacques Vallee, and other researchers whose past efforts provided inspiration and material for this book.

Special acknowledgments to Whitley Strieber for his kindness in providing the Foreward and to my dear wife, Margaret, who has lovingly tolerated my addiction to UFO research *for better or for worse!*

Introduction

This book is the third in a series that documents the reported UFO experiences of Betty [Andreasson] and Bob Luca. The very nature of its subject matter addresses the paradox surrounding the paraphysical nature of UFOs head-on.

The accounts recorded within the following pages must be placed in the category of ultrahigh strangeness. For the most part, they were extracted through a new series of hypnotic regression sessions. In order to facilitate a smooth presentation of this sometimes bizarre material, I elected to tentatively take it all at full face value. This has given me more freedom to provide some imaginative speculation along the way. I will save personal reaction and comment for the Epilogue.

In *The Watchers,* I will move from being an independent *observer* to that of a *participant* in the UFO abduction phenomena. Personal hypnosis sessions confirm youthful memories of encounters jolted from my mind when first confronted with Betty's childhood UFO experiences. UFO-related events that have occurred within my family will be discussed. They will reveal a pattern only just being discovered by UFO abduction researchers.

Not too many years ago, I would have placed a book like this in a section of my library reserved for the lunatic/hoaxter fringe of ufology. Back then, I watched in dismay as a number of respected UFO researchers moved from a *physical* to a *parapsychological* interpretation of the bizarre UFO phenomenon. Little did I know that my own views would also slowly but surely be honed to accommodate ever deeper levels of the psychic component found in the UFO experience. This process began in earnest when I first became intimately involved with the UFO abduction experience that has become known as *The Andreasson Affair.*

During the Phase One and Two investigations of this classic abduction case, the alien entities reportedly began to release segments of a *Message* to mankind. Heretofore, much of their so-called message had been purposely locked up within the hidden recesses of Betty's mind. Other abductees also had some aspects of their message hidden in their minds. The aliens allegedly have programmed it to be released over a period of time like the contents of a timed-release medical capsule. This Phase Three investigation contains the culmination of the Message. Its bittersweet contents graphically reveal the identity, purpose, and motivation behind UFO visitation. They are far beyond anything that any of us could ever have conceived. I present—*The Watchers*!

Prologue

In order to better set the stage for those who are reading about the subject of UFO abductions for the very first time, some orientation about this bizarre facet of the overall UFO phenomenon is in order. Several questions should be briefly addressed and answered right up front.

What is a UFO abduction experience? What is hypnosis and why does it play an important part in the investigation of abduction cases? What are the major proposed alternative hypotheses to actual real-time abductions of humans by alien beings.

Abductions

Researchers are encountering an ever-increasing number of sane and credible witnesses who claim not only to have observed but to have been taken aboard a UFO by alien creatures.

In most instances, the alleged abductee claims to have been examined and operated upon with foreign instruments. Almost always, communication with the aliens is accomplished by telepathy.

Some abductees believe that their very thoughts and memories have been somehow tapped and recorded by alien machines. Others report even more bizarre experiences, such as those recorded in this book. Unbelievable as these may first appear to researcher and layperson alike, such reported happenings provide what finally seems to be the definitive answer to the long-standing UFO problem.

Most, but certainly not all, UFO abduction experiences must be retrieved through the use of hypnosis. This is because a typical abduction scenario involves an alien-induced amnesia. Usually, the witness only remembers a close confrontation with a UFO and/or its alien occupants. Following this experience is a coincidental period of unaccountable missing time.

Hypnotic regression of the witness to relive this type of UFO experience often is successful in breaking through this amnesiac barrier. Under hypnosis, the witness remembers and relives an abduction experience. Since hypnosis is necessary to retrieve an abduction event in 70 percent of these cases, it would be helpful before proceeding further to say a few introductory words about this technique.

Hypnosis

Statements concerning hypnosis from equally well-qualified professionals range from "hypnosis does not exist" to "hypnosis can provide total recall of past events without error." The answer, in my opinion, lies somewhere between these two extremes. The late Dr. Benjamin Simon, psychiatrist and a leading expert in hypnotic regression, has stated that:

> Under hypnosis, experiences buried in amnesia may be recalled in much shorter time than in the normal course of psychotherapeutic process.[1]

He stressed that hypnosis was not a magical road to truth but that:

> Hypnosis is a pathway to truth as it is felt and understood by the . . . percipient. . . . This may or may not be consonant with the ultimate truth. *Most frequently it is.* [italics mine][2]

A growing number of law enforcement agencies use hypnosis as one of the many tools available to help solve crimes. It is usually used when a witness has difficulty recalling exactly what he or she saw at the scene of a given crime. It is especially useful in cases of rape and attack in public places where the experience might be too painful to recall consciously.

David Cohen, writing in *New Scientist,* states that the Israeli police have been using hypnosis on a regular basis since 1973. Dr. Eitan Elat, head of the Israeli Police Scientific Research Unit has claimed that in about 70 percent of cases, hypnosis helped witnesses recall details of crimes that led to conviction.

Opponents of hypnosis would argue that it is also possible for hypnotized persons to be easily influenced by leading questions or unconscious clues given by the hypnotist which, in turn, may lead to false answers given to please the questioner. This, of course, could be true in some cases. But it is also true of nonhypnotic intensive cross-examinations. In either case, such exceptions do not negate the fact that hypnotic regression can and does reveal true past experiences when performed carefully by a skilled hypnotist. This is especially true of excellent hypnotic subjects who not only recall but *relive* past experiences in excruciating detail with emotion in the first person.

It is possible that a person could lie under hypnosis, although professional hypnotists have methods that enable them to discern this. But it is also possible for a person to lie during nonhypnotic cross-examination. Again, these possibilities do not negate all results obtained under hypnosis. In either case, it really depends upon the morals and honesty of the subject. An honest person seeking only the truth would not willfully lie under hypnosis.

I now can finally describe hypnosis from the viewpoint of a subject. Since my staunch Christian ethics preclude willful lying, I had no desire to lie while under hypnosis. In fact, I found myself exceptionally careful to be painstakingly accurate in everything that I said. I also noticed on a number of occasions during *The Andreasson Affair* hypnosis sessions that both Betty and Bob would correct the hypnotist if he intentionally [as a test] or inadvertently misquoted their statements or descriptions.

During hypnosis, I found myself back in time *reliving* my childhood experiences. I *felt* the overwhelming emotions, the literally overpowering mental blocks and the stark-naked fear of whatever some of these memories represent in reality. Memory flashbacks have taken place during the posthypnotic periods. I definitely felt that hypnosis put both my body and mind in a highly relaxed state. It increased my powers of concentration, so that my conscious mind could retrieve memories and emotions held in the library of my subconscious.

In conclusion, I believe that the accuracy of memories hypnotically retrieved by a skilled hypnotist is directly related to the psychological makeup of the subject. Dr. Mark Rhine, a professor of psychiatry at the University of Colorado Medical Center, was on the staff of the University's Air Force-sponsored UFO Study. He correctly assesses the situation when he writes in the Study's final report that:

Hypnosis can aid in bringing to conscious awareness material that has been repressed. But persons who cannot distinguish their fantasies from reality will under hypnosis only reveal more of the same fantasies.[3]

If the subject is of sound mind, is a good hypnosis subject, and has a strong moral character, then I believe that hypnosis will most likely be successful in retrieving true and accurate memories.

Ideally the hypnotist should be a psychiatrist or psychologist with clinical experience so as to better assure the subject's health and well-being. However, trained hypnosis technicians are employed regularly to perform highly successful uses of hypnosis for habit control, time regression, and anesthesia. Hypnosis and its results should be taken very seriously when the conditions are correct.

Alternative Hypotheses

Critics have suggested a number of explanations for the abduction phenomena other than extraterrestrial visitation. Familiarity with the major alternative hypotheses will help the reader better assess the reality of this phenomenon.

Imaginary Abductions

Advocates of this theory preselected individuals who were generally unaware of the content of UFO abduction reports for their investigations. These individuals were then hypnotized and asked to describe their being abducted by a UFO. Each one of them described an imaginary abduction. While there were some parallels between these imaginary abductions and alleged real abduction accounts, there were significant differences. Unlike alleged real abductees, the imaginary abductees:

1. were told to imagine their abduction.
2. usually controlled their emotions and merely described their fantasy.
3. displayed no physiological effects or reactions.
4. had no conscious recall of a real UFO sighting followed by amnesia.
5. did not describe the typical aliens reported by real alleged abductees.
6. did not believe that their experiences were real.

I am of the opinion that if one preselected the same individuals and asked them to sit back and imagine being abducted by a UFO *without hypnosis,* similar results might be obtained.

Fantasy-Prone Personality

This hypothesis suggests that UFO abductees must belong to that 4 percent of the population who have been classified as *fantasy-prone personalities.* Such persons, usually from childhood, have secretly indulged in a parallel fantasy life. Such a personality might be the catalyst for vivid dreams. Living in a make-believe world, believing in fairies, having imaginary companions, seeing apparitions, and believing oneself to possess occult powers are all characteristics of this type of personality. Outwardly, these people appear to be socially aware, normal healthy individuals.

There is no doubt, as Dr. Rhine has just stated, that such people could easily fantasize, report, and relive a UFO abduction experience under hypnosis. They would really believe that such an event occurred and could easily pass a lie detector test!

I have met several people who could fall into this category during my long years of UFO investigation. However, such persons, *if undetected* by UFO researchers, would not prove that all of the hundreds of abductee reports originate from fantasy-prone personalities. It is a bit much to state categorically that all abductees fall into this small percentage of our population. Indeed many abductees, including Betty, have been psychologically screened by competent professionals and have taken psychological profile tests which do not reveal fantasy-prone personalities. Dr. Leo Sprinkle, director of counseling and testing and professor of counseling at the University of Wyoming, has subjected well over two hundred abductees to a number of psychological tests. Most of these individuals were American adults and their scores reflected that they fell into the overall personality norm for American adults. In particular, and relevant to their reported experiences, Dr. Sprinkle stated that the test results did not support the hypothesis that abductees are persons who are "experiencing neurotic or psychotic reactions."

The psychological tests employed by Dr. Sprinkle include the *Minnesota Multiphasic Personality Inventory, Sixteen Personality Factors Test, Adjective Checklist, Strong-Campbell Inventory,* and the *Strong Vocational Interest Blank.* The results of these tests were independently refereed by other professionals.

Psychosis

This hypothesis is similar to the fantasy-prone personality hypothesis. Advocates would assert that UFO abductees are persons who are experiencing neurotic or psychotic reactions. The same arguments applied to the fantasy-prone hypothesis are also applicable to this position. Psychologists and psychiatrists who have tested a number of alleged abductees would be quick to say that the results of psychological testing do not support this theory.

Birth Trauma

Adherents of this hypothesis would suggest that hypnosis awakens the subjects' subconscious traumatic memories of their births. Abductee accounts of tunnels, womb-shaped rooms, cervix-like doors, bright lights and of being probed by aliens with instruments all would correspond to the birth experience of a fetus. The fetus moves through the birth canal [tunnel] into a bright room [hospital] containing strange creatures [doctors and nurses] who prod and poke with instruments. This hypothesis also attempts to account for the fetus-like appearance of reported alien beings!

One of the chief proponents of the *birth trauma* hypothesis postulates that abductees, such as Betty, have described aliens with fetal characteristics because of hypnotically induced birth imagery. A number of objections can be leveled against such a possibility. Many nonabductee witnesses have consciously seen and reported fetus-like creatures in association with a UFO. Many abductees remember part or all of their experience without the aid of hypnosis. Two studies reveal that between 29 and 33 percent of 232 cases involved abductee recall of their experiences *without hypnosis*. I might also add that abductees who were born via caesarian operations would not experience the alleged imagery associated with normal births. Most embryologists would totally discount the theory that a fetus would have the ability to see its own image.

The Collective Unconscious

Noted psychiatrist and analyst Carl Gustav Jung pioneered the idea of a *collective unconscious* that somehow links all of mankind since time immemorial. Jung, although not denying the extraterrestrial origin of some UFOs, also theorized that they might have a psychological origin. He suggested that UFOs are archetypal images shared by us all. Some UFOs, according to Jung, are psychic projections that enable mankind to bring wholeness and serenity to a fragmented and violent world.

Those who hold to this hypothesis would also include other concepts detailed within UFO abduction accounts as being generated by the collective unconscious. These would include the shape of UFOs, tunnel imagery, and OBEs (out-of-body experiences). Adherents of this view would state that such a collective unconscious explains the similarity between modern UFO abductions and the abduction motif found in man's folklore, which tells of dwarf-like entities with supernatural powers who kidnap human beings, who need human assistance in giving birth, who are interested in genetics, and who can control time.

Jungian theorists would dismiss much of the UFO phenomenon and its abduction subset as nothing more than a new mythology instigated by the collective unconscious. However, Jung himself admitted that he would be hard pressed to place radar-visual, physical trace, and photographic cases in this category. Nonetheless, some Jungian extremists would insist that the powers of the collective mind could produce such physical effects including the *scars* found on abductees! This, of course, cannot be demonstrated scientifically. Somehow I find it hard to believe that the major governments of the world have been spending much time, energy, and money to investigate mental projections from our theorized collective unconscious.

Hoaxters

There will always be those who attempt, sometimes quite successfully, to perpetrate a hoax when it comes to UFOs. Some do it for notoriety. Others do it to fulfill some deep psychological need. A few hoaxes are merely an intended joke that somehow get out of control. Surprisingly enough, statistics compiled by military and civilian researchers alike indicate that genuine hoaxes comprise only a small percentage of any kind of UFO reports.

All of the alternative hypotheses that have been offered fall far short of explaining all UFO abduction experiences. In most cases, such hypotheses represent genuine attempts to account for reported experiences that most would rather not acknowledge as being grounded in reality. Sometimes those who offer such explanations have no real depth of knowledge of the UFO phenomenon at all. Some might be reflecting an underlying denial reaction to the strangeness and implications offered by such abductions. I am probably safe in asserting that the majority of those who offer such explanations have already prejudged the reality of UFO abductions. Their starting point would be that this could not possibly be happening. They would then proceed to build their hypothesis around their prejudiced proposition. I say this because sometimes some extremely irrational explanations are offered to make certain aspects of abduction reports fit a given hypothesis.

It is noteworthy to mention that at the 1987 meeting of the American Psychological Association in New York, participants agreed that a detailed study of alleged UFO abductees revealed them to be *normal* people from all walks of life. It was concluded that their experiences could not be accounted for strictly on the basis of psychopathology. Thus, what we end up with are both professional and nonprofessional *normal* people, cutting across the total social strata, who really believe that they have been abducted by aliens from a UFO. Their stories bear striking similarities. Many have identical scars in the same location on their bodies. In some cases the scars correspond to recalled memories of being probed in these locations by alien instruments. The scars, unlike pyschosomatically produced stigmata, etc., do not disappear. They are *real,* permanent scars. Real flesh has been removed from those scars categorized as *scoops*. In some cases there are physical traces left behind by the UFO itself. Such traces are identical to those traces left behind after well-witnessed UFO physical-trace cases that do not involve abductions. Significantly, as mentioned, about a third of UFO abductees are able to remember their experience without the aid of hypnosis. Their experiences tally with those experiences retrieved by hypnosis.

Do these and other strikingly parallel aspects of UFO abduction experiences constitute *proof* of their physical reality? No. They do, however, provide extremely strong *evidence* that such abductions are really happening whether or not people like you and I want to believe it. Belief or disbelief in the validity of such evidence, contrary to the reactions of some, does not negate the evidence itself. If we were dealing with something down to earth and more mundane, most would probably have no problem in accepting its reality based on such evidence. But we are not. We are being confronted by a phenomenon that runs diametrically counter to our mind-set. Regardless of the many alternative hypotheses offered to account for UFO abduction experiences, *actual* UFO abductions best account for what is being reported *if* we take the evidence at full face value. In the following pages you will be examining the most classic abduction case in UFO history. Weigh the experiences of Betty Andreasson Luca against the alternatives to a real-time physical abduction by aliens. You be the judge.

Prologue—Notes

1. John. G. Fuller, *The Interrupted Journey* (New York: Dial Press, 1966), pp. x, xi.

2. *Ibid.*, xi.

3. E.U. Condon, director, *Scientific Study of Unidentified Flying Objects* (New York: E.P. Dutton & Co., Inc., 1969), p. 596.

Recapitulation

A number of years have passed since the publication of *The Andreasson Affair—Phase Two* in 1982. This book was the incredible sequel to an equally incredible book that was entitled *The Andreasson Affair* which was originally published in 1979 and reprinted in 1988. Both books are based upon years of inquiry by a team of competent researchers.

The Phase Two investigation had ended abruptly when UFO abductee Betty Luca (formerly Betty Andreasson) suffered a painful mental block during a hypnotic regression session. This occurred when the hypnotist, behavioral psychologist Fred Max, attempted to regress her to a UFO event she apparently had experienced sometime in the early 1970s. The dreadful pain so unnerved Betty that she refused further hypnosis. For all intents and purposes, *The Andreasson Affair*, a classic UFO abduction case, had come to an untimely end. This was a bitter disappointment to researchers and readers alike. So many questions remained unanswered—questions that the aliens had said would be answered through Betty. Why had further probing of Betty's liaison with the aliens been prevented?

From time to time my mind has drifted back to that last Phase Two hypnosis session. Fred Max's gentle yet firm voice had filled the silent room of expectant investigators.

Fred Max Just relax, deeper, deeper, deeper. I want you to go to your *next encounter*. I will count from one to three. One, two, three . . .

Everyone watched and listened with bated breath. Thus far, hypnosis had unveiled six separate encounters with aliens from Betty's mind. These spanned the thirty-three years between 1944 and 1967 at ages 7, 12, 13, 18, 24, and 30. All of us wondered whether or not she had experienced further UFO encounters after her abduction in 1967. Only part of the answer was forthcoming at that time.

> *Fred Max* Where are you?
>
> *Betty* I'm in my bedroom. Ooooooh! [*Betty's face suddenly grimaced with pain*]
>
> *Fred Max* Where's the bedroom? Where do you live?
>
> *Betty* Ashburnham.

Suddenly, Betty became extremely agitated. She seemed to be in great pain. Fred immediately responded to this surprising situation and tried to relieve her.

> *Fred Max* I want you now to relax.
>
> *Betty* Ohhhhh. Ooooooh!
>
> *Fred Max* Just relax, deeper, deeper, deeper . . . What's the matter?
>
> *Betty* I can't go anyplace.
>
> *Fred Max* Okay. Why can't you?
>
> *Betty* Because . . . Oh my hands! Oooh, oh, oh!

After unsuccessful attempts to ease Betty's discomfort, it became apparent that this was as far as we were being allowed to go. It seemed that Betty had been programmed by the aliens to experience pain when Fred attempted to retrieve information that was not ready to be released.

Apparently, the alien race that is interested in our planet and its life forms has its own timetable to release information to humanity as part of a long-term conditioning process. It was not the correct time to release certain information then but *it is time now*. The painful mental block has been released! How did this come to be? What has been happening to Betty and her family during the years that followed the termination of the Phase Two investigation?

The answers to these questions are the basis for this book. Utterly amazing events have occurred, events that are of great significance to the survival of the human race. But first, for the benefit of those readers who are unfamiliar with *The Andreasson Affair*, a recapitulation of Betty's life and her UFO experiences are in order. Such a synopsis will also provide those who have read my books on this case with a concise review of the events leading up to the new UFO experiences recently unearthed during my continued study of this thought-provoking case. First, a biographical sketch of Betty .

Betty was born on January 7, 1937, at Fitchburg, Massachusetts to Waino and Eva Aho. Betty's father had immigrated from Finland as a young child. His parents, like so many others, sought a better opportunity in the United States. They managed to buy and operate a dairy farm in Massachusetts. Waino met his future wife, a native New Englander, during a stint in the army. Betty Aho was the second to youngest of five offspring.

Betty was brought up in a devout Christian home, a condition that would greatly influence her adult worldview of reality. She was both tomboy and nature lover and spent hours exploring the woods, fields, brooks, and ponds that surrounded several different childhood homes in rural Massachusetts. Her next homes were the adjoining towns of Leominster and Westminster, Massachusetts. At Westminster, she met and married James Andreasson, the boy next door. The newlyweds bought and renovated a small rundown house in South Ashburnham, a small town in northern Massachusetts. It was here that Betty would raise a large family and seek to instill her strong Christian beliefs and ideals within them. Sadly, this was done against a tragic backdrop of marital difficulties. It was also at South Ashburnham that Betty would experience her apparent first UFO abduction which has become widely known as *The Andreasson Affair*.

The encounter took place on the evening of January 25, 1967. Betty was in the kitchen. Her parents and seven children, whose ages ranged between 3 and 11, were in the living room watching television. Betty's husband was in a local hospital recovering from an automobile accident.

At about 6:35 P.M., the house lights began blinking on and off and then went out. A pulsating reddish-orange light shined through the kitchen and pantry window that faced a huge field located to the rear of the house. Betty made her children and mother stay in the living room while her father went to the pantry window to see what was causing the eerie pulsating light. Waino Aho saw more than he had bargained for. The light came from the side of a little hill in the back of the house that led to the field. Coming from that direction were a group of strange-looking humanoid creatures. In a signed statement, Mr. Aho stated:

> These creatures that I saw through the window of Betty's house were just like Halloween freaks. I thought they had put on a funny kind of headdress imitating a moon man. It was funny how they jumped one after the other—just like grasshoppers. When they saw me looking at them, they stopped . . . the one in front looked at me and I felt kind of queer. That's all I know.

The four creatures then entered the house by passing *through* the wooden door as if it were nonexistent. They were identical, except for the leader, who appeared taller. The creatures varied between three and one half to four and one half feet in height. They had gray skin, large, oversized, inverted pear-shaped heads, and their faces were mongoloid in appearance. Large, catlike, wraparound eyes stood in stark contrast to less prominent facial features: holes for noses and ears, and fixed, scarlike mouths. They wore shiny dark blue, form-fitting uniforms. Each left sleeve was adorned with an emblem that resembled a bird with outstretched wings. Their three-digited hands were gloved and they wore high shoes or boots. Very little was *consciously* remembered other than this. Betty instructed those who had seen the creatures not to talk about it. She was ignorant of UFOs and interpreted the experience as a visit by *angels*! Eight years passed before Betty reported the incident to UFO researchers.

In 1975, astronomer and Air Force UFO consultant Dr. J. Allen Hynek founded the Center for UFO Studies. He began advertising in newspapers throughout the country for UFO sighting information. His request appeared in Betty's local newspaper and her family persuaded her to write Dr. Hynek about this strange experience. The letter was finally acted upon in January of 1977 when I put together a professional team to investigate Betty's experience.

During a total of fourteen sessions, a professional hypnotist regressed Betty and her eleven-year-old daughter back to relive the weird 1967 experience. Both Betty and her daughter, Becky, relived a complementary detailed, mind-boggling UFO experience in the first person with vivid emotion and trauma.

The aliens had quickly mentally tranquilized Betty's initial fear and placed the rest of the family into a state of suspended animation. They established telepathic communication with Betty and, taking control of her will, took her outside and into a small oval craft. The craft accelerated upward and mated with a larger craft. Betty was taken inside and was subjected to the effects of strange equipment and devices both before and after a physical examination. Then she was taken through a dark tunnel which egressed into an alien place. There she experienced what seems to have been a holographic recreation of the death and rebirth of a Phoenix-like bird, the same bird that was pictured on the uniforms of the aliens. She was told that she had been chosen to show the world something important that would affect all of mankind. Then she was returned home where she found her inanimate family guarded by an alien. All of the family, under some kind of mind control, were put to bed in a state of unawareness before the aliens left the house.

During the aliens' physical examination of Betty, a long flexible needle was inserted into her nose to retrieve an object. It was the size of a BB and seemed to have tiny wires sticking out of it. We wondered how it had got there. Its presence hinted at a possible earlier encounter with the aliens. However, when the hypnotist tried to find out when it had been originally placed inside Betty, she experienced such excruciating pain and trauma that he refused to go any further.

Our investigation came to a halt when Betty moved to Florida to live with relatives. Her husband had deserted her and they later were divorced. We prepared a 528-page, three volume report for researchers. Betty and Becky had withstood a rigorous character reference check, lie detector tests, and an intensive analysis. A medical doctor declared Betty perfectly normal with no psychiatric problems. The case seemed solid. It was no hoax. The witnesses certainly believed the event had occurred and had hypnotically relived it in realistic detail. I wrote the book entitled *The Andreasson Affair*. It highlighted segments of the hypnotic regression sessions and presented an analysis of the case in laymen's terms.

I kept in constant touch with Betty over the ensuing years. I documented a large number of paranormal and odd events that plagued both Betty and her new husband, Bob Luca. She had met Bob under seemingly alien-prearranged circumstances. He too had a conscious recollection of a UFO encounter that had also occurred in 1967.

When Bob and Betty returned to New England, I quickly initiated the Phase Two investigation. Behavioral psychologist Fred

Max conducted a series of thirteen follow-up hypnotic regression sessions between March and June of 1980. The results were alarming. They bore out what other independent UFO researchers were discovering. Adult abductees had a history of UFO encounters starting from an early age.

We discovered that Bob Luca had an encounter at age five during the summer of 1944 in Meriden, Connecticut, and an abduction experience at age twenty-nine during the summer of 1967. The following is a recap of Bob's childhood experience. He was approached by a disk-shaped object with a transparent dome while on a swing at the edge of some woods. Two gray-skinned aliens with large heads communicated a message to him by telepathy from within the disk's transparent dome. During the hypnotic regression session, Bob was asked what the aliens were saying to him as he sat totally paralyzed on the seat of the now motionless swing.

> *Bob* They said first that I shouldn't be afraid. Telling something be good when I am older.
>
> *Fred Max* What would be good when you are older? What is this?
>
> *Bob* I can't say yet.
>
> *Fred Max* What else did they say to you?
>
> *Bob* They visit other people, and they're going to visit other people, too.
>
> *Fred Max* Where are these other people?
>
> *Bob* All over.
>
> *Fred Max* What do you mean, "all over"?
>
> *Bob* Like in school there is a kid from a different place. He didn't always live here. They visited people from all over, not just here.
>
> *Fred Max* Why do they need to meet other people?
>
> *Bob* Prepare us something good. Going to be for mankind. . . . In time, people in the light [UFO] will be back and the people that have seen them before will not be afraid when they come back.
>
> *Fred Max* Are you to speak of this often as you get older? So you can more or less seek other people who had similar experiences?
>
> *Bob* Forget 'till time. Forget!

The child's voice emanating from the mouth of adult Bob Luca was adamant. He had been programmed to *forget*. Fred Max tried every trick in the book to dredge out the complete message that the aliens had given Bob but to no avail. Somehow, they had induced a strong posthypnotic-like block that would only be released at a time of their own choosing.

Further hypnosis revealed that Bob's sighting of a cylindrical object releasing a descending disk-shaped object in the summer of 1967 was only the conscious tip of a UFO abduction experience. Bob was 29 years of age. He too underwent a physical examination on board a UFO. Bringing this experience to his everyday memory so terrified him that he refused further hypnosis.

Coincidentally or perhaps purposely, Betty too was found to have had her first UFO encounter with aliens in 1944. She was 7 years of age and was living at Leominster, Massachusetts. One day, while waiting inside a playhouse for her friend Didi to come and play with her, Betty was confronted with a miracle of technology. A tiny, luminous marble-sized ball flew into the playhouse and flew around her head with a soft buzzing sound. She was terrified but could not move to defend herself. Here is an excerpt from one of the Phase Two hypnosis sessions.

Fred Max What's the matter?

Betty There's something like a bee buzzing all around me. It's going round and round, but it's bright.

Fred Max Is it small?

Betty Yes! It keeps going around and it goes around my head. I think it's a bee! Ouch.

At this point Betty became terrified. Fred had to take immediate measures to calm her. The squeaky frightened voice of a little girl coming from the adult Betty Luca sent a chill through all who were present. Fred spent time conditioning Betty to step out of the event and describe the scene as if she were watching, not experiencing, it. Betty kept on slipping into reliving the experience and Fred kept on easing her back to being an observer. Finally, Betty was able to describe what was happening in a more dispassionate manner.

Betty I'm sitting there eating some crackers looking at the blue flowers outside the hut, and I'm waitin' for Didi to come over and play. And then all of a sudden I see a bumblebee or something, but it's bright light and it keeps on circling my head. Maybe it's after my crackers, so I drop the crackers. But it keeps on going round my head and then it came and it stuck there. . . . It was cold and it was making me fall backwards and I felt very sleepy.

Fred Max Okay, go on.

Betty I'm lying on the ground there and I *hear something*. There is a squiggly feeling in my head, and there is a voice speaking to me. There is a lot of them, but all talking together. . . . And they are saying something. . . . They have been watching me, and ah, I'm coming along fine. And they're talking to me and telling me that I'm making good progress . . . and they were getting things ready. . . . But it wouldn't be for awhile . . . about five years or so. . . . I would be twelve. . . . They would see me later.

The next alien encounter did occur when Betty was twelve. Her family had moved to nearby Westminster, Massachusetts. Betty was checking on a trap that she had set by a hole in the woods when she was confronted by a small alien being in a peculiar uniform. It had a number of orifices and pushbuttons on its chest area. Startled, Betty stepped back, reached for some stones and threw them at the frightening entity. What happened next scared her even more.

Betty I took some of those stones out of my pocket. I thought it was an animal coming out. I started to throw stones at it, and, ah!—The stones hit something and *stopped in midair* and just fell down! And there's a little person standing there, a strange-looking thing!

Instantly, the dwarf-sized being pressed one of the pushbuttons on its suit. A glowing marble-sized ball shot out an orifice in the suit and floated over to Betty. It attached itself to her forehead.

Betty I feel sleepy and I'm slowly falling backwards.

Betty again heard voices in her head discussing her.

Fred Max What are they discussing?

Betty Me.

Fred Max Go on.

Betty They're checking me and they're saying another year.

Fred Max Another year? What does that mean?

Betty I don't know . . . They just said, "She's got another year."

. . . They say that they are preparing things for me to see, that it may help people in the future.

When Fred later regressed Betty to relive her next UFO encounter, it turned out to be a very detailed abduction experience. We were about to find out when and how the aliens had placed the BB-sized object in Betty's head. It would not be a pleasant revelation.

In summary, Betty, age 13, got up early one morning at her home in Westminster. The rest of the family was still in bed. She decided to walk to a nearby pond. As she started out she sighted what seemed to be the moon in the sky. It soon became apparent that it was not the moon. The round object got larger and larger as it moved across the field toward Betty. She tried to run but found that she could not move. The next thing she knew she was in some kind of a room in a tranquilized state of mind that released her from the raw fear that she had just experienced. In the following excerpt from one of the Phase Two hypnosis sessions, Betty relives the beginning of her childhood abduction by alien beings.

> *Betty* . . . There's a *big huge moon* right over the top of the hill. [*Betty's voice then changes from puzzlement to stark terror.*] . . . It gets bigger and bigger! And it's coming toward me! It's like a big bubble, but it looks like the moon. And it's coming toward me and I can't move! And it's just coming closer. I can't seem to move! [*Suddenly, Betty's tense body and facial expressions relax.*] Ooooh, oooh. I'm standing in some kind of a room and it's all white and *I feel very relaxed*. And, oh! There's, there's little people coming in the room toward me, *just sliding along*. They're stopping in front of me. There is three little people standing there. And they are funny.

At this point, Betty lost her composure again as if the weird sight of the small entities jolted her back to reality. She became tense and began breathing heavily. Then she shouted.

> *Betty* If you hurt me, my father will get a hold of you!

Then, inexplicably, she again became very relaxed. It was almost as if the beings were somehow applying some type of mental control in a persistent attempt to calm her down. It would be impossible to even summarize all of the things that Betty experienced during her abduction as a teen within this short chapter. I'll try to mention what I believe to be the highlights of the experience.

The aliens placed Betty on a soft, rubbery, cushion-like mat on the floor of a section of the craft that was roofed by a large transparent dome. A mouthpiece was installed that kept her tongue held down. When describing it to us under hypnosis, she actually talked as if something were holding her tongue down. Betty began sinking into the rotating circular mat as the craft accelerated upward. Incredible as it may seem, her body actually sunk into the hypnotist's chair! The psychosomatic effects on Betty's face and voice were fantastic to behold. All present were amazed to actually see the effect of the g-forces on her face. The skin got very tight around her face and her mouth was pulled back. She experienced difficulty talking.

The craft then entered water and proceeded under water until it egressed in an underground complex. One of the bizarre things that Betty was allowed to see was what seemed to be a *museum of time* that depicted a chronological review of the different stages of mankind. The figures were lifelike and in glass-like cases. The clothes on the figures were typical of different eras. The exhibit cases also contained real-to-life habitats that corresponded to the pertinent era of each figure.

> *Betty* There's all people in these different things. There's an Indian in there.
>
> *Fred Max* What kind of scenery does the Indian have?
>
> *Betty* There's some rocks around, and there looks like some shrubs of some kind, I don't know, but it's not solid like the people are. . . . It looks like they're in the ice, and they're staying still.

Betty was subjected to the probing of many strange instruments which may have been used to examine her reproductive system. At one point she seems to have been given an object lesson that demonstrated that the aliens could create life from inanimate life forms. They told her that the object lesson was "for you to remember so mankind shall understand." Clearly, the aliens are telling us things about themselves and their relation to life on earth through Betty's experiences. This will become more clear as we attempt to consolidate their revelations later on in this book.

One of the most emotional segments of Betty's abduction experience as a teenager involved her meeting with the *One*. The aliens told her that it was now time for her to go *home* to see the *One*.

Betty We're coming up to this wall of glass and a big, big, big, big, big, *door*. It's made of glass.

Fred Max Does it have hinges?

Betty No. It is so big and there is—I can't explain it. It is door after door after door after door. He is stopping there and telling me to stop. I'm just stopping there. He says: "Now you shall enter the *door* to see the *One*."

At this point, much to Betty's amazement, she underwent an *out-of-the-body* experience!

Betty And I'm standing there and *I'm coming out of myself*! There's two of me! There's two of me there! . . . It's like a twin. But it's *still*, like those people I saw in those, those ice cubes. [i.e., the persons she saw in the glass cases that I have called *The Museum of Time*]

Betty then entered the door and moments later a rapturous, beatific expression of pure, unrestricted happiness came over her face as she apparently met the mysterious personage that the aliens referred to as the *One*. Fred tried over and over and over again to persuade Betty to tell us what she was seeing but to no avail.

Betty It's—words cannot explain it. It's wonderful. It's for everybody. I just can't tell you this.

Fred Max You can't? Okay, why can't you?

Betty For one thing, it's too overwhelming and it is . . . it is undescribable. I just can't tell you. Besides it's just impossible for me to tell you.

Fred Max Were you *told* not to share it with me?

Betty It is like even if I was able to speak it, I wouldn't be able to speak it. I can't. I'm sorry.

Betty's abduction as a teenager also had its terrifying moments. The worst of these was during one of the physical examinations. It was during Betty's reliving of this segment of her experience that we finally found out how the BB-sized object got into her head. If you recall, it was removed with a long flexible needle during her abduction as an adult in 1967 at age 30.

Betty He says now I'm ready, and he said to follow him. A door opens up from the wall. It goes up, and we're going into another bright, bright room. And in the middle of this bright room there's a box. . . . And he says that I will be getting on there. I'm floating up and lying on it and I feel like I'm stuck to it. And I see some of them coming in . . . and they're in silver clothes . . . and he's telling me to relax. They'll only be a little while and they're going to give me something and he put his hand on my forehead. And there's three of them around me, and he said to be still and that—one of them is coming by my eyes. Opening my eye. No! No!

Betty let out a loud scream. Everyone looked on helplessly and hoped that Fred would be able to calm her down.

Betty No! I don't want you to do that!

Fred Max Calm down, Betty. Just relax. I want you to imagine yourself moving apart from the situation. Move yourself out. Move yourself out. [*Betty's body begins to relax.*] Very, very good. Imagine it happening to someone else. . . . Okay? Just relax. Now, tell me what's happening to her. It's happening to her, not you.

The experience was so traumatic that Betty could not become an observer. Her voice trembled with fear and great emotion. We soon found out why. It sent shudders through us!

Betty [*screams*] They're taking my eye out!

Fred lost no time in relieving the shrieking, sobbing teenage voice from the past. He quickly eased Betty out of hypnosis and brought her back to the present. However, at the next session, he was able to slowly but surely induce Betty to describe what had happened next.

Fred Max Okay, and what did they do when your eye was out? You're all right. You made it through.

Betty They took a long, long needle. A *light* needle. . . . It was all *light* [i.e., glowing]. . . . And they had one of those tiny glass things on the end of it. They put that needle *in my head* through where they had taken my eye out and I can feel it in the back of my head. . . . Oh, there's bright colors all around every place. . . . And they are pulling out that needle light and now they're on both sides there. They got some long steel needles that they're holding toward my head. Now they've taken them away and putting them over there. And they're coming back and they're *putting my eye back in*. Ohhhh! Then I'm just lying there and they're floating me up.

One has no idea of the emotions that well up within just from listening to tape recordings of this and other traumatic segments of Betty's hypnotic reliving of her experience. I have put together an audio-visual presentation using slides of Betty's drawings coupled with pertinent recorded segments of the sessions. I've seen grown men cry when listening to her recorded account.

In any event, after Betty's eye was replaced, she was subjected to a battery of tests on strange instruments before being returned. She was set beside the pond that she had originally set out for during that fateful morning in 1950.

Fred continued his chronological probe of Betty's past UFO encounters. At age 18, in 1955, she had experienced hearing a strange voice calling while she was in her trailer home at Westminster. At age 24, in 1961, she relived a more substantial experience.

Betty was mopping the floor and happily singing hymns. Her husband was at work. Her daughter Becky was in school. The rest of her children were napping. Suddenly, she heard a weird sound outside. She felt compelled to go to it and left her children all alone as if it were the natural thing to do. She headed for nearby woods in a zombie-like state.

Fred Max Describe it. [i.e., the strange sound]

Betty I can't. I don't know what it is! I put the mop to the side and I'm going outdoors. I don't know what it is. My word! What is it? I'm just walking along and looking around. There's some kind of strange sound. . . . I feel strange like something is pulling me along. I'm walking up this hill. It's hard to get up here. There's all pine needles, and I'm slipping. I keep on walking and I'm climbing over this stone wall. I don't know why I'm doing this. I'm jumping down and walking over in the woods there and going over by the big rock. And over to the side of—Ohhhh!

Fred Max What's the matter?

Betty There's a strange *being* standing over there and I'm afraid of it. . . . It's staring at me, and *I can't move*! Oh, Jesus be with me!

The alien being communicated with Betty by telepathy and told her not to be afraid. He seemed to have a keen interest in Betty's religious beliefs.

> *Betty* He's telling me that I have been *watched* since my beginning. I shall grow naturally, and my faith in the Light will bring many others to the Light and Salvation because many will understand and see.

The appearance of the alien was typical of the others that Betty had encountered. He warned her that there were other aliens that were not friendly to mankind. Many of the things that were related to Betty were difficult for her to comprehend.

> *Betty* He's telling me that for every place there is an existence . . . that everything has been formed to unite and I don't, I can't really understand. . . . He's telling me I'm going to go through a lot of different things and for me not to fear, to keep my faith. . . . He says that I *will understand* as time goes by.

After a lengthy one-way conversation, Betty was told that for the time being, she would forget him and all that he had said. She was commanded to go back to the house.

Fred continued the chronological journey through the recesses of Betty's mind and soon she was again reliving her next encounter. It turned out to be the original *Andreasson Affair* experience when she had been abducted as an adult from South Ashburnham on the night of January 25, 1967. It was really uncanny to listen to her. It was like listening to an exact tape recording of a session that we had recorded years ago when initiating our investigation. Since we had fully documented this particular experience, Fred stopped her and attempted to probe Betty's mind for any other UFO encounters that may have occurred after 1967. It was at this point that we encountered the previously mentioned powerful block that brought the Phase Two investigation to a premature halt. All that we had uncovered was that Betty seemed to have had some kind of a UFO encounter in 1975.

But in 1987 we discovered that the painful memory block mysteriously disappeared. The investigation was resurrected. Betty was found to have had encounters with the aliens in 1973, 1975, and onward into the 1980s. Let us now examine the extraordinary events that finally led to the initiation and conclusion of the Andreasson Affair—Phase Three, which, for reasons that will become obvious, I have entitled *The Watchers*.

The Face

After the publication of *The Andreasson Affair—Phase Two* and another flurry of publicity appearances, Betty and Bob went through a difficult phase of adjustment. During this period, they shunned public discussion about their encounters with UFOs. They became modern day nomads, selling and moving from one house to another. Long trips were taken with their trailer. The hypnotically revived memories of their bizarre liaisons with alien beings, the occasional ridicule by the media and the lack of official response to their plight weighed heavily upon them. Added to this was the apparent harassment by some unknown agency. Black unmarked helicopters flew low over their home, followed their car, and even buzzed campgrounds where they were in residence. Apparent telephone taps at home and at work and the opening and resealing of their mail caused them great concern. Even more frustrating and frightening were the periodic paranormal happenings that plagued them: periods of missing time, apparitions of figures and objects appearing and disappearing, the sighting of unconventional objects in the sky, an out-of-the-body experience. Both continually experienced an anxious intuitive feeling of being watched. Even their dog sensed and seemed to watch the movement of invisible entities or forces in their house. Their situation was extremely unnerving to say the least.

I continued to monitor these events through the mutual exchange of letters and phone calls. They looked to me for help but

I felt completely powerless to do anything to alleviate the situation. The best that I could do for them was to be a good listener—an empathetic sounding board.

From time to time I would ask Betty if she would be willing to undergo hypnosis again. I felt that there was so much more hidden in the recesses of her mind. I felt convinced that her repressed memories would help unlock the mysteries engendered in the UFO phenomena. But each time that I asked, I would receive a polite but firm *no* for an answer. Then, almost as if caused by someone flicking a switch, Bob and Betty's temperaments dramatically changed to a renewed active interest in UFOs.

Both began soliciting media interviews. Betty created lifelike papier-mâché models of the alien beings and painted almost photographic representations of her experiences. Bob began collecting and studying UFO data released via the Freedom of Information Act. He undertook a detailed study of hypnosis and over a period of time became extremely proficient in its use. This would prove to be of great value later on.

Betty and Bob's resumption of interest provided new hope for the resurrection of research on *The Andreasson Affair*. But the real break in this deadlocked case came about in a totally unexpected and unrecognized manner. It began with a troubled phone call from Betty, who told me that she was experiencing flashbacks and dreams of a *face*. With trembling voice she told me that it was the face of a young woman with jet black hair. What disquieted her so much was the expression of intense fear on the woman's face. The eyes of the woman literally cried out for help. Betty tried her utmost to remember who the woman was, because she had an innate feeling of having seen this pleading face somewhere before.

When Betty phoned me about *the face*, I'm afraid I didn't take her concern very seriously. I had heard so many strange stories from her over the years that my mind was saturated. I felt that she probably did have an original vivid nightmare about the woman. But, as far as I was concerned, Betty's obsession with the woman's face was probably a paranoic byproduct of the emotional turmoil caused by her UFO experiences. But her letters and phone calls about the woman continued. The contorted face continually haunted her, so much so that she literally felt compelled to undergo hypnosis to attempt to discover her identity. Needless to say, I was delighted that Betty's preoccupation with the face had overcome her fear of hypnosis. Fred Max was contacted and a hypnosis session was scheduled for November 16, 1987.

Most of the session was taken up with pleasantries designed to put Betty at ease as she got reacquainted with Fred. At the end of the session, Fred put Betty under hypnosis for several minutes. I'm afraid Betty's interest in the face was put on the back burner. Our primary interest was to discover whether or not the *mental block* separating us from further exploration of Betty's UFO experiences was still in place. Fred decided not to push things, but just to ask a few simple questions about Betty's post-1967 encounters with aliens. Fred brought her back to her next encounter and gently questioned her about it.

Fred What are you wearing?

Betty I'm wearing a nightgown—a pink, nylon type nightgown.

Fred Do these *beings* look familiar to you?

Betty Yes. They look like the ones that came in my house in South Ashburnham [her 1967 adult abduction] only they're smaller, and they don't have the blue suit on. They've got a silver suit.

Fred Are they gentle with you?

Betty Yes, they're just standing there. . . .

Fred . . . Are you scared?

Betty No, because they're—they *make* me feel comfortable and not afraid.

Fred Do you feel as though you know them?

Betty Yes. Yes, and I feel, I feel as if it's coming to a *closing* or something . . . that *now was the time.*

Betty's words that "*now* was the time" created a ripple of excitement. Was it finally time for the aliens to reveal their purposes to us through Betty? My mind raced back to Betty's 1967 abduction experience when she had just finished observing the holographiclike representation of the death and rebirth of the legendary Phoenix. Betty had heard what sounded like a multitude of voices blended into one booming voice.

Voice You have seen, and you have heard. Do you understand?

Betty No, I don't understand what this is all about, why I'm even here.

Voice I have chosen you.

Betty For what have you chosen me?

Voice I have chosen you to show the world.

Betty Why was I brought here?

Voice Because I have chosen you.

Betty Why won't you tell me why and what for?

Voice The *time* is not yet. It shall come.

I thought back again to when the leader of the aliens, Quazgaa, bade Betty farewell before she was returned to her home in South Ashburnham. His last words, according to Betty, had been portentous.

Betty He says . . . he is locking within my mind certain secrets. . . . They will be revealed when the *time* is right. . . . He's putting both hands up on my shoulders. And he's saying, "Go child and rest."

Had *the time* for these revelations arrived? Unfortunately, we would have to wait for the answer because of time. The session had already gone beyond the time Fred had scheduled. It was frustrating. In any event, Fred gently brought Betty back to the present. But before doing so, he left her with a strong posthypnotic command in the event that Bob would have to continue hypnosis himself.

Fred I want you to relax. Very calmly. Very calmly. I want you to imagine your mind feeling relieved of external pressure such that as you sit, you feel free. What you and I have said here . . . *is on tape* . . . and, like a dream that you can revisit, more of the parts will be revealed to you as you sit and hear the tape. The tape is not to be heard while in a moving vehicle or while operating machinery. It has a calming effect, a *powerful calming effect*.

The tape recorder was left on while the session was briefly discussed afterwards. Betty was not at all happy that no attempt had been made to identify the face that was haunting her day and night. That was the reason she had come to Fred.

Fred explained to her that he wanted to keep this initial session simple because of the painful block that Betty had experienced at the last Phase Two hypnosis session.

Fred There's a *shunt*.

Betty There's a what?

Fred A *shunt*. Something that keeps you from talking . . . so I keep the story simple.

Betty Well, what do you think we ought to do then? Ah, have another session? And find out?

Bob I think we should get another one in and find out about *that woman*.

Betty I'd just like to know. Even if it has nothing to do with the UFO phenomena.

Bob I'd like to know if anything has happened *since that time*.

In reality, it seemed as if this remarkable breakthrough could not have come at a worse time. Betty and Bob were in the midst of packing for an annual winter trip to Florida. There was barely time to fit in one more session. Adding to the frustration, because of Betty's persistence, it was decided that the face would have first priority at the session. This was done despite the pressing need to explore what could turn out to be the sixty-four thousand dollar question underlying the study of UFOs. *Why* were they here? Little did we know that the face and the answer to this thought-provoking question were intimately related. Exploring the enigma of the face would ultimately lead to the key that would unlock the mystery of the UFO phenomena.

The next session took place on the evening of November 19, 1987. An air of expectancy filled the room. All of us knew that it would have to be the last session with Fred. Fred was prepared to go overtime. Betty was determined that the precious time be dedicated to identifying the mysterious face that obsessed her like some forgotten specter of the past. Betty was very tense. We wondered whether or not Fred could continue to get by *the shunt* that he sensed during the last session. Slowly but surely, he eased Betty into a deep state of hypnosis.

Fred I want you to relax as though your mind was floating in space. And, in your mind, you could see *that face* again. You could see it and you could even place it six feet away from you. You could have it stop there. And, you can peacefully take a look at it. What are you seeing?

Betty I'm seeing a woman's face. [*pause*] And she's looking to me for help. [*pause*] And she's trying to say something. [*pause*] Ooooooh! [*Betty's voice became stressed.*] She's on a table and she's

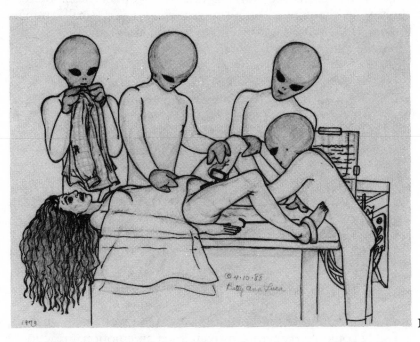

1

being pinned down! [*pause*] [*Betty spoke to the woman as if she was actually with her.*] "You're okay. Okay, okay, okay. Sh-h-h-h-h. You'll be fine. It's all right. Sh-h-h, Sh-h-h-h. Okay, sh-h-h-h." [*Betty's voice now became very apprehensive.*] It's a woman. And she's laying on this table. [*Betty's voice now became alarmed.*] And, she seems to be afraid! I'm trying to comfort her. Oh! There's, there's *beings* working down near her feet. I don't know what to do to help her! She looks so afraid! [Figure 1] I'm putting my forehead down near her forehead, ah, to try to make her feel calm or at ease. [*Betty sighed.*] And I'm just patting her temples and she's starting to relax a little bit. And, I'm looking down and—[*Betty suddenly became terror-stricken.*] Oh! Boy oh boy! Oh brother! That's awful! It's awful what they're doing. I feel so bad for this lady. Oh! "Sh-h-h-h, you're going to be all right." [*Betty sighed.*] One of the *beings* is coming over, and, ah, he's putting his hand on her forehead. She doesn't like it. She's looking over at me to stay with her. The *being* keeps putting his hand on her forehead. . . . [Figure 1]

At this point, the audiocassette tape came to an end. During a short break to change the tape, Betty continued to describe forgotten memories that unfolded before her: An alien brings her down to where other aliens are working near the woman's legs. Betty is shocked to the core to see them removing a very small, strange-looking *fetus*. What they then do to the infant horrifies her. By this time, the audio tape was running once again and we pick up from there.

> *Betty* Oh no! They're putting something on that baby's mouth! It's so tiny. [*Betty began to breath heavily and her voice was anxious.*] Oh! One of the *beings* is saying they have to do it this way. [*saying telepathically*] They can't allow the baby to take a breath of air. [*Betty sighed.*] Oh! Ooooooooo! Ooooooh! Don't do that!

Betty was on the verge of hysteria. Fred felt that he must intervene to ease her trauma.

> *Fred* Calm down. Calm down. What are they doing to it? Are they actually hurting the baby? Or, are you afraid they're hurting the baby? Are they actually hurting the baby?

Betty was now sobbing uncontrollably. One wondered what she possibly could be seeing to instigate such an emotional reaction.

> *Betty* They're putting needles in the top of its head and its ears!

Momentarily taken aback, Fred immediately regained his composure and continued his attempts to calm Betty.

> *Fred* That might be . . . Wait a minute. It might be acupuncture. They may not be *hurting* that baby. *Are* they hurting that baby? Take a look at it. Step back from the scene. Whatever it is that you saw, just see the *truth* of it.

Fred wiped her tears with a tissue as his gentle yet commanding voice homed in on Betty's state of emotional shock.

> *Fred* Just see the truth of it. Whatever the truth is . . . Just go for the truth. That's the safest thing in the world. Take it easy. Take it easy. Listen. The truth is always the safest thing for your mind to go to. If it's a really bad thing, just say "it's a bad thing." Then look at that.
> *Betty* [*Betty sniffled. Her voice trembled.*] They're—Oh! They put those long needles right in the soft spot of the baby and in the two

ears. And they got something around its nose and mouth. O-h-h-h! [*Betty again starts sobbing.*] And they're cutting the eyelids away!

Fred Is the baby making noise?

Betty No.

Fred Why not?

Betty It's not making any sound!

Fred Okay, do you remember the time that *your eye was out*?

Fred was referring to Betty's teenage abduction when the aliens had removed her eye and used a long needle to implant a tiny BB-sized object in her head.

Fred Do you remember that?

Betty Yes.

Fred Okay. Do you remember how scared you were?

Betty Yes.

Fred Can you *see* today?

Betty Yes.

Fred They did not harm you, did they?

Betty No.

Fred They don't seem to harm—[*Betty interrupted.*]

Betty It, it's so little!

Fred Hold it. Hold it. Hold it. Don't read too fast. Okay? Read slow and read the truth, whatever the truth is. [*Betty is agitated again.*] Only read the truth. If *they* are *beings*? Whose baby *is* this? That woman's baby?

Betty Yes.

Fred How does she feel?

Betty [*Betty spoke in a tired, strained voice.*] She's fast asleep now. She looked afraid before. I tried to comfort her. [*Betty started to cry again.*] I didn't know they were doing *that*.

Fred Okay. Allow yourself to drift on for several minutes.

Betty was so upset that Fred decided to move her ahead in time and beyond this emotion-ridden event.

Fred Tell me what happens in several minutes. In other words, what's happening, what's the *next* event?

Betty [*Betty has calmed down a bit.*] They're standing in—front—of a *glass case*. And there's another baby there. A *fetus*. It's very tiny. And it's just laying there inside this liquid. And—But its eyes, they've circumcised the lids. . . . They circumcised the eyelids of those babies and their eyes look so strange. [Figure 2]

Fred What's the next event? Who wakes up first, the mother or the baby?

Betty [*Betty gave a long sigh.*] The baby's just in there. And, it looks like, ah, I don't know, it's just—It's just so tiny. It—But, the eyes have been—The eyelids have been cut . . . and the *beings* are saying . . . that the baby—the little ones are not allowed to take a breath of air.

Fred That doesn't mean they're suffocating though.

Betty No.

Fred Okay, so you need, you need to view this more as *they* view it than as *you* would view it—As if it were happening to you. You know what I mean? It isn't like you are suffering. Do you have reason to believe the baby was suffering?

Betty I don't know. It seems as if it *was* moving about. And now, it seems very still and calm and not moving.

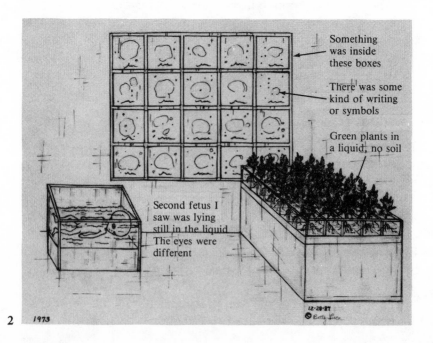

Something was inside these boxes

There was some kind of writing or symbols

Green plants in a liquid, no soil

Second fetus I saw was lying still in the liquid The eyes were different

12·28·87
© Betty Luca

Fred If we take what we've heard at face value, they are very skilled. They would have calmed the baby prior to doing their surgery.

Betty In this room, there are these, ah *glass cases*. And they have also in here, different kinds of plants and things, and something on the wall with some kind of—like sectioned off—with little symbols of something all through it. [Figure 2] It feels very cold in here. Oh-h-h. They're telling me they have to do this. And I'm saying— "Why do you have to do such a terrible thing?"

No one could have predicted the electrifying answer given to Betty in response to her agonizing question. It still rings like a death sentence in my mind. There was no conditioning of her mind for their reply. It was direct and matter-of-fact which made it just that much more cold and calculating.

Betty And one of them is saying—"We have to because as time goes by, mankind will become *sterile*. They will not be able to produce."

My initial reaction to these words was shock and disbelief. This aspect of the aliens' message to Betty was totally unexpected and my mind rebelled against the possibility of its authenticity. But, as I sat at the tape recorder and replayed Betty's words, flashbacks of weekly newscasts raced through my mind. It seemed that ever since I had begun to write this book, radio and TV news and specials that described frightening threats to life on earth had proliferated. Perhaps the aliens' message about the future sterility and extinction of Man had some foundation. Such threats include drugs, acid rain, pesticide poisoning, animal and plant extinction, ocean and shoreline pollution, the greenhouse effect, the depletion of the ozone layer, inadequate space for waste disposal, AIDS, and the accidental/intentional radioactive leaks from atomic power plants.

One news story about the North Sea's dying seal population was of particular significance. The North Sea is essentially dead because of pollution. Its entire seal population is now being decimated by unknown causes. However, marine biologists suspect that extreme water contamination has affected the seals' immune system.

The televised report showed North Sea seals being plucked from the water. They were taken to laboratories to be probed, tested, tagged, and released for further study. This was all in a supreme effort by humans to save a lower life-form from extinction. The striking parallel to the aliens' apparent genetic operations upon human life is only too obvious.

Even as I write these words, the latest breaking story on threats to our environment concerns radioactivity. For years the government had been covertly allowing dangerous radiation to leak from atomic energy plants in the interest of national security. Our own government [and probably others] is willfully exposing its population to radioactive poisoning in order to maintain the manufacture of materials required to produce and rejuvenate atomic weapons.

As I think of the implications of ever-increasing worldwide environmental problems, I am reminded of a Biblical story that I learned in Sunday School. A mysterious hand appeared and wrote on the wall of the Babylonian King Belshazzar who was desecrating the sacred worship vessels of the temple of Israel. The inscription on the wall was interpreted in part to read *You have been weighed in the scales and found wanting.* Mankind too is desecrating sacred things—the very things necessary to promote and sustain life on this planet. If the aliens' message is accurate, Man too has been weighed on the scales of the intricate balance of nature. He too has been found wanting.

The aliens' emotionless response to Betty's question had also unnerved her. She began shivering all over. Fred took time to calm Betty down before proceeding with his patient probing of the unimaginable events deeply repressed within her mind.

> *Fred* Imagine yourself feeling relaxed, very relaxed. Allow yourself to feel yourself feeling warm. Feeling comfortable. The *beings* appear to be peaceful—peaceful people who recognize necessity and act on it in their mind. This child required something. You need not judge it. Merely view it and see the truth. What happens next?
>
> *Betty* They're taking me out of that room where different plants are, and that one baby is, and those things on the wall sectioned off with symbols on it. We're going back in that room. Oh-h-h, I feel so sad for that little one. He's [an alien] got that little tiny baby. And it's strange. It's got real black eyes. And it's got a needle stuck in the top of its head—through its soft spot—and two needles in the ears. And they got something around the nose and the mouth. It looks like it's just dangling inside of the liquid. [Figure 3]

Betty is a talented amateur artist with a keen eye for detail. Her natural ability to draw was further enhanced by specific posthyp-

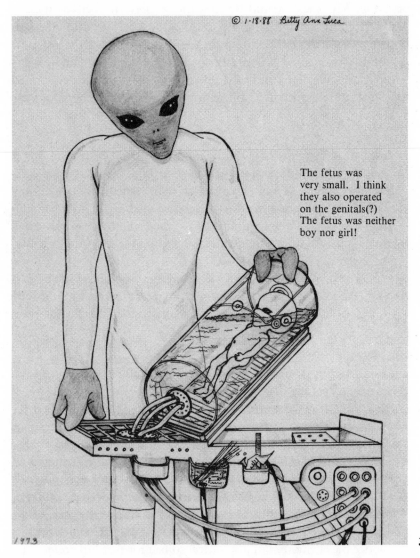

© 1·18·88 Betty Ann Luca

The fetus was
very small. I think
they also operated
on the genitals(?)
The fetus was neither
boy nor girl!

/973

3

notic suggestions to remember and sketch significant segments of
her experiences. The rough sketches done while under hypnosis
were later reworked with care and precision.

But what had Betty just drawn? Was the glass tank filled with
liquid an artificial womb? If so, how did the fetus receive nutrients
to keep it alive and growing? It no longer had an umbilical cord and
the mouth and nose were covered. What was the purpose of the
needles in its head and ears? A professional biologist who examined
the narrative and drawings found the alien apparatus and its use

puzzling. My guess would be that the strange device was used to place the fetus in a temporary state of suspended animation for transit to an artificial womb and controlled growth to term.

Betty's continued description of the weird equipment was just as unfathomable. This and other alien machinery will provide much food for thought and discussion amongst UFO researchers for years to come.

Betty And there's a thing on the top there. It, ah [*Betty paused for a minute.*] One of the *beings* is taking something over and it looks like thin strands of stuff with tiny lights or something on it in his hand. And he's bringing it over to where the baby is. And he's putting it on top by the thing on the top there. All these sparkly tiny, tiny lights. And these thin hairlike things on the top. And it looks so weird.

And they're putting it inside that thing that's above the head. [i.e., the fetus's head] And they're really pleased with, with this little thing because its eyes are *big and black* when they cut the lids—*like theirs*. [Figure 4]

Fred Uh-huh.

Betty And they said that the *splicing* took good on this one. And they're telling me that mankind gets so upset when they take the *seed*. And, really, the very first part that man and woman, when they came together, was to *bring forth*—was not for their pleasure, but to bring forth. And mankind keeps on spilling the seed of life over and over again. And they cannot understand why man gets so upset when *they take the seed*. [*Betty then sighed deeply and continued.*] And the woman is now being moved. She's sitting upward and being moved off the table. They only had a cloth covering her. And they're bringing her into another room. She doesn't even seem to notice me anymore. I'm just—I feel so bad for that little *thing* there.

Suddenly Betty just stopped talking. She looked as if she were in deep thought. During a very long pause she apparently had been reviewing the whole episode in her mind for when she once again started talking, her voice reflected sheer panic.

Betty They wouldn't even let it breathe to come alive! They rushed it from one place into that liquid! They said they had to do that!

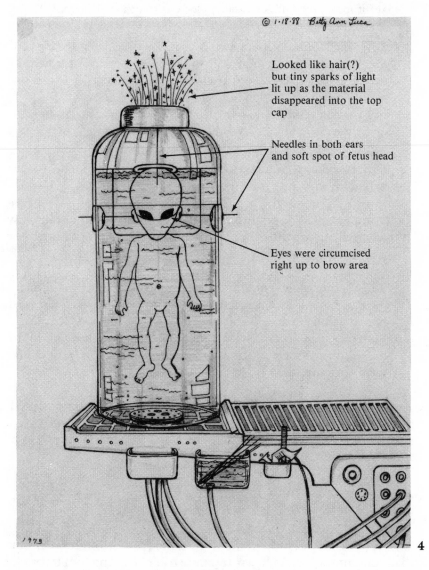

© 1·18·88 *Betty Ann Luca*

Looked like hair(?) but tiny sparks of light lit up as the material disappeared into the top cap

Needles in both ears and soft spot of fetus head

Eyes were circumcised right up to brow area

4

Fred again broke in to quell Betty's severe emotional reaction to the bizarre events that she had witnessed.

Fred Hang on! Sometimes, when we're in the snow, we get stuck in a rut. Then, someone comes along with chains, or sand, or a shovel, and we get out of the rut. And we realize we can drive in the snow. And this child is not necessarily deceased. It is merely in a liquid. They may have a more kind purpose than *you* might normally associate with having an infant in a liquid. And, look for that.

See if it's there. And it's easier to look at things in their most favorable light.

Betty They seemed very pleased over it. They seemed more pleased over this one than the other one in the other room. That lady had two little babies. They don't really look like babies. They're too small. Their heads are kind of *big*—like a *fetus*, I guess.

They have this thing over their mouth and their nose—comes up by the ears and they have those needles pressed right into the poor little thing's ears. [*Betty became upset again.*]

Fred Remember! You don't *know* if that child is suffering. Go *ahead* in time. Is that child truly suffering?

Betty immediately obeys Fred and moves ahead in time. She now finds herself *outside* the craft. Unfortunately, we did not know *how* she got there at this point.

Betty I don't know. I'm, I'm outside. And I see that lady is sitting there with her legs underneath her—like crisscrossed—and her head bowed with her hands on her knees. We're like in a wooded area. And, there's another, there's another—looks like another craft off to the side there. There's two craft there—the one we came out of and there's one over there.

One wondered just what Betty was talking about. Fred interrupted. He wanted to make sure that Betty was still reliving the same event. No one knew how far she had *gone ahead* in time in response to Fred's previous command.

Fred What year is this?

Betty 1973.

It was the same year and perhaps the same episode but session time had run out. Bob quickly wrote a note to Fred asking him to briefly check whether or not Betty had had any recent UFO experiences in the past year or two. Fred complied but as soon as Betty began reliving what appeared to be an experience in 1986 or 1987, he again encountered the mysterious but effective painful block.

Betty My hands and my feet and my legs again!

Fred decided to end the session but it was too late. Betty was now making gasping sounds and was in great distress.

Fred Relax, relax. . . . Tell your body that I'm going to leave it alone for now. Tell your body that I'm going to leave it alone for now. Tell your body—[*Betty interrupted and raised her voice in painful distress.*]

Betty Oh! I want to leave this alone! Oooooooh! It hurts!

Betty was trying to respond to Fred's command but whatever was happening seemed to still have her in its agonizing grip.

Fred Letting it go, letting it go, letting it go. Imagine, like the time you had a headache, you took the aspirin. The next thing you know, someone mentions the headache, and, you say—"I had one. Oh, I had it and it's gone." It's gone. It's—[*Betty interrupted and screamed in pain.*]

Betty Oooooooooooooooooooooo!

Fred Imagine it away! Know it's away. Know it's away. Know it's gone. Relax, relax, relax.

Betty Oh, it still hurts!

Fred I know, but nowhere near as much.

Betty It's not as bad but it still hurts.

Fred Let the, the rest of it go. Let it go. If you relieved it a little, you can relieve it more. Let it go.

Betty [*burst out crying*] I'm trying!

Fred I'm not criticizing you. Take it slow, take it easy. Let it happen. It *does* happen.

Fred continued and finally was able to relieve Betty of the terrible pain and bring her out of hypnosis to the present time. However, continuation of the recently initiated Phase Three investigation of *The Andreasson Affair* now seemed impossible. Betty was terrified after again having suffered excruciating pain while under hypnosis. Betty and Bob were to leave for Florida in a few weeks. Fred suggested that Bob take over the sessions as he had become proficient in hypnosis. In fact, Fred had already left Betty with a posthypnotic suggestion that would help Bob carry this out.

Fred Induce yourself with the tape. Bob can be with you . . . and can even ask you questions. In that way you can actually even get more and more out of this. . . . You can do it. You're seeing the method. If you stumble a few times, you stumble, but the tape will always bring you back.

I was wary of this. Had I been dealing with unknown witnesses, it would not have been acceptable. However, after years of knowing and investigating Betty and Bob, there was no question of possible collusion in my mind. My greatest concern was the possibility that Bob might inadvertently ask Betty leading questions while she was under hypnosis and possibly contaminate the accuracy of recalled events. I felt caught between the proverbial rock and a hard place. It was either my waiting for months to renew the sessions with Fred or having Bob continue where Fred left off.

Two things were in favor of the latter: Fred was confident that Bob would be able to do it and I deeply respected his professional opinion. Secondly, Betty, though apprehensive of further hypnotism, felt comfortable with the situation.

It was a difficult decision on my part and one which will raise objections by peer and critic alike. I decided to use Bob and am quite ready to take some criticism for this decision. I feel strongly that under the circumstances it was both essential and desirable to use Betty's husband in this way.

First, I had little choice. For years Betty had strongly objected to ever being hypnotized again. The totally unexpected advent of the *Woman* memory flashback, Betty's persistent, overwhelming desire to probe this nagging memory, and the schedule incompatibility of the Lucas and Fred Max forced me to strike while the iron was hot.

Several other things were also taken into consideration when making this decision. First, as mentioned, Fred Max, who had performed the initial sessions, wholeheartedly endorsed the idea. He rendered his opinion that Betty was an excellent subject and that Bob Luca was fully capable of performing the remaining sessions. Fred Max is a professional hypnotist with a background in behavioral psychology. He was employed as the hypnotist for the earlier Phase Two inquiry. Secondly, Betty was reliving some very painful and traumatic experiences. She felt completely at ease with her own husband. Thirdly, Bob and I worked out a routine that would all but negate any leading questions during the follow-on sessions.

I do want to make it painstakingly clear that I would never employ such a methodology on unknown percipients in a new case. Betty and Bob had already been thoroughly investigated during the Phase One and Two inquiries. Character reference checks, cross-

This is a sketch of what the woman, they took the two fetuses from, looked like.

Her hair and brows were black, eyes were brown. She looked French-Indian, and had a space between her top front teeth.

examinations, lie-detector tests, psychiatric interviews, and the vivid, highly detailed, internally consistent experiences relived under hypnosis performed by professionals convinced an objective team of investigators that Betty and Bob were credible persons who really believed that they had experienced UFO abductions.

Thus, I consider the Phase Three inquiry to be a belated completion of an open-ended investigation. In retrospect, as one who has monitored a number of professionally conducted hypnotic regression sessions, I was very pleased with Bob's performance during the follow-on sessions. The methodology we agreed upon involved relatively open-ended input from Betty with a minimum of questions. This method was very time consuming but it virtually eliminated the possibility of Bob asking leading questions.

In the meantime, Fred went out of his way to schedule one more session with Betty before she and Bob left for Florida. I was relieved. We seemed right on the verge of finally discovering the purpose behind the UFO phenomenon. Their cryptic conversation with Betty about the future sterility of mankind and their obvious references to genetic tampering with Man were revelations which raised a multitude of questions. Why is Man going to become sterile? Why should an alien race care? What was the strange infant? How could a human being mother such a thing? What were the circumstances that had led Betty to meeting the woman of her dreams—the face? [Figure 5]

CHAPTER

Three

Alien Housecall

Betty and her first husband, James, had moved from South Ashburnham to a newly built home on Russell Hill Road in nearby Ashburnham in 1970. It was located only a few miles from the site of the original *Andreasson Affair*. [Figure 6]. I remember driving out to examine the new house and its surrounding area during the Phase Two investigation. By this time, however, Betty had sold it and had moved to Connecticut to live with her new husband, Bob Luca.

Betty's former home is beautifully situated on the top of a relatively secluded hill. It is surrounded by fields, woods, and a nearby lake [Figure 7]. A number of strange, consciously remembered events had taken place within the house and on and above its grounds.

From time to time *inside* the house, members of the family had witnessed loud noises and *balls of light* floating around. *Outside*, while working in her vegetable garden behind the house, Betty had been confronted with an unmarked helicopter. It flew in over the property, descended, and hovered right over her head for a few minutes before moving away. One of the weirdest events took place on June 8, 1978. It involved the apparent surveillance of the house by some rather peculiar-looking gentlemen.

At 5:35 P.M., Betty and her daughter, Bonnie, were all alone in the house. They happened to glance out one of the front windows and were puzzled to see two strange-looking men standing in the

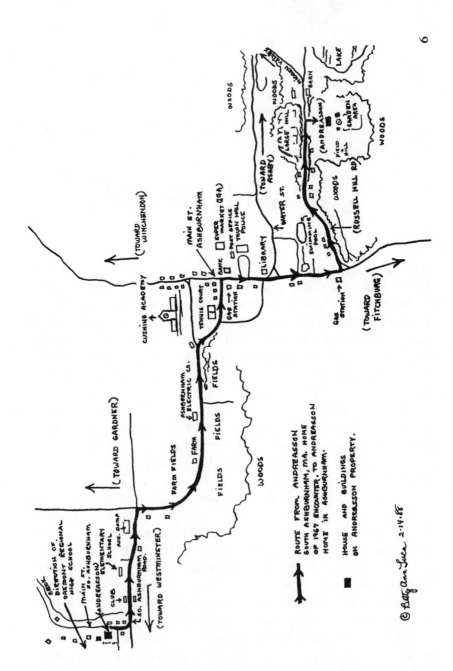

(TOWARD WINCHENDON)

(TOWARD GARDNER)

CUSHING ACADEMY

MAIN ST. ASHBURNHAM

BANK

SUPER MARKET (IGA)

POST OFFICE
TOWN HALL
POLICE

LIBRARY

TENNIS COURT

GAS → STATION

ASHBURNHAM ELECTRIC CO.

FIELDS

FARM FIELDS

FARM

FIELDS

FIELDS

WOODS

(TOWARD WESTMINSTER)

(L.SO. ASHBURNHAM ROAD)

MAIN ST. SO. ASHBURNHAM

CLUB (ANDREASSON)

ANDREASSON ELEMENTARY SCHOOL

ASH. PUMP

DIRECTION OF OAKMONT REGIONAL HIGH SCHOOL

WOODS

WOODS

(TOWARD ASHBY)

BAXTER ST.

SWIMMING POOL

WOODS

GAS STATION →

(TOWARD FITCHBURG)

NORTON DRIVE

LARGE HILL

(ANDREASSON)

FIELD HILL

BARN

GARDEN AREA

WOODS

LAKE

(RUSSELL HILL RD.)

WOODS

↑ ROUTE FROM ANDREASSON SOUTH ASHBURNHAM, MA. HOME OF 1967 ENCOUNTER, TO ANDREASSON HOME IN ASHBURNHAM.

■ HOUSE AND BUILDINGS ON ANDREASSON PROPERTY.

© Betty Ann Luca 2·14·88

6

SIDE VIEW OF ANDREASSON HOME IN ASHBURNHAM, MASS. 1973

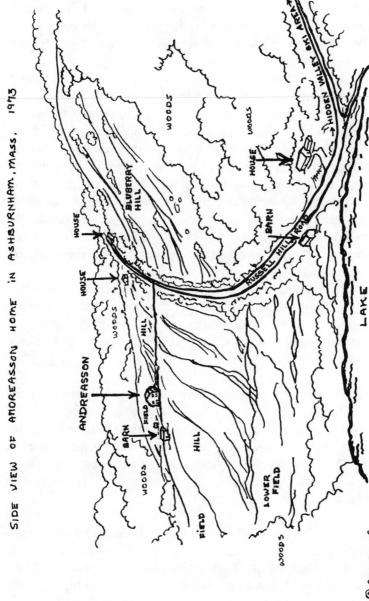

© Betty Ann Luca 2·14·88

driveway looking over the house and grounds. Puzzlement soon changed to fear when they noticed how odd they looked.

One man was very tall and dressed in a black, smoothly pressed suit. He had an extremely high forehead and jet black hair which contrasted sharply with his exceptionally pale face. His companion walked behind him with a strange shuffling motion. He was very short and wore a khaki jacket. The appearance of the two men was unnerving, especially when the black-haired one periodically raised one of his arms up in a stiff, unnatural motion.

Both Betty and Bonnie thought seriously about calling the police but felt foolish about doing so. Neither dared go outside to question their presence. Relief came when several cars came up the hill and began passing their driveway. The bizarre-looking figures immediately ducked into some bushes. The tall man again raised his arm as if to point. But he seemed to do so *without bending his elbow*. Then they walked stiffly behind a nearby stonewall and sandbank. Moments later, two cars that had been hidden from sight drove away. Another unearthly event in the saga of *The Andreasson Affair* had come to an end.

The Ashburnham site had indeed been the location of some very peculiar happenings. However, I was soon to discover that these events were only the conscious tip of a repressed iceberg of mind-shattering experiences buried deep within the mind of Betty Andreasson.

Nearly three weeks passed before Betty again sat apprehensively in the large soft chair that Fred used for his clientele. During this time Betty and Bob rode a whirlwind of activity trying to fit in the many last-minute things that demand attention when one leaves home for several months. The Christmas season is not the best time to plan such trips. It was December 8, 1987 and again Fred's soft but authoritative voice was directed at Betty.

> *Fred* Imagine the year 1973. . . . You are in Ashburnham, Massa-chusetts. You're in your home. . . . Focus on a moment of time in 1973. A moment that you'll feel coming to you, one that you'll be able to comfortably talk about. What are you experiencing?
>
> *Betty* [*Betty gave a long, deep sigh.*]
>
> *Fred* What are you experiencing? Allow yourself into that moment in time where something unusual comes to your attention. Allow yourself.

Betty I'm in my bedroom. I'm laying down. And it's night. And—
[*Betty sighed again.*] There's light coming in the window. I think
somebody must have driven in, in the driveway, because light is
shining right—And I can see it reflecting off the mirror [*sigh*]. And
I'm sitting up and wondering who it is.

Betty's matter-of-fact tone of voice now started to express anxiety as
she vividly began to relive her experience.

Betty And I'm shaking Jimmy. "Wake up! Somebody's in the drive!"
And I keep shaking him and he just doesn't wake up. "Get up!"
And he just doesn't move. He just doesn't get up. Those lights,
they're so bright and they're so close to the house. [*Betty paused and
her voice now sounded puzzled.*] Somebody's driving on the other
side. They're going on the other side of the house. That, that don't
seem right. [*sighs*] Oh! There's—those lights are *strange*. They're
weird. They're *not car lights*!

Betty now is frightened and literally shouts at her husband to wake
up. He doesn't hear her and seems to be in a strange kind of stupor.

Betty Wake up! [*now breathing heavily*] Wake up! Wake up!

Fred Calm down. What happens next?

Betty Oh! He just won't wake up! I'm putting the covers over my
head and crawling underneath there.

Fred Is the light coming from one window or all windows?

Betty It seems to be coming from all three windows.

Fred Equally bright?

Betty No, it's brighter down by the foot—Down there now. That
one window there. [*sighs*] And I'm covering my head with the covers. Whatever that is—"Go away! Go away! Lord Jesus! Lord Jesus!
Make it go away. Whatever it is, Lord Jesus." [*breathing heavily*]
Ooooooo! Oooooooo!

Fred [*Almost whispers*] Take it easy.

Betty Something's in the bedroom and it's pulling my arm! Oh!
Oh!

Fred Is it pulling hard or soft?

Betty It's pulling at my left arm.

Fred Hard or soft?

Betty Oh! I should have covered my arm up too.

Fred [*Loses his composure and laughs softly.*]

Betty Oh, I'm scared!

Fred Is it pulling you hard?

Betty It's pinching on my left arm, sorta. [*breathing heavily*] Something's pulling the covers off my head. [*Betty lets out a long deep sigh.*]

Paradoxically, Betty's terrified voice suddenly becomes very calm, almost serene.

Betty I feel very relaxed.

Typically, the aliens somehow alleviated Betty's fear as they had done to her and other abductees in the past. Betty now began to speak matter-of-factly as if what followed was a normal everyday event.

Fred What do you see now?

Betty There's those strange *beings* again. And one is still pulling at my arm and telling me to get up. They look little—big heads—big eyes. They're telling me I'll be all right. It's sort of dark but I can see them there and [*sighs*] I'm getting up. [Figure 8]

Fred How many are there?

Betty literally strains to make out how many were in the darkened room.

Betty Three, maybe four and they're leading me out into the hall-way and around the door, the cellar door.

Betty and the aliens do not walk. They *float* just above the floor!

Betty And they're going down the stairs [cellar stairs] and I am with them. And one of them touched the telephone on the post and I heard a "ping-ding" or something. The one in front.

The leader of the group touched a telephone mounted on a post in the cellar which caused its bell to sound in a muffled tone. One wonders if this temporarily disrupted it.

Betty And I'm just following them over the cellar floor to the back door. We're just moving along and we're going out the door. "How did they open the cellar door? I had that locked." Now we're in the backyard and there's an aircraft or machine over and above. We're brought over the grass and down aways. And a light is coming out of the bottom of the craft and we're standing in that light—And we're *in* the craft! [*surprised tone of voice*] And two of them are talk-ing very excitedly because another joined them.

I wonder if the excitement is because of what is about to happen. Perhaps they have brought Betty just in the nick of time for their purposes.

Betty And they're bringing me into that one room. [*sighs*] Setting me in some kind of a chair. And, ohhhh, for some reason I feel sick to my stomach. Uh! Oh Boy! I feel pressure all over me. And they're setting me in that chair and two of them are standing by. Oh-h-h, I feel like I'm being squished. So heavy. I could vomit.*

* Mutual UFO Network (MUFON) astronautics consultant John Schuessler, Project Manager for Space Shuttle Operations at McDonnell-Douglas Company and Deputy Director of MUFON, confirmed my

Betty once again became very upset. Her facial features and voice, coupled with her description of her feelings, indicate that her body was undergoing the effects of g-forces. The craft was apparently moving upward at a high speed. I assume that the chair they placed her in was used to protect her body from being seriously harmed. Fred immediately stepped in to help Betty.

> *Fred* All right, remember, this is an experience in the past. Allow your body to now feel comfortable as you step back from it a little and view the scene. Allow your mind and body to move back out of the immediate scene—out of the immediate scene. Relax, relax, relax, relax.

Fred again placed a strong posthypnotic suggestion in Betty's mind designed to help Bob work later with Betty.

> *Fred* In fact, when you hear this tape again, you can see how to pull everything out. You can bring yourself to places like this. You can even stop the tape that's playing in the room and *you* [i.e., Bob Luca] can take her a couple of inches at a time yourself. Okay, I just wanted you to know that you had a *tool* to bring you *in*—A tool to bring you *out* [i.e., in and out of hypnosis]. And you can use your own, whatever, wherever, you like. Now, *what's happening next?*
>
> *Betty* They have me in that chair. And they said they *had* to do it this way. Oh, I still feel kinda sick. [*sighs*] They're standing by, watching me and I just feel dizzy from it all. Oh, that one's coming over and placed something—fingers on my ears. And it's *hot* on that part of my ears. Oh! I feel something like *pulsing* in my back.
>
> *Fred* Is somebody touching you? [i.e., at that moment?]
>
> *Betty* No, I just feel something going *pulsing*, like, right in my back.
>
> *Fred* What do you see around you? Are you with people?
>
> *Betty* There's two of them there watching me. One just put something, like, to my ears—his fingers or something else. [*sighs*] Now, now, I'm getting up from the chair. And one is getting in front of me and the other one is in back.

suspicions that Betty appeared to be experiencing the effects of high acceleration.

The aliens' positions in relation to Betty are typical of how they had moved her along during her other abductions. In the 1967 event, they entered the house in a line. When they left the house, one entity had stayed behind and there was an obvious open *slot* that Betty was whisked into just before floating in line out of the house. One wonders how many years, or perhaps eons, are represented by such supernatural-like technology. Then again, perhaps such voluntary movement is the product of such a highly evolved brain that the aliens are able to produce controlled super-telekinisis at will! In any event, it is indeed a marvel to watch the various operations of these highly advanced entities through Betty's eyes and words.

> *Betty* And I'm being brought into another room and I see somebody laying on a table there. They're bringing me over by the—there's a person and—[*Fred interrupts.*]

From time to time, Fred tests Betty's recall for accuracy in the way of internal consistency.

> *Fred* You're in the backyard?
>
> *Betty* No.
>
> *Fred* Where are you?
>
> *Betty* I'm inside a room.
>
> *Fred* How did you get in there?
>
> *Betty* By that *light* underneath that machine.
>
> *Fred* Could you see this machine when you were outside it?
>
> *Betty* Yeah, it was big and it was—looks silvery. [*Betty lets out a long sigh.*]

At this point, Fred pulled a table over to Betty, gave her paper and pen, and asked her to sketch the object.

> *Fred* Just relax. Without affecting your travel, I want you to do a few things. I want you to draw me—without affecting your trance—open your eyes—and draw me a picture of what the craft itself looks like. Here's a pen. Here's some paper.

Betty took the pen and quickly did a rough sketch of the hovering craft. [Figure 9]

9

Fred [*pointing at sketch*] Are these stars?

Betty Yeah, it's nighttime.

Fred Relax. [*Fred takes the sketch and continues.*] And now you're in this room. And what's happening next?

Betty There's a lady lying on a table over there. And they're bringing me toward that person and she's looking at me. [*Betty's voice starts to quiver.*] She looks so-o-o-o-o afraid. She looks like she's crying out for help to me. And I feel I can move my hands and everything up to my waist. But, the bottom part of me is like, like stone. It feels like stone. That poor lady. She seems so afraid. And I'm calming her down.

We had now come full circle, back to the starting point of the last session when we had discovered the catalyst for Betty's preoccupation with the *face*. Fred let her continue in the event more details would come to light. Later he would home in on Betty's curious statement made at the last session. Namely, that she and the woman were *outside* the craft.

Fred What is she afraid of?

Betty [*sighs*] I don't know. She looks so afraid. Uh, there's some of those *beings* down by her feet. And, her legs are up. And, ah, she's so afraid. She's looking at me and I'm trying to calm her. [*Betty is now getting very upset.*]

Fred Sh-h-h-h. [*Fred tried to calm her down.*]

Betty And I put my forehead down on her forehead. And I tried to rub her temples to calm her down. She looks so afraid.

Fred Where did you learn that—to rub her temples?

Betty Long ago, when *they rubbed my temples.*

Fred When was that?

Betty When I was very young.

Fred How old?

Betty When I was thirteen.

Betty, of course, was referring to her abduction experience as a teenager when the aliens had removed her eye and placed a probe in her head.

Fred What was your name? [*Fred tests for accuracy.*]

Betty Betty Aho [Betty's maiden name].

Fred That was the *first* time that you saw them?

Betty No.

Fred Where was the *first* time that you saw them?

Betty I saw them up in the woods—*one* of them.

This was, if you recall, when Betty met an alien in the woods at Westminster, Massachusetts, when she was twelve years old.

Fred When you see them *now*—now that you're taking this lady and you're rubbing her temples—is it helping her?

Betty Yes, she's relaxing. And, I'm putting my forehead down on her forehead and I'm telling her "Sh-h-h-h, everything will be all right." And she's starting to calm down. And I'm lifting my head up and stroking her hair—trying to show her that *I'm there for her*.

This apparently was one of the reasons that Betty was abducted. The aliens seemed to want a human being to help and comfort the woman through childbirth!

Betty And, one of the beings are coming over. He's placing his hand on her forehead. She's going fast *asleep* now.

The *laying on of hands* seems to be the channel for an inherent energy that can be used to control the nervous system of human beings.

Fred now decided to let Betty again relive the trauma that she had experienced at the last session. It had occurred when she had witnessed the birth and the apparently bizarre treatment of two infants.

Fred What was she upset about?

Betty Oh, no!

Fred What do you see?

Betty They're taking something from her? Looks like a *fetus*. [*Betty is visibly shaken and again becomes terrified.*]

Fred Let me tell you something—[*Betty interrupts.*]

Betty Oh! They're taking it and putting something in its—oh-h-h! [*Betty starts to cry violently.*]

Fred Okay, okay. You don't need to observe this part. I want to ask you something, though. Before, when you were in bed—How long ago was that when you were in bed? When the light came, how long from this moment? Minutes? Hours?

Fred attempted to kill two birds with one stone. First, he wanted to divert Betty's attention from the traumatic experience that she was undergoing. Secondly, we wanted to know the time duration of the event up to that point.

Betty I woke up and there were car lights, only they weren't car lights. I tried to get Jimmy up and he wouldn't move.

Fred Where did the *beings* touch you in the arm? Where on the arm was it? Show me with the other hand. Show me with one of your hands where on your arm you were touched.

Fred's diversion had worked. Betty had calmed down but the time duration was overlooked as Betty continued to relive her experience.

Betty He touched me right here [*Betty points.*] and they were trying to pull me out of bed.

Fred Did they pull hard?

Betty Well, it felt pinchy and they're pulling me.

Fred Now, if they've seen you so many times, don't you somewhat know them when you see them?

Betty Yeah, but I don't wanna have any more needles. They gave me needles before. I don't want to have any more needles! [*Betty starts to panic.*]

Fred Okay, now, you're not getting needles.

Betty Not yet. [*Betty sounds doubtful.*]

Fred Okay. Well, allow your mind to wander ahead since you're ahead of that now. Do you get more needles?

Betty I don't know.

Fred Okay, so take it slow. Now, what year is this?

Fred wanted to make sure that she hadn't moved ahead to another experience when he asked her to wander ahead.

Betty 1973.

Fred '73? Okay. And?

Betty And they're putting that baby in that—that fetus in the water. And—[*Betty's voice starts to tremble*] and, they're putting needles in its head. In the soft spot and in the ears. And they've got something around its mouth and nose connecting to the ears. And they've circumcised the eyelids. And that little fetus has big black eyes. And he said that they had to put it in water, that liquid, whatever it is. The gray stuff. They weren't allowed to let it breathe the air. And they're putting some kind of a—looks like long strands of either hair or wire that has sparkles in it—in the top.

Again, the aliens tried to explain to Betty their purpose in performing such operations. Betty found it hard to understand even though the aliens tried to accommodate her lack of knowledge by using human terms. It was just the beginning of a series of revelations that, if true, would be a bitter pill for the human race to swallow in more ways than one.

Betty And they're telling me that they're doing this because the human race will become sterile by the pollution and the bacteria and the terribler things that are on the earth. They're telling me that they have to extrapolate and put their protoplasma in the nucleus of the fetus and the paragenetic. [*Betty stops and sounds completely frustrated.*] I don't understand them. Something like the paragenetic will utilize the tissue and nutrients to—I don't know—transform the creature or something like that. I don't understand what they're saying. They're saying also about man, that he gets so upset and, and in the beginning that it meant for bringing forth children, not for pleasure. And, they are taking the seeds so that the human *form* will not be lost—That they too are made of the *same* substance [*sighs*] and, that some of the female fetuses don't accept the plasma very well and that they have to—I don't understand what they're saying—something about——I can't understand and I'm just trying to repeat what they're saying.

Fred Are they saying that—[*Betty interrupts.*]

Betty That poor baby.

Fred Are they saying it gently to you?

Betty Yes. But it doesn't look very gently how they're treating that little thing. They seemed pretty pleased over it though. And— [*Betty expresses surprise.*] they have another one! That lady had two fetuses.

Fred The, the woman had twins?

Betty She had two fetuses.

Fred Same gender?

Betty I don't know.

Fred Do the *beings* have blood?

Betty No. They said they utilized the blood and tissue and nutrients that are there and the *form* and the fetus for the growth of the *new creature*. [*Betty gives out a long sigh.*] And, some females [alien females] just don't accept the protoplasma all together. So, they grow and use them to carry them, to carry other fetuses but they are very weak and cannot be artificially inseminated like humans.

Artificial insemination of humans? Could it be that the woman who gave birth to the two fetuses was used as a surrogate mother for alien genetic experiments with the human form? Why? The answer came with Fred's next question to Betty. Its implications are enormous and almost impossible to believe.

> *Fred* What happens to the fetus? Do, do they keep it there, or?
>
> *Betty* The fetuses *become them*—like them. They said they're *Watchers* . . . and they keep seed from man and woman so the human *form* will not be lost.

The fetuses become them? *The Watchers?* My mind continued to reel from this rapid fire of statements embodying such high strangeness. What could all of this mean?

At this point some of the implications were beginning to dawn on me. It would be a challenge to put the pieces of this mind-bending alien cryptogram together. First, the reader must be exposed to the rest of Betty's incredible testimony. Then and only then can we put it all together. I shall attempt some speculation in future chapters, but now let us return to Fred and Betty.

Fred too was continually taken aback by what Betty was reliving under hypnosis. It was hard to retain his composure but he continued calmly asking pertinent questions.

> *Fred* Where's the father of the child?
>
> *Betty* I don't know.
>
> *Fred* Do you know anything about the father?
>
> *Betty* I don't know. [*Long silence*] And they're taking me into the other room. And there's another little fetus. Their eyes are different. They've circumcised that fetus's eyes too. But it has like *white* around it and just a regular eye [i.e., not big and black like the eyes of the other fetus]. After I come out of that other room, they're having that lady get up. And she was only covered with some kind of a covering [*sighs*] and they're taking her into the other room. And, in that other room—Oh, my! My legs feel just like stone. They're just like stone.
>
> *Fred* Do they have permission to take that baby? Did they ask that woman if they could take her baby?
>
> *Betty* I don't know. I just was, just there. They brought me there, I think, to help her so she wouldn't be so afraid. I didn't talk to her ex-

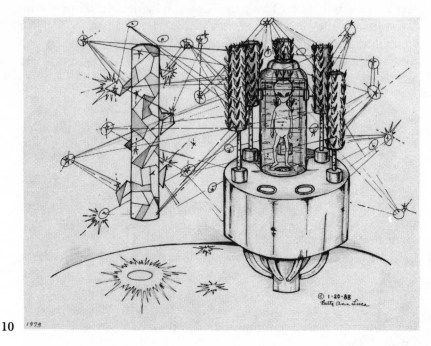

10

cept for trying to calm her. And I don't think I would have been able
to get an answer back. I couldn't even hear her voice, if I was to ask.
Oh, my legs. They're like stone. I'm in that other room by the *beings*.
And they wheeled that *thing*, [i.e., the tank containing the fetus]
pushed the thing, whatever it was . . . in the room with us—with
that baby that's hanging by those needles—in that thing—around its
face—in a liquid. And they push it. [*Betty groans and sighs.*]

Fred The baby might be fine. The baby might be fine.

Betty They got these five things around it. It's got, like—it looks
like—they look like—um-m-m-m, briars or something on these cylinders that come out of the smaller thing. And there's something
that comes down. And it's a cylinder-type thing with—[*Betty pauses*]
These things come out of it, and lights streak out of it and bounce.
Oh-h-h, my legs hurt.

Fred Out of what? Out of what?

Betty The light comes out of that cylinder thing that they moved
forward and they bounce through the room and hit some of those
pointy things. [Figure 10]

The description is so strange that Fred wondered if Betty was still
living the 1973 experience. He checked Betty out.

Fred What are you wearing?

Betty My nightgown.

Fred What's the lady, the other lady, wearing?

Betty She didn't have anything on but that cover.

Fred What cover?

Betty Just the cover they had over her. When I came in there, she was covered. But then, when they took her out, she didn't have any clothes on. Just that cover was there. And—[*Fred interrupts.*]

Fred How did they get that fetus from her?

Betty I don't know. They were working by her feet and legs. And, I just saw the *thing* come out and they plunged it in the liquid or water, whatever it was.

Fred Stay off of that. Stay off of that. [*Fred interrupts to stave off any repeat of Betty's trauma.*] Is there blood around the woman?

Betty Doesn't seem so—very little if—She is very clean. There is, there is a clump of something. There's a big clump of something there and that looks kinda bloody. Yeah, but I didn't see that at first. They had it covered. [Most likely, the fetus's afterbirth—the placenta and associated membrane.] I feel so upset at that poor little thing. The woman's fast asleep.

I can only imagine what might be going on in the mind of the neophyte who is being exposed for the first time to a documentation of the UFO abduction experience. To the well-read layman and UFO researcher, however, Betty's recalled experience with the woman and the infant and her follow-on experiences give rise to a major breakthrough in solving the UFO problem.

Up until this time, each abductee's recalled experiences have been like scattered, unconnected pieces in a complex celestial jigsaw puzzle. To fully appreciate this fact, one should become fully acquainted with the abduction literature. Due to the limitations afforded me in this book, I can only provide an overview of pertinent facets of such reported experiences.

Investigators of alleged abductees have known for some time that the aliens have displayed a major interest in the human reproductive system. From the earliest accounts up until the present time, abductees have described operations on their bodies that specifically were oriented to the examination of the genitals and the extraction of sperm and ova. Obviously related to these accounts is the startling discovery by researchers that a number of female abductees have become *pregnant* after UFO encounters. These pregnancies, in turn, resulted in medically confirmed anomalies of high strangeness.

One young lady, age thirteen, investigated by well-known abduction researcher Budd Hopkins, had a confirmed pregnancy. But, inexplicably, her gynecologist found that her hymen was still intact. She insisted that she had not engaged in sexual intercourse. Technically, she was still a *virgin*. The fetus was aborted. Under hypnosis, she relived a vivid UFO abduction experience during which she was artificially inseminated by alien beings. She described them as the typical small, large-eyed gray entities reported by Betty and many other abductees.

Another case study performed by Budd Hopkins involved yet another woman with a confirmed pregnancy. After two months, she chose to have an abortion for career reasons. During the operation, however, her doctor could not find any fetal tissue. Strangely, there were no signs that she had ever been pregnant.

A number of women now on record have had pregnancies that coincide with UFO encounters. All of these have suffered early *apparent* miscarriages. Under hypnosis, all of these women have relived abduction experiences that involved gynecological operations performed by alien creatures.[1]

As if this were not too much to believe, several female abductees have either dreamed or have relived under hypnosis even more fantastic events. Each told of postabduction visitations by the aliens who showed them strange-looking babies. None of these women had ever met or communicated with each other, yet their descriptions of the babies were extraordinarily similar. The babies were abnormally tiny. They had grayish skin and were oddly proportioned. In essence, they looked only partially like a human baby.[2]

Why were these surrogate mothers allowed to see their artificially sired infants? One reason given by their abductors was that they believed the hybrid offspring needed to be touched and caressed by their real mothers. It was felt that this was very important for the infants' well being. Another reason was to show mankind exactly what the aliens were doing and why. It is interesting to note that one surrogate mother was told by her captors that there was a critical need for self-survival involved in their operations. This cryptic remark, as we shall see later, alludes to the strangest truth behind the UFO visitation.

Thanks to Betty's just described experience we now have evidence that the mystery of the missing fetuses carried by abductee mothers has been solved. These fetuses were removed during yet another abduction experience. They were removed in exactly the same manner as witnessed by Betty Andreasson during her 1973 abduction from Ashburnham, Massachusetts. Betty was privileged to both witness and report on what newscaster Paul Harvey would call the *rest of the story*. This event and its implications, however, was just the beginning of the aliens' message to mankind.

Now, let us return to the office of Fred Max. The hypnotic regression session time had just about run out. Still to be explained was Betty's puzzling comment about being *outside* the UFO with the woman. Also unexplained was how and when Betty returned to her home at Ashburnham, Massachusetts. Curious, Fred decided to work overtime to find out before bringing the session to a close.

> *Fred* Okay, how do you get back? What happens between then and the time you go back to your own place?
>
> *Betty* We're, we're in that room where that cylinder comes down. The lights are bouncing all over the place. They're saying some things to me. I just can't, I just don't understand it. I don't know what they mean. I just don't understand it. They're bringing me out of that room to another place. And we're going out!

Betty's voice expressed surprise at suddenly being ushered out of the craft. She had previously mentioned being outside the craft during the November 19 session. Fred had brought Betty out of trauma by moving her ahead in time. When Betty told us that she was *outside*, we thought she perhaps had moved ahead in time to *another* experience. Fred, however, had Betty confirm that it was in the same year, 1973. Now we knew that Betty had been reliving the same experience. One wondered what would happen next. Betty had mentioned seeing another craft outside:

> *Betty* Outdoors! And there's that lady again. She's . . . [*Betty pauses*] Now she's got some clothes on. She's got a, a shirt, a man's shirt, it looks like. And it's plaid, or something or other—faded, faded shirt. She's, she's got her head kinda bowed down—Her hair streaming downward and her legs crossed. She's sitting there with her legs crossed and her hands on her knees, like. The *beings* that come out had *balls of light*. One is standing over by her and now one is standing by me. And [*pause*] there's *another* craft over there—Right next to the one we came out of. We're—there's woods

surrounding us. And we're in like, in a clearing. And there's a big lake. And there's two balls of light! The *beings* put two balls of light over the lake—Right by the edge of the lake—They are just hanging in midair over the lake. And they've got these hoses or something or other. I think they're hoses coming out from some place from underneath the ship, or the craft, whatever you call the airplane, whatever it is, and they're [the hoses] leading to the water. They're working on some of those hoses and I'm just standing there. And I don't know what they're doing but they've got all sorts of hoses.

Suddenly, Betty's body jerked in the hypnotist's chair.

Betty Oh! Oh! Oh! Oh! Oh! There's a loud, loud, loud bang!

Fred Okay, what is it?

Betty Oh, it's such a bright light. Oh, I can see right *through* my fingers and my hands. Ohhh—[*Betty sighs*] oh, is that weird! Oh, everything is so black but there is, like tiny balls of light . . . rushing all over the place . . . like streams of electricity coming out of it. Oh, oh, oh, wow! Oh, it's so bright.

Fred What do you smell? Take a whiff. What do you smell in the air?

Fred wondered whether Betty could detect the smell of a pungent gas called ozone which is created by the interaction of electrical sparks and air. Betty literally began sniffing but could only smell the sweet scent of evergreen trees that grew nearby. Fred again tested Betty's account for accuracy of recall.

Fred Are you alone?

Betty No . . . that lady's sitting right there and the *beings* are around, and I'm asking—"What happened?" I'm still seeing everything in reddish color. And they said, they had something, something about a *transversal shock* from something. I, I don't know if— from those hoses, the water or what. It's starting to come through now. I can see a little better.

Fred Are you inside the ship or outside the ship?

Betty I'm outside.

Fred And the lady's outside also?

Betty Yes, she's sitting right there. [*Suddenly, Betty becomes very excited.*] Something's coming! Looks like another ship is coming!

Another, another ship is coming! Oh, it's *whining*—awful whine sound to it. Oh, it's giving me a headache.

Fred Relax.

Betty [*Betty's tone changes from excitement to pain.*] Oh, I'm getting an awful headache.

Fred Relax, relax, relax. Take it easy.

The session time was up and Fred felt that this was a good point to stop. He had been helping Bob learn the art of hypnosis and gave Betty another posthypnotic suggestion to help Bob bring her back to this moment in the event after they arrived in Florida.

Fred Bob can bring you back to this moment in time also. You can go back to the moment in time where you've gotten out of the ship. You're standing outside. You're with this other woman and you see another ship come by. There's just been a loud noise— bright lights. And, relax. You can even go there slowly. And, you can even imagine hearing this tape at night and feeling more of the memories when you wake up in the morning. You can always take yourself out. You can always say "I'm Betty Luca. Today's date is—I wish to go back. . . ." You can always come back whenever you want to. You always have that power.

Betty But, I'm feeling such pain in my right eye. . . .

It was Betty's right eye that was removed by the aliens when she was thirteen years old.

Fred Okay, let that relax.

Betty . . . In the *inner* part of my right eye.

I wondered now whether or not the BB-sized object that the aliens had removed through Betty's nose in 1967 really was the same object that they had implanted behind Betty's eye in 1950. Could it be that the eye implant was a different device somehow connected to Betty's optical nerve? Is it possible that such a device was just one of several monitoring devices planted within abductees such as Betty? Perhaps the device placed behind Betty's right eye allowed an alien monitoring device thousands of miles away to actually record all that Betty Luca herself *sees*!

Fred Today is December 8, 1987. Imagine your mind forward feel-ing comfortable and relaxed. December 8, 1987. Feeling comfortable, relaxed, as though a part of you makes more sense to you and you feel a comfort and feeling of relief. Feel that feeling of relief. Relax, relax. . . . Allow yourself to relax and gradually and gently return to a comfortable place, feeling wide awake and feeling in a very, very comfortable mood.

Slowly but surely Fred's quiet voice brought Betty gently yet firmly out of her deep hypnotic trance. The last session with Fred Max was over. When he had asked Betty to describe what had happened between the time she witnessed the delivery of the fetus and her return home, he had underestimated the time it would take to bring this all out. As we shall soon see, Betty was not immediately returned home. There was much more for the aliens to show mankind through Betty. What she was to experience next, our scientists would give their proverbial eyeteeth to see and understand. Betty is indeed a privileged woman.

In any event, we have left Betty, in her mind's eye, outside a landed UFO in a secluded area. She is watching the arrival of yet another alien spacecraft. What was the purpose of this secret nocturnal rendezvous? What would Betty be privy to next? I would have to wait until after the Christmas holidays to find out.

Chapter Three—Notes

1. Bud Hopkins, *Intruders* (New York: Random House, 1987), p. 185.
2. *Ibid.*, 186–91.

CHAPTER

Four

Secret Rendezvous

Bob phoned me several days after he and Betty had arrived at their winter getaway in Florida. They had driven down with their trailer and set up house in a delightful trailer camp. Bob was about to start work as a service manager with a local automobile dealership. Very few people knew where they were located. Their annual pilgrimage to the south was normally a time of relaxation and escape from the wintry blasts of New England. It would be different this time, however. Betty would relive a number of UFO experiences that would sometimes leave her tired and distraught.

Bob assured me that just as soon as they felt settled, he would begin the series of hypnosis sessions. We put together a simple twofold game plan. First, he would only put questions to Betty that were absolutely necessary to instigate and move Betty along in her experiences. Secondly, Betty would be asked to relive her experiences chronologically. We agreed that it would be best just to let Betty talk without any unnecessary interruptions. We both realized that this procedure would probably be very time consuming and that it would require much patience on both their parts. In the meantime, all I could do was wait and ponder over what had been revealed thus far during the sessions with Fred Max.

During the hustle and bustle of the Christmas season, I somehow found the time to listen to and transcribe the audiotapes of the past hypnosis sessions. Sometimes, while listening intently to the tapes, I felt as if I were living in another world until being

57

shocked back to the current norm of life around me. If the recalled memories of UFO abductees like Betty actually reflect genuine physical events then our comprehension of reality is indeed limited. We could be compared with lower animals that experience life within the constraints of their particular physical and mental capabilities. Such animals are completely oblivious to the coexisting world of man and his technology. Even so, the forces that operate behind UFOs appear to be functioning on an infinitely higher plane of awareness that man is just becoming aware of through experiences like Betty's.

Christmas and the New Year passed before the mailman knocked at the door with a package sent to me via certified mail from the Lucas. It contained tape recordings of two hypnotic regression sessions performed by Bob Luca on December 28, 1987 and January 23, 1988. They were the first of a number of tapes that I would be receiving over the months that followed.

I shut myself in my study and placed the cassette tape in my recorder. My finger hit the play button. I waited anxiously and in just a few moments I was riveted to the voice of Bob Luca speaking in my headphones. His voice surprised me for a moment; I had been so used to hearing Fred Max conduct the sessions. I was impressed with the air of confidence Bob's voice expressed as he eased Betty into hypnosis like an old pro!

> *Bob* Imagine yourself very, very relaxed. Imagine yourself basking on a warm sunny afternoon. You're very, very comfortable. Totally, totally relaxed. . . . Even though you journey back to the past, you'll remain in control and be able to move back to the present very easily—At my suggestion or at your own will. Totally, totally relaxed. . . . Let's go back now to 1973. You just had an unusual experience involving a woman who had two fetuses removed. You are now by a lake and you're sitting there and there's just been a loud noise. After the loud noise, what happens? What do you see?
>
> *Betty* A bright light [*sighs*]. Everything went all dark except those *balls of light*. There's like tiny streaks—tiny streaks of lightning coming out of the center *ball of light*. And there's small balls of light—and—going into a reddish color. And it's starting to come into view again. [*Betty is beginning to see clearly again after temporarily being blinded by the bright light.*] And I can see some *beings* underneath the craft. And they're moving those hoses around that lead to the lake.

Bob Did they tell you what those hoses do?

Betty I asked—"What happened?"—And they said there was a *transversal shock*. They are taking some water from the lake. And they're, ah, *clear*-looking hoses and *green* and some *black* ones.

Bob Did they tell you what they are going to do with the water they've taken?

Betty No.

Bob What happens next?

Betty I'm standing there. And I can see that other lady over there sitting there to the left of me. And there's one of the *beings* with one of the *balls of light* over there too. [*sighs*] And she's just sitting with her head kinda bowed and sitting with her legs all crossed-like. And I see some of the *beings* stop [i.e., stop working with the hoses]. And they're looking over in the distance there. And I can see a *light* coming. I think it's another craft. It's coming over the trees way over there. And it's coming closer and getting bigger.

Betty, at this point, became very excited and her voice expressed wonder at what she was observing.

Betty It is! It's another craft! It's another craft coming toward us over the lake in the distance over there. They're pulling me over too. They want us to get into the craft again quickly.

Suddenly, Betty sounded surprised as somehow she found herself lifted just above the ground almost instantaneously!

Betty We're moving toward the craft!

Bob What? How are you moving?

Betty We're just floating! But there's, there's—she's gotten in front of me and the other one is in front with the *ball of light*. And there's one in back of me with a *ball of light*. And we're moving toward the craft. And it looks like they're working really quick underneath the craft with those hoses—very quick. They're pulling some in or something or other. And they're bringing us back into the craft and we're *swooping up* into the craft. And we're in that entrance room, I guess. And we're going through that room again, to the left there where I saw that, that *fetus*. And it's all clear now. There's nothing there except for the—looks like glasslike walls. Oh, wait. There is something there. It's in back of the glasslike wall. It looks like—it looks like plants, like, ah, like a whole bunch of plants there and even a tree! It looks like—but I can't make it out too much 'cause it's hazy. And we're keeping on going. They're escorting us in—into that room again where they took the fetuses from her. And they're stopping me. . . . And they're making her get back up on the table. And she's looking over at me with her eyes. And I can't go over to help her 'cause I'm just there. [*Betty's voice begins to sound helpless and panicky.*]

Bob Just relax.

Betty And [*pause*] And they have her laying down on the table. And now they're moving me toward the end of the table there. And they're making her put up her legs again. One *being* is by her head with that *ball of light*. And she doesn't seem to be resisting so much this time. They're taking something and—[*pause*] I think they're spraying her inside. They're spraying something inside, something inside her and on the outside. And I'm just standing there watching. And they move very quickly and precisional [sic]. And they're working there. And they're starting to put away those instruments that they used to spray her with and whatever else they did. And they're putting her legs down and the other *being* is stepping aside with the *ball of light*. And she's all of a sudden getting up. She's looking over at me to make sure I'm there with her. They're taking her off the table and we're being escorted into that other room. And that *baby* is not there anymore and neither are those plants. The *wall* looks different [i.e., the glasslike sectioned wall that she saw plants growing in]. They're telling her that she has to take off her shirt. And—[*pause*] she's doing it. [*Betty gives a long sigh.*] Oh, no! They want me to take my nightgown off too and I don't want to! They're moving her over to the side—to the center side there. And they're telling me that I have to take off my nightgown for there's,—"I'm not taking off my nightgown!"

Bob What do they say when you tell them "no"?

Betty They said "For my protection." "I'm not taking off my nightgown!" They asked me to please take off my nightgown and that it's for my protection. Again, I said "No!" They're just moving me over by that girl. And we're just standing there. Oh! There's something. There's [*pause*] like a glass tube or something coming up around us very slowly. [*pause*] And there's something coming out of the side of the wall there—swinging out like. [*Betty sighs and there is a long pause.*] It's coming down. It's connecting to that glass tube. And there's like little holes or something on the floor. I can

Swings out of
the wall somehow
to fit the glass
cylinder we
were in

feel them with my feet. And it looks like it goes down, way down, underneath us. Oh! They're starting to sprinkle this thick *jelly* liquid all over us, like raindrops or something. [Figure 11]

Bob What color is it?

Betty Clear. It's splashing all over us.

Bob Is it something like you've seen before?

Betty [*pause*] It could be. I don't know.

Bob Okay, how does this stuff make you feel?

Betty I just feel regular except for the heaviness in my waist down. And my hair is getting all wet and my nightgown is getting all wet from the jelly stuff that sticks to you. The only thing is that it doesn't feel sticky. It feels sorta like water but it's jelly.

Bob Okay.

Betty And it keeps pouring down on us so we're sopping wet with it. [*pause*] And it's just pouring down. [*pause*] It's starting to let up. [*pause*] It's stopping. And the *thing* is pulling upward and—[*pause*] swinging back into the wall there. [*sighs*] And the cylinder, glass cylinder-thing is going down into the floor. And it's down now. And I'm stepping off of the side of the things and *floating*. And the *being* says "We must have your nightgown." [*pause*] And I said "No! I don't want to!" And he said "You must because of *static electricity*."

Bob So they—[*Betty interrupts.*]

Betty "The *charge* would be very high on nylon."

Bob Do they know what nylon is?

Betty They just said the charge would be very high on nylon.

Bob Okay.

Betty Oh—[*pause*] I said, would they give it back to me? And I *have* to take off my nightgown. I feel so embarrassed. They're moving us out. The girl's in front of me and the—Ohhh! Shiny, shiny from that stuff all over us.

Bob Like—Is it like—if you put suntan oil all over your body?

Betty Even shinier. It's just so shiny.

Bob Okay.

Betty And we're moving out of that room where that table is, where they had put her on. And the *being* in back has her shirt and my nightgown and he's laid it on the table there. And they're escorting us to that room again. And I can see, like *plants* in back of that wall. [*Betty once again sees the vague shape of plants through a translucent wall.*] But, it's like a *hothouse* and it's all like hay and grass, I guess. And we've moved out of that room to that little room there, the little hallway and room. And the door is opening. [*Betty panics.*] Oh no! They're going to take us outside without any clothes on. [*sighs*]

Bob There's no one there, is there, besides the *beings*?

Betty The lady is there. I don't like this! And they're *floating* us down, and—Oh! I can see that big, big ship [i.e., the one she had seen previously approaching them]. It's hovering right over that smaller one.

Bob The big ship, now, that you saw—You've seen the Goodyear blimp, close up—Is it bigger than that or smaller than that?

Betty It's smaller than that.

Bob Okay.

Betty But it's bigger than those others—the two that are sitting on the ground here that they had out then. They led us back to the same place as where we were. And [*sighs*] she's sitting down.

Bob You mean the same place you were *before* you went in the ship?

Betty Yeah.

Bob In the woods?

Betty Yes, and that craft is right over above—so quiet. Oh, and a door is opening to that other craft [i.e., the other craft on the ground near the one she came out of]. And—[*Bob interrupts.*]

Bob The big one?

Betty No, the smaller one underneath it.

Bob Okay.

Betty It's opening and there's some *beings* coming out. And they have . . . [*Betty pauses, her voice sounds very puzzled.*] They've got these long things in their hands and they look like *jacks*—Long things. And they, they're putting them surrounding the smaller or lower craft—[*sighs*] about ten feet away from it.

Bob And you say these look like *jacks*? You mean the kind of *jacks* we played with when we were kids?

Betty No.

Bob Like a car *jack*?

Betty Like *jacks*—house *jacks* or something.

Bob Okay.

Betty But they got, like, pointed bottoms and they stick them in the ground. And, when they do, these things on the sides pop out. And they don't even have to pump them down into the ground. It pumps itself down. And, it's got a flat, flat three-sided thing around [the bottom] like a bowl, a flat three-sided bowl.

Bob Okay, later on, you will remember perfectly what these look like and you'll be able to draw them. [Figure 12] Go ahead. What happens next?

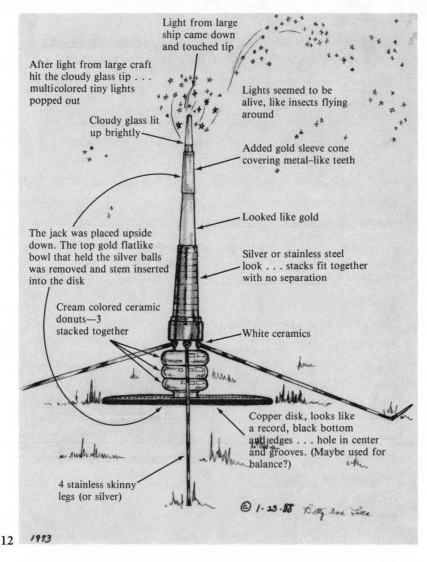

Light from large
ship came down
and touched tip

After light from large craft
hit the cloudy glass tip . . .
multicolored tiny lights
popped out

Cloudy glass lit
up brightly

Lights seemed to be
alive, like insects flying
around

Added gold sleeve cone
covering metal–like teeth

Looked like gold

The jack was placed upside
down. The top gold flatlike
bowl that held the silver balls
was removed and stem inserted
into the disk

Silver or stainless steel
look . . . stacks fit together
with no separation

Cream colored ceramic
donuts—3
stacked together

White ceramics

Copper disk, looks like
a record, black bottom
and edges . . . hole in center
and grooves. (Maybe used for
balance?)

4 stainless skinny
legs (or silver)

© 1·23·88 Betty Ann Luca

12 *1973*

Betty They're taking those *jacks* or whatever they are and they're ten
feet away from that bottom craft. That big craft is bright. It's lighting up the whole area—More than those *balls of light* did over the
water. And they're bringing those *jacks* around the lower craft. Oh,
no! Oh my word! Tch!

Bob What's happening?

Betty There's a *being* coming out. And there's a *man* with the *being*
and *he's naked too!* Oh, this is, this is awful. This is so embarrassing

and odd. [*sighs*] That poor man. I feel so sorry for that man. He's walking over, like trying to walk but he's *floating* with his walk. And they're bringing him over to the side. And, he saw, he saw us over on this side and oh, that is so embarrassing. And they're having him sit down off to the side too. And he's terribly embarrassed and he's bowing his head as he's sitting there. And there's more *beings* coming out. And they've got [*pause*] They've got some silver— Looks like silver balls they're carrying. And they're going to those, to those *jacks*. And they're putting those silver balls on those *jacks*. [Figure 13] [*Betty pauses as she reviews the procedure.*] And that craft is still on top there [i.e. hovering above the other smaller craft]. And there's some more *beings* coming out. Oh, a real *skinny being* coming out with those others. And that *skinny being* might be a lady [i.e. a female alien]. And—[*Bob interrupts.*]

Bob Okay, I want you to relax. And, I'm going to bring you back to today. . . . You will be able to remember and draw everything that you've told me—especially the craft, the *beings*, the woman, the *skinny being*. When I count back to one you will be wide awake, relaxed and comfortable.

Bob's voice slowly but surely prompted Betty to leave the past and come back to the present.

Bob Four—You can move your hands and your head. Three—relax [*Betty interrupts.*]

Betty I can't move my legs yet.

Bob Two—You're coming out of it more and more to December 28th, 1987, right here in the comfort of your trailer. One—Your eyes are beginning to open. You're feeling better and better and more and more awake.

Betty My legs aren't.

Bob They may have fallen asleep from being there.

Betty's legs had indeed fallen asleep. The circulation soon came back and she felt very relaxed but filled with wonder at the new memories that hypnosis had brought to light. The posthypnotic suggestion to remember specific segments for future sketching was a great help to Betty. She was able to draw things in great detail for us so that we could see as well as hear what she had witnessed. In some cases this was essential because words alone could not convey

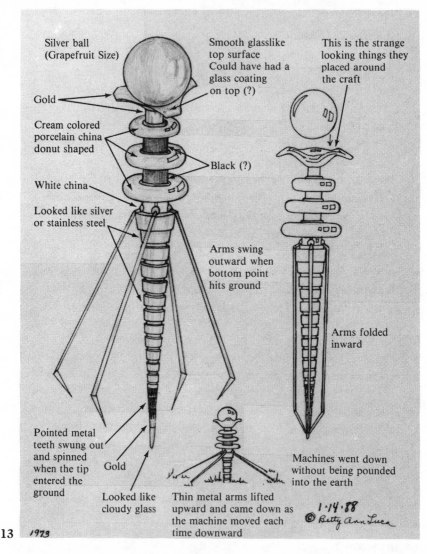

Silver ball
(Grapefruit Size)

Gold

Cream colored
porcelain china
donut shaped

White china

Looked like silver
or stainless steel

Smooth glasslike
top surface
Could have had a
glass coating
on top (?)

Black (?)

Arms swing
outward when
bottom point
hits ground

This is the strange
looking things they
placed around
the craft

Arms folded
inward

Pointed metal
teeth swung out
and spinned
when the tip
entered the
ground

Gold

Looked like
cloudy glass

Thin metal arms lifted
upward and came down as
the machine moved each
time downward

Machines went down
without being pounded
into the earth

1·14·88
© Betty Ann Luca

13   1973

some of the fantastic things she saw. She sketched the face of the
mysterious woman and the *skinny alien* standing with the *beings*
that were putting the mysterious *balls* on the house-jacklike stands
that had been stuck in the ground around the other landed craft
[Figure 14]. This latter procedure is almost unique among the
thousands of UFO events reported. I know of only one other report
where a human being was witness to this type of alien operation. In
this particular case, the witness accidentally happened to be in the
right (or wrong!) place to observe it.

14

The event took place at Hilliard, Ohio on February 5, 1967. Interestingly enough, this was only eleven days after Betty's first adult abduction from South Ashburnham, Massachusetts on January 25, 1967. The Hilliard event was reported by a witness to the National Investigations Committee on Aerial Phenomena [NICAP]. NICAP was the leading civilian UFO research group at that time. I served NICAP as the Director of the NICAP Massachusetts Investigating Subcommittee. The report was printed in the May–June issue of NICAP's bulletin, the *UFO Investigator*.

A lone male witness heard a strange noise coming from above concurrent with a nearby dog barking excitedly. He glanced up and saw an oval object gliding on a descending path into a field. He pushed his way through underbrush to the field and peered through the bushes at the unknown landed craft. It was sitting on strutlike landing gear. He felt paralyzed with fear, especially when a door in the side of the craft opened and several nonhuman entities emerged. He did not dare to move as he watched them start to place small *balls* on the ground all around the craft. He moved inadvertently in the bushes and made a noise. One of the entities looked in his direction and noticed him. In a moment several were at his side dragging him toward the parked UFO. Suddenly, something startled his abductors and they dropped him, picked up the balls and took off in the craft.

The terrified man first contacted the Air Force and Air Force investigators were sent on-site to investigate. When he reported the incident to NICAP he stated that the officers had examined a strange *burn mark* on the back of his neck which he had received during the short-lived scuffle with the aliens. Apparently, this man was not supposed to witness this operation. Who knows what would have happened to him if he had been taken aboard the alien craft? Based on what we have learned about alien behavior through the study of abduction experiences, I would speculate that no harm would have befallen this unfortunate fellow, and the incident would probably have been mercifully erased from his mind.

Betty, on the other hand, seems to have purposely been shown a number of examples of alien technology. And, at the proper time, she has been allowed to describe them to mankind to fulfill alien purposes.

In any event, I was highly pleased with the way that Bob had handled his first hypnosis session and intrigued with all that Betty had reported to us. I wondered what would happen next during the *secret rendezvous* of three silvery craft from an unknown world.

CHAPTER

Five

Scientific Miracles

I pondered long over the fantastic content of Bob's first hypnotic regression session with Betty. I thought about the strange house-jack objects which drove themselves into the ground by their own inherent power. Why did the aliens place them around the craft with the silver balls resting on top of them? Were they some sort of an electrical grounding device? What was the unknown liquid that was used to douse both Betty and her companion? How did it protect them from static electricity? The glasslike cylinder in which they were sprayed with the liquid seemed especially designed for use on human beings just as other devices Betty had witnessed during prior abductions. This would imply that they were used often on human beings.

What intrigued me most was the fact that the balls of light had the ability to fly and maneuver. In the past, these alien devices have been used to interact with the human brain to induce mind control. For example, similar glowing spheres were used by the aliens to control the movements of Betty and her family during her 1967 abduction experience at South Ashburnham. At that time they were always held by the aliens. This new revelation that they also have flight capability may solve another long-term mystery.

During World War II, both allied and enemy pilots reported being approached and followed by similar devices. Each thought they were the secret weapon of the other side. Allies dubbed the strange aerial balls *foofighters*. A typical encounter was made by

Charles Odom, a former B-17 bomber pilot who now resides in Texas.

The appearance of disk-shaped objects in the skies back in 1947 reminded Odom of the globe-shaped objects he and fellow pilots had sighted during their bombing runs over Germany. He told the Houston *Post*, datelined July 7, 1947, that the objects "looked like crystal balls, clear, about the size of basketballs." He stated that the glowing spheres would approach to within three hundred feet of plane formation and then "would seem to become magnetized to our formation and fly alongside. . . . After awhile, they would peel off like a plane and leave."

One of the early classic sightings in the annals of UFO history took place on October 1, 1948, over Fargo, North Dakota. There, Air National Guard pilot, Lt. George Gorman was approached by a glowing aerial ball of light. The curious pilot initiated a thirty-minute dogfight with the foreign object. His acrobatic maneuvers were witnessed by two control tower operators, and a doctor and passenger flying in another aircraft.

In the publicized statement made to his commanding officer, Gorman said that he was absolutely convinced that there was rational *thought* behind each maneuver performed by the glowing aerial ball. The fantastic incident received national press coverage as did hundreds of other so-called flying saucer reports that flooded the world. As fast as such reports were made, the government stepped in to counter their reality with mundane explanations designed to quell public interest and unrest. Lt. George Gorman's "thinking" sphere was explained away as a lighted meteorological balloon. In reality, the fact that it was a real machine of unknown origin was kept secret through security classification.

On January 29, 1985, almost thirty-seven years after the unearthly incident, researchers using the Freedom of Information Act were able to obtain the declassification of this incident. Air Intelligence Report No. 100–203–79 was classified *Top Secret*. It is entitled *Analysis of Flying Object Incidents in the U.S.* and dated 10 December 1948. Listed among other intriguing UFO sightings was the Gorman case. The Air Force, contrary to its public explanation stated that: "Investigation eliminated the possibility that this incident may have been another aircraft or a *meteorological balloon*." I mention this typical example to illustrate just how desperate the government seems to be to keep official data about UFOs from the public. One cannot help but wonder what is contained in the voluminous government files that still remain classified.

In any event, UFO researchers have often wondered whether or not there was a connection between early reports of *foofighter* balls of light and the larger structured craft that the Air Force dubbed UFOs. Betty's experience reveals that these examples of an advanced technology are a more integral part of the UFO phenomenon than has ever been imagined. Indeed they are a standard instrument used by the aliens for a variety of purposes including *defense*.

My mind raced back to a South American event that took place in Buenos Aires, Argentina, almost exactly five years after Betty's 1973 abduction. The incident was described in a report datelined July 27, 1978, in the Peruvian newspaper *El Comercio*, published in Lima. A translation was provided in the January 1980 issue of the *MUFON UFO Journal*. Note the similarities with what Betty saw and heard.

> Buenos Aires, July 26 [EFE]—Members of the provincial police force fired machine gun shots against the three crewmen of a flying saucer which landed early this morning in the neighborhood of an airport, according to a report in today's edition of the newspaper *El Popular* of the city of Olavarria.

The news story goes on to state that a little after 2:00 A.M., a wide sector crossing what is known as the Tapalque Valley was lit up by a very bright light in the sky which was accompanied by a strange sound that became very intense. A local chief of police witnessed the strange phenomenon and armed himself and four others before proceeding to the area in a jeep.

> Once there, they ascertained with surprise, a few meters above them, the maneuvers of an oval-shaped object, flat and with some feet on its edges, which was emitting multicolored rays. . . . It landed . . . behind the runway used by the military on emergency occasions.

Three strange beings in silvery suits emerged and started toward a nearby military garrison.

> The chief of police, surprised and fearful, tried to stop the *crewmen*, firing on them a burst of machine gun fire, unfortunately without hitting the target.

Then, while the unknown personages lifted their hands at the
same moment, showing a small *luminous ball*, all the witnesses felt
themselves invaded by a sensation of listlessness and tiredness that
rendered them incapable of using their weapons.

The newspaper adds that the occupants of the craft went back up to
it, and went away at great speed on a zigzag course. Concurrently,
the witnesses then recovered their faculties. The police squad
returned to Olavarria, where they reported the unusual happening.

The above incident reveals at least two significant facts about
the aliens' intentions and knowledge. First, they chose not to harm
or kill their attackers. Second, they must have an intimate knowledge of the human nervous system to be able to harmlessly paralyze
an individual. We have seen both of these aspects again and again in
the Andreasson case and in others. Again, one could easily surmise
that a number of the capabilities of their ball-shaped instruments
were designed around the mental and physical makeup of humanity.

Another fascinating aspect of the last recorded segment of
Betty's experience was her description of the aliens drawing water
from the lake into one of the craft by means of colored and
translucent hoses. I wondered whether or not such an event had
been reported before. I searched my files and found a number of
cases where UFOs had been reported hovering over or resting on
ponds and lakes. However, I only found one case that bore a
striking resemblance to the water-drawing operation that Betty had
been privileged to witness. The case was mentioned in an internal
newspaper published by the Steep Rock Iron Company, Ontario,
Canada. In the September 1950 issue of *The Steep Rock Echo*, its
editor, Mr. B. J. Eyton, stated that he had been unable either to
verify or disprove the story given the company newspaper by an
anonymous employee. He printed it because there were a number
of well-witnessed UFO sightings being reported in the area at the
time. Here is the story as printed for comparison with Betty's
report.

In the dusk of July 2, 1950, I and my wife had drawn up our boat
on the sandy beach of a tiny cove in Sawbill Bay, where we had
gone fishing.
    Cliffs rise on all three sides of the cove. Small trees and bushes
concealed us and our boat from sight of anyone overhead, in a
'plane, had there been one round that evening. We had snacks and
a thermos flask of tea, and, as the dusk was drawing on, we talked

of going home. Suddenly, the air seemed to vibrate as if from shock waves from a blasting operation at the local iron mines. I recollected, however, that the mines were too far away for that.

The witness clambered up the rocks until he could find a vantage point that looked out over the bay. He continued:

I was amazed at what I saw. As I peered through the cleft, taking care to make no noise, I could see out on the bay a large shining object resting on the water. It was in the curve of the shore line, about a quarter of a mile away, across the top end of some narrows. I got down from the cleft and sped back to my wife. She was startled as I came running up. "Why what on earth is the matter?" she asked. "Come and see if you see what I see," I said, grasping her by the arm. "And make no noise or show yourself." I drew her by the hand to the cleft. We both peered through it.

The shining thing was still resting on the water. It looked like two saucers, one upside down on top of the other. Round the edge were holes like black ports, spaced about 4 feet apart. We could not see the underside, because the bottom of the thing was resting either on the water, or close to it. On top were what looked like open hatches, and moving round over its surface were ten little figures. They looked queer, very queer. Rotating slowly from a central position, and about 8 feet up in the air, was a hoop-shaped object. As it rotated, to a point directly opposite to where my wife and I were peering through the rock cleft, it stopped, and the little figures also stopped moving. Everything now seemed concentrated on the little opening through which we were peering. We were about to duck down, as we thought these midget figures might see us and take alarm, when, on the opposite side of the cove, a deer appeared, came to the edge of the water, and stood motionless.

We again peered through the cleft in the rock. The little figures and the previously rotating circle were aligned on the deer. But now the circle moved to the left. We ducked down, counting twenty, and took another peep. The thing was gyrating and the figures moving; but the deer didn't seem to trouble them. . . .

It looked as if the whole machine were worked from a central point below the circling ray. The operator was a midget figure on a small raised stand. . . . I should say the figures were 3 feet 6 inches to 4 feet tall, and all were the same size. We could not see their faces. . . . The figures moved like automata, rather than living beings.

Over their chests was a gleaming metallic substance, but the legs and arms were covered by something darker. These figures did not turn around. They just altered the direction of their feet. . . . One of the midgets picked up the end, or nozzle of a vivid green hose. . . . And now the air hummed in a high-pitched note, or vibration. Maybe water was being drawn in, or something was ejected. I do not know if something was being extracted from the water of Sawbill Bay.

Next time we peered through the rock cleft, we found that all the figures had vanished, and the machine was about 8 feet up in the air. I noticed that the water of the lake, near where the thing had rested, was tinged with colour combined of red-blue-gold. The disc . . . tilted at an angle near 45 degrees. . . . Now there came a rush of wind. . . . A flash of red-blue-gold, and it was gone, heading northwards, and so fast that my eye could not follow it. It was now quite dark. We decided to call it a day, and got into our boat and went out into the bay where the saucer had rested on the water. I had aligned two trees to estimate its size, which, I think, was 48 feet.

The similarities between Betty's experience and that of the Canadian man and wife are striking. The size and color of the craft. The *green* hose. The size of the entities and their ability to *glide* rather than walk. The loud bang or explosionlike sound that the aliens told Betty was due to a *transversal shock*. The loud whining, vibrating sound. The bright colors. Betty, of course, witnessed the operation at close range and at night whereas the man and his wife observed from a distance with periodic peeks through a small cleft in a rock. Little did I know that there would be even more similarities reported by Betty during the next hypnosis session.

Bob had recorded the next session on January 23, 1988. I anxiously placed the tape in the recorder and sat back, pencil and pad in hand, to transcribe the continuing saga of Betty and her interface with beings of unknown origin.

Betty responded easily to Bob's voice and was soon in the deep state of relaxation that is called hypnotic trance.

Bob Now, what happened from the time *they* put these things in the ground? Just tell me, at your own speed and will, what you saw. And remember, you're in control and there is nothing whatsoever to fear. Where are you?

Betty Ah, outdoors.

Bob What's going on around you?

Betty There are two similar ships on the ground. One that the *beings* took me in, with that other lady with the long wavy black hair, out of one. And there's a huge one that is hovering over that other one over there. And the *beings* have taken out these things, these *jacks*. And they've placed them in the ground around the second craft or ship there. And they automatically sprung, like, these arms, out, on them. And without even pounding them into the ground. They just *work themselves* down into the ground. And the arms that lift up and go down—lift up and go down. And they place them about ten feet or more away from the ship, around it, surrounding it. And, then they had these *silver balls* about the size of grapefruits. [*sighs*] And they placed one in each one of those *jacks* on the very top. And, also, a *man* came out with some of the *beings*. And, he was naked and it was so embarrassing.

Bob How old was this man? How old did he look?

Betty He looked in his mid-thirties, I think. He was kinda tall with light blondish-brown hair. And he was embarrassed and we were embarrassed.

Bob Okay, what happened after you were all out there?

Betty He's sitting down on the edge over there. And another *being* comes and the *being's* skinny and tall. And it looks sort of *female*. But, it might not be; because [*sighs*] before [during the 1967 abduction] they said they could *opulate* and *deopulate*—Make themselves thinner or fatter or what now.

During Betty's 1967 abduction from South Ashburnham, the creatures told her that they could make things smaller or larger and used these two strange terms to describe the process. Betty interpreted this to mean that they could change the size of their own bodies. At this time, the entities were referring to changing the size of their craft. However, time would soon tell that they had the capability to do both!

Betty And the man is all *shiny*, just like us [i.e., from the liquid which was sprayed on them]. And all of that *beings* are stepping to the side. And there's *beings* beside me and beside that lady that they took the *fetus* from. [*pause*] And that huge craft is hovering silently right over that second craft on the ground, and—[*pauses*] and, there's things like legs coming out, or arms coming out, from underneath the big craft. And they're coming down and they're clamping on to the edge, the edge, of the bottom craft. And it's like sitting there. And I'm standing there watching those other people [the lady and man] sitting. And I'm trying to communicate through my mind because I can't speak out as to what's going on to one of the *beings* by me. Oh!

Bob What does he say?

Betty He's not saying anything. I'm just seeing that there's something coming *out* of the big craft on the bottom. And there's something coming *up* from the smaller craft underneath—in the center. And it's starting to move. It's starting to move counterclockwise.

Bob What is, the big one or the little, or the thing in the middle?

Betty The thing in the middle. The, the two. The big ship and the small ship. They're, they're not moving. But, the thing in the middle is moving *counterclockwise*. And it's starting to, it's starting to spin and spin and spin.

The scene that Betty described was somewhat similar to the Canadian report where witnesses watched a hoop-shaped object hovering and rotating over the UFO on the water.

Betty I'm wondering what it is. And, and the *being* says they are purging and lining the *cyclonetic trowel*. [phonetic rendering]

Bob Is the *cyclonetic trowel* part of the craft?

Betty I, I think it's that thing that is spinning counterclockwise, I don't know. It keeps spinning and spinning. Oh, and there's, there's—It, it looks just like *water* spinning around it, on it, on this smooth thing. It looks like water going around and round.

Bob Okay, I want you to stop. Relax a minute. I want you to fix this in your mind, exactly what you're seeing now, so that later on you will be able to draw it in great detail. Just take a second or two. Relax. Look it over real well. Fix it in your mind and then, when you're ready, continue on. [Figure 15]

Betty [*pauses*] It's spinning around and round and water's with it. And, what's happening is, these *silver balls* are starting to *light up*, that are on those *jacks*. It's like bright white light there. The *balls* aren't silver right now. They're white light and—[*pause*] They're

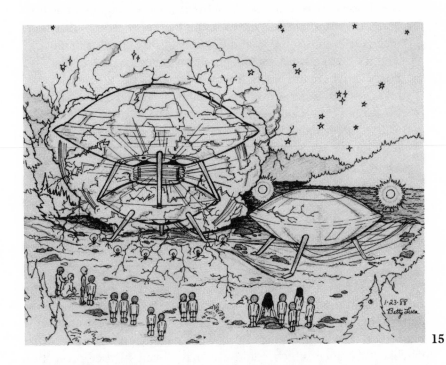

15

raising up in the air above the *jacks*. And they're just hovering in the air with white around them. And they're white light. And just—They're there, above the *jacks*. And they're raising up higher above the *jacks*. But, it looks like that spinning is causing *steam* or *mist* all over—Sending out, like, cloud or puffs of *steam* or something. [*sighs*] And it feels like it's starting to get warm here. Ah, it's getting warmer for some reason. I'm warmer. [*sighs*] The *being* says: "Balancing the oscillating telemeter wheels and leveling." Ah, I just can't understand some of that.

Bob That's okay. Just, just try to repeat what you're hearing, even if you don't understand it.

Betty But, I, I don't know the words to use.

Bob Okay.

Betty tries her utmost to catch the phrases that the aliens are using to describe their ongoing operation but finds it almost impossible to do so.

Betty Rotating series of semi-full swing back. Liquid line? Magnetic rings [*pause*] and the depolarized rim. And there was something else, I don't know. [*sighs*] And, oh! Is that something. Oh, this is beautiful, beautiful! Tch, there's bright light now right *in* that spinning part in the center? And the steam? It's like clouds all around. And it's causing *rainbows*. Ohhhh, this is beautiful. There's like bright, bright light coming from that spinning thing—and the middle—with water or something spinning around and round. And it's causing clouds all over the place and, and *rainbows*. And those *balls of light* hanging in the air over those *jacks* are turned, like, a *blue* color [*pauses*]—Real bright blue, blue. And, oh, it, that— Those *rainbows* are so beautiful! [*sighs*] Oh, this is so beautiful. But it is warm, so warm too. It's getting [*pause*]—You can hardly see anymore though because of the, [*pause*] the fog. That stuff is causing such a fog all over now. There's so much foggy fog. It's so warm, it's almost smothering. Whew!! And there's *lightning* coming all over the place! OOOOOOOh, that's scary!

At this juncture I wondered whether or not this was the reason Betty's nightgown had been forcefully removed because of the danger of static electricity. The aliens had also removed the black-haired woman's shirt. Both were naked but covered with a jellylike substance which could also have been further protection from static electricity associated with the frightening electrical display that they were witnessing.

Bob Okay, just relax.

Betty Oooooh, there's lightning all over!

Bob The lightning will not hurt you.

Betty Yeah, but it's going all over the place! Oh, it's scary! [*Betty is now exhibiting raw panic.*]

Bob Okay, I want you to step back and just observe. You've already been there and no harm has come to you.

Betty [*continues to talk excitedly*] There's lightning! There's lightning coming out of that whirling thing. And it's going so fast. And it's coming out of the clouds. You can see streaks of lightning all over the place. Oh, oh, I'm so glad we're back this far [i.e., from the craft]. Oh, there's lightning all over!

Bob It's pretty to look at though—isn't it?

Betty It's scary. It's too much lightning. I don't like it! The lightning. It's too strange—All over the place.

Bob Okay.

Betty It's even hitting those *balls*, those blue *balls*. Those blue *balls* *of light*. And, and going all over it. Oh!

Bob Okay. Now, just relax. Let's go—

Betty [*interrupts*] Oh, it's scary! The lightning.

Bob Let's go further ahead—

Betty Ohhhh!

Bob—after the lightning stops. Let's go to where the lightning stops. We're moving ahead in time now. The lightning *has* stopped. The lightning *is* gone.

Betty stopped talking. There was a long pause and she eased forward in time becoming relaxed once again. Then she spoke without further prompting.

Betty It's raining. We're getting drenched. Oh, I'm so drenched. It's just heavy, heavy rain—like buckets of rain coming down on us. [*sighs*] But it's cooling us off because it was so warm. Oh, it's raining, it's just raining. It's starting to slow down a little but I feel drenched.

It seems as if the quizzical operation performed by the aliens may have produced a localized artificial cloudburst.

Bob Are the *beings* out in the rain also?

Betty Yes. They're just standing there and the rain is just coming down. It's starting to go real soft now. Oh, and it's washed off all that shiny stuff off of me. My hair is soaking wet from it. It's starting to let up. And that bigger craft is—the spin is starting to slow down. The water is going round and round and it's going slowly. And the rain is just very lightly now. I can see on the big, big craft—There's like huge indentations, like windows. They were spinning—Big silvery-colored craft. It's slowing. And it's just slowing down. And it's stopped. Oh, I feel prickly. All over my body feels prickly. [static electricity?] Oh, oh, that feels just like my whole body is fast asleep. And it's, oh, it's all prickly, prickly, prickly feeling—All over my—[*Bob interrupts*]

Bob Are you still outside?

Betty Yeah, next to that *being*. The lady's there. [*sighs*] All her *shine* is gone too—Just sitting there and they're wet. And the center thing stopped. And now it's starting *clockwise* very, very slowly. [*pause*] Very slowly. [*pause*] Very slowly. [*pause*] Still going clockwise. [*pause*] And it stops. [*pause*] And swinging back again to *counterclockwise*. [*pause*] Slowly. [*pause*] Stops. [*pause*]

Bob Do the *beings* indicate what the purpose of this is? Why it's stopping and going back and forth?

Betty No. I don't know. It's going forward— [*Bob interrupts.*]

Bob Okay.

Betty Clockwise. It stops. [*pause*] The *balls of light* are still hanging in the air and they're white now—and over those things [i.e., what Betty has been calling *jacks*]. And the *beings* are going over now and collecting those *balls of light*. And they're going up into the bottom craft [i.e., the other landed craft under the larger hovering UFO]. [*pause*] They're coming out after those [*pause*] *jacks*. And they somehow twist the top and the things start picking up those skinny arms. And I don't know if it moves itself up, or they are folding them with the top of their hands. And it works its way out of the ground [i.e., automatically]. They're bringing one of them over [*pause*] and setting it on the ground by us. The rest are folding those arms up, like [i.e., the arms on the *jacks*] [*pause*] And the—A *being* that went in the craft that we were in is coming out now. And he's got, he's got my nightgown and that lady's shirt. And he's giving it to us. And he's also got a round thing, like a record, in his hand. And I'm putting on my nightgown. I'm still wet and my hair feels so wet. [*pause*] And she's putting on her shirt [*pause*]. And the *being* is taking that record, ah, like a black record—black on the inside. And it's, it's got copper on the other record and it's just—[*pause*] He's putting it on the ground and taking that gold [copperlike] thing off the top of that *jack* [the one that the alien had left on the ground]. And he's placing it upside down on top of that record [i.e., the *record* is like a stand for the *jack*]. And the thing slides down somehow. Oh, and he's putting, like a sleeve or something to cover those tiny little teeth there that were all buzzing around there when they put it in the ground. [Betty is describing the motorlike mechanism that drove the *jacks* into the ground automatically.] And he just set it there.

Bob Does he say, or do you know, what this thing is for?

Betty No. That man over there. They're telling him to get up or something cause he's getting up and he's following the *beings* into that craft that they came out of. He's still very ashamed and it's so embarrassing. They should let him have some clothes too. They're going inside and that tall skinny one is following in. [*pause*] One of the *beings* in that ship is coming over and talking with the crew of that—In the ship we came in.

Bob Can you tell what they're saying?

Betty No. They don't use, move their mouth.

Bob Do you hear anything in your mind?

Betty No, but he's going over and taking the *ball of light* from the one that's beside that lady. And that lady's getting up. They're taking that lady too—they're taking her over to the craft that that man was brought into. [*pause*] That cylinder, silvery thing is separating now from the big, big craft and that little bottom craft. It's pulling up inside and going down inside the top of the smaller one. [*pause*] And the legs are lifting up off of—unclamping themselves from the small craft. [*pause*] And two, three of the *beings* are out and they're pulling in those hoses that were connected to the bottom craft [i.e., the one under the large hovering UFO] to the water. Somehow they're just moving very easily. Just moving, sliding along.

Bob Do you get the impression when you look at them—are—do they look like they're made out of rubber or glass or plastic? Do you have any ideas?

Betty They're black and green and clear color. They look sorta either glass or plastic. And some—The glass one's look, ah [*pause*] It looks sorta, ummm [*pause*] like rubber.

Bob That's okay. If you can't describe it, that's okay.

Betty They pull those in so you can't see them anymore. And one of them's coming over to the *beings* that were with us. He's talking with the others, I guess, cause they're face to face. There's three of them listening to what he's saying. And yet they're not moving their mouths. He's probably gonna come and get me too. [*pause*] And they're standing there [*pause*] and one of them turned and looked at me. [*pause*] And then turned back to them. He's leaving. He didn't come over to get me. [*Betty sounds puzzled.*] He's going over into a, the craft, too. The others are going into the craft there that were with him. They left one of those *jacks* upside down. That big, big craft or ship is, is just hovering now over the smaller one. [*pause*] And suddenly the lights on the circular part of it all went on! Lit up the whole bottom up, the bottom of the top craft. [*Betty sounds amazed.*] They're *shrinking* that craft! That ship is getting smaller from those lights around the edge in the bottom of that big ship. [Figure 16]

Bob Do you have an idea as to how small it gets?

© 1·23·88
Betty Luca

Craft was shrunk to the size of a car!
(with the man and lady in it!) and the beings

16

Betty It's about the size of a car almost.

Bob Uh, huh.

It appears that Betty has witnessed what the aliens call *deopulating* first hand!

Betty And now that big craft is just putting off those lights that beamed down on. It's lifting upward. And the smaller craft is start-ing to—starting to lift off and lift upwards. And its, its legs go in. It's like going in a circular motion and it's taking off over the lake. [*pause*]

As Betty watched the craft lift off the ground and retract its landing gear and move off, her voice began to sound worried. Betty wondered if she was going to be left behind.

Betty I don't know why. I don't know why I wasn't able to go with them too. [*pause*] But the craft [the large one] is just hovering way above, and I'm just standing there. And a *being* comes over and he's taking that, that, [*pause*] *jack* and with the *record*like on it. And he's bringing it over by where the big craft is.

Bob Okay.

Betty And the big craft is just hovering there and it shoots out some kind of a light toward the tip of that thing [jack] on the ground. And when it does, all these sparkling lights—tiny, tiny, beautiful, beautiful, beautiful, ah-h-h—Oh, that is beautiful!

Bob Okay, again I want you to stop right here.

Betty [*Gives a long, long sigh*]

Bob I want you to relax for a minute and look at these beautiful, beautiful lights. Fix them solidly in your mind so that later on, it will come back to you very clearly. And, you will be able to draw it in detail. You may go back when you are ready.

Betty [*pause*] It's so beautiful. That light that came out and hit the very tip of that thing [jack] is all like sparkles, sparkling, and lights just floating all over the place—Like, like fireflies that are lit all the time. And they're all sort of colors. Tiny, tiny lights—just all over the place and it's beautiful, beautiful, beautiful. They're just like swarms of bees but they're light! Tiny light! Like swarms—Just [*sighs*] beautiful! They're just flying all around and they're like in streams. And now the, the light is being taken back up to the ship [i.e., pulled back in a telescoping manner as if it were solid!], so that it's not shining down on that tip there [i.e., the tip of the remaining *jack*]. But there's still a continuation of tiny, almost like bubbles, coming out. But they're tiny lights just flowing out of that. [*pause*] And they're floating around [*pause*]. And that craft is opening up the door—on the one I came out of. And the lights are like swirling around and going into the craft. [*pause*] Oh, it's just beautiful. It's like a stream of all colored tiny lights. It's just fantastic [*pause*] Oh! All the lights are going out. There's no more tiny lights outside. And the door is closing. [Figure 17]

Bob felt that Betty had undergone more than enough for this session and slowly but surely brought Betty back to the present time.

Bob . . . I want you to slowly come back to January 22, 1988. You're in the trailer lying on the couch, perfectly relaxed.

Bob eased Betty back to her normal state of awareness and told her that she would remember her experience in detail and would awaken totally refreshed and relaxed.

Betty [*Awakes and yawns*]

Bob Watch your eyes, I'm going to turn on the light.

Betty Oh boy!

17   *1973*

I echoed Betty's "oh boy" and just sat dumbfounded for several
minutes in front of the now-silent tape recorder. Who would
believe such things could happen? Each session seemed to be more
incredible than the one before. Later I went over Betty's experiences
in this chapter with MUFON's consultant in astronautics, John F.
Schuessler, B.S.M.E. John is the Deputy Director of MUFON and
directs MUFON's *Project VISIT* which attempts to extract technological data for study from UFO reports. He is also Project
Manager for Space Shuttle Operations with the well-known aero-
space company, McDonnell-Douglas.

Phonetic renditions of words like "Transversal Shock," "Cyclonetic Trowel," "Magnetic Rings," "Depolarized Rim," and other terms repeated by Betty and other abductees meant nothing to John. He found Betty's description of the rendezvous with other crafts at a lake fascinating. He speculated that the taking on of water and obvious electrical phenomena described around the spinning cylinder on one of the craft *possibly* could have been some kind of atomic energy *fusion* process. In any event, we mutually agreed that it would very difficult for even man's best minds to understand what Betty had experienced. It would be analagous to a primitive aborigine being confronted with television or some other marvel of twentieth-century technology. It would be magic to the aborigine and a *scientific miracle* to the Ph.D!

CHAPTER

S i x

Visit to
the Nursery

As I waited somewhat impatiently for the next tape to arrive from
Florida, I wondered how many other people had been privileged to
witness what Betty herself had experienced. Since the publication
and reprinting of *The Andreasson Affair* books, hardly a week or two
goes by that I don't receive a phone call or letter from possible
abduction victims. Typically, these people have experienced periods
of missing time after having sighted a UFO. Whitley Strieber,
author of *Communion*[1], has received hundreds of letters from
alleged abductees. Granted, letters and phone calls comprise only
raw data. I have, however, referred a great number of such people
to qualified UFO researchers who have documented cases similar to
the Andreasson case. The aliens told Betty that they were interfac-
ing with many other people to prepare them for a helpful role in
their overall plan for mankind. But Betty, as far as I can ascertain,
has been specially chosen to somehow, as the aliens put it, "show
the world." Show the world what? This was the question that
hounded me as I listened to the tapes and reviewed the complete
saga of Betty (Andreasson) Luca in my mind's eye. The next tape
arrived in early February. It was dated February 7, 1988. Again I
plugged in my recorder and entered the twilight zone of overall
UFO phenomena.

The voice of Bob Luca shattered my reverie as he datemarked

the next hypnotic regression session. The quality of reproduction was pleasing as compared with prior tapes. I was soon to find out why. It would make things easier for me.

> *Bob* This is . . . February 7, 1988, 10:30 P.M. This is the first session that we're making with the new equipment. Hopefully the sound will be much clearer and easier for you to transcribe.

The Lucas had finally invested in a good quality tape recorder. After Bob's welcome announcement, he patiently and gently brought Betty back to the time where she had left off at the last session.

> *Bob* I would like you to go now, back to the time we discussed a short while ago, when you were seeing some beautiful lights. And there was something on the ground. And the lights were just beginning to fade. I'd like you to tell me what you're seeing. [*There was a long pause and no response from Betty.*] This was in 1973. A woman and a man had just been taken away and you were left. And you were seeing some beautiful lights. Tell me what you saw from there.
>
> *Betty* It has this machine that they sat down on the ground. [i.e., what she has referred to as the *jack* and the attached *record*]. It was one of those *jacks*. And they had taken the top off. That one *being* had this thing that looked like a *record*. And it looked like copper on one side and black stuff on the bottom. And he had put it in the top of the machine—that *jack*—the top. He had turned it upside down and it's just there on the ground. And that big, big craft— after that little one left—that, that big one had shrunk it to about the size of a car. And that *man* and that *lady* and the other *beings* in it left. That small craft left. The bigger craft is over. And light came out of it and hit the tip of that upside down *jack* and went. That light went back up.

Betty then began to describe again the myriad multicolored lights which became visible after the light from the large craft had hit the *jack* on the ground. Bob let her continue to describe them in real time. It was like listening to a tape recording of her description from the last session. Rather than repeat her prolonged description, I've elected to record the events that occurred after the swirling colored lights entered the door of the craft in which Betty had come in.

Betty They're all going into the craft and in the door [*pauses and gives a long sigh*]. And the door is closing. Now . . . I can't see any more of those little tiny lights. They've all gone inside the craft. And the door is shut. And now, one of the *beings* is over working underneath the craft. And one is going over and taking up that *jack* and is folding up that *jack*. And he's taking off that recordlike thing and bringing it over where I am. And, and he's taking that bowllike thing and putting it back on top of it. Now, they're, they're going off to the side—all of them. They must be talking about something. They're looking up at the bigger craft and it's just hovering. No! It isn't hovering there anymore [*sounds very surprised*]. Oh, it's moving over, over, close to, um, almost above the craft in front of me. Oh no! Oh no! I got this nightgown on and there's—If they're going to do the same thing and they're not remembering!

Betty remembers the aliens' prior warning about static electricity and her nightgown. She is afraid that the aliens are about to repeat the dazzling electrical display with the other craft but have forgotten to have her take her nightgown off.

Betty The big craft is hovering over on top of the smaller craft there. Oh, they're coming over toward me—a couple of them. And the other one's coming over. And I'm getting in back of one of them and following. And there's one in back of me.

Betty's movements, for the most part, were completely involuntary. The aliens just floated her around at will. Again, the familiar stance was repeated when they moved her. One got in front of Betty and the other in back. They seemed to move as a single unit during this procedure.

Betty And we're going inside the craft, the smaller craft. We're going to go inside. But that big craft is right above us—Right over the small craft. [*pause—Betty sounds worried.*] I wonder if they're gonna shrink us too! We're just moving toward the craft—And that one with that machine [*jack*] now. The door's opening and he's swooping into the craft [i.e., the *being* with the *jack*].

Again, the aliens got in the now familiar stance with Betty in preparation for transportation up into the craft. Betty was always floating just above the ground. An invisible force moved the *beings* and Betty up into the craft. During this momentary swooping flight, Betty felt a distinct drop in temperature.

Betty And we're getting in line and swooping in. And, ohhh! It feels so strange, just *cool*, moving upward into the craft. We're all inside and the door is closing. [*sighs*] And we're just standing there. And that one with the machinelike thing [*jack*] went into another room. And the door just went up—and out he went—and down the door comes! You couldn't even see where the doors are.

Time and time again, during this and other of her UFO experiences, Betty is amazed at the seamless doors that are invisible until they are operated. Other abductees also have mentioned this facet of alien technology.

Betty The other ones are standing to the side. [*sighs*] One is in back of me. I think, think they're talking but I don't know what they're saying to each other. [*sighs*] One is coming over to me [*pauses and sighs*] and saying: "Follow me please." And he just gets in front of me and I'm moving along with them—and one in back. And the others are leaving out the other door. That door there, to the right, where the other *being* went through with that *jack*. And then we are going to another door right straight ahead. Oh! [*pause*] We're—[*pause*]

Bob What are you seeing?

Betty We're in the room, that ah—There's, um some things whizzing round. A big round—seems like a round room.

Bob Okay. I want you to stop for a minute and take a real good look at this. And I want you to remember every detail that you can, so that later on, you can draw me a picture exactly as you see it. Just take your time. Look around. And you may go on when you've had a good look.

Betty [*pauses*] This room, it has—It looks like this, this white light in streaks keeps circling. And the very center, it looks like, looks like, looks like *water-light*! It's—I don't know how else to explain it. Looks like water-light, just going down.

Many times, Betty was confronted with technological marvels that were beyond her power of description. Her drawing shows a cylindrical curtain of luminescent light that literally flowed downward like a waterfall. This in turn was girdled by a whirling circle of streaks of white light.

> *Betty* I'm just standing there for some reason watching it and I feel all tingly. [*pause*] They said—[*sighs*] "They're working a *shield* for us."—whatever that means.
>
> *Bob* They're working a *shield* for you?
>
> *Betty* Yes, they're working a shield for us to go through. So, we're just standing there. I don't know what they mean but—[*pause*]
>
> *Bob* Okay, and then what?
>
> *Betty* Just standing there waiting. And that light keeps whirling round. A whole bunch of light, white light, just—[*pause*] a real round circle, it keeps making.

It is apparent that whatever Betty was observing was dangerous to touch. She felt an electriclike sensation coursing through her body. Suddenly, the threesome began to move toward the circle of whirling white light which inexplicably thickened into a vibrating, glowing doughnut. Concurrently, her tingling sensation stopped and a *pathway* appeared through the doughnut of light. It was as if a finger had tripped a switch in an alien control room which somehow consolidated the whirling energy and neutralized a segment of it for them to pass through. [Figure 18]

> *Betty* And oh, we're going to be moving and we're just moving, floating like . . . and the tingly feeling is gone and we're moving *through* that whirling white light [the *doughnut*].
>
> *Bob* Do you feel anything when you are in the light?
>
> *Betty* No, it's like a *path*—like it's breaking through the light. And I don't know how they're doing that. . . . The light doesn't touch us. . . . We're just moving onward and we passed that ring or circle or doughnutlike thing of light . . . and it didn't touch us . . . and now we're coming up to that waterlike
> light . . . almost like a waterfall but it's not water, but it's light. I don't know what it is.
>
> *Bob* Don't worry about it. . . . You'll be able to draw it as it appears to you. Just continue on. [Figure 19]
>
> *Betty* We're going through it. And inside, it's all—[*pause*] hollow! And we're in a cylinder-thing with all that water-light around us in a circle, like it's a—[*pause*] Um, I just can't explain it. It just is so

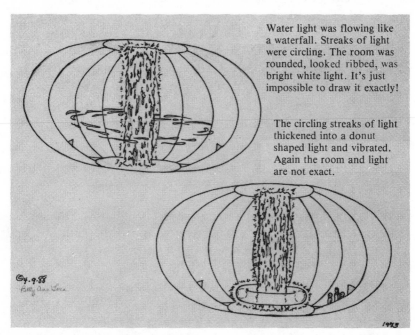

Water light was flowing like a waterfall. Streaks of light were circling. The room was rounded, looked ribbed, was bright white light. It's just impossible to draw it exactly!

The circling streaks of light thickened into a donut shaped light and vibrated. Again the room and light are not exact.

18

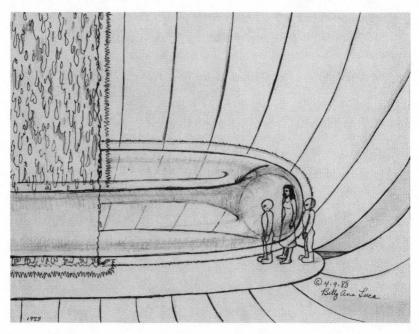

19

strange. We're just standing there, and in the center. [Figure 20] And—Oh, we're starting to move. We're moving *upward*, very slowly, very slowly upward. Very slowly going up and up. Oh, it's beautiful. Oh, there's those, um, those multicolored lights. Seem to be, um—[*pause*] like—Oh why can't I explain this better? It's like the tiny lights are—[*pause*] floating upward with the liquid water, liquid light, liquid light. I don't—It's just like, um, oh—[*Bob interrupts*]

Bob That's okay. What words cannot describe, you will be able to draw.

Betty Oh, it's so weird looking. We're just moving upwards some more and more. It feels like we're going a long distance.

At this point, I wondered if Betty were just being moved to another floor or to the larger craft that hovered above the craft she had entered. Evidence seems to point to the latter.

Betty Oh this is gorgeous. Oh, it's just so gorgeous. [*pauses*] We're stopping. [*pause*] And turning. [*pauses and sighs*] And we're going *through* that liquid water again—the one *being* in front and the other *being* in back of me, moving onward. And we're in some kind of a hallway. But it's, it's [*pause*] just different. We're moving along this hallway, and—Oh, we're coming into a room and I see some things up ahead.

Bob What kind of things do you see? Can you describe them to me?

Betty They look like *capsules*. They look like glass *capsules*.

Bob I see.

Betty And there's some stuff in it. There's like a, a board or something that these things come out on the bottom and on the top. And there's like, in front of it, there's a, a big round thing that is, is sort of like a, oh, um, a big round thing. And it goes like—Oh, it looks like, ah, it looks like it's, it's in the floor. And it can tilt. And it's got like, ah—[*pause*] It's got like—looks like jelly, like, like, ah, gray or jelly around the bottom part of it. And it can move it.

Bob Okay, I want you to take a minute here again and look real closely at these. And later on, you will recall totally what you see. And you will be able to draw it. You may go on when you've had a good look.

Betty My shoulders and my arms are very—Oh, they feel like pres-

We went upward as the water light poured downward, and the tiny multi-lights swarmed around going upward too.

©4-9-88
To Betty Ann Luca

1973

20

sure or lame or something. Oh, [*sighs*] I feel lame. And my feet and my hands and my legs feel fast asleeplike. I don't know. But my shoulders even feel lame, pressure or something. [*gives a long sigh*] Ohhh, and there are three [*pause*] big capsules to the right there. And it looks like a big open window, ah, not open, but open so that I can't see anything out of it.

Betty had entered a long corridorlike room with curved sloping walls. Along the floor were a series of round hatches that reminded her of manhole covers. Three tall glasslike cylindrical capsules stood in a row off to one side. They were located in front of an oblong opening like a covered window. She also noticed pipes running along the corridor which seemed to fit the contour of a segment of the oval craft. We couldn't quite picture what she was describing until she drew it for us. [Figure 21]

> *Betty* And, [*pause*] there's like, um, [*pause*] stuff on the floor there. And we're just passing through. Oh! I see on the *screens* on that first one [i.e., the first transparent capsule]. I see, like the ground and trees and stuff like that and stone. They have four of them lit up and other lights and writing. [Figure 22]

The screens that Betty referred to that were lit up in the first capsule seemed to have been remote viewing monitoring screens.

> *Bob* What, ah, what does the writing look like?
>
> *Betty* I don't know. It's not like ours.
>
> *Bob* Okay, I want you, I want you to remember the writing. And, later on—[*Betty interrupts.*]
>
> *Betty* My eyes are sore. My eyes feel sore. Them—[*Bob interrupts.*]

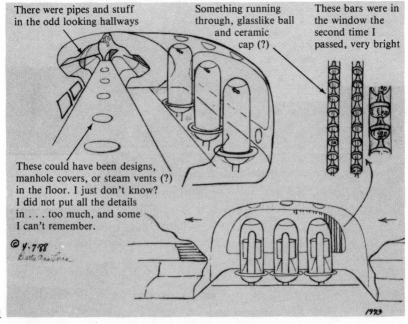

There were pipes and stuff in the odd looking hallways

Something running through, glasslike ball and ceramic cap (?)

These bars were in the window the second time I passed, very bright

These could have been designs, manhole covers, or steam vents (?) in the floor. I just don't know? I did not put all the details in . . . too much, and some I can't remember.

© 4·7·88
Betty Dan Luca

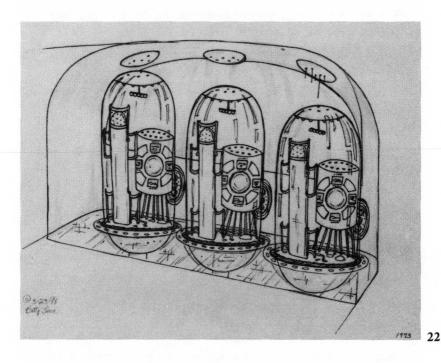

22

Bob And later on—[*Betty interrupts.*]

Betty Like sand is in them. Ohhhh!

According to MUFON consultants Lt. Commander Thomas Deuley, USN Retired and Major Richard C. Niemtzow, M.D., USAF, Betty's reaction might have been due to nonionizing radiation. Thomas was in the USN Nuclear Program and Richard is a USAF doctor/radiation specialist. Both explained that ultraviolet radiation could cause weak eyeburn at the molecular level which would literally feel like *sand* in one's eyes.

> *Bob* Okay, that's all passed. Just relax and step away from it. You may look at it as an observer.
>
> *Betty* Like thick sand. [*sigh*] And I pass. And I can see the second one too. And that's four screens. And it's got, it's got, it's like water. It's like water and ground or something or other [i.e., the scene depicted on the screens]. And the same thing. There's lights and some kind of weird writing. [*sighs*] I can't look at that. It's so bright. It hurts my eyes. Whew! Oh brother, it hurts. Whew! [*sighs*] And we're going past that third one [capsule]. That third one is lit up too. And it looks like just—[*pause*] I guess, the sky. The clouds.

I don't see anything else. Just looks like the sky. Oh yeah, and there's one with the stars.

Bob Are these screens in color? Or, are they in black and white? What do they look like to you?

Betty They're in all sorts of colors but you can see that it is, is like the sky or water.

Bob Okay.

Betty And also the trees and the ground—the first one. But my eyes feel—My eyes are hurting.

Bob The feeling in your eyes will pass. That feeling *will* pass.

Betty And we're just slowly moving on. [*sighs*] Ouch! Whew! Eyes hurt. It's like I've got something in my eyes. We're moving onward, and, [*sighs*] we're going through a door. Oh, it's beautiful! Oh my word! [*a long pause*]

Bob What is so beautiful?

Betty Oh my word! I'm in the woods. I don't know how I got here from there but I'm in the woods.

At this point, Betty thinks that she is back on Earth in a wooded area. However, she is still aboard the craft. Betty has entered a huge *vivarium*, an enclosure for keeping or raising plants or animals indoors. Perhaps this is what she had seen earlier behind a translucent wall in the smaller craft. However, it could just as well be a larger version contained in the bigger craft that was hovering above the small craft. It depends upon whether or not she was just raised to another floor, or to the larger craft when she and the aliens took the elevatorlike ride up through the glowing curtain of water-light.

Betty Oh, it's so green and beautiful. And there's a pond right there. And it's, it's just like, just so beautiful.

Bob Are these woods like the woods near your house or are they different in any way?

Even Bob thinks that the craft had landed back in Ashburnham and that Betty is describing the woods behind her house.

Betty Unnnnnnn! It just seems like woods. It just is so beautiful and it's so nice to breathe. Ohhhh! [*Betty takes a deep, deep breath of air.*] Oh! It feels like my lungs are opening up for a change. . . .

It's just so green. . . . The water is so clear. I, I can see fish there. Oh, wow! There's—It's just loaded with fish. Loaded! Loaded! . . . All sizes of fish in there. And such a small pond too. Oh, and I can see ferns. And it just is so beautiful. And, oh, I can just so—I can breathe here. [*Betty sounds excited and inhales and exhales vigorously.*] It feels so good. It feels so good.

One wonders why Betty reacted so strongly to the atmosphere within this biosphere. Was the oxygen content higher than the air elsewhere within the craft? Perhaps it was just the same overpowering freshness of air that one experiences when first entering a greenhouse full of plants and flowers. In any event, it really made quite an impression on her.

Betty I don't know how I got into the woods that quick.

Bob was still confused as to the whereabouts of Betty. Was she on earth? Was she on another planet?

Bob Are you alone?

Betty [*gives a long sigh*] No. The *beings* are there. There're two of them there and they're just standing. Oh, it just is so—Oh my whole body feels so good. Oh, it feels so great here.

Bob Is the sun shining?

Betty [*sighs*] No, there's no sun shining.

Bob But is it light?

Betty It's, it's not, it's not bright sunlight. It's just perfect. It's just perfect.

Bob Can you see any bright spot in the sky?

Betty [*sighs*] No, it just feels just perfect. Ohhhh.

Bob But, do you see any light source? Where is the light coming from?

Betty No. Oh! That door is opening again and there is light coming in. There's a—There's two *balls of light* floating in. They look, they're, they look like the *balls of light* that were over that lake [i.e., where the craft had landed previously near a lake]. And they're making it bright in here, brighter. One's over the pond and the other one went way, way down there in the woods. Looks deep in the woods. Oh, it's so—It's just so beautiful. I can just really breathe so good. Ohhh.

Bob Do the *beings* tell you why they're showing you this? Or do you know why they're showing you this?

Betty No. I don't know why. They're just standing there. Oh! And here come all those tiny, tiny colored lights. Multicolored lights. Oh, they're just [*pause*] floating in the air. Oh, and they're whirling around that *ball of light* over the pond. And now the other white *ball of light* has come up [i.e., the one that had gone into the woods]. Oh, it is so beautiful. I wish you could see this. [Figure 23]

Again, the familiar *balls of light* have appeared and continue to display yet another facet of their innate abilities. Betty again was about to witness another spectacular display.

Betty It's soooo beautiful. Those, those tiny multicolored lights are forming tiny balls around the big—bigger balls of white light. And they're just *circling* it and moving around. Oh, it's so beautiful. I mean, it is just so gorgeous. Makes me feel like Christmas with all the lights. [*sighs*] And the *being* is telling me to sit down here on the grass. Oh, it feels so comfortable. It is just so perfect. And those, and those balls of light are just like *tiny* balls of light—of all

(Pond)
1. Tiny lights
   formed balls of multi-
   lights and circled
   the large white lights.
   One hovered over the pond

© 7·1·88
Betty Luca

23

multicolored lights—just slowly swirling around the white *ball of light*. They just move around [i.e., orbit the larger ball]. Oh, it's so peaceful. [*Betty gives a long sigh. There is a long pause.*]

Betty appeared to be observing something with her mind's eye. Her face looked puzzled.

Betty The water. It, it looks like the, it looks like the water is going down. [*pause*] It looks, it, like the water is, is getting lower. Oh, and the fish. It's loaded with fish. [*pause*] Water is like going down. They must have opened a, some kind of a dam or something. [Figure 24]

Betty was still unaware that she was looking at an artificial pond enclosed within a tank on board the craft.

Betty But the water seems to be going down. [*pause*] Oh! The fish are kinda [*pause*]—They're all like flipping around. It's getting less and less water in the pond. [*pause*] What is happening? Those fish will die. There's no water for them. It's getting so down. [*long pause*] The lights [balls] are just hanging over the pond as these fish

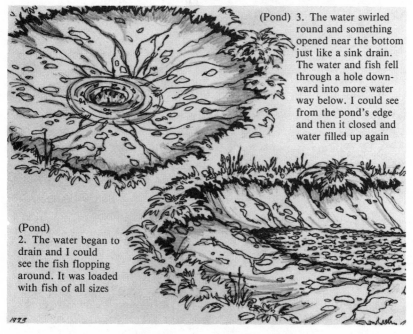

(Pond) 3. The water swirled round and something opened near the bottom just like a sink drain. The water and fish fell through a hole downward into more water way below. I could see from the pond's edge and then it closed and water filled up again

(Pond) 2. The water began to drain and I could see the fish flopping around. It was loaded with fish of all sizes

24

are flipping upwards in the air. And, they're, they're—They don't have very much water left in that little pond. Oh! [*long pause*]

Bob What do you see?

Betty Oh, the fish. There's something opening and the fish are falling down. Looks like they're falling way, way down. [*pause*] Like, there's, like, there's water there, way, way down.

Bob Okay.

Betty Like a, like it's, like fish are being [*pause*] put into another place or something. They're all falling into that water, way, way down there. There was no *hole* there before. [Figure 24]

Bob What are the *beings* doing?

Betty They're just standing there turned toward it. Oh, and now I got cramps in my legs for some reason. Ohhhhh.

Bob Okay, that will pass. The cramps will pass. Relax.

Betty The fish are all gone out of the pond and so's the water. And there's like a, an opening there. And I can see—looks like water, way, way down. [*sighs*] It's starting to close or something. And I'm just sitting there. And those lights [balls] over above it. [*pause*]

Betty looks at the *beings* and asks them to explain what is going on. She doesn't get an answer at first but her persistence pays off. One of them responds to her question.

Betty "What is going on?"—Why won't they answer me? "What are you doing?" They said they are just *replenishing*, just *replenishing*.

Bob Do they say *what* they are replenishing?

Betty No. . . . They just said only that they are just replenishing. Oh, now those tiny lights are leaving the pattern they were in [i.e., their orbiting of the larger white ball of light over the pond]. Those tiny balls. And they're settling on, on some of the trees there and on different parts of the ground. And there's water coming back into that pond. It's starting to fill up again.

Bob Where is the water, where is the water coming from?

Betty I don't know.

Bob It's not raining?

Betty I don't see any. I don't see any rain and I don't see any, any brook. It just seems as if the water is coming in again, just filling up.

Again, obviously the pond is a landscaped tank that was being replenished with fresh water. Most likely the water was siphoned from the real lake outside the craft through one or more of the hoses Betty had seen going from the craft into the lake when she had been really outdoors.

Betty Oh, it is so beautiful. All those tiny—Looks like Christmas. All those tiny lights all over the trees over there and on the ground. And, [*pause*] the *beings* are going out the door and they're leaving me there.

Bob They're going out the *door?*

Betty Yeah.

Bob There's a door in the woods?

Betty Yeah, there was a door there but you wouldn't know there was a door. But there was a door where we came and there was a door where those lights came in.

Bob still had not realized that Betty was still inside the craft within a huge vivariumlike section.

Bob I want you to remember the door—where it is—so that you can draw it for me later. Okay? Take a good look at it.

Betty I don't think I can draw it.

Bob Just memorize it. Look at it. Study it.

Betty But it, it *blends* and I, I don't think, I don't think I could draw it.

Bob Just remember it the best you can.

Betty And now just the lights [tiny lights and two hovering balls] are there and me. Just sitting there. And it looks like that pond is almost half full. I can even see the lights reflecting from the trees in the pond. And it's so beautiful. . . . Oh, it feels so good to breathe so clearly here.

Left alone, Betty became curious and decided to disobey the alien's command to sit on the grass. Little did she know that she was being monitored and that she would be stopped dead in her tracks by strange luminous streaks of energy.

Betty I think I'm going to try and get up and walk over to the side there, closer to the pond. [*There is a very long period of silence from Betty.*]

Bob [*wondering what was going on*] Where are you now?

Betty [*did not answer; another long period of silence*]

Bob Where are you now?

Betty [*in a strained voice*] I'm, I'm trying to get up and—

Betty tried over and over again to lift her body from the ground but found that she could not. Bob wanted to know what was holding her back.

Bob . . . When you tried to get up, it felt like what?

Betty Like pressure. And like, [*pause*] pressure. And I'm still trying. [*sighs*] At least I can breathe real clearly in here. This woods is just gorgeous. And I'm trying to stand up. And I'm, I'm able to stand up a little—But the pressure! I'm going to try to go down to the edge of that pond. That pond is all filled up now and I'm trying to take a step.

Suddenly, Betty is surrounded by swirling ribbons of light. She cannot move.

Betty Oh! There is a—I don't know if it's those lights or what but there's these lights on—ribbons of light circling me.

Betty's movement might have tripped off an alarm system which reacted instantaneously to her body's movement. However, this is speculation on my part.

Betty And they just keep on circling me. These different colors of ribbons of light. I don't know if they're some of those tiny lights or what they are but they're flat—like ribbons. They keep circling me. [Figure 25]

Warned by their alarm system, the two *beings* reentered the area. One of them carried a small, square, sparkling box.

Betty And, and these *beings* are coming in again, the two of 'em.

Bob [*still confused*] You say they're coming *in*? Are these woods *inside* something?

Betty I don't know. It seems like I'm out in the woods.

Bob [*puzzled*] Okay, okay, continue.

25

Betty Maybe I came out of something into the woods. I don't know. And the *beings* came in. And one of them have a, ah— Those ribbons are—They're beautiful but I can't move when they're circling me. I tried to take that step and they just suddenly appeared around me. The *being* has something in his hands that—He's coming over and touching. And it, and the ribbons go inside that thing that he's got. [*long sigh*] And they're just standing there off to the side. And I'm there in the woods. Oh! Ohhhh!

26

Betty's voice expressed utter astonishment at what she saw. I must admit that what she described next strained my already credulous mind to the brink of disbelief.

Bob What are you seeing?

Betty The *beings* are sitting me down. Telling me to sit down. I'm sitting down, and, there are—there are *babies* here! Little, little tiny babies. Oh, there's such—They're just tiny babies. And they're *walking* around. They're so small! They're looking over at me. They're in the woods and they're just looking over at me. Some of, ah, them look as if they want to come over. They are sooo small.

Bob Okay. Again, I want you to remember what these babies look like. Take a good look. [Figure 26]

Betty They look *human*! Oh, they're so beautiful but so small. [*pause*] And they, they, they're so beautiful. How can they be walking? So tiny?

The babylike entities, although small, are perfectly proportioned and are able to walk like adults. Betty found it hard to describe them.

Bob When you say tiny—Are they like a six-month-old baby? A year-old baby? Are they bigger or smaller?

Betty They are small.

Bob Are they smaller than a six-month-old baby?

Betty They look about, maybe—[*pause*] I don't know. Maybe twelve or sixteen or eighteen inches tall. They're just so tiny.

Bob If you were standing up, and one stood next to you, would he come up to your knee or higher?

Betty Oh no, they wouldn't come up to my knee. They'd be small. And they're coming out of the woods. And there's a whole bunch of them. They just look so *curious* at me. They're so cute. Oh, they're beautiful. I just keep on seeing more and more of them come out around some bushes and [*pause*] some stones and some trees. They're just little tiny things. They're so beautiful.

Bob Do the *beings* tell you anything about these babies? What they are? Who they are?

Betty No, they're just standing there.

Bob Do you have any feeling about these babies—What they are? Who they are?

Betty They look beautiful, they're just beautiful. Little things. Walking! It doesn't seem possible that they could be walking, like, and moving around. They're just too small. [*pause*]

It is obvious that Betty was not watching infants. Whatever they were, they were fairly mature but of extremely small stature.

Betty And one of the *beings* is coming over to me now. And he has something in his hand. And he's stretching it out to me and opening it up. It looks like some kind of a box. A beautiful, beautiful box. Looks like *crystal* with sparkles all over it. He's opening it up and there is something in it. [*pause*]

Bob Could you tell me what's in it?

Betty He's telling me to take that thing that's in there. I don't know what it is. [*pauses and sighs*] It's like, ah, I don't know. It's got a handle and it's beautiful glasslike and feels so smooth. And it's got like a [*pause*] rounded thing, like, on top. And they told me—Oh, it feels so good to breathe in here. I can breathe so good. Oh, those babies are so cute. Oh! And they're coming over to me. [*Betty laughs out loud.*] It, it looks so funny. It's touching my knee. [*Betty roars with laughter.*] Something is *odd* to them about *me*. Almost, like, I was a—[*pause*] something they never saw before. [*pause*] Just touching my knee. A couple of them.

Betty is so entranced about the tiny creature that she momentarily stops describing the wandlike instrument that one of the alien *beings* had asked her to hold.

> *Bob* What do they feel like? Are their hands cold or warm or moist or dry?
>
> *Betty* I don't know. It feels like a—just like a person. Like a little baby hand. Oh, and they're moving out. And they're running down with the others there. And they're all lining up for some reason. [*pause*] And the *being's* saying to take the [*pause*]—I don't know what he called it. [*pause*] That thing in the box there.
>
> *Bob* Okay, take a good look at that because I would really like for you to draw it for me later. Okay? [Figure 27]
>
> *Betty* And he's telling me to hold it in my right hand. [*pause*] And I'm supposed to—[*pause*] direct it towards the lights. And I'm raising it towards those lights in the trees there and pointing it at it. And, as I do, those lights all *shimmer*! Oh, it's beautiful. They're like—They're shimmering. They're like they're alive. Like those lights are living.

Whatever Betty is pointing at the lights seems to be able to remotely control them. Why they are letting Betty use the device is anybody's guess. It might be analogous to our giving a child a TV remote control to see its reaction during its operation.

> *Betty* And he told me to raise it up higher. And as I raise it up higher, those tiny lights are starting to come off the trees, that were shimmering. And they're going all through the air. Oh! They're landing on those little tiny babies—Right, right between their eyes. [Figure 28] They're, they're landed right between their eyes.

One is immediately reminded of Betty's experiences at ages seven and twelve when the aliens communicated with her through a tiny glowing floating ball that affixed itself between her eyes.

> *Bob* Did you ask the *beings* what is the purpose of this?
>
> *Betty* [*pause*] I don't know. They're not saying. It's something to do

with the *spirit* of man. [*pause*] All those lights now. Each one of those little tiny [*pause*] babies, I guess. They don't—I don't know if they're—They look like babies but they're too small. They got one of those lights, different colored lights, right in between their eyes. And they're standing in line. And they're moving now. [*pause*] They're moving. They're going someplace. Oh, there's a bright white streak of light up ahead there in the woods. A bright white streak of light. That's where they're going. They're going to the

28

white light. Oh, I feel so sad to see them leaving me. But, they
seem as if they're excited or happy about going where that white
light is. And that light is beautiful up ahead. It's just a—[*pause*] it's
just a *slice* in the forest, in the green forest—A slice of white
light. . . . And they're moving toward it. [*pause*] And they're go—
they're going. [*pause*] They're so little. They're all going. I don't see
them anymore. And that bright slice of white light now [*pause*] has
disappeared.

In retrospect, Betty seems to have been describing a distant door
which opened to admit the herd of tiny childlike creatures.

Betty And all that's left is—Oh, the lights are starting to disappear
too. The tiny lights. [*pause*] They're all going. It's like the lights are
going out—[*pause*] into the trees, into the grass. The lights are all
disappearing now. [*sighs*] And now I'm putting down that—I don't
know what they called it. I'll call it a *stick* but it's not a stick.
[*pause*] And the *being* is coming over to me with the box. [*pause*]
and telling me to please put it back into the box. I'm putting it
back in. [*pause*] And they're leaving me there for [*pause*] a while
because they were bringing those boxes in, in there. They're coming back for me, he said.

Bob decided to end the session for Betty's sake. She appeared tired. It had been a long but worthwhile probe of the events hidden in Betty's mind. Slowly but surely Bob eased Betty back to the present.

> *Bob* . . . Relax now. I want you to relax and remember this point. And next time, I'll bring you back to this point very easily, very easily. For now, I'm going to count to three. When I get to three, you'll be fully awake, here in the trailer, February 7, 1988. One— you're starting to feel a little bit awake. You're feeling movement in your feet, working up your legs into your hands. Two—You're starting to feel more and more awake. You can move about a little bit now. There's a feeling of relaxation and happiness coming over you.

> *Betty* [*stirs and starts yawning*]
>
> *Bob* You feel relaxed and yet you feel joy. You're starting to open your eyes. [*Betty's eyes open.*] Move them around. And, three— You're wide awake and very relaxed.
>
> *Betty* [*gives out a long sigh and comes out of hypnosis*]
>
> *Bob* And that's it, and that's it for this evening.

I stared at the silent spinning tape on my recorder, still dumbfounded at what had reportedly transpired. I wondered what went through Betty's mind that evening as she made the mental transition back to a Florida campground from an extraterrestrial nursery.

Chapter Six—Notes

1. Whitley Strieber, *Communion* (New York: William Morrow, 1987).

CHAPTER

S e v e n

Return from Oz

The sudden intrusion of these hidden memories bursting into Betty's consciousness left her emotionally drained and introspective for days. She would lie awake at night for hours rehearsing these events over and over again in her mind in an attempt to fathom their ultimate meaning for her and for mankind. It was a heavy cross to bear. Many UFO abductees seek help and empathy within abductee support groups because of the memories that they now have to live with.

As I reviewed Betty's relived experiences to date, I could not help wondering who would believe that such things could really happen to human beings. Many would treat her account as a modern-day version of Frank Baum's classic *The Wizard of Oz!*

Oddly enough, there were a few broad parallels between Betty and Baum's Dorothy if one wanted to stretch the facts a bit. Both were whisked to a strange place in the sky populated by small creatures who stood in awe of a powerful being. In Dorothy's case, it turned out to be a charlatan who posed as a wizard. Betty, on the other hand, was taken to meet *the One* but was prevented from telling us about her rapturous meeting. I had instructed Bob to try to unwrap this mystery sometime in the future. Only time would tell whether or not he would be successful.

In Baum's story, Dorothy was told that all she had to do was click her magic shoes and wish that she were back home if she wanted to return to her aunt and uncle in Kansas. Betty, however, was oblivious to even the concept of home while under the mind control of her alien captors.

When we left Betty, during the last session, she was still in the larger alien craft. She was sitting on the grass that covered the floor of an incredible *vivarium* where both atmosphere and lifeforms blended perfectly. It would have taken more than a wish and a click of her heels to bring her home. Still, I wondered. Betty must have been away for two to three hours. Soon morning would be breaking at the Andreasson household back on Earth in the little town of Ashburnham. Surely the aliens would be returning her soon. When would they, and how would they do this? It wouldn't be until med-February that I would receive the next tape which described Betty Andreasson's incredible return from Oz.

It was Wednesday, February 10, when Betty was ready to undergo another hypnotic regression session. Bob soon eased her into a deep trancelike state as she reclined comfortably on a couch in their trailer.

Bob We're going to go now, back to a time in 1973. A time when you were by a lake. And you saw the *beings* . . . remove the fish from that lake. You saw what looked like ribbons of light. And the *beings* had left you for a short time. And now, they're coming back for you. I want you to tell me what happened from that time forth.

Betty [*utters a long sigh*] I'm in the wooded area. And the *beings* have—two *beings* had gone out with the boxes in their hands and they said they would be back in a little while. And I'm just waiting for them. I can see the pond and the woods. And it's so peaceful. [*Betty takes a deep breath.*] I'm able to breathe so good here. It feels so good. It's so green. It's so beautiful. The water's so crystal. And I'm just wait—Oh! What's that? [*sighs*] Oh! That—I wonder what that was? [*pause*]

Bob What did you see?

Betty I, I, don't know what it was. It was a—I don't—It was like something spurted out of the water and different places. And, and something from the ground was moving some. Some of the ferns and some of the, the trees. I don't know if it was like a burst of air in different places or something. [*pause*] I don't know what it was. sigh] I'm just waiting for the *beings* to come in and—There it goes again! [*pause*] It's like, um, it's like air being forced upward or something causes it to move the trees and the ferns. I don't hear anything but—and also the water. There's four or five places in the pond. . . . There it goes again . . . like air blowing up.

Bob allowed Betty to continue to describe the puffs of air as Betty relived the incident in real time. It took time to conduct the sessions in this way but such a procedure negates the possibility for a hypnotist to ask leading questions. However, after a while, even Bob became a bit impatient and decided to break in to get Betty to move on to the next event. It seemed as if the aliens were now replenishing the atmosphere within the vivarium by pumping in fresh air from the outside. If so, it would mean that the craft was still in the desolate area that Betty had described when she was outside. As mentioned, the water in the artificial pond was probably replenished from the lake outside via the same kind of hoses that Betty had seen drawing water into the smaller craft she had arrived in.

Bob Okay! Does anything happen between now and the time the *beings* come back for you?

Betty The *beings* are coming in now from that door into the woods.

Bob [*sounds relieved!*] Okay, and what happens from this time on?

Betty They're coming over to me and—[*pause*] I'm just *raising up*! [floats up] And one is standing still and the other one's getting in front of me and I'm moving [floating] along with them. And the other one has gotten in back of me. We're going over to the door. Looks like part of the woods even. [*sounds puzzled*] And it doesn't really look like a mirror. It looks like part of the woods.

The walls and the door seem to give off a perfect holographlike, three-dimensional reflection that astounded Betty.

Bob Okay.

Betty And I'm going through that door into that room. That room we came out of. And, there's those three *capsules* up ahead. [*pause*] Oh! There's a *being in* that first capsule there.

Bob Does he look like the others?

Betty Yes. He's inside it. He's like standing up inside that capsule. There's two of them there. The one on both—There's one on both ends inside those capsules. We're coming up to the . . . capsules where they're, they're standing, not sitting there. [Figure 29]

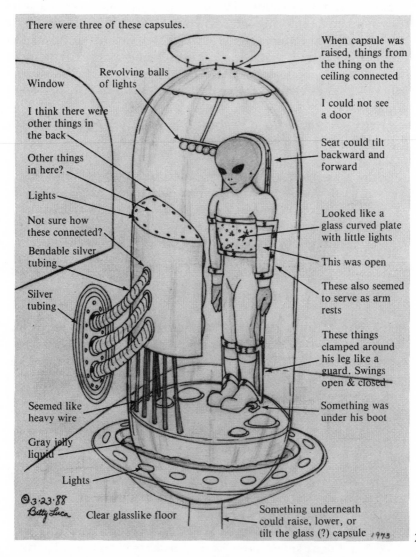

There were three of these capsules.

When capsule was raised, things from the thing on the ceiling connected

Window

Revolving balls of lights

I could not see a door

I think there were other things in the back

Seat could tilt backward and forward

Other things in here?

Lights

Looked like a glass curved plate with little lights

Not sure how these connected?

This was open

Bendable silver tubing

These also seemed to serve as arm rests

Silver tubing

These things clamped around his leg like a guard. Swings open & closed

Seemed like heavy wire

Something was under his boot

Gray jelly liquid

Lights

© 3·23·88
Betty Luca   Clear glasslike floor

Something underneath could raise, lower, or tilt the glass (?) capsule 1988

29

Betty is referring to the three capsules that she had passed earlier, when on the way to the terrariumlike area. This time, two of the capsules each contained an alien. Both were in a standing position and were attached by clasps to a back board. The capsules seemed to have been units that contained instruments essential to the operation of the ship. They seem to have been designed with the capability to absorb the effects produced by the craft when accelerating or performing rapid turns and maneuvers. Each capsule rested on what appeared to be some sort of shock absorber and each could tip in any direction. The only function Betty noticed were televisionlike monitoring screens. Power and data apparently were received and transmitted via heavy cables and three flexible silver tubes. It appeared that the craft was being prepared to move because both aliens were strapped in and gazing at the instrument panel located directly in front of them. Perhaps at last, Betty was going home.

Betty continued to describe the interior of the craft as she floated along in line between the alien creatures.

> *Betty* There's something coming out of the walls, ah, in front of that windowlike—From the top part of the walls. The walls and the ceiling seem to go right in together [i.e., they were seamless]. Looks like long things stretching downward, almost like bars but they're not bars. They look like they're, they look like they're [*pause*] porcelain or—[*pause*] They're close together like—[*sighs*] I don't know, they're just—[*pause*] They shot down from the, the wall and ceiling downward.

Betty seemed to be describing some kind of protective struts that slid down over the closed windowlike opening in front of the three capsules. Perhaps they were used to reinforce the structure of the craft during its flight. Again, this operation seemed to indicate further preparations being made for travel.

> *Betty* They're all the way down now and we're passing the second capsule. There's no being in the second capsule and there's one in the third one. And there's all, like these—It looks like bars, but they're not bars, that are in front of that—The window that was in front of those capsules. And boy, it feels cold in here suddenly. Ohh [*her voice shivers*]. We're moving onward, but, ah, the room suddenly got awfully cold. Maybe because of those bars that came down. I don't know. [*Betty continues to shiver.*] Oh, whoa, I'm cold! We're moving onward. Ohhh, it's cold in here.
>
> *Bob* Relax, relax for a minute now.
>
> *Betty* Ohhh. [*shivers all over*]
>
> *Bob* I want you to relax. Step out of that scene. Back away, back away.

Bob decided to attempt to have Betty describe the event as an observer rather than an actual participant in order to relieve her of the cold temperature that she was experiencing.

Bob Now, you're standing behind a curtain. Just like in a theater. You're warm and comfortable. Now, what I want you to do is to just take a peek through that curtain, back into that cold place, and let me know what's happening. But you're on the outside of the curtain and you're comfortable and warm. So, just look through there and tell me what's happening?

Betty [*gives out a long sigh*] For some reason, when I step back behind this curtain? Away from it? I felt like [*pause*] something *leaving my body, like.* [*pause*] It was a very strange feeling, stepping away from that cold, in back of this curtain where it's comfortable. I could feel it all through my chest. Like something, something left from my body. Like a—Oh, wow. I wish I could explain it. That was a strange sensation.

Bob That's okay. You're safe. You're warm. And, you're comfortable.

Betty But that sensation was so very strange.

Bob That's okay, as long as you're warm and comfortable.

Betty Something rushed, like, through my body. Something rushed through my body and I became very comfortable.

The strange sensation that Betty felt was akin to having an out-of-the-body experience as she mentally left being a participant to become an observer watching *herself*!

Bob Okay, what are the *beings* doing?

Betty They're just moving on and we're floating. And I can *see myself* floating in between the other two!

Bob Okay.

Betty And we're moving past that third capsule and now we're into a hallway. Very—I don't know—peculiar, odd hallway.

This was similar to the same unconventionally shaped hallway that she had passed through before when on the way to the *nursery*.

Bob Does the hallway look warm and comfortable or is it, would it be cold too?

Betty I don't know. It is just very—It looks like some pipes and stuff in this hallway. And it was shaped funny. [*sighs*] And I can see myself just floating along. [*sighs*] There's one in front of me—a *being*. One in back—just floating. And we're going through another door into a very small cylinder room. It—I think it's an elevator. We're just standing there, [*pause*] waiting there, for awhile. [*long pause*] Waiting there for awhile. [*another long pause and sigh*] The elevator is going downward. [*pause*] Oh, and I'm getting a headache. My head hurts. It feels funny. It hurts. And my eyes are hurting from something. I don't know what it is. My eyes hurt and my head aches. And my eyes still pain in the back of them. And my head aches.

Betty again slipped from being an observer to being an actual participant again. Bob immediately came to her aid.

Bob Back away from the scene and look at it as an observer.

Betty I am, but I'm still feeling in pain. [*sighs*] And it's going downward slowly. [*pause*] And we're stopping. I can see, ah, me, standing there with the *beings*. [*pauses*]

Bob What's happening?

Betty [*sighs*] I'm just standing behind this curtain and watching myself and the two *beings* going out of the elevator.

Bob And where are they going?

Betty They're in the *round* room. [*pause*] Everything seems to *slow*.

Bob Slow? What?

Betty Everything seems to be so slow watching them from here [i.e., from behind the hypnotically induced *curtain*].

Betty could have been experiencing the extra effort that her mind was making to reprocess her memories from those of a participant to those of an observer.

Bob Do you want to go back to your body?

Betty [*does not answer*]

Bob If it's not uncomfortable, and you wish, then just move yourself back into the scene.

Betty [*Betty gives out a long sigh and complies*] And we're moving along and [*sigh*] we're on the outer part of that round room and we're stopped. And all of a sudden, that elevator is lifting upward, so there's no elevator there.

No sooner had Betty floated out of the cylindrical elevator than it reversed direction and disappeared into the ceiling of the round area that they had entered. As she continued floating along, something else started to come down from the ceiling. Again, the various devices that she witnessed were just too foreign to her to explain. It is indeed fortunate that Betty not only has a photographic memory but also a natural talent for drawing. If this were not the case, UFO researchers and those exposed to this case would be utterly baffled by mere verbal descriptions of the nearly indescribable!

> *Betty* Something else is coming down. I can't explain what it is. [*sighs*] And they're turning and I'm turning with them. We're moving through a door. We're coming into another room. And it looks like the same room in that craft that they brought me there in. When I first was brought into the craft. There's that *chair* there.

As mentioned before, it seems that Betty had been first transported from this original small craft up into the larger craft that hovered above it. If you recall, the two had been connected by a mating cylinder as illustrated in Figure 16 (page 77). When Betty left the larger craft, it appeared that it was being prepared to separate for take-off. It is obvious that the smaller craft is also ready to leave, for again Betty is floated to the *chair* in which she experienced g-forces when the craft lifted off from the field behind her house back at Ashburnham, Massachusetts.

> *Betty* It's really like a stand-up kind of seat. And they're bringing me over to it and I'm sitting there and standing in a sit position.

In the past two abductions, Betty was placed on or within different devices to protect her from the effects of high acceleration and deceleration. When she was abducted in 1944 as a thirteen-year-old, a cushionlike unit was employed. During her 1967 abduction, at age thirty, she was placed in a tank containing liquid and including breathing apparatus which was connected to her. This *chair*, Betty was told later, was the only facility on that particular kind of craft for moving humans. The aliens would even apologize for not having better facilities!

> *Bob* Okay, I want you to remember everything that you see as best as you can. Later on, it will come back to you. And you will be able to draw any of these things you are experiencing. [Figure 30] Go ahead, you can continue.

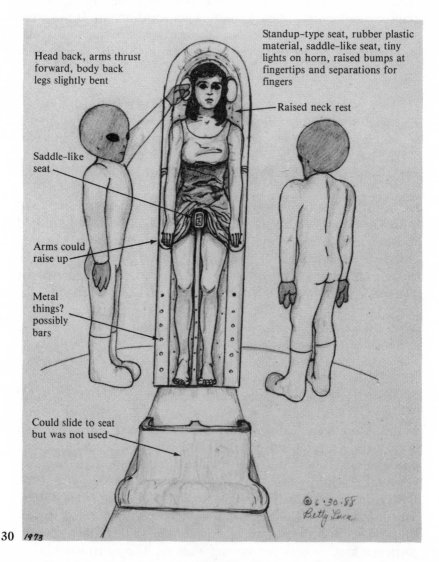

Head back, arms thrust forward, body back legs slightly bent

Standup-type seat, rubber plastic material, saddle-like seat, tiny lights on horn, raised bumps at fingertips and separations for fingers

Raised neck rest

Saddle-like seat

Arms could raise up

Metal things? possibly bars

Could slide to seat but was not used

© 6·30·88
Betty Luca

30 *1973*

Betty [*pause*] And the other *being* went out and left me there with only one. And that one *being* is communicating to me through the mind.

Bob What, what does he say?

Betty He's, very grateful to me. [*pause*]

Bob Why? For what?

Betty For being there. [*sigh*] That I helped the lady calm down, he says. [*pause*] It was very beneficial for the, [*pause*] fetus.

Betty, who had tried to communicate with the aliens several times without success, asked her unearthly companion questions relating to who they were and what they were doing. The entity's response, though incredible to the human mind, was related to Betty in an emotionless matter-of-fact manner.

Betty "Who are they?" I asked. I was trying to ask him. [*sigh*] He says that [*sigh*] they are the *caretakers* of nature and natural forms— *The Watchers*. They love mankind. They love the planet earth [*sigh*] and *they have been caring for it and man since man's beginning*. They watch the *spirit* in all things. . . . *Man is destroying much of nature*. . . . They are curious about the *emotions* of mankind.

Bob Do they have emotions?

Betty Not like man.

Bob But, didn't he say they *love* the earth?

Betty It is not the same emotion. It is a forever love—constant, continual. [*deep sigh*] And they are the *caretakers* and are responsible. And this is why they have been taking the *form* from man.

Bob How, how long have they been taking the *form* from man?

Betty For hundreds and hundreds of years.

Bob In their, their duties of *watching* over the earth in their craft— do they ever have problems with, um, the military from different countries, including ours? Has anyone tried to, to harm them?

Betty I don't know. He's just telling me what they're doing.

Bob I see. What else does he say?

Betty [*gives a long sigh*] He's saying that they have *collected the seed of man* male and female.

Bob Uh, huh.

Betty [*sighs*] And that they have been collecting [*pause*] *every species* and every *gender* of plant for hundreds of years.

The implications of such revelations are mind boggling and will be discussed in detail later on in the book. Somehow, Bob was able to keep his composure and continued his questioning calmly.

Bob Okay, and what happens after this conversation that you're having with him?

Betty I am in the, kinda, chair. And I'm feeling my—[*pause*] Oh! My hands and my feet. They are starting to feel so heavy. [*sighs*] Ohhhhh, pressure in my legs—my whole body! He's just standing by me.

As mentioned, MUFON consultant John Schuessler told me that the effects Betty felt are typical of g-forces felt during extreme acceleration and deceleration. Interestingly enough, the alien standing beside Betty did not appear to be affected.

Bob Okay. You know from past experience that this will pass.

Betty Um, okay. [*sighs*] I'm just sitting there. Oh, I can feel it. It feels like it just goes on gradual, but it goes! It's coming on fast! [*Betty gives a big sigh*] Such pressure! [*big sigh*]

Bob Okay. If it becomes uncomfortable, you may back away from it.

Betty [*sighs*] I'm just sitting there and he's just standing there watching me.

One wonders if the alien was unaffected by the forces that Betty was experiencing because of physical makeup or some type of invisible protective field of energy.

Betty Oh, I feel something of a let-up. Ohh, Ohh, feels better. Starting to let up some. [*pause*] Phew! Oh! Now it's just in my hands and my feet.

Bob Okay.

Betty [*sighs*] Ohhhhh! [*Betty is breathing heavily.*] Oh, please just rub underneath my lip. Oh, underneath my nose, and—It's itching so. I can't move my—[*Bob begins rubbing Betty*] Down, down, down and over to the left. To the left! Yeah. [*sounds very relieved*] Thank you. Phew! Thank you. Phew! Still can't move my hands and my feet.

Bob That's okay. That will pass.

Betty Oh, I feel as if it's letting up.

Bob Okay.

Betty Oh, another *being* is coming in now.

Bob Okay, what is happening?

Betty Another *being's* come in. [*pause*] And another one's coming in. [*sighs*] And the two are talking together and the one is still watching me. Another one came in. Ouch! My feet and my legs are—The life feels like it is beginning to return to my hands and my feet a little. [*sighs and pauses*] Oh, the one is saying to me— [*pause*] that [*pause*] in *our* terms, like, that *they're sorry*. But they don't feel the emotion. But, they say the words. That [i.e., the *chair*], that's all the craft had provision for was this type of [*pause*] *carrier*.

Bob Okay.

Betty And that's why I felt the pressure. [*sighs*] But there's three of them there now [i.e., in addition to the one standing by the *chair*]. The fourth one's going over. They're talking among themselves but not by their mouths, just with their minds. And they're looking over at me. Now the—One of them's coming over—Two of them's coming over now. And I'm being taken [*pause*] out of that seat and in back of the one. We're moving up a little bit and the other one's getting in back of me.

Again we note the typical procedure used to move Betty along which strongly suggests that the aliens combine some type of personal force field to move Betty along with them. Betty continued to describe her movement with them.

Betty Just floating along toward the—

Betty stopped short and gasped with surprise at what happened next.

Betty Oh! The door's opening! [*sighs*] And it's night outside. I can see down below. It's the grass.

The craft hovered silently above the ground. Betty then found herself thrust out into the night air!

Betty Ahhhhhhhhhhh! Going down out of the craft! Floating down to the grass. [*pause*] Ah, there seems to be [*pause*] three of them in back of me and one in front of me. We're moving [floating] along. Oh! We're back home! I can see the house. And we're moving toward the cellar [i.e., the cellar door]. We're moving across the lawn. [Figure 31] Um, I'm floating!

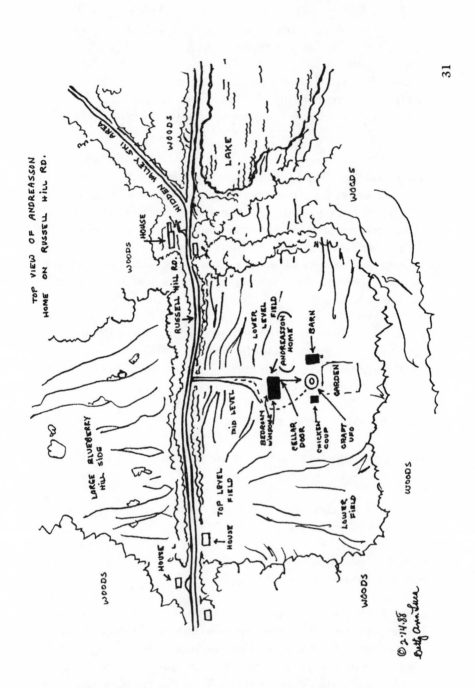

TOP VIEW OF ANDREASSON HOME ON RUSSELL HILL RD.

WOODS

HIDDEN VALLEY SKI AREA

LAKE

WOODS

HOUSE

WOODS

WOODS

RUSSELL HILL RD.

LOWER LEVEL FIELD

(ANDREASSON) HOME

BARN

N

MID LEVEL

BEDROOM WINDOW

CELLAR DOOR

CHICKEN COUP

CRAFT UFO

GARDEN

LARGE BLUEBERRY HILL SIDE

TOP LEVEL FIELD

HOUSE

LOWER FIELD

WOODS

HOUSE

WOODS

WOODS

© 2-14-88
Betty Ann Luca

31

Bob Okay, what happens when you—[*Betty cuts in.*]

Betty We're up, we're coming up to the door. The door is still open like it was when we left. We're in the cellar and it's dark. [*pause*] It's real quiet. [*pauses and sighs*] We're coming up to the stairs and I can see the partitions. Ah, the blanketed* partitions over there. . . . We're coming around [*pause*] and one of them is standing by the post and the telephone there.

This particular alien chose to remain in the cellar beside the telephone while the others floated up the cellar stairs into the house with Betty.

Betty And we're going up those stairs and so are they. We're going up the stairs. [*pause*] We're at the landing. We're up top there. We're going through that door. [*pause*] We're going around. I can see Jimmy's [her son] room there. And there's Becky's [her daughter] room there. [*sighs*] And I'm being brought back in my bedroom. [*sighs*] And they're standing there. And there's that other one that was down cellar—Now is in there with us. They all look alike but [*pause*] there was three at first and then there's four. And they're putting me back into the bed.

Bob Okay, I want you to relax here. I want you to relax and remember this part.

Betty [*gives a long sigh*]

Bob And remember this part. Remember this point in time. And the next time, [next hypnosis session] you'll very easily and comfortably be able to come back to this point in time. I want you to just relax. Just relax. Remember what happens as you approach your bedroom and from that point on.

Betty [*sighs*] We're moving into the bedroom and [*sniff*] I'm getting in bed and sitting there. And I can see that Jim is in the same position as he was when I left.

Her husband, and most likely everyone else in the house, was put into a state of suspended animation. It is an awesome capability to have this kind of power. Some abduction reports indicate that a

---

* Betty had sheets and blankets partitioning off bedrooms in the finished cellar for her children's privacy.

whole neighborhood has been affected in this way so that the aliens can carry on their operations completely undetected!

> *Betty* And one of the *beings* is coming over closer to me. And he's communicating with me. [*pause*] And he's telling me, I must, I must not, *I must not remember* this for a long time. Until they decide when it should come forth. I must not, I must not remember this, [*sniff*] until *they decide.*

As I listened to the aliens through Betty, I suddenly felt queasy. It was as if deep within my own subconscious I had heard similar words. Indeed, when I first delved into investigating *The Andreasson Affair*, over a decade ago, I received flashbacks of eerie nighttime visitations by unknown entities. They were vague impressions that seemed to rise to the surface of conscious memory and then sink elusively as I tried to grasp and hold them. The feeling was akin to that of waking up from a vivid and interesting dream that quickly sinks into oblivion before one can retain its content. I had shared this with other researchers who urged me to undergo hypnosis myself, but for some reason I had put it off. Even as I began writing this book the flashbacks continued. I determined once and for all to explore these fleeting memories to ascertain whether they reflected dreams or reality. The results of this personal plunge into the unknown will be discussed later on in the book. In any event, let us now return to Betty.

Again the aliens reminded Betty of their mission on planet earth and again they revealed that they had complete control over how and when its purpose would be revealed to man.

> *Betty* . . . And that I *would be used to carry much of the information to the world.* [*pause*] And they would clear the way. [*pause*] They would make the way clear. [*pause*] So, when the time came for me to remember, the human race would accept and receive and believe [*pause*] although many would not understand. [*pause*] I must not, must not remember this for a long time—*my* time—until the time was right.

The alien's words spoken through Betty also caused a strange unfamiliar emotion to trickle through my body—a hidden, instinctive feeling that I too was part and parcel of some alien conditioning process so complex that it strained the mind even to think about it.

I tried to regain my composure as I strained to concentrate on Betty's words recorded on the slowly spinning cassette tape.

Betty And so I'm looking at them and I feel myself suddenly laying down. And I can see them standing there but [*pause*] they seem to be growing dim [*sniff*] or else I'm falling asleep. I don't know-w-w-w-w-. [*Betty's voice trails off to nothing. There is a long pause. Then Betty jumps!*] Oh! The telephone. It's ringing. It's downstairs. [i.e., in the cellar] I gotta get up. [*long pause*] "Hello?"

Bob What are you hearing on the phone?

Betty [*sounds puzzled*] I'm hearing this high-pitched woman's voice and she said: "Ees Jimmy they-a?" And I asked: "Junior or senior?" [*sighs*] And she hung up. And I'm walking up the cellar stairs. Oh boy!

Oh boy is right! As we shall see later on, the aliens used such distractions to suddenly divert Betty's attention and thus reinforce the strong posthypnotic suggestion to forget the events of that fateful night. They had also used this technique during Betty's 1961 encounter in the woods at Westminster, Massachusetts. If you will recall, Betty was twenty-four years of age and mopping the floor when she heard a strange sound. She was literally compelled by the sound to leave the house and wander into nearby woods where she came face to face with one of the *beings*. After a lengthy, mostly one-sided conversation with Betty, the alien entity commanded Betty to forget.

Betty I will forget. I will forget all that he has spoken and I will forget him. And, I am to go back now to my house and I will not remember *at the ring* [i.e., of the telephone].

If one accepts the reality of such events at full face value, it is painfully obvious that the aliens are capable of knowing everything about us and can actually tailor their operations and plans by controlling the thoughts and will of the human mind. Indeed, if this were not enough to strain one's credulity, in the next chapter we shall discover that somehow they are able to know the future! Needless to say, this not only provokes some pretty hefty philosophical questions but it also raises equally mind-straining questions about the nature of *time* itself. Poor Betty's immediate future was not bright. Few people could weather the terrible tragedies that she soon would face.

CHAPTER

E i g h t

Portents of Tragedy

The next hypnotic regression session would bring back heartrending memories of tragedies that Betty had experienced during the Phase One and Two investigations. It also would shed new light on some of the mysteries that we had encountered then. Its contents would also reveal just how closely knit Betty's relationship was with the aliens. They appeared to have not only been monitoring every facet of her life but also seemed to have been able to motivate her very actions in order to carry out their plans. The actual session took place on February 16, 1988. Bob, in accordance with our gameplan, moved Betty chronologically to her next encounter with the aliens.

Bob I want you to move on now, [*pause*] from 1973 [*pause*] to the very next time that you had any communication with the *beings*. But, I want you to relax a minute and think about it.

Betty [*starts breathing very heavily*]

Bob Okay, I want you to go from 1973 to the very next time you had any communication with the *beings,* whether you saw them or heard them, ah, in your mind or otherwise. And tell me when it was and what you experienced.

Betty It's dark out and I'm in my bedroom.

Bob What year is this?

Betty 1975.

Bob And where are you in your bedroom? Where is your home?

Betty Russell Hill Road in Ashburnham.

Bob Okay, and what happens there?

Betty And Jim is, is sleeping there and I see the lights come in. Somebody's driven in the yard. [*pauses and sighs*] The lights are coming awfully close to the house! And they're coming off to the side there. [*pauses and sighs*] And it's stopping [*pause*] and Jim doesn't seem to want to wake up.

For a moment, Bob thought that Betty was back reliving the 1973 abduction experience. The scenario was nearly identical. However, it was not. In fact, we had even started to retrieve this event from Betty's mind at the close of the Phase Two investigation but were unable to continue because of the painful mental block that Fred Max referred to as a *shunt*.

Betty [*pause*] It's so quiet.

This sudden quietness that descends over the area during UFO encounters is puzzling. During Betty's abduction in 1967, when a UFO landed outside her house at *South* Ashburnham, not only was there an electrical power cut but, as Betty then described it under hypnosis: "It seemed like the whole house had a vacuum over it. Like stillness all around . . . like stillness." Many other witnesses have reported identical phenomena.

Betty [*pause*] Ohhhh! The *beings* are in the bedroom with me. [*sighs*] They're standing there and they're communicating to me [i.e., by telepathy].

Bob Can you tell me what they're saying?

Betty They're telling me [*pause*] it is *now time.* They're setting things up—Putting things in motion. [*pause*] They're saying also that I'm going to have to go through a short period of *hard time.* [*pause*] They have watched, watched me and seen what I have gone through [marital problems] and seen my loyalty. [*pause*] They're telling me different things. [*pause*] That I must [*pause*] *move* [i.e., from her present home]. That I will be *motivated* in certain ways and not realize or understand. It will be *them* in the background. [*pauses and lets out a deep, long sigh*] Very soon, I will *begin to remember.* . . . And they're saying, soon, very soon. [*pause*] They're *setting things in motion.*

As I pondered the aliens' words, I literally shook my head in wonder, for it was in 1975 that things were indeed set in motion. At that time, Betty had received mental flashbacks about her 1967 abduction. Astronomer and former chief scientific consultant to the United States Air Force on UFOs, Dr. J. Allen Hynek, had solicited UFO encounter information in the national press. Betty saw his newspaper article and on August 20, 1975, responded to it.

> To Dr. Hynek:
>
> I am so happy to read someone is finally studying about UFOs. Now I can tell someone of my experience . . . an encounter in 1967 with UFO occupants.

Dr. Hynek received Betty's letter and filed it for many months before it was sent to our investigating team for action. The rest is history. First, a 528 page, 3 volume report was prepared and sent to major UFO research organizations. Then, I wrote *The Andreasson Affair* which was published in this country and abroad, including an edition in Japanese. The book and a nationwide radio/television publicity tour brought the knowledge of Betty's encounter with alien entities to millions of people all over the world. The *New York Times* termed the book: "An unforgettable experience" and stated that it "must rank with the great classics of scientific revelation." Betty's mission to *show the world* had begun. Behind the scenes, the aliens would be orchestrating it to the very end!

The 1975 encounter was short-lived. The aliens had appeared to give Betty a simple but far-reaching message. Placed within her subconscious, it would provide help for her when she experienced the hard time that they had forecast for her. When they allowed the message to come to light, at the present time, it was to show us that they have been and are in control of all the information stored within the deep recesses of Betty's mind.

As usual, Betty's memory of the encounter was temporarily blocked by something akin to a strong posthypnotic suggestion. Again, their block or *shunt* was reinforced by the distraction of an identical enigmatic phone call. It was getting all too familiar.

> *Betty* And he's coming over to me and he's [*pause*] pressing my— between my eyes and my forehead.
>
> *Bob* Does he say anything while he's doing this?
>
> *Betty* [*begins to breathe heavily*] I, I don't know. I'm just laying there.

Bob Are the *beings* still there?

Betty [*sleepily*] Yeah, it seems like they're there but I can't see them.

Betty apparently had fallen asleep. Suddenly, the telephone rang and she jumped up.

Betty Oh! The telephone. I've got to get the telephone. [*long pause*] "Hello?" [*pause*]

Bob What do you hear on the phone?

Betty There's a high-pitched female voice, it seems like. And she's asking me "Eees Jeemy there?" And I'm saying, "Junior or senior?" [*pause*] And she's hanging up. And I'm kinda irritated because I'm wondering—cause I'm wondering now—what's Jim up to?

This is now the second time that Betty was awakened by this strange-sounding female voice asking for her husband. Betty became very suspicious.

Betty Why would, would a woman be calling this early?

Bob Is there a clock in the room? Can you see what time it is?

Betty No. It's early in the morning.

Because of the identical phone call to the one she has received immediately after her 1973 abduction, Bob wondered if Betty had somehow slipped back into the 1973 experience. He decided to check this out and asked Betty what year it was.

Bob And, do you know what year it is?

Betty It's 1975.

Having determined that Betty was still reliving a new experience, Bob continued the session.

Bob Okay. What do you do after you answer the phone?

Betty I got back in bed and I'm real peeved.

Bob Are the *beings* still there?

Betty, reliving the experience in real time, has now advanced to that point of time where she has forgotten the encounter. She just ignored Bob's question and continued on with her then current thought pattern.

Betty And I'm shaking Jim and telling him that a woman just called and asked for him or Jimmy Junior. I'm wondering why somebody would be calling like that here.

Bob Does he wake up?

Betty [*sighs*] He wakes up, but groggily, and just turns over and goes back to bed.

Bob Okay.

Betty And I'm just laying there irritated.

Despite the *shunt* and the alien-produced distraction of the phone call, Betty still had a nagging feeling that something unusual had occurred, but she couldn't fathom just what it was.

Betty And I don't know. Something's strange . . . like somebody was in the room. I can almost sense that there is somebody in the room.

It was as if Betty was experiencing a fleeting mental afterimage of what she had experienced just minutes ago.

Bob Okay. Is there anyone there now?

Betty Just Jim and I.

Bob Okay, I want you to relax.

Betty [*sighs deeply*]

Bob Deeper, more and more comfortable.

Betty [*starts to breathe heavily*]

Bob More and more relaxed. Now, I would like you to tell me the very next time that you either saw the *beings* or had communication with them or had anything to do with the *beings*. What was the next time?

Betty [*gasps and sounds very excited*] I'm in my bedroom and it's the weirdest thing.

Bob Where? Where is your bedroom?

Betty In Ashburnham.

Bob And what year is it?

Betty It's 1976.

Bob Okay. What seems strange or weird?

Betty It's so quiet in here and, and I—a while ago I heard, heard, the kids out in the other room and the television going.

Again, the oft-reported *quietness* occurred as yet another encounter with the aliens took place. However, the vacuumlike stillness was only experienced by Betty. The activities that she had just been hearing continued to go on unabated. Only she was affected by this curious side effect of alien visitation.

> *Betty* It's Aino and Alice's anniversary party tonight, today. That's why I'm getting ready. And, I, I just have to put on my shoes and I'm all set. But, it's just so *quiet* in here and I just can't *move*.

Concurrent with the uncanny stillness that had enveloped her like an invisible vacuum flask, Betty found that she was completely paralyzed from head to foot!

> *Betty* I'm sitting on the bed there. I'm all dressed in my, in my, my navy blue dress with the white polka dots. And I did my hair and makeup . . . just putting on my shoes. [*pause*] There's, there's a *being* standing there. [*pause*] He's communicating with me.
>
> *Bob* Could you tell me what he is saying?
>
> *Betty* He's saying—I've gone through enough. [*pause*] Things are going to change. There will be some hardship in it. And, that I am to go in the other room [*pause*] and turn the television knob to seven.
>
> *Bob* And did you do this?

Betty apparently had already forgotten that the alien had appeared and continued on just as if nothing had happened.

> *Betty* [*long pause*] I'm sitting on the bed and putting on my shoes there, my blue heels. And I'm just finished putting on my second one. The kids are out in the kitchen. They're playing there—couple of kids—Bonnie and Cindy. I don't know if they have cards or what they're doing there. And I can hear the TV going.

The eerie quietness that had settled around Betty had dissipated. Family sounds and the blare of the television filled the air once again.

> *Betty* And I'm just about ready because pretty soon Jim and I will be going to the anniversary party.

Betty then interrupted her own train of thought. She experienced a strong compelling impulse.

> *Betty* I gotta get up and go in the other room. [*a long pause*] That was strange! I wonder why I did that? [*sounds surprised and puzzled*]

Betty had obeyed the subconscious posthypnoticlike suggestion implanted within her mind by the alien. Again, this tactic of diversion, like the phone calls, seemed to have been employed by the aliens to strengthen and enhance Betty's programmed amnesia regarding the alien visit.

> *Bob* What was it you did that was strange?
>
> *Betty* When I got up, I went through the kitchen there and went into the living room. And Jim and Dad are sitting there watching a *Western* until I get ready. And I just went over to the television and turned the knob and changed the station. Oh, that was rude of me. I don't know why I did that.
>
> *Bob* What station did you put it on?
>
> *Betty* Channel 7.
>
> *Bob* What was on Channel 7?
>
> *Betty* I don't know. I just went in and, I, I changed the knob and walked right out. That I—Oh, Jim is going to be furious. [He was!]
>
> *Bob* It's okay.
>
> *Betty* I don't know why I did that. That, that is so strange.
>
> *Bob* Is the *being* there anymore?
>
> *Betty* What *being*?

Betty had no conscious recollection of the alien's brief visit and message. Again, it was locked within her subconscious to help her deal with what soon would happen between herself and Jim. It would also show us again, as Betty relived the event, that the entities had the uncanny ability to know and influence a number of *future* events. Later, it would become painfully apparent that these powers had certain limitations. They could warn Betty of impending tragedies but they could not interfere on her behalf to stop them.

The alien had told Betty that she had *gone through enough*. Looking back in retrospect, there existed, as in many families, a serious problem involving alcoholism. For years it had weighed heavily upon the security and well-being of the family and marriage. Indeed, on that very evening, after the anniversary party, the old problem once again reared its ugly head and the scene escalated into violence. The police were called, restraint was issued without arrest, and Jim was placed in jail for the night. When he was released, he did not return home. He disappeared without a trace for four months until he phoned Betty from Florida in January of 1977. Betty had begged him to come back and undergo treatment. She desperately wanted to keep the family intact. He refused. When she finally discovered where he was residing in Florida, she flew down and attempted again to persuade him to return home. He refused but did turn over ownership of the house to Betty. However, already overburdened with financial pressures, Betty was forced to sell the lovely home.

Both of these events had been predicted by the aliens. During her 1973 abduction, Betty was told that she would have to move. Now, during the 1976 encounter under discussion, an alien had told her that the problems she had endured for years would come to an end. Concurrently, she was warned that there would be hardship, but that steps had to be taken. She had *gone through enough*.

During Betty's reliving of the 1976 encounter under hypnosis, she had unwittingly supplied enough information to determine its calendar date and to corroborate several of her statements. Information that can be checked against real-time records helps to validate the efficacy of hypnosis.

In the original Phase One investigation, a number of Betty's relived events were confirmed through the examination of hospital, television, power company, and weather records. In this case, Betty had mentioned that an anniversary party and the showing of a TV Western had occurred on the day of the 1976 encounter. She also told me that her husband had been taken into protective custody by the police just after the anniversary party.

Armed with this information, I was able to track down the Andreassons' friends who had celebrated their anniversary. They told me that their anniversary date was on September 1 and that to the best of their memory, the party had taken place on the last weekend of August 1976. This left me with two dates—August 28 and 29.

Betty had not asked the police to search for her missing husband until early October. This was only after she had exhausted all leads to his possible whereabouts. Both relatives and the police assured her that his absence was probably temporary. The story was carried in the local newspaper. A search found the article in the October 13, 1976 issue of the Fitchburg-Leominster *Sentinel and Enterprise*. It was captioned "Area Man Still Missing." Pertinent excerpts are extracted below.

> Andreasson was taken into protective custody from his home on the night of August 29 . . . and kept overnight at the Fitchburg Police Station. Fitchburg police released him at 9:40 A.M. on August 30. Since then he has not been seen by members of his family or friends.

Thus, the date of the 1976 encounter was confirmed as being August 29, 1976. But, one further check still had to be made. Betty had mentioned that the event had occurred shortly before she had obeyed the posthypnoticlike command of the alien to switch the television set to Channel 7. She stated that when she had accomplished this, her husband and his father were engrossed in watching a Western. Other than Channel 7, only two other channels were well-received in that area in 1976—Channels 4 and 5. However, a check of *all* channels again confirmed the accuracy of Betty's account. An examination of television records for the date of August 29 revealed that a Western had indeed been shown in the afternoon. *Union Pacific*, a well-known Western, had started at 2:30 P.M. on Channel 4 during that fateful afternoon. This was the time period that Betty had received a *portent of tragedy* during her fleeting encounter with an alien! The worst, however, was yet to come. Betty's first conscious intimation of it was during a phone call with the new man in her life—Bob Luca.

In the first chapter, I mentioned that Betty and Bob met under circumstances that appear to have been prearranged by the aliens. For the benefit of those who have not read my prior two books on the Andreasson case, I will summarize the circumstances that led to their meeting and the events that followed. Both have a direct bearing on Betty's next relived experience and are part and parcel of the overall *Andreasson Affair*.

Bob Luca himself had a remarkable UFO sighting in June of 1967. He was driving through a wooded area on the way to a beach in Connecticut when something in the sky reflecting light caught his eye. Glancing up, he was amazed to witness two large cylindrical-shaped objects outlined against a blue, cloudless sky. He watched incredulously as two smaller oval objects suddenly dropped out of the two cylinders. One oval object sped off toward New Haven and the other in the opposite direction. A few miles up the road, Bob saw one of the oval objects drift downward toward his car. It descended with a *falling leaf* motion behind some trees just to the left of him. The next thing he knew was that he drove into the beach's parking lot three hours late. This incident had been a near constant source of puzzlement for years.

In the fall of 1977, Bob and a friend took an extended vacation to drive from Connecticut to California. On the way back, Bob felt a strange compulsion to abort his plans to go directly back to Connecticut. Instead, he went to Florida to visit friends.

Betty, because of her husband's desertion, had also gone to Florida temporarily to stay with relatives until she could get established in a job. This would enable her to move her family where it was warm. Betty had told one of her friends at work about her UFO experience and our investigation. It just so happened that Betty's co-worker was the person that Bob and his friend were visiting! She mentioned to Bob that Betty had some kind of a UFO experience. Bob felt that he had to meet and share his experience with Betty. Thus, another of the amazing synchronisms that pursue some who are involved with UFOs brought Betty and Bob together.

Upon returning to Connecticut, Betty arranged with us to meet Bob. It was decided to conduct an investigation of Bob's UFO experience. When we move back to discuss Betty's next encounter, we will find her recollecting a telephone conversation with Bob just after he had spoken with our investigators. Let's return to where we left off during the hypnosis session with Bob on February 16, 1988.

Bob Okay, I want you to relax.

Betty [*gives a deep sigh*]

Bob Relax. Now, I would like you to move, if you will, to the very next time that you saw the *beings* or heard them or communicated with them in any way. Can you tell me when that was?

Betty [*Begins to breathe heavily. Long pause.*] It's 1977.

Bob And where are you?

Betty I'm in Ashburnham. And I'm on the telephone talking with

Bob. It's around ten o'clock, I think. And he's [*laughs*] all excited on the telephone. He's just—He's telling me about—He went to the investigators and told them exactly what happened to him. They put it all down. And we're talking there. He's so sweet. [*pause*] Oh! [*long pause*]

Bob What's happening?

Betty [*Betty relives it in first person.*] Speak up so Bob can hear you.

Bob What are you hearing?

Betty It's, it's some of the *beings* and they're angry. Very angry. They broke into Bob's and my telephone conversation. And I can make out what they're saying: "It's finished. It is done." And they're really angry. Oh, they're really! They're talking very plainly but it's in a strange language, almost like a mad hornet.

It was the sound and intensity of the language that made Betty think that the aliens were angry. Although the language was unfamiliar, Betty received the same mental impressions that she had during other alien encounters.

Betty [*panicky voice*] And I told them to speak up louder so that Bob could hear even more clearly. And I heard—click, click—and they did speak louder. And it went—click, click down—and they kept on speaking. And then Bob is saying that he'd better get off the phone and, and call the investigators right away because they had told him that if anything strange or unusual should happen, to call them right away immediately. And so he's hanging up and I'm hanging up. And, as I do, I'm hearing tones, like, ah, musical tones of some kind on the telephone.

Bob did call and tell us about the bizarre voices heard during his phone call with Betty. Betty, in the meantime, was thoroughly shaken and blurted out what had just happened to her children.

Betty And, [*pause*] Becky and Todd come running over to me and—the—as I'm on the telephone in the hall. And they say: "What's the matter, Mum? What's the matter?" And I said: "The *beings* just interrupted Bob's and my telephone conversation." And Becky said: "Well I'm sleeping in where you are!" And then we went into the kitchen. And Toddy starts clowning around. And he's, he's laughing. And he's saying: "Come get me! Come get me!" [to the aliens, in jest] And, ah, I told Toddy: "Stop that Toddy!

Stop it!" And Becky's all upset and she's got Niccie there. [Becky's daughter]

It was fascinating to listen to this particular event because Betty had already reported it before during the Phase Two investigation. Now, she was actually reliving the experience and it tallied perfectly with what she had told us earlier. However, what we did not know then was that Betty again would have a nocturnal visitor with a tragic message. In retrospect, what was to occur next would help explain one of the mysteries encountered during the Phase Two inquiry.

Bob Just relax, relax, totally relaxed.

Betty And so, all the kids are around.

Bob Just relax. I don't want you to continue with anything that's disturbing. If the *beings* are not there, then I want you to move on to the next time that you communicated with them, or saw them, after this point.

Betty [*gives deep sigh*] The kids are gathered around me and they're saying: "What happened, Mummy?" And I told them that the *beings* had interrupted Bob's and my conversation on the telephone and for them not to be afraid because Jesus is with us.

Bob That's right.

Betty The Lord loves us. And, so we're sitting around. And, it was getting later, around ten-thirty or so. And so we decided to go to bed. But everybody wanted to sleep up in the large living room. And so, because we had sold a lot of the furniture, the kids brought their heavy blankets and laid them on the floor, and their pillows. And they made beds in the living room where I had the two or three beds set up. And the kids were all going to bed. And we're saying goodnight and giving kisses and saying our prayers. And we're all laying down. [*pauses and sighs*] And everybody seems to be dropping off to sleep. And suddenly, there's a light that shines into the window. And everybody's very *quiet* as if *time stopped again.*

At this juncture in Betty's life, Betty was selling the furniture and had the house up for sale because she received no support from her husband. Again, note the typical *quietness* as the UFO event begins. The Phase Two investigation had covered everything up until this

point because Betty remembered it all consciously. She had been
made to forget the UFO event.

> *Betty* And again, there's a *being* standing by me, by the bed. And—
> [*Betty starts to cry.*] It's telling me [*Betty is now sobbing hard.*] that
> they *could not intercede*. Something was going to happen! [*There is a
> pause as if Betty is listening and then she begins crying violently.*] They
> could not intercede but it would all turn out all right. It would be
> okay. My faith would see us through. They're telling me that—
> [*Betty gives a long sigh and stops talking and crying.*]

Betty had fallen asleep, but not for long. She is awakened by Becky
to witness a frightening spectacle. This too was remembered
consciously during the Phase Two inquiry and was reported by
Betty. Now, she was actually reliving the event under hypnosis.

> *Betty* Ohhhhhh! And Becky is—Becky's yelling: "Ma! Ma!" And
> there's all sorts of noise all through the room like trains or—Oh!
> There's all sorts of noises like trains or planes crashing or some-
> thing! And—[*Betty now is in total panic.*]
> *Bob* Relax.
> *Betty* And there's bright lights all through the living room! And
> Becky's yelling: "Ma! Ma!" And I'm sitting up and saying: "Becky,
> it's all right. I know what is going on. It's okay! It's okay!" And as I
> do, all those lights in the room gather together and a huge ball of
> white light goes whooshing around the room and over my head
> and out the window. And I said: "Becky, it's okay. You're okay,
> honey. It's okay, it's okay! Jesus is with us." The other kids start
> waking up because Becky was really shook. She was very upset.
> And I'm trying to calm them all down: "Everything is going to be
> all right. Everything is going to be all right." And, that—Bonnie
> and Cindy are up too. And, and the sky out there is just beautiful.
> It's, it's like lightning—heat lightning or something. But it's pinkish
> in color. Pink and orangey and yellow.

It would seem that side effects of the forces that had enabled the
alien to enter and leave the room were seen and heard by Betty. A
recent check with the National Climatic Data Center confirmed that
the sky over and around Ashburnham was overcast and foggy. The
weather station at Worcester, about twenty miles from Ashburnham reported lightning between 8:58 P.M. on October 19 to 3:58
A.M., October 20, 1977. Betty observed it from a distance.

Betty And all the kids are starting to calm down now and lay down. And I'm sitting up still, on the edge of the bed and looking out in the sky. It's just so wondrously beautiful. . . . [*Betty sighs*] And now I'm laying down.

Betty began breathing deeply. She had fallen asleep.

Bob Okay, relax now. I want you to relax. Totally, totally relaxed. [*pause*] The next time that we do this, I'll bring you to a point *after* this incident. When I wake you up, you'll feel refreshed, relaxed. You will be in good spirits. And you will be comfortable enough so that you'll get a good night's sleep this evening. And, none of what has happened tonight will disturb you. For it is, after all, in the past. I want you to relax now. Just relax.

Bob mercifully stopped the session. He knew the tragic event that was just around the corner in Betty's life and did not want her to have to go through the pangs of reliving it.

It is obvious now that the alien had actually told Betty what was going to happen and that there could be no intercession on the alien's part to stop it. Betty woke up on the morning of October 20, 1977 in a deep state of depression. Of course, she had no remembrance of the nocturnal visitor and his message in her conscious mind. But buried deep within was the foreknowledge of an impending tragedy that tried desperately to surface. Betty became distraught and phoned me for help. I told her that she would be welcome to come and talk to me about it on the following day. I felt that perhaps an empathetic chat would help her, and, it was an opportunity to meet her new boyfriend, Bob Luca. My investigators had already interviewed him and I was anxious to talk to him firsthand.

Betty was visibly upset when she and Bob arrived. Her voice quavered as she related to me what had happened on the telephone and what had happened later on in the night when she and her children witnessed the loud noises and ball of light. I sat listening as I recorded her description of the events and her general conversation. In essence, she believed that something awful was going to happen and all my attempts to dissuade her from this premonition were to no avail. I had no idea, at that time, that this feeling of foreboding was due to a warning by one of the alien entities. We talked far into the night. I was very impressed with Bob Luca. When they finally left for their respective homes I, too, wondered what on earth was going on. It all sounded so utterly unbelievable at the time. However, just twenty-four hours later it became all too believable and terribly disturbing. Betty's fears had been realized. The bold headlines of her local newspaper, *The Gardner News,* spelled out the tragic news in terse fashion: WEST-MINSTER CRASH KILLS TWO BROTHERS.

Shortly before midnight on the night of October 22, 1977, two of Betty's sons—James, age 21, and Todd, 17—were killed in an automobile accident. It was a terrible shock to all of us. It also portrayed in the most graphic way possible the probable authenticity of Betty's experience with the alien creatures and their supernatural ability to personally predict tragedy.

CHAPTER

Nine

UFOs and OBEs

Part I—The Terms Defined

UFOs—Unidentified machinelike objects which violate the earth's airspace. OBEs—Leaving one's body and entering another realm of existence. What could they possibly have in common? Paradoxically enough, evidence has been steadily accumulating in recent years of UFO research that the UFO experience and the out-of-the-body experiences are intimately related. No where does this astonishing revelation come across more emphatically than the experiences contained within *The Andreasson Affair*. Those already familiar with my previous books on this case or who are already well acquainted with the OBE are asked to bear with me as I lay the groundwork for Betty's next UFO experience and its relationship to the OBE. First some official definitions are in order.

Definitions

> *Unidentified Flying Objects* (UFO) Relates to any airborn object which by performance, aerodynamic chracteristics, or unusual features does not conform to any presently known aircraft or missile type, or which cannot be positively identified as a familiar object.[1]

The abbreviation *OBE* has been aptly defined by the well-known researcher, Robert A. Monroe. Monroe has been a pioneer in exploring out-of-the-body experiences. His first book, *Journeys Out of the Body* has become the undisputed classic in the field. He is the founder and executive director of the Monroe Institute, located in Afton, Virginia. The Monroe Institute is internationally known for its work on the effects of sound wave forms on human behavior. One of these effects is the OBE. Monroe defines an OBE as:

> An event in which the experiencer seems to perceive some portion of some environment which could not possibly be perceived from where his physical body is known to be at the time, and, knows *at the time* that he is not dreaming or fantasizing.[2]

Part II—Prelude to the Incredible

The first obvious example of an OBE took place during Betty's abduction from Westminster, Massachusetts, in the fall of 1950. Betty was thirteen years of age. Early one morning while her family was still sleeping, Betty left for Crocker Pond, one of her favorite woodland haunts. As she entered a large field, her eye caught sight of what seemed to be the moon in the sky over a nearby hill. The following is a portion of her experience as she relived it under hypnosis for Fred Max and investigators during the Phase Two investigation.

> *Betty* There's a *big huge moon* right over the top of the hill. And it was strange because it gets bigger and bigger. And it's coming toward me . . . and I *can't move!*

In an instant, young Betty found herself in a strange room. Her fear quickly dissipated as the tranquilizing effect of an alien technology took merciful control of her mind.

> *Betty* Ooooh, ooooh! I'm standing in some kind of room and it's all white and I *feel so relaxed*. And, oh! There's, there's little people coming in the room toward me, just *sliding along*. They're stopping in front of me. There are three little people standing there and they are funny.

The bizarre sight of the small creatures caused Betty to temporarily lose the induced composure that had quickly settled over her. She shouted at them in a frightened, shaky voice: "If you hurt me, my father will get a hold of you!" The aliens soon persuaded her not to be afraid and they took her to an *underground base* through an underwater entrance. There, the young girl participated in a number of traumatic events including the aforementioned eye operation. But none of these events corresponded to the aliens' chief purpose for abducting her. This reason had already been hinted at during her previous encounters with the small gray-skinned beings.

The aliens' purpose was first revealed to Betty in the summer of 1944 at Leominster, Massachusetts. At that time, Betty was only a child of seven. If you will recall, a tiny marble-sized buzzing ball of light had landed on her forehead. The glowing device caused her to enter a state of semi-consciousness during which she heard many voices speaking as one voice. Betty recalled their message to her during a Phase Two hypnosis session.

Betty Something about five years or so or I would be twelve and I would be able to see the *One*. I would be able to see the *One* and everything was being prepared and I was not to be afraid. They would not hurt me and they would see me later.

The voices then told Betty that she *would not remember* the incident. True to their word, the aliens did contact Betty again five years later. The year was 1949. Betty was twelve and lived at Westminster, Massachusetts. While walking in the woods, she was confronted by one of the creatures who directed an identical tiny ball of light at Betty. Again it landed between her eyes and put her into a trancelike stupor during which she heard the familiar chorus of voices. The voices repeated their plan for Betty to meet an unknown personage known to them as the *One*. Under hypnosis, Betty relived the unearthly episode.

Betty They're checking me and they're saying *another year* . . . They said I will learn about the *One* . . . They said they are preparing things for me to see, that it may help people in the future.

Then, sure enough, in 1950 during her abduction at thirteen, Betty met the *One*. This segment of her abduction was briefly summarized in the first chapter.

She was brought before a huge door embedded in a tall wall of glasslike material. Then the unexpected happened. During this very *physical* UFO event, young Betty Aho experienced an *OBE*. This is how she described what had happened to her while under hypnosis.

> *Betty* And I'm standing there and *I'm coming out of myself!* There's *two of me* there . . . and the little person is saying: "Now you shall enter the *Great Door* and see the glory of the *One.*

As mentioned, during her visit with the *One,* Betty's face literally radiated with joy and amazement at what she saw and felt. Fred Max tried his utmost to hypnotically persuade Betty to describe what she was experiencing but to no avail.

> *Betty* I went in *the door* and it's very *bright.* I *can't take you any further.*
>
> *Fred* Why?
>
> *Betty* Because . . . I can't take you past this *door.*
>
> *Fred* Why are you so happy?
>
> *Betty* It's just, ah, I just can't tell you about it. . . . It's—[*pause*] Words cannot explain it. It's wonderful. It's for *everybody.* I just can't explain this. I understand that *everything is one.* Everything fits together. It's beautiful!

This facet of *The Andreasson Affair* has always frustrated me. I wanted to know what Betty had seen behind the *Great Door* that had been too overwhelming to describe. On an impulse, I asked Bob to try once more to unlock the mystery of Betty's visit to the *One.* Bob agreed to give it a try by inducing Betty to be an *observer* rather than a *participant* of the experience.

On July 10, 1988, Bob hypnotized Betty and told her that the trip to see the *One* had been recorded in detail by a television camera. He then asked her to watch a replay of her visit on television. The results of his attempt were both astonishing and frightening:

> *Bob* Relax, just relax. You're going to go back to a time, to this one incident when you were before a *Great Door.* You're going to see the *One.* I want you to go back to that incident and then go right by it and sit down again with Bob and the television. The camera has gone behind the *Great Door* with you. It has photographed everything you saw. It has picked up all the thoughts, all the sounds. We'll be able to play back that one part on the television and it will come out very clearly on the screen so that you can describe it. I

want you to sit down with Bob now. The event has already passed and we'll turn on the television from the time that you're going in the *door*. I just want you to watch the television.

Betty [*sighs*] Ohhhhh! There's a bright light coming out of the television! This is weird! There's rays of light, bright white light, just [*pause*] like they've got a spotlight coming out of the television! It's hurting my eyes!

Bob Okay, let's turn the brightness down a little bit on the television so it's not so bright.

Betty Ohhhh! I can't. It just comes out like a spotlight! It's so bright! [*Betty is now very agitated.*]

Bob Okay, we'll put a dark glass over the TV screen and that will make it darker.

Betty It doesn't help! This light just absorbs that black glass! [*Betty is getting hysterical.*]

Bob Okay, then, then, let's relax, just relax.

Betty [*screams in pain*] It's too bright! It's hurting my eyes!

Bob Okay, we're going to shut off the television now and you're going to relax. The TV is off. Just relax.

Bob eased Betty back to the present time. She had a terrible headache and her eyes ached for several days after our attempt to discover what was behind the *Great Door*. We should have known better than to have tried. It was obvious that we were not meant to know at this time.

What is this *Great Door*? Where is the underground installation in which it is located? In retrospect, it is very interesting to note that during our original investigation of Betty's 1967 abduction experience, she had alluded to a *Great Door* when the hypnotist was probing her past memories.

Investigator What is the *Great Door*?

Betty It is the entrance into the *other world*. The world where light is.

Investigator Is that available to us as well as to you?

Betty No, not yet.

Betty's cryptic comments about the *Great Door* during our previous Phase One and Phase Two investigations are indeed thought-provoking. If we take them at full face value, they indicate that someday *everyone* will enter the so-called *Great Door*, and like Betty, will experience what she experienced when she met the *One*. Equally thought-provoking was the *word* that the aliens used to describe the realm of the entity known as the *One*. Just moments after thirteen-year-old Betty Aho had been whisked into a UFO from the edge of a field near her home, the aliens made a quizzical statement.

> *Betty* Ah, they're just standing there looking at me with their big fat brown eyes . . . and they said, "We're going to take you *home*."

Betty hadn't a clue as to what the little *beings* meant. After all, she had just been standing in the field behind her house on her parents' property. That was home to her.

> *Betty* I said, "I am home!" And they said, "Don't fear, don't be afraid, you're all right."

The aliens used the cryptic word *home* on several other occasions during this same abduction experience. After she had been escorted through various sections of the aliens' underground base, one of them informed Betty that "You're getting closer to *home*." He then floated her into an unknown man-sized container that was shaped like an open clamshell. As she reclined in the strange device, she suddenly could see many images of herself reflecting back from a mirrorlike interior. The top of the container snapped down enclosing Betty inside. In a moment, the top was again opened and Betty was floated into a different place that seemed to be constructed out of a glasslike material. Somehow the clam-shaped box had been used to transport her there. In this place, Betty was shown glasslike models of many kinds of life found on earth. The aliens gave her an apparent object lesson that demonstrated their ability to give life to inanimate life forms. Utterly amazed, Betty asked them how they could do such a marvelous thing. When an alien answered her, he again referenced a place called *home*.

> *Betty* He told me that I will see when I get *home*. . . . It is time for me, they said, for me to go *home* to see the *One*. . . . He said, "*Home* is where the *One* is." . . . He says, "We are drawing closer to *home* where the *One* is."

The implications of Betty's OBE during an obvious abduction of her *physical* body are mind-boggling, especially when viewed in the light of her visit to the *One*. What are these startling implications?

First, in order to visit the *One*, Betty had to leave her body behind to enter the *Great Door*. Secondly, the place where the *One* resided was called *home*. Thirdly, Betty was told specifically that *everybody* would share this experience. In retrospect, there are only two things that we know for a fact that *everybody* on earth experiences: *birth* and *death*!

I recently retired from the defense industry as a manager of program planning and scheduling in the development of major weapons systems. When scheduling weapons programs, planners would gather together in brainstorming sessions and discuss what are known as *What If* situations. We would plan different actions and work around situations based upon a number of circumstances that might crop up during a given program. I would like to apply this same philosophy to Betty's OBE visit to the *One*. What *if* it were grounded in reality? What might it mean? Could it possibly be that the aliens are telling the world through Betty that the origin [*home*] of our life and our ultimate *destination* is the world in which she visited the *One*? My research and its conclusions have always centered on the so-called *nuts and bolts* or physical side of the UFO problem. However, if we take *The Andreasson Affair* at full face value, the evidence overwhelmingly reflects the *paraphysical* nature of what we have come to call UFOs!

As we examine certain segments of Betty's experience, we find that UFOs and their occupants are perfectly capable of traveling between at least two different *planes of existence*. The first hint of this was demonstrated during Betty's 1967 abduction experience at age thirty from her home at South Ashburnham, Massachusetts.

When the aliens entered and left her home, they did not bother to open the wooden door. Four blue-suited entities simply passed through it. This ability has also been reported in a number of other cases. But, it is Betty's description of the procedure that is so intriguing and which may hold the clue to just *how* they accomplished this fantastic feat. Here is her description of the event, given while under hypnosis during our original investigation:

Investigator How did they get there, Betty?

Betty They came through the *door*.

Investigator Did you open the *door* for them?

Betty   Uh uh.

Investigator   Did they open the *door?*

Betty   No . . . they came in like follow-the-leader . . . like form-after-form-after-form . . . right *through* the wood, one right after the other. It's amazing! Coming through! And I stood back a little. Was it real?

Betty stated that the alien entities would appear and disappear with a jerky motion as they floated through the door. As each disappeared and reappeared farther ahead, he would leave a vapory afterimage in his wake. It was as if each alien were moving in and out of our plane of existence and temporarily into an unseen parallel dimension in order to pass through the solid wood of the *door*. The question that immediately arises is—*Where* were their bodies when they disappeared? This question, in turn, raises still another— Where do humans go when they *leave their body* during an OBE? The sixty-four thousand dollar question would be—Are the two different planes of existence the *same place?*

Let us summarize some of the things we know about the OBE experience. In the typical OBE, the percipient enters a locale that co-exists with the physical world where the body dwells. The person in the OBE state can perceive but not influence the world he left behind, people in that world cannot see him. In the OBE, the experiencer's *other body* simply passes *through* physical objects of this world as if they were illusions. Betty, however, went one step further than the person who undergoes a typical OBE. Betty entered still another realm which the aliens called the *world of light* through a rectangular passageway capped by the so-called *Great Door*. Wherever she went was indescribably beautiful. What really boggles the mind is that there is a specific type of OBE described by thousands of people over the ages that parallels Betty's visit to *the One* in many ways. It is called the *NDE* or *Near-Death Experience*.

The NDE has been described in the literature and legends of different cultures over the centuries. In Western countries they were often referred to as deathbed experiences. Religious persons accepted such experiences as bona fide visions of the afterlife, but science, until fairly recently, ignored these widely scattered reports and placed them in the category of hallucinations induced by the fear of death and wishful thinking. With the advent of modern medicine and its technological array of life-resuscitating devices, however, the NDE has sparked new interest on the part of both parapsychologists and medical doctors. In the past, a large majority of people died without the benefit of resuscitation techniques and devices. In recent years, many, many persons who have technically died have literally been raised from the dead. A great number of them come back with memories of an experience very similiar to that described by Betty.

The NDE reportedly occurs when a person is pronounced dead at the scene of an accident, in a hospital sickbed, or during a number of death-dealing circumstances. Typically, an OBE initiates the NDE. The dead person reportedly *floats* above the inanimate body. In this state, this *other self* may watch and hear medics, doctors, and nurses converse with each other as they attempt to revive the lifeless body. For some, this is as far as they go. The body is quickly revived and the person floats back into it. Others, however, enter a second stage when the physical body is not revived quickly. They fairly consistently describe entering a tunnel or long dark void. Their *other self* is whisked along toward a brilliant light at the end of the tunnel. As the person egresses, there is a confrontation with a *being of pure light* concurrently with an overwhelming feeling of love. The person sometimes converses with the dazzling entity.

Some variations of the NDE include seeing a beautiful world of light with meadows, gardens, and cities. Some report seeing dead relatives or friends beckoning them to cross a barrier which separates them. In many cases, persons are somehow told that it is not time for them to be there and they are sent back to their body. Others are given the choice to stay or go back. The desire to stay is almost overwhelming but thoughts of the needs of loved ones cause many to decide to return.

When a person returns from an NDE to the revived body and awakes with its memories, they, like Betty after her visit to the *One*, express great difficulty in finding the right words to describe their experiences: "I can't even explain it."—"There is no feeling you experience in normal life that is anything like this." These are typical statements of persons who have had an NDE.

I have had a number of occasions to interview persons who have undergone OBE and NDE experiences. They include a cousin and a friend who attends my church. My cousin died while giving birth to one of her children. My friend was pronounced dead from the effects of postsurgical complications. Both related to me that they had first undergone an initial OBE. They floated about in the hospital room for a short time observing everything that was going on around their physical bodies. Then they ascended into a dark void and egressed into a beautiful realm where they were met by a radiant personage. Both wanted to stay but were told that their families needed them and they were returned to their bodies. One cannot avoid noting the similarities that exist between certain segments of Betty's otherwise *physical* UFO experience and the oft-reported OBEs of many people, especially the NDE type.

Such parallels continued after Betty returned down the tunnel from her other-worldly visit and egressed through the *Great Door* to rejoin her physical body. There awaiting her return were not the dwarflike entities but two tall persons that looked like human beings. The following is the pertinent portion of one of the Phase Two hypnosis sessions.

> *Betty* Okay, I'm outside the *door* and there's a tall person there. He's got white hair and he's got a white nightgown on and he's motioning me to come there with him. His nightgown is, is *glowing* and his hair is white and he's got bluish eyes. And it's bright out here, and I think I see two more of them over there.
>
> *Fred Max* Do they look like *people*?
>
> *Betty* Um, but tall. They are real tall and they got some ferns or something in their hands.
>
> *Fred Max* Do you speak to them?
>
> *Betty* He's beckoning me to come over there and there's like a *shell*, an open *shell*. But it's mirrors and mirrors and mirrors.

One of the robed entities placed Betty into the same type of apparatus that the small gray-skinned beings had used to transport her to where she was now. They then closed the cover.

> *Fred Max* When you were in the *shell*, what did you experience in there?
>
> *Betty* I could *see myself* quickly.

Moments later, the cover of the clam shell-shaped box opened. Betty again was floated out into another location and was greeted by the dwarf-sized aliens. Who were these strange Biblical-like entities that greeted Betty when she returned from her other-worldly visit to the *One*? Have such persons figured in other UFO and OBE cases? The answer is yes.

A huge wave of UFO sightings blanketed Italy in 1978. Of 500 known cases, 130 [about 25 percent] involved close encounters within 500 feet of observers. Over two dozen cases involved the sighting of humanoid entities in association with the UFOs.

The sightings led to unprecedented public discussion and debate, even in the Italian Parliament. For some reason, they were ignored by the major news media in the United States. I was particularly intrigued with one incident that took place on July 4 because it revealed that Betty's description of tall, robed human figures operating with alien dwarfs was not unique. The event was summarized in the November 1980 issue of the MUFON UFO journal.

> On July 4, military personnel from the Navy Air Base at Cantania felt a *compulsion* to ascend the slopes of Mt. Etna, and there saw three red pulsating UFOs, one of which landed. It was a *domed* disc about 12 meters [40 feet] in diameter with red and yellow body lights.

The Italian Navy personnel then sighted a bizarre group of entities near the landed UFO.

> The group then encountered two *tall* golden-haired, *white-robed* beings accompanied by three or four *shorter beings* wearing helmets and spacesuits. [italics mine]

The luminous, white-robed human-looking persons that Betty encountered as she egressed from the *Great Door* in an OBE state have also been described by people who have undergone an OBE during an NDE. Some were recognized as dead relatives. Others were friends or strangers. Some interpreted the identity of these robed figures within the context of their religious beliefs. Sometimes the percipient undergoing the NDE would find himself dressed in the same luminous garb as Betty herself would during a future encounter in 1978.

A number of professional medical doctors have and are making clinical studies of the NDE. Since MUFON has no consultants on such matters, I turn now to the studies of two nationally known specialists in this field for assistance. The first, Michael B. Sabom, M.D. is a professor of Medicine at Emory University and a staff physician at the Atlanta, Georgia VA Medical Center. The second,

Dr. Raymond Moody is a psychiatrist who is well known for his pioneering investigations into OBEs.

Dr. Sabom has documented a number of cases that involve *tall white-robed* personages. A few are described as follows.

> My Grandparents were all dressed in *white*—He was tall . . . and he had a *white robe* on—He was standing with a very *white robe* . . . his eyes were *blue*, very *blue*.[3]

In some cases, the place where those who were undergoing an NDE was called *home*. Dr. Sabom tells of a man who suffered a cardiac arrest in 1975. During his NDE, he saw his deceased mother and a man both wearing bright gowns saying: "Come on *home*. Come on *home*." [italics mine]

Like Betty, NDE percipients have described the world that they enter through a dark tunnel as a *world where light is*. The following examples are taken from a study of NDEs by Dr. Moody.

> I seemed to go up . . . a tunnel. . . . All of a sudden I was just somewhere else. There was a gold-looking *light* everywhere—I went through the dark tunnel . . . and came out into brilliant *light*—I actually entered this tunnel. . . . I entered the spiritual world where there is . . . brilliant light that surrounded everything. [italics mine][4]

Another striking parallel that exists between UFO abduction experiences and the NDE type of OBE is that people who return from death's door describe communication in the other world as being accomplished via *mental telepathy*. Dr. Moody states the following concerning a typical person that has undergone an NDE:

> If he meets *other beings*, he reports that they *know his every thought* and vice versa. He finds that in this state, communication is not mediated through words, but rather that thoughts are understood directly.[5]

I felt it necessary to include this overview of some of the parallels that exist between UFOs and OBEs to prepare the reader for Betty's next *abduction* experiences which occurred in 1978 and 1986. The 1978 experience is extremely pertinent to the subject at hand. *Both* Betty and Bob were sucked skyward to a huge craft somewhere in space during an utterly amazing *dual* out-of-the-body experience.

The 1986 event would introduce another type of OBE event, perhaps unique in the annals of UFO literature.

Up to this point in my investigation, the hypnosis sessions had stretched over a period of almost seven months. Our methodology of allowing Betty to relive each incident in near real-time was a lengthy, time-consuming process. It was also rough on Betty. I became impatient to know in advance just how many more UFO events remained in Betty's life. I proposed a temporary change in tactics to Bob. I asked him to conduct a special session in which he would have Betty briefly relate her remaining UFO experiences in chronological order. This special session was conducted on May 13, 1988, and produced a number of encounters that took place in 1978, 1981, 1982, 1984, and 1986. Bob could get no further than 1986 due to time constraints and because of terrible pain experienced by Betty during the 1986 event. Later, Bob did succeed. The results will be revealed later on.

After studying the recording of this special session, it was decided to first probe the 1978 and 1986 events in detail because of the astonishing OBEs that they contained. The following is extracted from three detailed hypnotic regression sessions that took place on May 13, 22, and 24, 1988. I could find no other word to describe the contents of the rest of this chapter except *incredible!* First, let us examine the 1978 event which took place at Meriden, Connecticut.

Part III—The Meriden Incident

In October of 1978, shortly after the event had taken place, Betty had phoned me and excitedly related what had happened. I made a brief mention of the event in my sequel to *The Andreasson Affair.*[6] Little did I know back then that what they could *remember* of the incident was just the conscious tip of an iceberg of nearly indescribable buried memories.

Betty had briefly related the following during the special chronological-overview session of May 13, 1988.

> *Bob* Just go forward in time to the next event or happening where you witnessed the *beings,* the *angels,* after this.

Bob at times used the term *angels* to accommodate Betty's persistent religious interpretation of the events that had befallen her.

Betty I was on Draper Avenue. We had a little blue house there.

Bob And what happened on Draper Avenue?

Betty A lot of strange little things kept happening: problems with electricity, the doorbell [*sighs*] and the louver doors in the bathroom going up and down. No wind at all there.

Bob Okay, but at any time did you actually see or have contact with the *angels* on Draper Avenue in 1978?

Betty Yes.

Bob Okay, and when was that? What happened?

Betty [*sighs*] Bob and I were upstairs in our bedroom. And I was in the bathroom brushing my teeth. And he was over by the bed. And he was putting on his socks or taking them off. He was down on the floor kneeling. And there came a loud, [*pause*] dull *whirring sound* over the rooftop over the bedroom. Very, very loud. And I turned to look at Bob and he glanced up at me and suddenly, [*pause*] he came out of his body so that there were *two* of him! And he rushed toward me and toward the bathroom and stopped abruptly at the door.

Up to this juncture was all that Betty had remembered consciously when she had phoned me about the event back in 1978. It had been puzzling. I knew of no other OBE where an onlooking person could actually see the *other self* leave a person having an OBE. What she had described did not make sense. The reverse is always reported. The *other self* is able to see *both* the physical world it has left *and* the new realm that it has entered. However, the puzzle was resolved during this session. Betty had seen Bob's *other self* only because she too had a concurrent OBE. It was her *other self* that saw her husband. They both co-existed in the other-worldly realm of the OBE!

> *Bob* What was going on?
>
> *Betty* [*long pause*] Oh! [*sighs*] Oh!
>
> *Bob* Just relax.
>
> *Betty* [*becomes very agitated*] Whew!
>
> *Bob* Relax.
>
> *Betty* [*now breathing heavily*] Oh!
>
> *Bob* Relax. You can move away from the situation.
>
> *Betty* [*calms down—long pause*]

Bob What happened?

Betty [*again becomes very agitated*]

Bob Okay, relax. Relax.

Betty [*with a scared voice*] I just see *myself*. I see myself *coming out of myself too*! And I'm reaching out to Bob. I'm holding on him tightly. [Both are in the OBE state.]

Bob Don't be afraid.

Betty Ohhhhh!

Bob It's okay. This has already passed.

After much persuasion, Bob was finally able to keep Betty in the role of an *observer* long enough to see what had happened next.

Bob You have already been through this and you've made it just fine. Relax. Distance yourself from it. Look at it as an observer. You *are* an observer. That's better. Relax. Can you tell me what you saw?

Betty again described the sequence of events over again but this time was able to continue for a brief moment of time.

Betty . . . And I'm just holding and hugging around him— holding on. And it feels like we're being *lifted up* somehow! [*pause*]

Bob Okay, just relax.

Betty Oh! It hurts! Oh! Oh! Oh! Oh! Something is hurting me!

Bob Does Bob go with you?

Betty [*sighs*] We're both being lifted up somehow.

Bob Okay, Bob is with you. Don't be afraid.

Bob brought Betty back to relive the event from its beginning to the time both were lifted up in the OBE state, but each time he brought Betty to that point, she would scream in agony. Frustrated, he moved her on to briefly describe future events and then ended the session.

Betty did not feel up to another session for over a week. During that time, Bob thought up a new technique that might help Betty to see and relate what had happened as an *observer* so as to negate the pain that she had experienced. The scheme worked marvelously and Betty was able to painlessly describe the incredible events that unfolded during their dual journey into another plane of existence with the alien beings.

After Bob had conducted the next two sessions, he phoned to tell me that he had just put the tapes in the mail. He also warned me that their contents would strain my credulity to its limits. I wondered what on earth he was talking about. I was soon to find out that whatever he meant, it certainly did not take place on this earth. In any event, the tapes arrived. I placed the first one on my recorder, put on my headphones and began to transcribe its eerie contents.

Bob put Betty into a deep hypnotic trance and began his questioning.

> *Bob* I'd like for you to go back to a time in the house
> at . . . Draper Avenue in Meriden, Connecticut. You are in the
> bathroom. Bob is sitting on the bed nearby.

And then Bob initiated his new technique to allow Betty to relate what had happened comfortably and without pain.

> *Bob* I want you to imagine that in the next several minutes some-
> one is *videotaping* everything that happens. Everything. Bob went
> out of his body and rushed toward you in the bathroom. I would
> like you to go well past this point in time. Be seated downstairs in
> the living room watching the television and tell me what you see
> from the point Bob rushed over to the bathroom door. And, re-
> member, you *are an observer* and you're going to watch this video-
> tape which will show you everything that happened. Why don't you
> tell me what's on the television?
>
> *Betty* I am standing in the doorway. Bob looks very concerned and
> Betty . . . is brushing her teeth. She has a toothbrush in her
> mouth and she's looking at him puzzled. And . . . Betty *came out
> of her self* and she reaches out toward Bob and throws her arms
> around his stomach and, is like, holding on, And suddenly, the two
> of them start to raise upward and they're going right *through* the
> ceiling. And it looks weird! And they're going upward into the
> *misty light* and it's, um, like wind is blowing all around them, wind,
> as they're going upward in the *misty light*. And they're being pulled
> apart then they're being pulled apart and Betty is holding on—
> trying to hold on but the wind is so strong. They're being pulled!
> Bob is being pulled over to the side upwards and Betty is being

pulled to the other side. And, she's holding on and trying to grab hold of his arms as she's being pulled upward and he's trying to reach out and hold on to her hands and he can't. He tried to catch her feet and he can't. And they're both going upward in different directions. [Figure 32]

Bob's technique worked. Betty, in her imagination, sat comfortably, dispassionately describing to Bob the events on the hypnotically

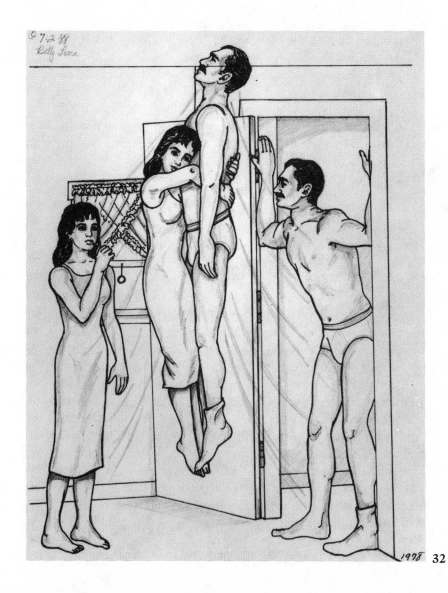

32

induced television set. He decided not to interrupt unless it was absolutely necessary.

Betty [*sighs*] And I see Betty. She's going upward and yelling for Bob. She's saying "Honey! Honey! Honey!" And I see her raising upwards and it's so misty. I don't see where Bob is. I don't see him on television. . . . And suddenly the area is a bluish color—blue haze all over . . . and it's starting to get a lavender color to it. And Betty is starting to *lose color*. She looks almost *ghostlike*. [Figure 33] Her color is gone . . . and there's lavender light like and it's like wind and haze. She's being lifted up into the purple, purple color and she looks like a . . . whitish-gray ghost. . . . And she's starting to come into golden color, and as she does, *all her features are disappearing* and her whole body looks like it's becoming *light*!

At this point, Betty began to get agitated and breathe heavily. Even as a passive observer, the sights on the TV caused chills to course up and down her spine. Still, Bob did not step in to calm her. He let her continue unabated.

Betty . . . And there're other *forms* that look like people but *they're light* and there's a golden area—Beautiful golden color! . . . They're just like *human forms* but they're *light*! There's no features . . . and they're all standing around in this golden area. They're—[*pause*] They seem to be touching hand to hand. [Figure 34] They're moving now . . . into a, a room. But it's, it's—The room is like, um—This is strange! I don't know what it— how to explain this. The room looks sorta like a *domed thing*. But it looks like a *walk* around it and they're all going on to this *walk* around the room.

Betty had watched the humanoid forms of light enter a huge round room capped by a domed roof. The *walk* that she referred to was similar to a catwalk which ran around the room's middle circumference. The outer circumference of the round room revolved slowly in a *counterclockwise* direction, whereas the inner or middle circumference, including the *walk*, revolved slowly in a *clockwise* direction. The circular *walk* encompassed and looked down on an amphitheaterlike setting where a number of the dwarflike aliens were huddled around three long tables. A person covered with a sheet or blanket lay on each of the tables.

(Ghostlike)

© 6·1·88
Betty ann Luca

1978

33

Betty And it's revolving very slowly and there is, like, um, a banister. Oh, this is hard to explain what it looks like. It's so unusual. And they're just, they're just touching hand to hand and they're walking now on this—looks like a huge revolving, um, [*pause*] porch. I don't know what you would call this. I don't know— balcony or something. It just keeps slowly revolving with them on it. And a couple of them are going off to the edge to look over and look way down what's down there. There're some *people* down there and there's some *beings* down there. And their feet and legs are

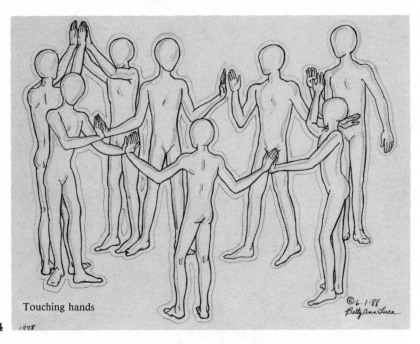

Touching hands

34 *1988*

bare. And there's blankets or something white over them . . . but I can't see the other half of them cause there's, there's *beings* that are over them—big-headed *beings* with grayish-white skin.

Bob Okay, I want you to look at this scene on the TV carefully now so that later, you can remember it and then you'll be able to draw it. It's only on television. It's only on television.

Later, Betty was able to make a basic sketch of the huge round domed room and its contents. [Figure 35] Betty became frustrated because she could not see what the *beings* were doing to the persons lying on the tables. [Figure 36]

Betty There's a bright [*pause*] light with all sorts of lighting—tiny lights—and cylinders and stuff coming out of it that's over those three people. . . . The *beings* are over them and they seem to be standing over them watching them. . . . And it's so bright down there . . . and if the *beings* would get out of the way, I could see more. . . . I just can't see from here. They're standing in that light. [*pause*] I, I, I just can't see. They're working around the top parts of those three—[*Betty becomes very frustrated.*]

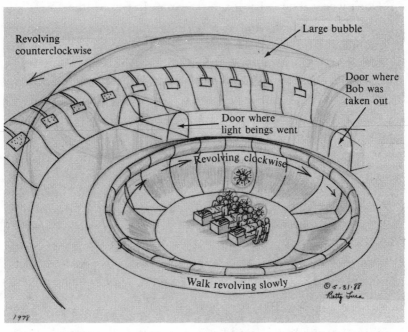

Revolving counterclockwise

Large bubble

Door where Bob was taken out

Door where light beings went

Revolving clockwise

Walk revolving slowly

© 5·31·88
Betty Luca

1978

35

1978

© 5·31·88 Betty Luca

36

Bob That's okay. Watch the television. Just watch the television. Don't worry about what it shows or not. Just watch the TV.

Betty I'm watching. And, they're still looking down at the round room and those three tables are there and those three . . . are on there [*pause*] and I'm trying to see more but I can't see more because the *beings* are all at the top there with those lights all over the place.

Bob That's okay, just move along and see what the TV shows after that.

Betty It's strange 'cause those *forms* [glowing human figures] are all alike. I don't know where Betty is and I don't know where Bob is and those *beings* [light forms] are just standing all around the railing looking down as that thing rotates very, very slowly. [*sighs*] It's rotating around. [*pause*] Ahhhhhh! I see over there! I see over there on that side! There's Bob over there! He's on that side. [*pause*] And, and one of the, one of the *light forms* people are waving, waving, waving to him. [*pause*] And he's just standing there with two *people* like, like,—Boy, this is weird. [*pause*] The thing keeps revolving. [*pause*] They're taking him now to that side door again. [*pause*] And, [*pause*] I still can't see who those people are down there. [*pause*] They've got such bright lights over them. [*pause*] Ahhhhh! Oh no! Oh, no, no, no, no, no!

Bob It's okay.

Betty Oh no!

Bob You're only viewing this on the television.

Betty [*starts breathing heavily*]

Bob This has already come to pass and it's just being played back on television.

Betty Oh no! [*pause*] Ohhhh! [*pause*] I don't want to watch it any more.

Bob Okay, let's—I'll turn off the television. I want you to relax now. The TV is off. I want you to relax. Totally relaxed.

Betty [*sobs uncontrollably*]

Bob You are on the beach. The sun is shining. On the beach. Relax, relax.

Bob slowly but surely eased Betty out of her trauma as he had her imagine herself lying on a beach enjoying the sunshine and the sound of the surf. What Betty had seen that caused her violent reaction was that the three persons lying on those tables below were members of the family! She insists their names be kept anonymous.

At the next hypnosis session, Betty insisted that she not be made to relive what had troubled her so again, so Bob moved her past the upsetting event and asked her to continue her description of what was happening on the imaginary television set.

> *Bob* We're at Draper Avenue. The TV was turned off at [that point]. . . . It's already happened. . . . Let's turn the television back on . . . and tell me what happened from that point. What does the TV show you?
>
> *Betty* [*long sigh*] The wide circular platform. It's slowly revolving . . . I see one of the light-forms, form-*beings*, at the railing's edge looking down. . . . And, suddenly the other *beings* that are all light come over to the one and start to touch that one all over the shoulders and back and head as if to caress that one light-*being*. They're all stepping back—some holding hands acting very much like children watching out for each other. And the platform, the upper platform-thing, keeps revolving slowly. And now they are holding on hands and walking ahead. But they don't seem to really have *touched* the floor part. Some are skipping and they're all bright light and they're just a *form*. I don't see any eyes or nose or mouth or ears or hair—just a light-form about five feet tall.

As I listened to Betty's voice, my mind rebelled at the fantastic things that she was describing, especially within the context of UFOs. For years I had separated the psychic from the physical elements in UFO reports. But since my involvement with *The Andreasson Affair*, I found myself reluctantly accepting the paraphysical nature of the UFO experience. The *nuts-and-bolts* side of UFOs seemed to have at least made sense. UFOs were undoubtedly highly advanced *machines* from a neighboring star-system manned by a super-technological race of *physical* beings. Now, I was beginning to question even the concept of the term, *physical*. The same attributes that we apply to our physical world could equally apply in the invisible realms described by out-of-the-body, near-death, and some UFO experiences. What Betty described next just added more fuel to the fires of my confusion.

> *Betty* Oh! A *door* is opening and they're [light beings] are all filing in. Looks like a, almost like a *glass* passageway. And they're all go-

ing into another—I don't know how to explain it—sort of a *balcony* but it's [*sighs*] *round* like a wheel. It's big. And it too is revolving but the opposite way. It's like, looks like glass, and it—the floor— swerves up and goes like around the banister area. And there are— Oh, this is so odd! It's hard to explain this. There's like *squares* embedded in the glass banister—like with all—looks like all twin- kling multicolored lights in that square. And out of each square, there's like a band of light that goes up and over the banister. It goes over the banister and it goes way down. Oh, it drops way, way down. And I see something way down there off to the side. It's like *rings* of white light. All—Each one of those light-*beings* [*long sigh*] are leaning against that square thing of multicolored light and that, that strap or something. I don't know. Each one [square] has a strap of different-colored light attached to it. One after another after another after another. And the *beings* are putting their backs up against it and laying sort of curved. And they're—It's so peculiar! They're all laying down on that banister. On that square thing, in that strap of—That long, long strap of *light*. Each one is getting on that square-thing-like, with their back. And they're bending their heads forward.

I must confess that I wholeheartedly agree with the old adage that a picture is worth a thousand words. Until I received Betty's drawings, this and other things that she had described were almost impossible to visualize. Happily, Betty supplied a sketch of what she had just described. [Figure 37] I waited with bated breath to see what happened next. Each time I felt that I thought one of her experiences had reached the limits of strangeness, another would come along and better it. This was one of those instances.

> *Betty* Oh my word! Is that weird! Oh my word! Is that weird!
>
> *Bob* What are you seeing?
>
> *Betty* Oh, that is so weird. Those *beings* just seem to *roll into a ball of bright light* and roll over that strap! And that strap came undone with all those multicolored lights. And they just roll down the strap of bright, bright light. Just rolled and *consumed* the strap as it went down and came down to the floor there. And there's like a *ball of light* just sitting there! [Figure 38]

At this juncture, Betty was talking very excitedly. The tone of her voice expressed the utter amazement that she was experiencing as

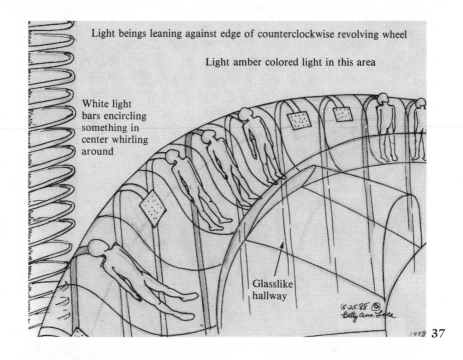

Light beings leaning against edge of counterclockwise revolving wheel

Light amber colored light in this area

White light bars encircling something in center whirling around

Glasslike hallway

5·25·88 Ⓒ
Betty Ann Luca
1988   37

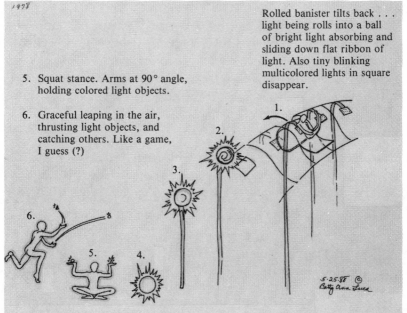

1978

Rolled banister tilts back . . . light being rolls into a ball of bright light absorbing and sliding down flat ribbon of light. Also tiny blinking multicolored lights in square disappear.

5. Squat stance. Arms at 90° angle, holding colored light objects.

6. Graceful leaping in the air, thrusting light objects, and catching others. Like a game, I guess (?)

5·25·88 Ⓒ
Betty Ann Luca

38

she watched the incomprehensible scenes that flashed on the hypnotically induced TV screen.

Betty This is fantastic! The *balls of light* that were all just sitting there—All of a sudden they changed back into those *beings* . . . those forms of light. And they're holding their arms out and hands out and they're, they're—I don't know how to explain this. This is so strange. And their hands are up and they're, they're, they're not kneeling but they're—I don't know what! It's just in a, a—Their legs and feet are in a strange sort of stance. Not even standing. It's squatting in a sidewise squat. And its hands are upward. And in them are these bright lights. But, each one has different colored lights in their hands. And, they're *different shapes*. They're, they're— One's got like a little tiny *sphere* and, and, then on the other hand is like a *pyramid*. [Figure 39] Another one's got something that's shaped all *pointed* all over it in one hand and it looks like a square or a *cube*. And another one's got like a, a *curlicue* thing and a, in the other hand, a *diamond*-type thing. And there's one there that's got this strange, strangelike *bar*, or, or, or, bar or a pole—small pole— that's bright white light. And it's real black on the other side and they both have *points* on it. Real pointy. And they're all, they're all, ah, strange *squat*. [*sighs*] Now they're just, they're just *leaping*! And this is so odd! This can't be happening! It's just so peculiar! Too odd! It's, it's so, so odd.

Bob [*stepping in to quell Betty's agitation*] It's just what you're seeing on the TV.

Betty They're flinging those shapes of different colored light around. Oh, the light makes different angles and they leap up as if they're *playing* and grab the light.

Bob Okay.

Betty And they keep on passing it through all different ways. It's just so unusual! They seem so *happy*. They just, it seems as if they're happy cause they're just—They just look so free-e-e! [*sighs*]

Bob Is there emotion on their faces? A smile?

Betty There's no eyes or nose. Their face, they're all *light*. And they just—But they are just so graceful. They just seem so happy with what they are doing.

Bob Okay, that's fine.

Betty And the one with the long *bar* with the pointed ends—

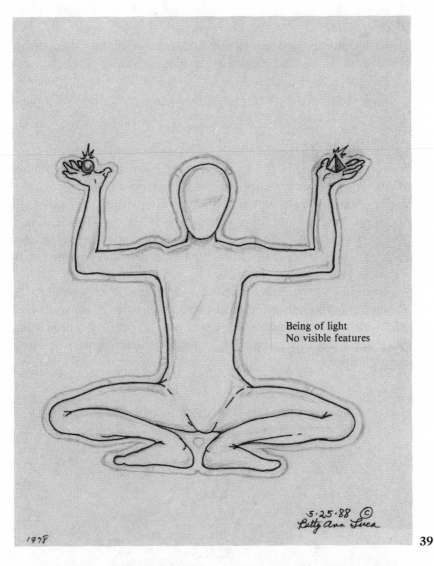

Being of light
No visible features

5·25·88 ©
Betty Ann Luca

1978

39

Looks like it is different than the others in movement. It seems to be just *floating* out. Oh! The *bar* just attracted, oh, one of those *spheres* and is pulling it toward it and it's circling, circling, circling— Comes to the point and goes *on the bar*! Is this strange! This is so strange but beautiful. This is—Oh it just—I've never seen anything like this before. They just keep on bouncing those lights. Oh, and—it—That bar's catching another. It's catching, catching another one of those *shapes* of light! And it's being penetrated into that point there. [i.e., on the *bar* held by one of the light-*beings*] It must be the, that, that, ah, *being* of light must be the one *collecting* all of these. Cause it, ah, just is like floating, almost like swimming, but floats out you know. It—[*pause*] Oh, this is so unusual. Oh! One of the *beings*, ah doesn't have any more *shapes* for their hands. It's going over to that, ah real round, big thing, like bars of light circling something that's whirring round and round. And that *being* of light is just *holding on to the bars.*

Again, we found it very difficult to visualize Betty's verbal description of the unearthly things that she was witnessing. She talked concurrently about a cylindrical tower of whirling energy encircled by many bars of light and a single bar of light held by one of the glowing entities. I asked her to draw both for me in order that I could better visualize what was going on; first, the ringed tower of energy [Figure 40] and secondly, the bar of light held by the entity. [Figure 41]

Incredible as it may seem, the light-forms appeared to be playing and enjoying some kind of a game! Why Betty was being made privy to this made no sense to me. In fact, I wondered just *where* Betty was observing these events. She had mentioned catching a glimpse of Bob on the *television* but up to now, she had not

5.25.88 ©
Betty Ann Luca

40   *1978*

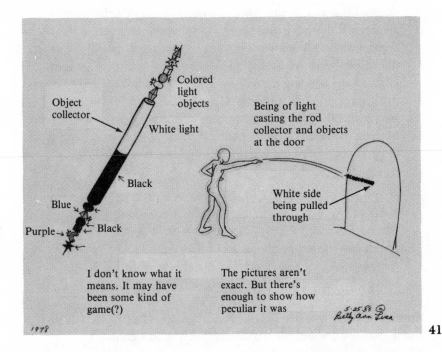

Object collector

Colored light objects

White light

Being of light casting the rod collector and objects at the door

Black

Blue

White side being pulled through

Purple → Black

I don't know what it means. It may have been some kind of game(?)

The pictures aren't exact. But there's enough to show how peculiar it was

5.25.88 @ Betty ann Luca

1978

41

seen herself. Where was she? She had to be there somewhere to witness such things. The answer was soon forthcoming. Again, it raised her bizarre experience yet another level in the scale of strangeness. Let us continue with Betty's account.

Betty There goes another one of the *beings* holding on to those, that bar over there. Those bars that encircle that thing that looks like a whirling—something whirling—going around and round inside of it. I don't know what it is. It's very tall. Goes way, way up. And that *player*—I guess it's a *player*—seems to be collecting all those little *shapes of light* on that bar. Oh, well, there only seems to be a couple more lights left. And most of the *beings* of light now are over on those bars. [circular bars around the tower of energy] And there's only one more. Seems as if that *player*, I guess . . . doesn't want to give up that one [light-shape] and keeps bouncing it around. There it goes. . . . It's caught on the light-bar of light. Oh, this is really weird!

Bob Okay, let's move the videotape up to where they're done.

Betty They are, they are done with the lights. The last *player*, the last *being* with the bar of light in his hand is standing . . . and he's getting ready to throw that bar. He's flinging that bar. He hit a

door with it and all the other, the other *beings* of light are now
coming off those [circular] bars. And that one that threw the bar is
going over and holding on [i.e., to the circular bars like the others
did before him]. And the door is—Oh! That bar [the one thrown
at the door] is going right *through* [the door] and the only things
that's showing now is the black part of the bar with the black
shapes and the blue and the purple. [Figure 41] And the *beings* are
heading toward that door. And that other *being* now is getting off
those bars of light and following. Oh! [*long deep sigh*]

Bob   What's on the TV now?

Betty [*sighs*] Those *beings* of light, one at a time are going through
the door. And, as they do, *they're people* [have human features]! But
they're ghostlike looking. They're all sorts of people! They's, there's,
there's an *Oriental* person, it looks like. And, looks like there's—the
features look like a *black* person. But they're ghostly looking.
There's no colors at all, just ghostly looking.

Suddenly Betty gasped. Her voice rose to a high pitch of excitement. Now we would learn where Betty had been!

> *Betty*   And, Oh! That's me! That's me! That's me there! There I am
> too! There I am and I'm like a ghost. I'm whitish gray when I went
> through the door.

Fantastic as it seems, Betty had actually been one of the *light-forms*
that she had been observing play the weird game. She had been the
light-form that she had seen waving at Bob and who had gazed over
the railing to look at the alien operation below. And there was yet
another surprise to come as Betty again came face to face with
familiar personages that she had met as a teenager just after her visit
to the *One*!

> *Betty*   There is [*pause*] a very tall—looks like men in white robes
> with white hair that are escorting us to a door. And it's all purple
> and lavender. And the door is opening and I'm swooped through
> all by myself and it's whirring, whirring and whirring and whirring
> around.

Bob could sense in the tone of Betty's voice that she was rapidly
slipping from the state of an *observer* to that of a *participant* in the
experience. He stepped in immediately to help her.

Bob Okay. I want you to step back, step back and—[*Betty interrupts*]

Betty I'm whirring around. Oh, it feels so strange! Ohhh, I feel so weak!

Bob Relax, relax.

Betty Ohhhhhhh!

Bob I want you to step back, step back. You're viewing this on television. Step back. You are watching the tape on the television. You are looking at this as an observer on the television. It was taped earlier. Remember? You're viewing this on the television. Relax. Now, I want you to watch—[*Betty interrupts again.*]

Betty I *see myself* there going round and round. Oh, oh, my hands and my feet are hurting while I'm sitting here [i.e., in the imaginary living room watching TV].

Bob Okay, let's relax.

Betty Oh my hands and my feet hurt awful though.

Bob Okay, let's shut off the television.

Betty I feel weak. I feel funny.

Bob Okay, we're going to shut the television off. We're shutting the TV off. I want you to relax now. The TV is off. Relax. Let's go back to the beach. You're lying on the beach. The sun is shining down on your back. You feel warmth in the sun. A beautiful warm breeze is going over your back. You feel perfectly comfortable.

Slowly but surely, Bob eased Betty out of the extreme discomfort that she was experiencing. Then he brought her back to the present time and ended the session. It is assumed that both Betty and Bob were experiencing the same effects that they had encountered when they were taken out of their bodies and lifted *upward* to the strange alien installation. This time, however, the procedure was reversed. They were being returned to their bodies. Upon their return, the whole episode would be forgotten just as if it had never happened. One cannot help wondering how many others have had or will have similar out-of-the-body experiences but will never know what has happened to them. What is this all about, I mused? What is this all about?

Part IV—The Higganum Incident

During the May 13 *overview* session, Bob had to cut short an experience that Betty had undergone because of the pain and trauma associated with it. However, I will use excerpts from that session as an introduction to *The Higganum Incident*.

> *Bob* Okay, I want you to move ahead in time in your mind, only as an observer, to the *next* time that you saw or had contact with the *beings*. I want you to look, as an observer. You need not go into great detail. Just see what the *next* time was that you were in contact with the *beings*.
>
> *Betty* It's 1986. And I'm in the trailer. I'm laying down on the couch reading the Bible. And it's beautiful out. It's summer. I'm laying there. The wind is getting so violent outside. I, it's odd. It's so windy. I can see the trees whipping back and forth like—the branches there—right from the couch as I'm looking out.

Suddenly, Betty finds that her body has become totally paralyzed from head to foot. She cannot move a muscle!

> *Betty* I can't seem to move!
>
> *Bob* Okay.
>
> *Betty* And I'm hearing a dull whirring sound like a fan or something.

You will note that Betty has described the same sound that she and Bob had heard just prior to their OBE in the Meriden incident. As mentioned, because of the adverse effects felt by Betty, he decided to go no further with this incident at that time. Then about a month later, on June 8, Bob and Betty decided to give it another try using the new *television* technique with Betty as an observer. Betty again repeated her description of lying on the couch, noticing the strong wind and hearing a whirring sound like a fan motor.

> *Betty* [*watching herself on television*] And it's making a loud sound. Dull, fanlike sound. And I can hear the wind and I see myself sit up. Got up on one elbow and turn and look out the window toward the woods. And the trees are just moving so radically. The wind is so strong. And suddenly I see myself [*pause*] just *staring* as if listening to something. [*long pause*] I'm just on the couch there

listening to something. [*long pause*] Just on the couch. [*long pause*]
Oh! There's a *being* that has come in the trailer and standing next
to me as I'm laying on the couch. And I can see myself looking up
at the *being*.

As I listened to the tape, it suddenly dawned on me that Betty had
started to relive this same event in part for Fred Max. During the
November 19, 1987 session as it was coming to an end, Fred had
asked Betty if she had had any recent experiences. Betty responded
as a participant and as such, told us what the alien had *said* to her
as she listened. Since it fills in this gap in the session currently being
discussed, it is worth mentioning. Let's go back to the 1987 session
for a moment.

Fred Max   When do you see them?

Betty   Last year. [i.e., 1986]

Fred Max   Where?

Betty   In Higganum. I'm laying on the couch reading my Bible
[*long sigh*] and they're telling me that I'm going to be *transported* in
a much different way . . . because there's too many eyes and ears
[*sighs*] watching and listening.

Fred Max   Where's Bob?

Betty   He's at work. I'm in the trailer all by myself.

Fred Max   What day of the week is today?

Betty   It's a weekday. . . . We don't have a calendar in there. It
seems like it's a Thursday.

Fred Max   What month?

Betty   It is in July, in July.

Fred attempted to go further and realized that Betty started to
experience pain so he did not continue. However, this segment of
that session provided us with two pieces of information that would
supplement the session currently being discussed; namely, the
month of the year and the aliens' intention to *transport* Betty in a
way that would not be noticed by those living in the trailer park.
Let's now return to the June 8, 1988 session and continue where we
left off.

Betty   And suddenly, I'm standing up. . . . There's silence. I don't
hear anything on the TV. The wind has stopped but [*pause*] looking on the TV I see the leaves still moving [*pause*] very roughly.

Something obviously had happened to Betty. At the outset, she could hear the whirring sound and could both see and *hear* the wind blowing. Now, she could see the effects of the wind but could not hear it. Everything had gone silent. Betty's *other self* had left our so-called *physical* world.

> *Betty*   Oh! [*gasps*] I see myself standing and I see myself laying on the couch! The *being* had put a small box or something on the couch first and then I saw myself appear there.

Betty's OBE seemed to have been the product of a technology that transcends what we would call the *physical* and *spiritual*! However humbling as it might seem, both of these terms are just invented, descriptive nametags for states of being that we really know little about.

> *Betty*   I see myself standing up and I look a little bit astonished. I'm just standing there. [*pause*] It's very quiet. And I see myself moving toward the *being*. [*pause*] And then I turn toward the couch and I reach down to touch myself and—Ahhhh! [*gasps*]— when I do, my hand goes right through me! And I'm laying on the couch and I pulled it back, my hand back because—with a puzzled look on my face. [*long pause*] Very silent. Just standing there. It seems as if [*pause*] there is some communication going but I don't hear anything on TV. [Figure 42]

Betty, as an observer, not a participant, cannot perceive the telepathic thoughts emanating from the *being* as she had during the earlier session with Fred Max.

> *Bob*   Maybe you could turn up the TV a little bit and it might record with the special camera, *even mental telepathy.*
>
> *Betty*   [*long pause*] I don't hear anything but there is some kind of communication going on.
>
> *Bob*   Okay, just watch the TV.
>
> *Betty*   I'm just standing there. I'm standing up there with the *being*. And, there is a *form of me* laying down on the couch. And the form has picked up the Bible and is holding it in, in the hand. [Betty had laid the Bible down previously.]

This OBE was strikingly different. Betty's inanimate body on the couch became animate while Betty's other self was still out of it!

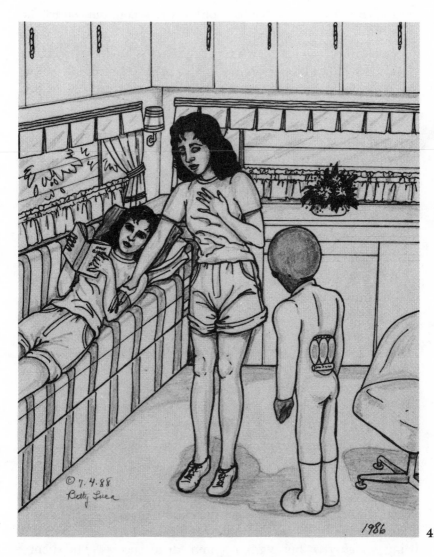

42

This type of OBE is known as a *doppelgänger* experience. It is a rare but well-documented phenomena that has been reported and investigated by researchers.

Betty   I, I, I don't understand it!

Bob   That's okay. You're just watching it on television.

Betty   [*long pause*] There's just some communication going on but there's silence. I can't hear it on TV. [*long pause*] The *being* is backing up.

Bob If, if you look at the *being* on the screen now, can you tell me what he looks like?

Betty Ahh, [*sighs*] he's got a very large hairless head, gray skin, big blackish-brown eyes—big eyes—sort of, sort of slanted; tiny holes in the, in the nose and sort of a slit in the mouth part. And he had a very large head. It goes down very narrow at the chin.

Betty, of course, was describing the same type of aliens that she had encountered over the previous years.

Bob Okay, what kind of clothing is he wearing?

Betty He's wearing tight-fitting clothes.

Bob And what color?

Betty It's a grayish-silver.

Bob Are there any marks or emblems or anything on his clothing anywhere that you can see on the television?

Betty No, but he's carrying something in the back by his waist. He's carrying something there in the back. It juts out a little, but at the side. I didn't see it at first. It's some kind of a wide belt that blends right in with his suit. [*long pause*] He's taking something out from the back there by his back and his waist. And he's pressing something and it causes, like a, a shower of sparkly light or something to go over him and over me. [*pause*]

Bob Okay, the camera will catch it all. Just watch the TV and see what happens.

As the shower of glittering light engulfed Betty and the alien, Betty instantly became a *participant* in the event. Again, she felt excruciating pain. Bob did his utmost to bring her back to the state of being an *observer* but with no immediate success. He spent a desperate time with Betty in a number of attempts to relieve her. Finally, he worked her back to the present time. Betty would not be ready to face another session for another month. I admired her for allowing herself to be used in this way. Her cooperation would help further our knowledge about UFOs and their mysterious occupants who were willfully violating not only earth's airspace but its citizens as well.

On July 9, 1988, Bob again tried to uncover the mystery surrounding the Higganum incident. This time he finally succeeded in keeping Betty in the role of an *observer*. She again relived the experience verbatim right up until the time the pain had caused Bob to terminate the session. We'll pick up the conversation from that point:

> *Betty* And he's facing me, and, and he's saying something but I *can't hear it* on television. [*pause*] Oh, there's suddenly, ah—it must have come from that thing on his back because suddenly, like a spray of sparkles just filled the area, like a—It shot up and it's sparkles all over the place. Oh! [*pause*] And it's like the sparkles are making us *lift up* a little but we're getting very *faded*. [*pause*] We're, we're faded away! The sparkles too! [*sounds very puzzled*] And I can, I can see myself just laying on the couch there and [*pause*] turning page after page after page of the Bible.

Incredibly, Betty's physical body continued to function while her *other self* faded away with the alien!

> *Betty* The television has just gone blank. [*long pause*]
>
> *Bob* That's okay. When it comes on again, see what else is on the tape.
>
> *Betty* It seems like it's just blank or snow or something. [*very long pause*] Oh! [*long pause*] I see, ah—[*pause*] There's, ah, I don't know how to explain this. I don't know what it is.
>
> *Bob* That's okay.
>
> *Betty* It's lie—[*pause*] There's nothing like this! I've never—There's nothing to compare these things with. [*long pause*] I seem to be floating in this—[*pause*] I don't know what it is! Everyplace and all around I see things. But, they're nothing I've ever seen before. [*pause*] And I can't even make a comparison to anything I've ever seen. [*sounds frustrated*]
>
> *Bob* That's okay. We want to know what the TV is showing. If you can't explain it, don't worry about it. Just relax.
>
> *Betty* It's very strange because I've never seen anything like this before. I see my body on the television just floating along and looking. And it looks as if my mouth is open as if [*pause*] I—this is so strange. How could that be on the television? [*Betty is a bit on edge at this point.*]
>
> *Bob* Just relax.
>
> *Betty* The things are just like nothing that I've ever seen in my life.

Bob   That's okay.

Betty   It's like I'm floating or flying or something through the area. [*pause*] It's so weird. It's beautiful. The only thing that, that looks and seems familiar is the light that's there. Everything else seems so unusual and unexplainable. And I'm coming up to just an open air. The stuff is—That stuff—I don't know what it was—It's behind. I'm just drifting like [*pause*] Oh! There's all sorts of—looks like *crystal spheres* way down below there. . . . I can't see, like any buildings or anything except those crystallike spheres down below. . . . I'm just, um, I've stopped now and it's like I'm suspended in space there.

When Betty stopped floating, she felt herself sink into something soft as if she had been borne along on something. At this point she saw a pinkish featherlike object appear under her on the TV. She was lying on it. Suddenly it began to sway back and forth. Betty saw herself descending on the fluffy object with a falling-leaf motion and settling on the crystal spheres that covered the ground. Then it happened: a vision or holographic presentation reminiscent of her encounter with the *Phoenix* during her 1967 abduction.

Betty   And there's sounds on the television like a *rumble*, like a rumble of thunder. And I see the look on my face. Ahhhhh, there's a huge *shadow* passing over me—huge, huge shadow passing over. And I look very frightened from it! There's specks of sparkles now in the air. And—Oh! They're, they're turning into little tiny lights and going down at my body. I can see them penetrating at my body. And I can hear like a *thunder*! [*long pause*] That, that *shadow* is, is, is crossing over, is crossing over. I can see it! I can see the shadow crossing all over my body, all over me. And, and the tiny lights have stopped hitting my body. And I see myself lifting my head and looking up. And I see, I see, I see the *wingtip of a bird*! A huge, huge wingtip of a *bird* on the television. It's huge! [*long pause*] I hear rumbling like thunder and those crystal spheres are *moving*. I can see them moving! And there's like steam or fog or something coming out from in between some of them making it awfully foggy. Ohhhh! There's a *baby* crying. I hear a baby crying on the television. And I can see myself looking to try to find out where it is. Ohhhh! [*gasps*] The crying is coming from me—from my chest—It's like the baby's in my chest! The cry of a baby! This is strange! [*long pause*] The baby's cry is echoing everywhere. Ohhh!

A loud voice is calling my name! "Betty!" And I look and, and it, it seems as if I can't answer. [*pause*] And the voice called again, my name. And I hear it say—"Equal balance, you're seven complete." [*pause*] The baby's stopped crying. [*long pause*] I see myself just laying there so still. It looks like I don't dare to move. I can see my eyes looking around and I look very frightened. It's so still and so quiet. [*pause*] I see myself being raised up. [*pause*] And I'm almost standing and I see two *beings* [typical dwarf-type], two *beings* coming toward me. They're floating over those crystal, [*pause*] crystal balls, crystal spheres that are on the ground. [*pause*] They're coming over to me.

Betty floated off the featherlike object and drifted down to join the two aliens.

Betty The one *being* is in front and one in back.

Bob Look at the screen good. See what the *beings* look like so you can draw them later.

Betty They look very much like the one that was on the screen [i.e., the one that originally took her from the trailer].

Bob Okay.

Betty They're moving and I'm moving with them. We're moving across these spheres. [*long pause*] And it feels as if, [*pause*] I'm watching them. It makes me feel like I've got a stomachache.

Bob Don't worry. Just watch it on the television.

Betty We're still just moving across these crystal spheres that are beneath. We're floating across, one in front of me and one in back of me. And you look over and all you see is like a vast open space with light, with some kind of fog and mist. [*pause*] I wonder what that [*pause*] huge, huge shadow was? We're still moving. And there's nothing around but light and, and there's mist, and underneath us, just those spheres. Oh, we're coming to a [*pause*] ball-shaped craft. It just looks a huge, huge ball like those spheres, those crystal spheres underneath, but only this is huge! [*pause*] And it's just hovering there. [*pause*] And I can see the mist and the light like movement around me. Huge ball-shaped craft. [*pause*] The movement of the mist and air and light, I guess. [*pause*] I'm almost up to it. [*pause*] A door is opening.

Bob Can you see on the television how the door opens?

Betty It just moves upwards and disappears but you can't see a door. It's only when it opens you can see that there's a door there. It looks almost, ah, mirrorlike. It's so shiny and we're moving inside, inside a room. And we're just standing there. The door is closing. [*long pause*] Again, there's just a *blank* on the television.

Bob Okay, well we can just move the tape forward until there's something on the TV again and then go from there.

Betty [*long pause*] All I see is a blank. [*pause*] Um, oh, I'm in a room. I see myself standing in a room. And there's one, only one of those *beings* in the room with me. I'm just standing there. [*starts to become agitated*]

Bob Watch the TV. You're already back home sitting down watching it on television. You're in the trailer in the nighttime. Just tell me what you see on the screen.

Betty Um, the *being* is talking to me there and [*pause*] saying something. I don't know what it is 'cause there's no noise but—

Bob How about if—Let's tune the television in so that it will even pick up the *being's* thoughts. And then we'll wind the tape through again and this time you'll be able to hear it on the TV.

Betty Um, it, ah, he's saying that I'm, I'm to forget. I'm not to remember. I'm not to remember this. I'm not to remember. Oh, there's another *being* coming in. Looks like the same *being* because he's got that *thing* on his back. And he's coming over to me and the other *being* is in back of me. I feel them touching my temples. And the other *being* is facing me. And he's just looking deep in my eyes. And he's telling me too that I should not remember. [*long pause*] I see that shower of sparkles again and it's coming up over me. I can feel it coming over me. [*becomes agitated*]

Bob Just watch it on the TV. You're already home sitting in the trailer with Bob. You're sitting in the trailer with Bob. I just want to know what you see on the television. This has already passed. This has already passed. You're already back. It's passed.

Betty [*pause*] I see all sparkles *in the trailer*. [*Betty is back again.*] And I'm just laying down on the couch there and it's as if I have fallen asleep or something. It looks like the Bible is laying on my stomach. And I'm sleeping and it's so windy out. You can see. The television is showing outside how windy it is! Oh, and the wind is starting to die down. And I'm waking up.

Bob Okay, I want you to relax now.

Slowly but surely Bob brought Betty out of the state of hypnosis. He was relieved that he had been able to keep her reliving the event as an observer and thus bypass the pain that she had experienced before.

I am at a loss to explain what the aliens tried to communicate to Betty through this experience involving a huge bird. Was it the Phoenix? The shower of lights and rumbling voice with a message for Betty was very similar to her past Phoenix experience. I can only hazard a guess as to what the crying baby and cryptic message meant. Betty had seven children but had lost an eighth which had to be aborted because of suspected cancer of the cervix. This had always bothered her. Perhaps she was being told that she was only meant to have seven children and that it was all right to have aborted the eighth. ("Equal balance—You're seven complete.")

It was frustrating not to know what the alien *beings* might have said to Betty during this experience. The *television* method used by Bob bypassed the telepathy used by the aliens. Betty was not able to pick up their thoughts on the *television* until Bob told her that she could by tuning the TV. By this time the experience was just about over. Betty had no desire to push her luck and try to relive the experience again by hypnotism. She was thankful to have gotten through the ordeal without pain. However, she did attempt through concentration and self-hypnosis to retrieve what the aliens had spoken to her telepathically. She sent me the results via a letter dated July 12, 1988.

Dear Ray,

This morning I was concentrating and trying self-hypnosis to determine what communication took place in the trailer between me and the *being* in 1986, being that it did not come out on the TV video as Bob suggested.

Although I did not see him during the sessions, I know now that another *being* was left behind in the trailer as a guard against any kind of intrusion when I was taken up.

I was told, through power, they can form illusions right down to movement, heartbeat, and breathing of a person for the sake of cover. If any outsider was to approach the trailer and look in, they would have believed the moving form on the sofa was actually me. The guard would activate the power to change the thought in the intruder's mind, to turn away. An intruder would have thought it was his natural decision and will, as not to disturb me. It would probably be some time later the person would question why. Just like they planted the thought in me to be activated in the 1975 experience to turn the TV to channel 7. I often have things happen where I say, "Now why did I do that? Why did I say that, or what am I doing here?" I realize it is not always their influence doing this but you wonder if it was really your decision or not.

What was revealed to me again is their power can control things for miles around to a small local spot. Something can be happening right amongst the busiest activities of a host of people and yet never be seen by some except those the *beings* choose to reveal it to. The *beings'* scanners and minds pick up any and all life forms within the immediate area of a target. They said they're keepers of form. They've been entrusted with and are responsible for the care of all natural form since the beginning. They know physically all there is to know about plant, animal, and human life form with the exception of human emotions which often activates the free will to do as it pleases. Emotions make man unpredictable. That's why it is not the immediate vicinity in their control that concerns them, but unexpected intrusion of someone entering the vicinity. Even though they can quickly gain control of the situation, they may be too busy to detect an invasion.

They have a problem in understanding the unpredictable free will of mankind. Again, I believe that was why a *being* was left behind in 1967 at South Ashburnham to hold at bay any unwanted visitors.

Their examinations of man are really checks for the environmental effects on our bodies (besides the restoration of form). The balance of nature, all nature, including man is in jeopardy.

When I realized they used illusion to control prying eyes, I asked (because of the ability to form an illusion) did they create illusions for me to see at anytime when they took me aboard their ship and to places? They said, "No, except for the illusion of the door into the forest." I asked, "Then how did we go through the wooden *door* and mirror in the cave [i.e., during her 1967 abduction]?" They said, "By controlled vibrational levels. It is very simple, those structures are very loose," he said.

I asked, "What did you mean 'too many eyes and ears watching and listening'?" He answered that—"The physical presence of eyes and ears is no concern for we control this easily. But, waves and manifestations of present energy cannot be erased. What is, is always there like grooves in the record of time. If the right tool or point is rubbed against hairlike warps and weaves, the recorded energy is artificially materialized. That is why we have to scramble the energy. When you are taken up, an excessive amount of energy will be scattered about us, masking the identity. This mask will blend and fill in any and all gaps and weaves during transition. Stay very still during the extensity of yourself," he said.

That was it, Ray. I didn't want to go any further in case I experienced the pain again.

In Christ Jesus,
Betty

Part V—Postscript

I have read and reread Betty's letter and have pondered much over the connection between the OBE and the UFO. Not too many years ago, I would have scoffed at even the mere suggestion that either had anything in common with the other. Now, I am being forced to reexamine the UFO phenomenon in light of its apparent paraphysical nature.

The paraphysical abilities of the aliens are mind-boggling. Their capability to materialize and dematerialize at will is most intriguing. This process of emerging into our space/time frame has been described as a conversion of energy and a change of vibration rate. Perhaps something akin to this process is inherent in the human OBE. The OBE appears to be a natural phenomenon for human beings.

A recent national survey conducted by the National Opinion Research Council (NORC) revealed that two million Americans have reported OBEs. One wonders how many go unreported in such a survey and how many occur without being recognized as such or remembered. It is possible that OBEs occur frequently during sleep but like most of our dreams fade from our memory upon awaking.

The human OBE seems to be transient and unpredictable in its occurrence. But what is most curious is the ability of the aliens to trigger OBEs in humans at will by a technical device small enough to be attached to a belt. Again, their intimate knowledge of the physical, mental, and spiritual makeup of man is both astonishing and alarming. They know more about our overall makeup than we do ourselves. This knowledge is reflected in both the design of their obviously human-adapted apparatus and their ability to control the human mind and body at will. This is most disturbing, as in the past such capabilities have only been attributed to the divine and supernatural.

Note that when a human being has an OBE, the physical body is left behind on our local space/time frame. It would appear that human consciousness travels to a different nonlocal space/time frame apart from the so-called physical body. But, in the case of the alien entities, it appears that their physical bodies make this same transition by a dematerialization process. Again, this seems to be instigated by technology. The same instrument attached to the belt of the alien in Betty's trailer initiated both her OBE and the dematerialization of the alien to a different space/time locale. Betty had left her physical body behind but still retained a body. The alien traveled with Betty in what appeared to be the same body.

Parapsychology and the New Physics are both relatively new branches of human science. Significantly, both seem to be revealing the bare rudiments of the super technology demonstrated by the aliens.

For example, parapsychological experiments indicate that the powers of telepathy, levitation, and telekinesis may be inherent but usually latent in the human mind. One cannot help but wonder how much more such powers would be manifested in a super-mind millions or billions of years in advance of the human mind. Most likely, such super minds would display exactly what Betty and other abductees have described—telepathy, levitation, and telekinesis.

A clue to their ability to perform such powers at will might be in a statement they made to Betty. They told her that their technology has to do with the *spirit*. Perhaps they have learned how to artificially enhance inherent mental powers via their technology. For example, artificial amplification of mental powers such as telekinesis and levitation might produce the equivalent of antigravity.

The New Physics, based upon quantum mechanics, also is revealing profound paradoxes, apparently already understood and applied by the aliens, in the physical world. For example, these super-intelligent creatures are reportedly able to manipulate the molecular structure of seemingly solid structures. They have been observed passing *through* doors, walls, and windows as if they did not exist.

Experiments within the context of the New Physics have made some startlingly and perhaps pertinent discoveries. All fundamental atomic and subatomic particles have been demonstrated to exhibit a paradoxical wave-particle duality. Waves are particles and particles are waves. Thus the physical solid stuff of the universe, including doors, walls, windows, and even ourselves, is only apparently solid.

What the aliens are reportedly able to accomplish is not that impossible if we grant them super minds and technology.

Another pertinent paradox indicated by theories embodied within the New Physics is also echoed in what the aliens told Betty about *time*. They insisted that our concept of time was *localized* and that time as we understood it did not really exist. The human concept of time was illusory. All is *Now*. Until recently such statements would have been scoffed at by scientists. But the New Physics seems to be hinting at this very concept.

Dr. Paul Davies is an internationally known and respected theorist specializing in the New Physics. He is Professor of Theoretical Physics, University of Newcastle-upon-Tyne, England, lecturer in applied mathematics at King's College, University of London, and visiting fellow at the Institute of Astronomy, Cambridge, England. He writes internationally for science magazines and journals and has authored a number of books. Concerning *time*, Dr. Davies writes that:

> There seems to be no strong reason for supposing that the flow of time is any more than an illusion produced by brain processes similar to the perception of rotation during dizziness. Accepting the passage of time as an illusion makes it no less important. Our illusions, like our dreams are very much a part of life.[7]

Dr. Davies and other theorists of the New Physics argue that the quantum theory reveals that in the universe there may be multiple ghost worlds which are alternate existences parallel to our own. Betty's experiences with the aliens appear to substantiate what human scientists are just beginning to probe.

Another affirmation of the paraphysical aspects of Betty's experiences can be found in our government's intense interest in the paraphysical properties of UFOs and their occupants. Such official interest lends credence to the experiences related by Betty and other abductees and deserves our examination.

For example, a recovered memo written by Wilbert B. Smith indicates such interest at the highest levels of the United States government. Smith was Superintendent of Radio Regulations Engineering for Canada's Department of Transport. He headed a UFO study dubbed Project *Magnet* which was part of Canada's overall UFO program called Project *Second Storey*. Much of Project Magnet's files remained classified but after Smith's death, researchers obtained a number of papers from Smith's home files from his

widow. Among them was a formerly classified *Top Secret* document
which Smith had kept for his personal records. It has turned out to
be one of the most important documents in UFO history for
obvious reasons. Pertinent excerpts are as follows:

> I made discreet enquiries through the Canadian Embassy staff in
> Washington who were able to obtain for me the following
> information.
>
> a. The matter is the most highly classified subject in the United
>   States government, rating higher than the H-bomb.
> b. Flying Saucers exist.
> c. Their modus operandi is unknown but concentrated effort is
>   being made by a small group headed by Doctor Vannevar
>   Bush.
> d. The entire matter is considered by the Unites States authorities
>   to be of tremendous significance.
>
> I was further informed that the United States authorities are
> investigating along quite a number of lines which might possibly
> be related to the saucers *such as mental phenomena.* [italics mine][8]

Another revelation of government interest in the paraphysical
connection with UFOs started with my receiving a phone call from
a Mrs. Irene Lombardi. She phoned me at my office on May 18,
1968, after reading about my interest in UFOs in a local newspaper.
At that time I rejected any notion of the paraphysical nature of
UFOs as being the fanciful ideas of occult practitioners, but what
the woman related made me sit up and take notice.

The telephone conversation started with a question. Mrs.
Lombardi told me that she had sat in on a NASA meeting in Boston
concerning ESP. According to her, the connection between ESP
and UFOs had been discussed. Her question to me was, what did
I know of such a connection? At first, I gave her my standard
"blame the occult" answer thinking that she was some kind of a nut.
When she persisted, I asked her who else was at the meeting and
how she happened to be there.

She told me that she was just one of a number of persons being
tested for *telekinetic* powers by the USAF and NASA. A list of
names was given to me to investigate. It included Everett Doyle and
Margaret Hill, Air Force Cambridge Research Laboratories, Bed-
ford, Massachusetts; Mrs. Giogrande, Instruments and Devices

Section, NASA, Boston; Dr. Miller at EG & G Company, and Dr. Charles Bufler.

Due to business and lingering skepticism, I did not get around to checking out these names until June 28, 1968. I found that Doyle, Hill, Giogrande, and Bufler all existed. I never did find Dr. Miller.

Mrs. Giogrande at NASA told me simply that the project was closed and did not care to comment further. Margaret Hill was a mathematician at AFCRL. Mr. Doyle was one of the USAF ESP Project leaders. Dr. Bufler was an independent parapyschologist who sought a NASA grant to work on ESP experiments.

The only individual that I could get to talk at any length was Mr. Doyle. He told me that he knew Mrs. Lombardi and that he was one of an AFCRL team sent to investigate her claim to have telekinetic powers. The AFCRL test consisted of asking such people to stop the spinning vane of a Crookes Radiometer. Light pressure causes the vanes to move. He said that the results were unsatisfactory and that the USAF ESP project had been terminated.

My curiosity now really aroused, I got back and interrogated Mrs. Lombardi. I recorded what she could remember for my files. The results are summarized as follows:

1. The team visited her on or about May 18, 1965.
2. She stopped the vanes once.
3. The team left the radiometer for her to keep a record of her hits and misses until their next visit.
4. When the team revisited, her ability to stop the vanes was intermittent. Mr. Doyle placed a 60 watt light source near the radiometer to cause the blades to spin faster. She was told to practice under this new condition and that they would return in six months. They did not return and informed her that they had been ordered to stop all proceedings.

Two additional significant bits of information came out of my conversation with Mrs. Lombardi. She mentioned that when one of the AFCRL team suggested she also get in touch with M.I.T. about her ESP abilities, Mr. Doyle gave him a dirty look and snapped "M.I.T. no longer works on ESP!" Curious, she phoned M.I.T. and was referred to someone who asked if she was officially connected to the project and had clearance. When she answered no, the person terminated the call. This, of course, is all hearsay but any ESP research at M.I.T. would most likely be government-sponsored.

The second piece of information may have a direct relationship with cases like *The Andreasson Affair*. Once, while casually chatting with an Air Force employee at a meeting, Mrs. Lombardi was told that all incoming phone calls to AFCRL's ESP project were taped. The tapes and all information about persons *really* exhibiting ESP were routed to Washington, D.C. by the C.I.A. because they suspected that a connection existed between UFOs and ESP. The employee also made the cryptic remark that the C.I.A. felt that there was a connection between some people that had ESP abilities and the *UFO occupants*! If this is true, then it lends further credibility to persons like Betty who report personal ESP experiences and abilities after being abducted by aliens. Was the C.I.A. using the NASA/AFCRL project to locate unsuspecting amnesiac abductees for special study?

A more striking leak of government interest in the paraphysical nature of UFO experiences involved a classic close encounter between an Army Reserve helicopter and a UFO over Ohio on October 18, 1973. The object was witnessed by the helicopter's four crew members and by five witnesses on the ground. In summary, the helicopter was approached by a sixty foot domed cigar-shaped craft. It had no wings, rudder, or stabilizer. It hovered above the helicopter and somehow dragged it upwards from 1700 feet to 3800 feet even though the controls were set for a dive!

Former Air Force scientific consultant and astronomer Dr. J. Allen Hynek dispatched Jennie Zeidman to investigate. Ms. Zeidman had been his technical assistant on the USAF UFO Project Bluebook which was in operation between 1952 and 1969. During the inquiry, the commander of the helicopter crew, Captain (now Lt. Colonel) Lawrence J. Coyne confided to Zeidman about a strange connection between the crew's witnesses and Pentagon officials. This connection further enhances the credibility of Betty's description of the paraphysical nature of her experience.

The following excerpt is extracted from Jennie Zeidman's 123 page report on the incident.

> Coyne told me that approximately three weeks after the event he
> received a call from a man who identified himself as being from
> the "Department of the Army, Surgeon General's office." . . .
> The caller said he was in the field of metaphysics, and specifically
> asked if Coyne or any of the other crew members had had any

unusual dreams since the UFO experience. Coyne, indeed, reported that he had had two unusual dreams; the first one, which he believed occurred two or three days after the event, he described as follows:

> I was sleeping peacefully, and I got up and walked into the hallway and stopped, and I turned around and I saw myself lying in bed; I was laying on my side, sleeping. It was like looking into a mirror, you know? I dreamed that I was conscious but that my body was sleeping. I got up—I *dreamed* I was getting up—and I started walking, and I turned around—and I was scared—I saw something laying in bed, and it was me [laughs uneasily] and I got so scared that I lay back down again and I said, "I better do this over again." You know, am I seeing something? Am I hallucinating? And I laid back down and then I woke up. When I lay back down it was like sinking into something.
>
> The other dream which was very vivid—and I talked to my wife for a week about this—was, a voice said, "The answer is in the circle." A very clear voice. I don't know whose voice it was. It was a very strong voice, a voice you have respect for, very sure. It said, "The answer is in the circle." And I was holding a *clear sphere* in my hand, a *round sphere*. A bluish-white *sphere*. [italics mine] This dream happened about two days later [after the first dream] and suddenly I started getting a little ridiculous and I told my wife about it and she said, "You're becoming a little absurd, you know."[9]

Another crewmember, Sgt. John Healey, also went on record concerning similar interest by the Pentagon. The following is an excerpt from a taped interview from the Zeidman report.

> As time would go by, the Pentagon would call us up and ask us, well, has this incident happened to you since the occurrence? And in two of the instances that I recall that they questioned me, was, number one, have I ever dreamed of *body separation* [italics mine], and I have—I dreamed that I was dead in bed and that my spirit or whatever was floating, looking down at me lying dead in bed, and the only thing that upset me was I was wondering what would happen to my two boys, but other than that I had no qualms about it—and the other thing [that the Pentagon asked] was if I had ever dreamed of anything in *spherical shape*. Which

definitely had not occurred to me. But every now and again the Pentagon—they haven't done it now for the past year, I guess, but every two months or so they'd call Larry [i.e. Commander Coyne], and they'd have a series of questions: had these certain incidents happened to you or had you dreamed of them since your incident with the UFO? And please contact the other people on the crew. And then Larry would call us up and ask about these things and then he would mail it back to the Pentagon. The Pentagon, from the way I gather it, believes us.[10]

Does all of this sound familiar? You bet it does! The OBE experiences of Coyne and Healey, Coyne's flashback of being given a round bluish-white *sphere* and the Pentagon's extreme interest in whether Healey had *dreamed* of seeing a *sphere* all reflect a detailed knowledge of the characteristics of abduction experiences. Surely these questions asked by the highest representatives of the military are based on official investigations of abductions within the ranks of the military and probably of NASA itself! This crack in government secrecy lends credulity to the authenticity of abduction experiences described by Betty and hundreds of others.

I trust that this rather long postscript on the reported paraphysical nature of alien beings has made their capability and Betty's recalled OBE abduction more intellectually palatable to the uninitiated and the skeptical. Perhaps in the distant future mankind will master the mysteries just being tapped in the new disciplines of parapsychology and the New Physics. Perhaps Man then will have mastered interstellar travel and will also cause primitive beings on newly discovered planets to wonder at his supernatural-like technology. I say *perhaps* because the very physical existence of mankind is dependent upon the reality and accuracy of the message of *The Watchers*.

Chapter Nine—Notes

1. Air Force Regulation No. 200-2, Department of the Air Force, Washington, 12 August 1954, paragraph 2a.
2. Robert A. Monroe, *Journals Out of the Body* (New York: Anchor Press/Doubleday, 1973), p. 3.
3. Michael B. Sabom, M.D., *Recollections of Death—A Medical Investigation* (New York: Harper & Row, 1982), pp. 21, 49, 76.

4. Raymond A. Moody, Jr., M.D., *Reflections on Life after Life* (New York: Bantam Books, 1977), pp. 15, 16, 20.

5. *Ibid.*, p. 34.

6. Raymond E. Fowler, *The Andreasson Affair—Phase Two* (Englewood Cliffs: Prentice-Hall, Inc., 1982)

7. Paul Davies, *Other Worlds* (New York: Simon and Schuster, 1980), p. 190.

8. Personal Files.

9. Jennie Zeidman, *A Helicopter-UFO Encounter over Ohio* (Chicago: J. Allen Hynek Center for UFO Studies, 1979), pp. 115, 116.

10. *Ibid.*, p. 116.

CHAPTER

T e n

The Watchers

Who are these UFO occupants that have the ability to transcend time and space? Where do they come from? How long have they been visiting our planet? What are they doing here? Such questions have plagued military and civilian researchers for decades.

Betty never was told exactly where her alien captors came from but she was given answers to these other provocative questions. It is now time to review their answers in a more detailed and cohesive fashion.

However, before we can appreciate the question of the legitimacy of their startling statements, it is important that we do some serious preparatory contemplations about the theorized nature of advanced alien lifeforms. In order to accomplish this, it will be necessary to examine a number of scientific disciplines.

Unfortunately, we cannot send an anthropologist to study alien cultures living in distant solar systems. The best that we can do is to have an anthropologist study UFO reports. Then theories relating to alien mind-set and motivation could be extrapolated from the contents of such UFO reports. One, of course, should select a leading expert in this discipline to accomplish this task. It just so happens that one of the world's most brilliant anthropologists performed such a study. Because of her privileged position in the world of science, she was able to sit in on official scientific discussion on UFOs. This person was none other than the late Margaret Mead, leading anthropologist and past president of the prestigious American Association for the Advancement of Science. Her statements on the subject of UFOs are highly pertinent. They provide an excellent introduction to the redevelopment of our perspective as it relates to mankind and super-intelligent extraterrestrial beings.

> "Do you believe in UFOs?" Again and again over the years, I have been asked this extraordinary question . . . a silly question, born of confusion. Belief has to do with matters of faith. It has nothing to do with the kind of knowledge that is based upon scientific inquiry. . . . Yes, there are unidentified flying objects . . . that even after the most cautious and painstaking investigations, *cannot be explained away.* Certainly a great many people are frightened by the idea that somewhere in outer space there are beings who are technologically more advanced than we are. Today, apparently, *it is precisely those who are best informed about our technological capabilities who are most disturbed by the idea that superior beings from some other unknown planet are taking an interest, an unexplained interest, in our planet earth.* Others deny that any creature could build a vehicle that could arrive here from anywhere in space. But a little quiet thought ought to convince us that, knowing what we now know about space technology, *the capability of reaching earth from somewhere else depends only on others having taken further steps into the unknown that are beyond our present capability.*
>
> These questions introduce a suspense element that is almost unbearable to us. If these creatures have been coming here for a hundred years, for thousands of years, *what are they doing it for?* The most likely explanation is that they are simply *watching* what we are up to; that a responsible society outside our solar system is keeping an eye on us to see that we don't set in motion a chain reaction that might have repercussions far outside our solar system. This is a plausible way of thinking to attribute to such living extraterrestrial creatures, that is, as plausible as any that we ourselves at present are capable of imagining.[1] [italics mine]

This intriguing hypothesis advanced by a learned anthropologist naturally raises an obvious but nonetheless provoking question: If an alien race has been *watching* us for many centuries, why have they been so covert about their operations instead of being more open and direct?

Early in the Air Force's study of UFOs, this frustrating

question—Why no contact?—was raised by military-contracted scientists. It was first supposed that the UFOs were making an initial assessment of earth's defense capabilities. But, this answer had its shortcomings.

> The lack of purpose in the various episodes is puzzling. Only one motive can be assigned: that the space-men are "feeling" out our defenses without wanting to be belligerent. If so, they must have been satisfied long ago that we can't catch them. It seems fruitless for them to keep on repeating the same experiment.[2]

As time went on, the Air Force proposed other reasons in an attempt to explain the aloof behavior of whoever operated the foreign craft that were invading the earth's skies. In 1968, the United States Air Force Academy advanced other possible reasons to their cadets as to why the aliens had not made contact with world governments.

> That question is very easy to answer in any of several ways. 1) We may be the object of intensive sociological and psychological study. In such studies you usually avoid disturbing the test subjects' environment. 2) You do not *contact* a colony of ants, and humans may seem that way to any aliens. (variation: A zoo is fun to visit, but you don't *contact* the lizards.) 3) Such contact may have already taken place secretly; and 4) Such contact may have taken place on a *different plane of awareness* and we are not yet sensitive to communications on such a plane.[3]

All of these conjectures, whether by Margaret Mead or Air Force studies, presuppose that UFOs are the product of a highly advanced culture. The Air Force's *Project Sign* acknowledged this obvious presupposition soon after it was organized to deal with the UFO problem.

> Instead of being a first port of call, Earth would possibly be reached only after many centuries of development and exploration with space ships, so that a visiting race would be far in advance of Man.[4]

As we continue to redevelop our perspective toward extraterrestrial life, it is essential that we consider the development of life on our own planet.

Since our sun is relatively young among the 100 billion or more suns in our galaxy, it is likely that a visiting alien race could easily be a billion years ahead of man in evolutionary development. The universe is considered to be fifteen to twenty billion years old. Our earth was born only 4.6 billion years ago. Life-supporting planets in other solar systems within our galaxy are probably five to fifteen billion years older than earth. Our planet and its lifeforms are still in the cradle of creation!

Intelligence seems to be an inherent byproduct of evolution. On our planet, life from its first inception has evolved *both* physically and mentally thus fulfilling a universal trend towards greater intelligence. This trend stretches from the earliest lifeforms, to fishes, to reptiles, and to mammals, culminating in primates and Man. Unless we destroy ourselves, this process should continue unabated into the billions of years that lie ahead. It might further help our perspective if we *summarize* the progressive development of lifeforms on earth.

Evolution began slowly but at a certain point suddenly accelerated. It took about four billion years for cells to achieve reproduction by sexual means. But it only took 600 million years to produce the variety and volume of life we know today. What caused this acceleration? It took Man 98 percent of his two to three million year existence before he engaged in agriculture. But it only took 16,000 years to produce civilization. What caused this acceleration? Let's put this matter in still further perspective.

If we compress the two to three million years of Man's existence onto the format of a normal January through December twelve month calendar, agriculture would not begin until December 28! Man's historical era, a brief six to ten thousand years, would be nestled in the last two days of the year! Let's take note of what has happened thus far on December 31.

During the early morning hours, Babylon, China, and Rome rose and fell. Socrates, Plato, and Aristotle lived around 9:30 A.M. Man's history rolled on through the afternoon hours into the evening. At 8:57 P.M., Columbus discovered America. At 9:16 P.M., Copernicus proved that the earth orbited the sun. At 10:27 P.M., Watts perfected the steam engine. At 11:09 P.M., Darwin formulated the theory of evolution. At 11:21 P.M., Fermi split the atom. At 11:41 P.M., the first computer was built. Between 11:43 and 11:48 P.M., man developed the airplane, the liquid fuel rocket, the artificial satellite, and the manned spacecraft. At 11:49 P.M., Man landed on the moon. It is now about 11:50 P.M. The science and technology curve is climbing straight up. What's next on Man's agenda?

One of the world's most prophetic thinkers along these lines of thought is Arthur C. Clarke. Clarke predicts a manned flight to Mars by A.D. 2005, the construction of space cities by A.D. 2010, a manned base on Mars by A.D. 2020 and manned exploration of the solar system by 2030 A.D.[5]

Fantastic you say? But we're only talking about the next five decades or so. This is not even a speck of dust on the cosmic scale of time. Let's continue to move ahead in time with other carefully thought out predictions of Man's space ventures in the centuries that lie ahead.

Some scientists predict almost incomprehensible things will happen during the next few centuries. James Oberg of the NASA Space Center in Houston writes that man will be capable of *Terraforming*—massive planetary engineering that will enable him to reshape other worlds to satisfy human physical needs.

With a set of well understood tricks-of-the-trade, and specialized tools developed for use on alien worlds, future planetary engineers will be able to carry out what we can only dream of today.

- evaporate the clouds of Venus, spin up the retrograde planet, cool it, and allow oceans to form.
- make rain fall again on Mars, turning the red skies blue and tinging the red rocks with the green of lichens.
- give an atmosphere to Earth's barren moon.
- dismantle the outer planets, using their hydrogen as rocket fuel and their rocky cores as material for a dozen new earths.
- collect comets, asteroids, and interplanetary dust—raw material for housing billions of our not-so-remote descendants.[6]

As our descendants leave our solar system and discover other solar systems, the then well-developed art of *terraforming* will transform lifeless planets into hospitable worlds. Earth lifeforms will be introduced from huge celestial versions of Noah's Ark. All of these ventures, including many undreamed of events, could take place during the next few thousand years or less. What are the implications for our step-by-step redevelopment of perspective concerning

Man's relation to the existence of and contact with advanced extraterrestrial beings?

If the earth is typical of planets in the universe, intelligent beings who live on planets a billion or more years older than the earth have already bypassed that advanced level of intelligence and capability that our successors will only achieve in the distant future. Interstellar space travel would have been surpassed long ago by intergalactic space travel. In short, such an advanced technology would exhibit capabilities that Man, in his infancy, has only attributed to supernatural beings. Such an alien brain would be inaccessible to earth scientists except on their terms. A NASA study conducted by the Brookings Institution, a government think tank located in Washington, D.C., admits that:

> If superintelligence is discovered, the results become quite unpredictable. It has been speculated that of all groups, scientists and engineers might be the most devastated.[7]

A graphic way to illustrate the intelligence and knowledge gap that would exist between Man and such aliens would be to go back one billion years and look at what existed in the fossil record. What would we find? One billion years ago, the highest form of life on earth was a simple wormlike animal. The creatures that dwell on planets only one billion years older than earth may possess an intelligence that surpasses us by as much as we surpass the worm! We could hardly expect them to land on the White House lawn to propose the exchange of ambassadors. As the Air Force Academy text so aptly puts it: It's fun to visit the zoo but you don't contact the lizards!

What would such creatures be like to human beings? Could we even begin to comprehend a mind so far in advance of ours? Dr. Robert Jastrow, founder and director of NASA's Goddard Institute, has stated that:

> If the UFO phenomenon is actually an extraterrestrial probe of some sort, they have to be technologically greatly in advance of us. And if this is true, whatever they do will not make complete sense to us. If it does seem completely logical and consistent, it is probably not extraterrestrial in origin.[8]

UFO researcher Budd Hopkins echoes Dr. Jastrow's remarks: "Only if their behavior seems paranormal are we possibly dealing with extraterrestrials." Those who have read my first two books on *The Andreasson Affair* and who have read this far in this book have probably long ago concluded that the actions and abilities of the aliens encountered by Betty are certainly paranormal. In fact, this would be an understatement of the highest degree! As a reminder, I have listed some of the abilities exhibited by the entities that were witnessed by Betty. They have the ability to:

1. Travel between star systems.
2. Exist in a timeless realm.
3. Control our time.
4. Predict our future.
5. Travel between different planes of existence.
6. Read and control human minds.
7. Communicate telepathically.
8. Place human beings in suspended animation.
9. Instigate OBEs in human beings and interface with humans' *other selves*.
10. Proportionally increase or decrease the size of humans and complex machinery.
11. Pass through *physical* objects with ease.
12. Levitate and move at will.
13. Transform their bodies into balls of energy and back again.
14. Conduct advanced complex genetic operations on human lifeforms.

These are just some of the paranormal capabilities exhibited by these uninvited lifeforms to our planet. Who could ever have conceived that such things could be happening in our midst? Who can believe it? However, to see and hear Betty relive her experiences with the aliens has made believers out of some of the most ardent skeptics. For example, one of my lead investigators on our Phase Two investigation was a hardboiled, no-nonsense police lieutenant named Lawrence Fawcett who is an expert in the art of investigation and interrogation. Lieutenant Fawcett stated for the record that:

> I first entered this case feeling that it could easily be explained as a very elaborate hoax. Of course, I hadn't met Betty, and this was a biased opinion on my part.
> After many months of intensive interviews in and out of regres-

sive hypnosis, I found all facts to be consistent. After hearing and listening back to all the testimony that was given, I feel that it would be impossible for an individual to concoct such an elaborate story and to be able to hold it together under the intensive interrogations that were conducted. It would be impossible for anyone to fabricate a story of this magnitude and remain consistent throughout. To the average lay person, this story may sound like a chapter of *Lost in Space*, but to this investigator, it is not only plausible, but true.[9]

How would such highly advanced living beings communicate with lowly man? What do the experts in the subject of communication with extraterrestrial life say about this?

In September 1965, a military electronics conference was held to discuss this very subject. The sessions were chaired by Dr. Harold Wooster, Air Force Office of Scientific Research. It was pretty well agreed that the type of communication most used by humans —*talking*—might be a physical impossibility because of the biological makeup of an alien's body. To *talk*, such an alien would have to have a similar tongue, vocal cords, teeth, certain cavities in their respiratory tract from the vocal cords up to the mouth and produce voice signals within a human's frequency range of hearing. Such an advanced race would probably have no problem in deciphering human languages and reproducing the sounds of a human voice artificially. However, one of the participants in this conference on communicating with extraterrestrial intelligence had something very interesting to say that is highly pertinent to *The Andreasson Affair*. Dr. William O. Davis is a highly respected physicist known for his *free thinking* on such matters. He has served as deputy commander of the USAF Office of Scientific Research and director of research at the Huyck Corporation, Stanford, Connecticut after his discharge from the USAF. He stated the following:

> In many respects the most probable encounter is with a higher form of life, or at least a more advanced form, because these beings would be more likely to reach us first than vice-versa. If we assume that they understand more about the mind than we do—and let's say they understand more about ESP or it turns out to be a human-type of phenomenon—they should be able to detect us. After all, we know all kinds of fields associated with the physical world, the world of entropy. It is not illogical to assume

that life may have as yet detected fields and radiation associated with it. They wouldn't have to scour the whole universe for us. They would simply focus their life-detecting device.

The nice thing about this hypothetical contact is that communication would be their problem. We wouldn't have to worry too much about it. They would come to us. As a matter of fact, *I strongly suspect that the first communication is very likely to be telepathic.* [italics mine][10]

Dr. Davis's statement is nothing short of prophetic. There are hundreds of cases on record similar to the Andreasson case where abductees report *telepathy* as the mode of communication between themselves and the aliens!

This ends the step-by-step attempt to redevelop our perspective concerning the existence of and contact with advanced extraterrestrial beings. It is now time to review *what* the aliens told Betty about their *identity* and *operations*. They were brief and to the point but what they revealed will revolutionize every aspect of our lives—science, religion, philosophy, sociology—nothing will be spared. For, if we take what the aliens told Betty Andreasson at full face value, mankind is on the verge of a revolution in thought of a magnitude far greater than the Copernican revolution. In fact, there can be little comparison.

The aliens' revelations to Betty were not given all at once. Indeed, these powerful entities seemed to have induced appropriate mental blocks within Betty's mind to prevent certain information from being released prematurely. They informed her that they have a specific time schedule. It is interesting to note that when pertinent information was given to Betty, it was done in a straightforward, sometimes casual manner. Betty did not receive any long classroom-like dissertations nor was she allowed to bring back the equivalent of a written message. In a real sense, Betty's relived experiences are the aliens' actual message. Betty Andreasson is the aliens' *living audio visual* to mankind!

During her childhood encounters, Betty was simply told that she would be used to help prepare mankind for something good that was going to be done for them. As mentioned, a similar message was given to her husband, Bob Luca, during his childhood encounter with alien beings. Bob Luca's encounters were documented in my book *The Andreasson Affair—Phase Two*.

Incredible as it may seem, the aliens have inaugurated what appears to be a mass conditioning program through individuals selected when children. These so-called abductees are then apparently periodically groomed and in some cases physically experimented with into adulthood. Messages for Man, like grains in a medical time-release capsule, will only be revealed according to a predetermined alien timetable.

During Betty's first *adult* abduction from her home in South Ashburnham, Massachusetts in 1967, the aliens' message became more specific. Betty was told in no uncertain terms that she had been chosen *to show the world*. Just prior to leaving the spacecraft during that abduction, Quazgaa, the leader of Betty's abductors, delivered a debriefing message to her.

> *Betty [under hypnosis]* He's putting both hands on my shoulders and is looking at me. And he says, "Child, you must forget for a while." He's telling me things.
>
> *Raymond Fowler* Did you feel dizzy or strange when he was looking at you in the eyes?
>
> *Betty* Yeah, it seemed as if he were going deeper inside of me—my mind. He says my race won't believe me until much time has passed—*our* time. . . . They love the human race. . . . All things have been planned. . . . They do not want to hurt anyone. But, because of great love, they cannot let Man continue in the footsteps he is going. . . . It is better to lose some than to lose all. . . . They have technology that Man could use. . . . It is *through the spirit*. But, Man will not search out that portion. . . . *Man is not made of just flesh and blood*. He says that he has had others here. . . . Many others have locked within their minds secrets. . . . He is locking within my mind certain secrets. . . . They will be revealed when the time is right.

In essence, Quazgaa informed us through Betty that there is an overall plan by the aliens to intervene to help mankind because of something undesirable that Man is doing. Others, like Betty, have been abducted but have had the experience erased from their conscious mind. Quazgaa also told Betty that Man is *more than just a physical being* but has not realized this truth because of lack of interest and research. He also made the quizzical statement that: "It is better to lose some than all." For years I wondered what was meant by this. When I found out the answer during this phase of the investigation, it was not pleasant news. In fact, it was devastating. In some ways, I thought, it might have been better not to have known.

If you will recall, during Betty's 1973 abduction, the aliens finally revealed their purpose in their abduction of human beings. It was done in a straightforward manner without emotion or fanfare. I would like to divide up their message into two segments. The rest of this chapter will deal with the first segment, namely: *Who* the aliens claim to be and *what* they claim to be doing on earth. The second segment in the next chapter, will deal with the most provocative question: *Why* are they doing this? It will be worthwhile to repeat Betty's conversation with the aliens at this point.

The following is extracted from the hypnotic regression sessions that recorded Betty's 1973 abduction from Ashburnham, Massachusetts. Betty had just been placed in a special seat designed to reduce the effects of g-forces during the craft's return to earth.

> *Betty* And the other *being* went out and left me there with only one. And that one *being* is communicating to me *through the mind.*
>
> *Bob Luca* What, what does he say?
>
> *Betty* He's very grateful to me. [*pause*]
>
> *Bob Luca* Why? For what?
>
> *Betty* For being there. [*sigh*] That I helped the lady to calm down. He says, [*pause*] it was very beneficial for the [*pause*] *fetus.*

Betty took advantage of this rare opportunity to communicate with the aliens and asked one of the sixty-four thousand dollar questions. One should consider their answer in the light of our new perspective of super-intelligent extraterrestrial beings and their capabilities.

> *Betty* "Who are they?" I asked. I was trying to ask him. [*sigh*] He says that [*sigh*] they are the *caretakers* of nature and natural forms— *The Watchers.* They love mankind. They love the planet Earth [*sigh*] and *they have been caring for it and Man since Man's beginning.* They watch the *spirit* in all things. . . . *Man is destroying much of nature.* . . . They are curious about the *emotions* of mankind.
>
> *Bob Luca* Do they have emotions?
>
> *Betty* Not like Man.
>
> *Bob Luca* But, didn't he say they *love* the earth?
>
> *Betty* It is not the same emotion. It is a forever love—constant, continual. [*deep sigh*] And they are the *caretakers* and are responsible. And this is why they have been taking the *form* from Man.

Bob Luca How, how long have they been taking the *form* from Man?

Betty For hundreds and hundreds of years.

Bob Luca In their, their duties of *watching* over the earth in their craft—do they ever have problems with, um, the military from different countries, including ours? Has anyone tried to harm them?

Betty I don't know. He's just telling me what they're doing.

Bob Luca I see. What else does he say?

Betty [*gives out a long sigh*] He's saying that they have *collected the seed of Man* male and female.

Bob Luca Uh, huh.

Betty [*sighs*] And, that they have been collecting [*pause*] *every species* and every *gender* of plant for hundreds of years.

When I first heard these provocative and astonishing claims, my mind was literally bombarded by the implications that they posed to every facet of mankind's history and to the development of lifeforms on earth. Such implications would certainly take another book to explore. Two questions immediately spring to my mind. How have they affected Man's *physical* evolution? Is it possible that they were responsible for some of the giant leaps in Man's *mental* development discussed earlier in this chapter? Let us first consider Man's physical development.

The aliens told Betty specifically that they had been on earth since Man's *beginning*. Is it possible that extraterrestrials, as envisioned in Arthur C. Clarke's classic *2001—A Space Odyssey*, were responsible for producing Man from his primate relatives? Noted UFO researcher Scott Rogo, lecturer in parapsychology at John Kennedy University and a prolific author, mentions this possibility in connection with questions raised by Pierre Teilhard de Chardin.[11]

A member of the Society of Jesus, de Chardin held positions as professor of geology at the Catholic Institute in Paris, director of the National Geologic Survey of China, and director of the National Research Center of France. He played a major role in the discovery of Peking man. This brilliant Jesuit priest and noted paleontologist raised questions about Man's evolution that were far in advance of his time. He dealt with these questions in two remarkable books: *The Phenomenon of Man*[12] and *The Appearance of Man*.[13]

The basic mystery that puzzled de Chardin was that there was no apparent evolutionary link between Neanderthal and Cro-Magnon man. Neanderthal was so far below the fully human Cro-Magnon that de Chardin could not understand how the first could logically have evolved into the second. The gap was too wide and the jump was too quick in the fossil record. Relatively speaking, Cro-Magnon man seemed to have suddenly appeared upon the earth. UFO researcher Scott Rogo comments that:

> Teilhard elaborates on this mystery. In Neanderthal Man, whom Teilhard considered the "utmost fringes of true fossil humanity," there seemed to be three racial types. Yet, when true *Homo sapiens* in the forms of Cro-Magnon, Grimaldi, and Chancelade men— representing our three modern dominant racial types—appear on the evolutionary scale, there is no evidence that these modern types evolved gradually from the Neanderthals which preceded them.[14]

Thus, the question that plagued de Chardin and others concerns the abrupt disappearance of Neanderthal culture and his replacement by Cro-Magnon and his counterparts as the planet's dominant species. In the light of the apparent genetic operations being carried on by aliens who claim that they have been on earth since Man's beginning, it is only logical to conclude that they may have had something to do with the mystery posed by Pierre Teilhard de Chardin. Was Cro-Magnon Man placed on earth intact or was he the result of a genetic transformation of Neanderthal Man by alien beings? If either case were true, it would go a long way in explaining the *genetics connection* manifested in UFO abduction reports.

Let us now turn to the question of the rapid *mental* development of Man. Is there evidence in Man's written records of extraterrestrial influence upon the development of civilization? If so, how do such legends relate to modern day reports of contacts between humans and nonhuman entities?

We have recently marveled at the fact that out of the roughly three million years of Man's existence, his historical era has been only a brief six to ten thousand years. It took 98 percent of Man's three million years existence before he engaged in agriculture. But, it took only 16,000 years to produce civilization. Legends, supported by the aliens' claims to Betty, imply that they may have been the so-called *culture-gods* believed to have been responsible for this dramatic acceleration in Man's mental development.

Legends abound from many parts of the world concerning contact with celestial beings who aided in Man's development of civilization. Such legends were the basis for the development of complex religious beliefs in the existence of gods from the sky. Bookstores and libraries are now full of books that attempt to link such legends with extraterrestrial visitation. Many are done in a popular, poorly researched manner and have to be read critically. But some scholarly works have been produced. Among them are *The Sirius Mystery*[15] and *Intelligent Life in the Universe*,[16] coauthored by Carl Sagan and the late prominent Soviet scientist, I.S. Shklovskii. Sagan and Shklovskii discuss a number of such legends but are particularly impressed with one originating from the ancient civilization of Sumer.

> Taken at face value the legend suggests that contact occurred between human beings and a nonhuman civilization of immense powers on the shores of the Persian Gulf, perhaps near the site of the ancient city of Eridu, and in the fourth millennium B.C. or earlier.[17]

Ancient records state that a nonterrestrial being:

> . . . used to converse with men. . . . He gave them an insight into letters and sciences and every kind of art. He taught them how to construct houses, to found temples, to compile laws, and explained to them the principles of geometrical knowledge. He made them distinguish the seeds of the earth and showed them how to collect fruits. In short, he instructed them in everything which could tend to humanise mankind.[18]

Of such legends, Shklovskii writes that:

> Despite the great dangers of confusion with legends generated in other ways, such hypotheses are entirely reasonable and worthy of careful analysis. Agrest [a Russian ethnologist] has boldly conjectured that perhaps a number of events in the Bible were in reality based on the visit of extraterrestrial astronauts to the earth.[19]

Even conservative-minded Carl Sagan admitted that these early legends, especially of the earliest civilizations:

. . . deserve much more critical studies than have been performed heretofore, with the possibility of direct contact with an
extraterrestrial civilization as one of the alternative interpretations.[20]

He also stated that Sumerian mythology conceived the universe:

. . . as a state governed by an apparently representative and
democratic assembly of gods, which made the great decisions on
the fates of all beings. . . . Such a picture is not altogether
different from what we might expect if a network of confederated
civilizations interlaced the Galaxy.[21]

It is interesting to note that Sagan considers Sumer as perhaps the
first civilization on the planet Earth and that near it lies the site of
the ancient city of Eridu. Why is this interesting? Because Eridu is
the so-called Babylonian Eden, the birthplace of Man! The Baby-
lonians were the successors to the Sumerians. Early Babylonian
inscriptions tell a story of Adapa, so strikingly parallel to the
Biblical story of Adam, that he is called the Babylonian Adam.
These inscriptions refer to him as: "Adapa, the seed of Mankind"
and "Adapa, the wise man of Eridu."

One wonders if there is a connection between such legends and
the aliens' statements to Betty:

They love the planet Earth and they have been caring for it and
Man *since Man's beginning.*

The Babylonian creation account, although polytheistic, has so
many points of similarity to the Hebrew [Semetic] account in the
book of Genesis, that both must have had a common origin. Are
highly advanced *beings* from outer space God's agents of creation on
this and other planets? Perhaps we should take the Genesis account
more literally when it states "let *us* make Man in *our own image.*" If
this is indeed a fact, it would certainly help explain some of the
mind-bending revelations covered in the next chapter. But what of
abductions and genetic experimentation on Man by such aliens?
Where is the evidence in Man's historical past for such incredible
things?

Obviously, if such alien operations involving genetics did take
place in Man's past, they would be interpreted within the context
and the limitations of nontechnological cultures. We would expect

that such events might be grossly distorted over centuries of time. But such events would be so extraordinary that a clear signal should remain that would override the background noise of ignorance and superstition. It is with these reservations that I can say with utmost assurance that Man's history is rife with *tales* of abductions, sexual intercourse, and strange operations that involve *nonhuman entities*. Many of these tales almost exactly parallel modern UFO abduction reports. Such stories are recorded in the religions, myths, and legends of many cultures.

It is certainly not within the bounds of this chapter to explore these ancient tales in detail. Others have done a fine job in this area. I would especially refer the reader to Jacques Vallee's book, *Passport to Magonia*[22] for an intriguing collection of such recorded tales. These involve humans being abducted by nonhuman entities invariably called fairies, gnomes, elves, and demons among other human tags for the unknown.

Concerning the legends of fairies, Vallee refers to a number of experts well-versed in fairy folklore. These include Walter Wentz, who wrote an extensive work in 1909 entitled *The Fairy Faith in Celtic Countries, Its Psychological Origin and Nature*. Concerning abductions mentioned in fairy folklore, Vallee quotes Wentz:

> This sort of belief in fairies being able to *take* people was very common. . . . A man whom I have seen, Roderick MacNeil was lifted up by the hosts and left three miles from where he was taken up.[23]

Significantly, as in the case of modern UFO abductions, the abductee was *made to forget* what had occurred during the abduction. Vallee states that:

> The mind of a person coming out of Fairyland is *usually blank* [italics mine] as to what has been seen and done there.[24]

A most startling parallel is recorded by another specialist in fairy folklore. Edwin S. Hartland authored a treatise in 1891 entitled *The Science of Fairy Tales—An Inquiry into Fairy Mythology*. In this book, Hartland relates a story strikingly analogous to Betty's 1973 abduction during which she was used by the aliens to assist a woman in child labor. Hartland tells of a Swedish book published in 1775 that contained a legal statement, solemnly sworn on April 12, 1671, by the husband of a midwife. He swore that his wife was taken to fairyland by a dwarflike entity to assist in an act of childbirth. The author of the legal statement was a clergyman named Peter Rahn. Vallee quotes Hartland as follows:

> On the authority of the declaration we are called upon to believe that the event recorded actually happened in the year 1660. Peter Rahn alleges that he and his wife were at their farm one evening late when there came a little man, swart of face and clad in grey, who begged the declarent's wife to come and help his wife then in labor. The declarant, seeing they had to do with a Troll, prayed over his wife, blessed her, and bade her in God's name go with the stranger. She seemed to be borne along by the wind.[25]

Hartland remarked that the tale ended with the midwife returning home with the troll in the same manner, that is, being "borne along by the wind."

In modern times, this incident might be reported as an abduction by an alien entity who entered a farmhouse and *floated* off with the abductee and returned in the same way. Just as striking is the description of the place where the midwife was taken. Reportedly, she entered an underground passageway through a *shiny metal door*! She told her husband that the *door* led to the home of the *little people* which was *filled with light* from an unseen source. Such a story engenders visions of certain portions of *The Andreasson Affair* itself!

Another common *abduction* theme that permeates folklore involves *changelings*. Although distorted by time and superstition, past belief in changelings may also have roots in UFO abduction of the past. Vallee again quotes Hartland:

> By the belief in changelings, I mean a belief that fairies and other imaginary beings are on the watch for young children or . . . sometimes even for adults, that they may, if they can find them unguarded, seize and carry them off, leaving in their place one of them.[26]

The abrupt personality changes that some abductees experience today might have also occurred in the past. This could have been the catalyst for the belief in *changelings* by our ancestors.

American researcher John Keel writes that similar stories abounded in Indian legends of the Northern Rockies according to studies performed by Dr. E.E. Clark.[27] Clark tells of various stories about three-foot tall entities who *abducted* Indian children. Reportedly, these beings also had the power to render themselves invisible. Keel also tells of the findings of anthropologist Brian Stross. Stross unearthed some intriguing *little men* stories while doing research on the Tzeltal Indians in Chiapas, Mexico. The dwarflike entities were called the *ihk'al*. The Tzeltals claimed that these small beings carried a device on their back which enabled them to fly. Reportedly they occasionally kidnapped women and *forced them to bear children*.

Thus, it is a documented fact that legends from many corners of the earth tell of little people who could fly, render themselves invisible, and control the human mind. Allegedly, these beings would abduct both children and adults for reasons having to do with *reproduction*. We will examine this latter theme shortly but we would be remiss not to discuss another capability attributed to the little people of yesterday that is also attributed to the little people of today.

Another provocative feature that emerges from these hazy tales from our past is that these dwarflike, nonhuman beings have control over what we call *time*. If you will recall, Betty Andreasson was told some very incredible things about the aliens and their relation to time. Some examples follow as excerpted from the Phase One and Two hypnotic regression sessions conducted on July 16 and 23, 1977.

> The future and the past are the same as today to them—Time to them is not like our time, but they know about our time—They can *reverse* time—Time with us is not your time. The place with you is localized. It is not with us. Cannot you see it?

In essence, the aliens informed Betty that they had the capability to freely move through time and space. The past, present, and the future are the same to them. *Time*, as we know it, does not exist for them!

Vallee calls attention to examples of ancient abduction tales from European and Chinese folklore that parallel modern UFO reports involving the relativity of time. I call the common theme of such tales the Rip Van Winkle scenario: A person mysteriously disappears for weeks, months, or years but upon his return believes that he has not lost any time at all. Vallee quotes Hartland's writings concerning Gitto Bach, a farmer's son who mysteriously disappeared.

> During two whole years nothing was heard of him; but at length one morning when his mother, who had long and bitterly

mourned for him as dead, opened the door, whom should she see but Gitto with a bundle under his arm. He was dressed and looked exactly as when she last saw him, for he had not grown a bit. "Where have you been all this time?" asked his mother. "Why it was only yesterday I went away," he replied.[28]

Gitto then proceeded to open the bundle and showed her a suit made of a material that resembled white paper. Incredibly, it had been made in such a way that there were *no visible seams*. Gitto then proceeded to tell his mother that the suit had been given to him by the *little people* that he had been with!

Modern UFO reports in many instances display the aliens' ability to manipulate time. Placing humans in a state of suspended animation, stopping and starting car engines and placing abductees into another space-time continuum during OBEs all hint at the aliens' ability to master time. For example, compare the tale about Gitto Bach with the well-known *time-relativity* report from a Chilean night border patrol. The patrol advanced to within six hundred feet of a glowing object that had descended and landed behind a small hillock along the Chilean-Peruvian border. The patrol leader Corporal Armando Valdes, took it upon himself to go over the hill for a closer look while his frightened men awaited his return. About fifteen minutes later, their leader appeared coming back over the hill in a dazed state. He was no longer cleanshaven but had a distinct beard growth. Paradoxically, his digital calendar watch was found to be ahead of time by five days!

Consider also the well-known Casey County abduction case thoroughly investigated by Dr. Leo Sprinkle, a professor of psychology at the University of Wyoming. This case involved the abduction of three women from Liberty, Kentucky. Louise Smith, Mona Stafford, and Elaine Thomas. After the abduction ended, Louise reported that the minute hand on her watch was *spinning* almost as fast as the second hand. Their abductors were the typical short humanoids with gray skin. Two of the abductees remembered being taken to what appeared to be a place underground into a room filled with bright light to be examined by the aliens, a scenario amazingly similar to the *home of the little people filled with light*.

As mentioned, another theme of fairy folklore that parallels UFO abductions in our time is in the area of *procreation*. Stories of copulation between nonearthly beings and humans persist all the way back to Biblical times. Early in the first book of the Bible entitled *Genesis* we read these provocative words.

And it came to pass, when men began to multiply on earth, and daughters were born unto them, that the Sons of God saw the daughters of men that they were fair; and they took them wives of all they chose.[29]

Throughout the Bible, the term *Sons of God* refers to celestial beings called angels (messengers). If taken at face value, such stories present a far-reaching implication. Such interrace sexual union would imply that these nonearthly entities were genetically compatible with Man. This is borne out as we continue to read that progeny resulted from this unlikely union.

There were giants in the earth in those days; and also after that, when the Sons of God came in unto the daughters of men, and they bare children to them.[30]

The Hebrew word for *giants* (nephilum) literally means the *fallen-down-ones* because these tall celestial beings *fell* from the sky. Their half-breed progeny and their descendants are often mentioned in the early books of the Old Testament until the last of them were finally killed off. They were known as the Rephaim, Emim, Anakim, Horim, Avim, and Zamzummim.[31] Some scholars speculate that this tradition of giants born from the union of gods and humans formed the basis for the demigods of Greek mythology. The Bible describes these tall hybrids as "mighty men (heroes) which were of old, men of renown."[32]

Stories and beliefs of sexual contact between nonhumans and humans were popular in the Middle Ages. In this period we find a strong belief in the existence of male incubi and female succubi who forced human beings to have sexual relations with them. Later, these beliefs continued in the guise of fairy folklore. Wentz, a scholar of such folklore, concludes from his studies that the fairies who entice mortals in modern times are much the same, if not the same, as the succubi of the Middle Ages. Modern times for Wentz was the nineteenth century!

One hundred years later we find the twentieth century counterpart to angels, demigods, incubi, succubi, and fairies of Man's dreamy past. Consider the well-known Antonio Villa-Boas case investigated and thoroughly documented by Dr. Olava Fontes of the National School of Medicine in Rio de Janeiro, Brazil. Briefly, Antonio was abducted by alien creatures while plowing his field on the night of October 15, 1957.

Antonio was brought aboard a UFO by dwarf-sized entities and brought to a small room furnished with a *couch* covered with a thick gray material. Blood was extracted from his chin which resulted in long-lasting scars. A gaseous substance was emitted through tubes into the room and Antonio was stripped naked and sponged with a liquid. A strange naked small humanlike woman entered the room and intercourse took place. The female entity then pointed at her stomach, then to Antonio, and then toward the sky as she left the room. Consider also a more contemporary case concerning a person named Dan (pseudonym). Dan's case was investigated and documented by well-known UFO abduction researcher, Budd Hopkins. Under hypnosis, Dan relived an experience very similar to that of Antonio Villa-Boas. The aliens appeared in his bedroom with a female described as half-human. Through mind control, Dan was forced to have intercourse with her. Flashbacks and nightmares about the experience finally led Dan to Budd for assistance. In bygone days, the female entities encountered by Antonio, Dan, and others would be called succubi!

One might very well ask at this point what kind of purpose was served or is being served by such abductions and sexual encounters? Is there a correlation between the reported *purpose* of yesteryear and that of today? Concerning the motive behind fairy abduction, Vallee again quotes Hartland who wrote back in the nineteenth century that:

> The motive assigned to fairies in northern countries is that of *preserving and improving their race*, (italics mine) on the one hand by carrying off human children to be brought up among the elves and to become *united with them* (italics mine) and on the other hand by obtaining the milk and fostering of human mothers for their own offspring.[33]

The motivation for the fairy abductions of the past and the UFO abductions of the present is one and the same—*Genetics!*

Today, however, their genetics program appears to have accelerated to vast proportions. *The Watchers* are diligently collecting the seed from earth's lifeforms. Their purpose is to preserve them for existence elsewhere because of their impending extinction on this planet. It has only been because of their past genetic interference that mankind has prolonged his stay on earth.

> *Betty* They have spliced into it [the seed] to prolong the form. . . . They have been collecting every species and every gender of plant for hundreds of years so that nothing will be lost [*pause*] when the last shall come. [*pause*] And that's all he's saying.

I am sure that what the aliens told Betty next was just as shocking to the reader as their announcement that mankind was to become sterile. Who would have ever imagined that human females were being used covertly to carry hybrid fetuses in their wombs because of genetic deficiencies in female aliens?

> *Betty* They too are of the same substance [as Man] and that some of the females [alien females] just don't accept the protoplasm all together. So, they grow and use them [human females] to carry other fetuses. They [alien females] are very weak and cannot be artificially inseminated like humans.

If you will recall, this conversation had taken place immediately after Betty had observed the aliens remove a strange-looking premature fetus from the woman that she had been brought to help during childbirth.

> *Fred Max* What happens to the fetus? Do they keep it there [i.e., on the craft] or?
>
> *Betty* The fetuses *become them.*

I still remember the cold chills that trickled up and down my spine when I first heard these alarming words. Again, my mind flashes back to Hartland's conclusion that the motive assigned to legendary abductions by nonhuman beings was the preservation and genetic improvement of their race.

What can be said about this and other such echoes from our misty past with any surety? Namely this: Throughout mankind's history there are undeniable motifs woven in and out of religious beliefs and folklore that are strikingly parallel to UFO abduction accounts of today.

It is true that time, superstition, and technological ignorance have distorted these tales from antiquity. But the sheer quantity of our contemporary accounts coupled with modern communications allow us to record and analyze their content in some detail. I feel confident if we could somehow magically transfer today's reports back to our past that we would be reading about them now in the legends of our predecessors. It is quite probable that these ancestral whispers from the abyss of time are confirmatory of the voices of abductees being heard today.

Could it be possible that alien lifeforms have really been living in such a clandestine relationship with Man? Are the so-called *Watchers* dependent upon us to perpetuate their own species? If so, it becomes quite obvious that their very survival is intimately linked with the success of their ongoing genetic engineering program. (Whoever created and commissioned these celestial caretakers made sure they were faithful to their task!) One also cannot help but wonder when this symbiotic kinship with Man originally came to be. How could Man be genetically compatible with an alien being? This intriguing question will be discussed in some detail as we continue to analyze the abduction phenomenon in the next chapter.

The dwarf-sized creatures that have abducted Betty and count-less others may have been dubbed many things by Man including nephilum, fairies, elves, gnomes, trolls, ihk'al, incubi, succubi, and aliens. But the name by which they call themselves stretches back to the dawn of civilization at Sumer in Babylonia.

The Chaldeans, an ancient and dominant people in Babylonia, believed in a certain class of angelic *beings*. These *beings* were responsible for watching over the affairs of Man on earth. The Chaldean name for this class of celestial entities is 'īr which translated means *Watcher*.

Chapter Ten—Notes

1. Margaret Mead, "UFOs—Visitors from Outer Space?" *Red-book*, September 1974, pp. 57–59.
2. J.F. Lipp, *Project Sign Technical Report No. F-TR-2274-IA, Appendix "D"* (Wright–Patterson AFB, Dayton, Ohio: AAF Air Material Command, February 1949), p. 35.
3. Donald G. Carpenter, Major, USAF, ed., "Unidentified Flying Objects," *Introductory Space Science* (Department of Physics, USAF Academy, 1968) Volume II, p. 462.
4. Lipp, *op. cit.*, p. 31.

5. Arthur C. Clarke, *1984: Spring—A Choice of Futures* (New York: Ballantine Books, 1984), pp. 147, 148.

6. James Oberg, "Terraforming," *Astronomy*, May 1978, p. 9.

7. House Report No. 242, *Proposed Studies on the Implications of Peaceful Space Activities for Human Affairs*, 1961, p. 225.

8. Budd Hopkins, "The Extraterrestrial-Paraphysical Controversy," *MUFON UFO Journal*, November 1980, p. 4.

9. Raymond E. Fowler, *The Andreasson Affair—Phase Two* (Englewood Cliffs, N.J.: Prentice-Hall Inc., 1982), p. 268.

10. Dr. William O. Davis, "Communication with Extraterrestrial Intelligence," *IEEE Spectrum*, March 1966, p. 162.

11. Ann Druffel and D. Scott Rogo, *The Tujunga Canyon Contacts* (Englewood Cliffs, N.J.: Prentice-Hall Inc., 1980), pp. 198–99.

12. Pierre Teilhard de Chardin, *The Phenomenon of Man* (New York: Harper & Row, 1959).

13. Pierre Teilhard de Chardin, *The Appearance of Man* (New York: Harper & Row, 1965).

14. Druffel-Rogo, *op. cit.*, p. 199.

15. Robert R. G. Temple, *The Sirius Mystery* (London: Sidgwick & Jackson Limited, 1976 and Futura Publications Limited, 1979).

16. Carl Sagan and I.S. Shklovskii, *Intelligent Life in the Universe* (San Francisco: Holden-Day, Inc., 1966).

17. Sagan-Shklovskii, *op. cit.*, p. 456.

18. *Ibid.*, p. 457.

19. *Ibid.*, p. 454.

20. *Ibid.*, p. 461.

21. *Ibid.*, p. 460.

22. Jacques Vallee, *Passport to Magonia* (Chicago: Henry Regnery Company, 1969).

23. Vallee, *op. cit.*, p. 100.

24. *Ibid.*, p. 87.

25. *Ibid.*, p. 101.

26. *Ibid.*, p. 104.

27. John A. Keel, *UFOs: Operation Trojan Horse* (New York: G.P. Putnam's Sons, New York, 1970), pp. 230–1.

28. Vallee, *op. cit.*, p. 107.

29. Genesis 6:1–3.
30. Genesis 6:4.
31. Genesis 14:5, 15:19–21, Numbers 13:23, Deuteronomy 2:10, 20, 21.
32. Genesis 6:4.
33. Vallee, *op. cit.*, p. 105.

Fitchburg-Leominster, MA, *The Gardner News*, October 13, 1976. This article documented Betty's former husband being taken into police custody and then deserting her. *Credit: Raymond E. Fowler*

Still Missing

ASHBURMHAM — Mrs. Betty A. Andreasson, 30 Russell Hill Road, has notified Police Chief Ronald LaPlante that her husband, James S. Andreasson, 43, is still missing. Mrs. Andreasson first reported her husband missing on Sept. 9.

Andreasson was taken into protective custody from his

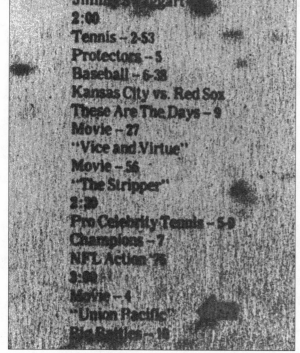

Photograph of the August 29 television schedule which verified Betty's hypnotic recollection that a western ("Union Pacific") was being shown that afternoon. *Credit: Raymond E. Fowler*

4 Dodge Court, Danvers, MA. The circle indicates the
window of the "big hall." *Credit: Frederick A. Fowler*

M EVENING NEWS

SALEM, MASS., MONDAY, JULY 7, 1947   Published in Salem For Salem, Danvers, Beverly, Hamilton Wenham, Ipswich, Topsfield, Middleton   PRICE FOUR CENTS

Flying Saucers' Reported
Seen in Beverly, Wenham

Two Mysterious Discs, Similar to Sky Objects Which Have Entire Country in State of Wonderment, Sped Thru Evening Sky in Wenham; Single Speeding Disc Was Seen in Broad Daylight at Beverly

Beverly, July 7—Mysterious, "flying discs," which are baffling observers throughout the entire country, have already appeared in this area where at least two reliable persons have reported them to The News. E. Meredith Chute, 348 Cabot street, Beverly, proprietor of a Cabot street bakery, and Albert Harry Pembroke, Dodge's row, Wenham, caretaker on the former Hollander estate, now the William T. Kemble estate, Wenham, for 50 years, were the first to report them.

Mr. Chute spotted a single disc in broad daylight while with friends in Magnolia Friday afternoon and Mr. Pembroke saw a group of them when he glanced out a window at 2:45 A.M. Thursday. Being were firm in their belief that they were seeing something unusual but hesitated about reporting to The News until they read similar reports in newspapers and heard radio broadcasts about them.

This photo was published in the evening edition of the Morristown Daily Record, Morristown, N. J. on July 10, 1947. If there had not been...

place standing on end. He said it was clearly visible to him for several minutes, although his companions could not locate it, and finally it faded out like a light being slowly turned off.

Mr. Pembroke stated that the several he saw looked like blue lights and appeared to be floating over Longham Basin. Suddenly they turned and drifted back toward his house and just as they came near the...

Salem Evening News, July 7, 1947. Banner headline of local UFO
sightings which may have been related to the author's daylight disc
sighting at Wrest Farm, Danvers, MA. *Credit: Salem Evening News
and Raymond E. Fowler.*

Ray Fowler, Bob and Betty Luca. *Credit: Peter Tomikawa Nagura*

Betty Andreasson Luca and hypnotist Fred Max. *Credit: Fred Max*

The Gardner News, October 24, 1977. Headline story concerning the death of Betty's two sons.

Two Brothers Killed In Westminster Car Crash

WESTMINSTER, Oct. 24 — Two brothers were killed and a third passenger was injured when the car in which they were riding crashed broadside into a tree on South Ashburnham Road late Saturday night.

James S. Andreasson Jr., 21, and his brother, Todd J. Andreasson, 17, both of 50 Russell Hill Road, Ashburnham, were pronounced dead at the scene by Dr. Joseph Hill.

Medical Examiner Dr. Arthur Kanserstein, who signed the death certificate, attributed James' death to a fractured skull and fractured ribs and Todd's death to a fractured skull. Time of death was placed at 12.05 a.m. Sunday.

Kelly O'Connor, 13, of 48 West Princeton Road, a passenger in the vehicle, was transported to Henry Heywood Memorial

Hospital by Woods Ambulance Service. She is being treated for a broken femur (thighbone) and is listed today in good condition.

According to Investigating Officer Vincent Puchalski of the Westminster Police Department, the 1974 Mercury Capri was operated by James Andreasson.

The vehicle was traveling south on South Ashburnham Road, Puchalski said, and approaching a slight left curve of the road when it crossed the right lane of traffic and then went back into the left lane and slid, hitting the tree broadside.

Officer Puchalski said he could not divulge the estimated rate of speed. The accident is being investigated by local police and Inspector Richard Smith with the Registry of Motor Vehicles' Fitchburg

office.

The accident was reported to police by a motorist who happened upon the scene minutes after it had occurred at approximately 11.54 p.m.

Services

The young men were the sons of James S. and Betty (Aho) Andreasson of 50 Russell Hill Road, Ashburnham.

James was born April 25, 1956, in Fitchburg. A 1974 graduate of Oakmont Regional High School, he had recently been discharged from the United States Navy and was a student at Mount Wachusett Community College. He attended Twin City Baptist Church in Lunenburg.

Todd was born in Gardner, Aug. 12, 1960, and was a senior at Oakmont Regional High School.

In addition to their parents, they leave three sisters, Mrs. Rebecca Anderson, Miss Bonnie Andreasson and Miss Cindy Andreasson, all of Ashburnham; two brothers, Mark Andreasson of May Port, Fla., and Scott Andreasson of Gardner; paternal grandparents, Selfred Andreasson of Westminster and Mrs. Dorothy Andreasson of Leominster, and maternal grandmother, Mrs. Eva P. Aho of Ashburnham.

Services will be held Wednesday at 11 a.m. in First Baptist Church. The Rev. Robert Westcott, pastor, will officiate. Burial will be in Forest Hill Cemetery, Fitchburg.

Calling hours at the Sawyer-Miller Funeral Home, 123 Main Street, will be tomorrow from 7 to 9 p.m.

Bust of the fetus-like alien head, designed and constructed by Fred R. Youngren and his daughter Faith, with the aid of Betty Luca. Compare with the photograph of an actual fetus *face-on*. *Credit: George J. Bethoney*

Human fetus. Compare with the bust of an alien.

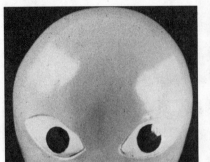

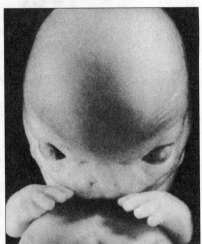

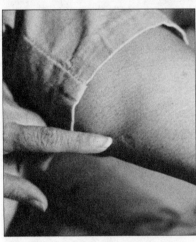

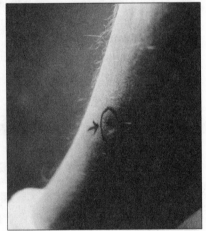

Typical scoop mark scar on Betty Luca's left calf. First noticed on June 1, 1987. *Credit: Bob Luca*

Typical scoop mark scar which appeared on Ray Fowler's right shin sometime during the night of August 16, 1988. This photograph was taken on the following day. *Credit: Raymond E. Fowler*

CHAPTER

Eleven

Anatomy of a Phenomenon

I am currently serving as director of investigations on the board of directors for the Mutual UFO Network [MUFON].[1] MUFON is an international organization which investigates, documents, and analyzes UFO reports. On its advisory board of consultants, there are specialists and scientists who represent a broad spectrum of disciplines. We depend upon their expertise to study, evaluate, and comment on those aspects of the UFO problem that are pertinent to their background. In this chapter, I shall draw upon the expertise of two MUFON consultants: Michael D. Swords, Ph.D., consultant on the history of science and technology, and Richard N. Neal, M.D., consultant on physiological and psychological effects of UFOs. Dr. Swords is a professor of natural science at Western Michigan University, Kalamazoo, Michigan. Dr. Neal is a specialist in obstetrics and gynecology at the Beach Medical Center in Lawndale, California.

Our analysis of the UFO abduction phenomenon must start with the question of the origin of Man himself. Why? This is when the aliens informed Betty that they were given the responsibility to be caretakers of the *forms* of life on earth.

Earlier, we speculated about the possibility that an advanced extraterrestrial race genetically interfered with an earth primate lifeform to produce *Homo sapiens*. It is possible that this same race created *The Watchers* at the same time and appointed them as caretakers. Evidence derived from certain scientific findings and the study of UFO abduction reports indicate that *The Watchers* were created from *Homo sapiens* himself. What is this evidence?

The latest thinking in the theory of evolution attempts to explain extensive changes in the structural appearance of evolving lifeforms as being caused by small changes in the regulatory genes. These are the genes that control the rates of growth and development. Dr. Swords writes that:

> When we compare the human form to that of our nearest genetic *cousin* on earth, the chimpanzee, we see many similarities, of course. But there are significant differences as well. And yet when we compare ourselves genetically to the chimps we are nearly identical. As someone has phrased this: the genes fit, but the bodies do not. How can this be? How can we have nearly identical structural genes, yet quite large structural differences in some areas of our bodies. The answer, it seems is *Neoteny*.[2]

Neoteny is the phenomenon of a fetal or a larval form of species that bypasses normal physical development and becomes sexually mature. This occurrence is quite common in animals today, including many species of amphibians. They are capable of it due to simple fluctuations in the temperature of the water in which they breed. Dr. Swords points out that sometimes the physical changes that occur are permanent and an apparently new physical lifeform pops up from nowhere on the evolutional landscape. It is one of nature's genetic tricks to produce leaps of structural difference called *punctuated equilibrium*. He notes that the retention of fetal or ancestral characteristics in such changed lifeforms is a basic characteristic of neoteny. But he is careful to note that the change is not in gene structures but in the mechanisms that govern the rates of their functions. Significantly, creatures with the same genes, but working at different rates, can appear remarkably dissimilar.

Back in the 1920s, an anatomist named Louis Bolk was intrigued by the similarities in structure, not of humans and chimpanzees, but of *fetal* humans and *fetal* chimpanzees. He pointed out that almost all of the readily apparent physical differences between Man and ape are much closer when comparing their embryonic forms. He theorized that *Homo sapiens* is physically a fetal ape which has become sexually mature. Now what does all of this have to do with what is reported about the abduction phenomenon?

The similarity between the physical appearance of the so-called *Watchers* and a human fetus is striking. A common description by abductees is that "They looked just like fetuses." This curious fact, coupled with the aliens' remark that they too are of the "same substance" as Man, provide two primary clues to unlocking the mystery of their origin. Let us follow up on these clues and see where they will lead us.

Dr. Swords speculates that through human genetic engineering breakthroughs in the future, *Homo sapiens* someday might look very much like the typical alien beings being reported by witnesses and abductees.

> In present day humans, it is theorized, fetal development proceeds for 9 months or so with the fetal brain consuming 50% of the total oxygen being sent by the mother during much of the pregnancy. Upon reaching a certain size, the mother can no longer supply sufficient oxygen and the fetal brain begins to mildly asphyxiate. As the fetus thrashes about (possibly sending chemical signals into the mother's blood) in protest of this insufficiency, the mother's system begins the birthing process. Over the millennia our species has matched this developmental phenomenon with the *pelvic size* of the woman and all turns out well.
>
> But there is ample evidence that human brain development during this fetal period *could go much further*. Modern nutrition and prenatal care is pushing fetal development along more quickly. Fetal heads are becoming too large for the birth canals of smaller women. Caesarian births are more common. As Bioscience advances, this trend can only become more acute. There may easily be pressure to avoid the problems and the limitations on our brain's development by going to artificial wombs when they are developed. And once such cultural choices become commonly made, the doors to artificial selection and genetic engineering are wide open.[3]

Through genetic engineering, our future descendants could bypass neoteny by natural selection and easily produce human beings of small stature and large heads very similar to the aliens being reported. The fetal head, allowed to develop and grow in an artificial womb, would significantly increase the size and the capability of the brain of the new *Homo sapiens*. Dr. Swords suggests that the aliens may actually *be* our descendants who have traveled back in time to their genetic roots [us] to revitalize their gene bank, which had been adversely affected by environmental changes. But the same capability of genetic engineering would be true for advanced extraterrestrials who have visited earth since man's beginning. These aliens, as we have speculated, may be very much like us and could have produced both *Homo sapiens* in their own image and *The Watchers* to be caretakers of the forms of life on earth. In fact, this can be deduced from the aliens' message to Betty that they have been here since Man's beginning. The creators of both Man and Watcher may be linked to the tall, blue-eyed, blonde humanlike entities often seen with the fetuslike aliens.

Betty was privileged to observe the birth of two *premature* fetuses. They were initially conceived in the womb of *the woman* and allowed to grow within her womb for several months before being removed. Betty watched horrified as they made an incision around one of the fetuses' eyes, placed something around the mouth and ears, inserted needles in its head and placed it in a highly sophisticated-appearing tank. The tank could very well be the *artificial womb* of Dr. Swords's imaginative look into the future. *The Watchers* may have been using this same procedure to procreate their species since their own conception in the same way, possibly by the tall human-appearing entities who may be their masters. This is obvious just by examining their physical description as provided by Betty and many other abductees. Dr. Swords comments that:

> A biologist looks at our . . . ufonaut and thinks: how did that ever get born? The large domed cranium seems far too big for the birth canal indicated by the pelvic width. There are only three scenarios which allow this:
> 1. birth could occur "earlier" in brain and cranial development than it would in humans, thereby making the birth diameter of the head very small.
> 2. sexual dimorphism in ufonauts could be very great with the females . . . having very large pelvises proportionately.
> 3. natural delivery could never take place in this hi-tech civilization, and the large domed craniums would be a result of their liberation of their genetic potential from the limits of their small birth canals.[4]

Dr. Swords dismisses scenario 1 since it would mean the birth of a very incomplete being that required a lengthy postbirth vulnerability period. He admits that scenario 2 is possible if female aliens have exceptionally large pelvises. However, if Betty is correct, then female aliens are even thinner than their male counterparts. As mentioned, she was told they had procreation problems, and it could be surmised that their thinness could be related to this problem. This brings us scenario 3 where the problem is overcome by advanced extraterrestrial technology: artificial wombs. As mentioned, *The Watchers* seem to be employing a procedure that man himself may use as bioscience advances over the years ahead. If he does, the result could eventually be human beings that are exactly like *The Watchers* themselves. What we would be like is what they are now! How could this be?

Dr. Swords explains that when such a drastic change becomes a reality (i.e., a neotenous artificial jump), our civilization would be so advanced as to allow certain physical qualities in the individual which would not be possible in a natural environment. For example:

1. The head-to-pelvis ratio already mentioned.
2. The diminution of sex organs, secondary sex characteristics, and a general "unisex" look; these characteristics are sometimes seen in pituitary gland abnormalities today. The sexual organs would not even have to be functional, since forms of genetic selection . . . do not require active sex cells.
3. In the human fetus today, the form of the voice box or larynx is incomplete, and if expressed in that form in an adult through a neotenous jump, it would probably eliminate communication by sound waves altogether. If telepathy exists, that would make the loss of speech unimportant.[5]

Dr. Swords, as mentioned, applies these characteristics to our descendants who have come back to visit us (their genetic roots) to revitalize their weakened gene bank. However, genetic engineering of a neotenous nature in Man's past could also have produced these alien caretakers. In either case, the Neoteny Theory would lay to rest much of the mystery of the typical description of UFO alien entities. It explains:

1. Their facial features.
2. Their physical proportions.
3. Their lack of hair and pigmentation.
4. Their sex-organ diminution.

5. Their head-to-pelvis anomaly and need for artificial birthing.
6. Their lack of speech and use of mental telepathy.
7. Their ability to breathe earth's atmosphere.
8. Their intimate association with alien humanlike companions. [The robed entities and others like them] [Figure 43]

Indeed, this latter point involving the observation of apparent human beings working in concert with the fetuslike aliens had presented a great mystery to UFO researchers. For example, in the classic Travis Walton abduction case, Travis described a blue-uniformed human being working with the aliens on board a UFO.

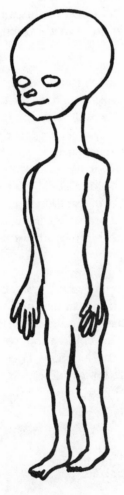

Credit:
Michael D. Swords

43

He was about six foot, two inches in height and wore a transparent helmet through which Travis could see his facial features.

> He had coarse, sandy-blonde hair of medium length that covered his ears. He had a dark complexion, like a deep, even tan. He had no beard or mustache. In fact, I couldn't even see stubble or dark shadows of whiskers. He had slightly rugged, masculine features and strange eyes. They were a bright golden-hazel color—but there was still something about these eyes that I could not quite place.[6]

There was no communication between Travis and the enigmatic tall man. He simply acted as an escort. He would not respond to Travis but did smile kindly in a tolerant manner.

It appears now that the mystery of these manlike creatures has been solved. Most likely, this person was one of many bred by *The Watchers* as part of their genetics program. Indeed, Betty was privileged to visit one of the onboard vivariums where small children were being raised along with other forms of earth life. As in the case of the two fetuses she had witnessed earlier, she observed that there were two distinct kinds of children in this alien biosphere. Some looked like *The Watchers* and others appeared more human. This also seems to explain the subtle differences and similarities between witnessed descriptions of UFO occupants.

The tiny children in the vivarium, like the newborn fetuses that she observed earlier, had no genitals. They might be hybrid in nature and possibly implanted and carried to partial term by human surrogate mothers. The birth that Betty was brought to witness may have been a product of genetic engineering and neoteny. When the aliens told Betty that "The fetuses become *them*," it could have been the literal truth. *The Watchers* and human beings may be genetically tailored variants of the same lifeform. The paraphrased words of the comic strip possum named *Pogo* might be appropriate here—"We have met the aliens and *they is us!*"

Revealing as this may be, however, we are still faced with another mystery that requires a solution. If we take *The Watchers'* statements at full face value, they have coexisted with Man from his very beginning. This being the case, we are confronted with the thought-provoking possibility that both *Watcher* and Man may be genetically related to a common ancestor.

Our common ancestors may be traced to a highly advanced race of extraterrestrial beings who discovered our solar system millions of years ago. In the course of their scientific activities on this planet, they may have genetically altered one of earth's primates to make it in their own image. This would explain the amazing similarities existing between fetal apes and fetal man that we discussed earlier. Have we any clues as to who these ancestors might be? Yes. Evidence indicates that mankind's heredity may be related to the tall, blue-eyed, blond, robed entities seen by Betty and others. It is apparent that whoever they are, the small fetus-looking Watchers are subservient to them.

It goes without saying that the evidence presented for Man's origin and rapid development in terms of extraterrestrial intervention is still highly speculative. Thus, it may come as a surprise to an incredulous reader that implications stemming from the modern discovery and studies of DNA independently support such evidence.

In 1963, Drs. Francis Crick and James Watson uncovered the structure of DNA. DNA is the master molecule that contains the genetic code. Both scientists received the coveted Nobel prize for this historical breakthrough in genetics.

The *nature* of DNA, however, presented its discoverers with a perplexing problem. Because of its tremendous complexity, Crick and others felt that there had not been enough time for it to have evolved *naturally* on earth. The September 10, 1973 issue of *TIME* magazine reported on a theory proposed by Dr. Crick and an associate that is highly pertinent to the subject at hand.

Were We Planted Here?

After winning the Nobel prize for helping to discover the structure of DNA, the master molecule of life, what does a scientist like Francis Crick do for an encore? He tackles something even bigger. With Leslie Orgel of California's Salk Institute, Crick has now taken on the mystery of the origin of life. . . . The two scientists theorize that life on earth may have sprung from tiny organisms from a distant planet—sent here by spaceship as part of a deliberate act of seeding.

This bizarre-sounding theory, called "directed panspermia" by its authors, results partly from uneasiness among scientists over current explanations about how life arose spontaneously on earth. Crick and Orgel note, for example, that the element molybdenum plays a key role in many enzymatic reactions that are important to life. Yet molybdenum is a rare element . . . [they] suggest that earth life could have begun on a planet where molybdenum is more abundant.

Crick and Orgel also ask why there is only one genetic code for terrestrial life. If creatures sprang to life in some great "primeval soup," as many biologists believe, it is surprising that organisms with a number of different codes do not exist. In fact, Crick and Orgel say, the existence of a single code seems to be entirely compatible with the notion that all life descended from a single instance of directed panspermia. . . .

Why would . . . some distant intelligent beings ever launch a panspermia project? To demonstrate technological capability, say Crick and Orgel—or, more probably, out of "some form of missionary zeal."

Dr. Crick theorized that mankind might seed life in the same way on some planet in the distant future. Again, one can not help wondering if the tall, blond, robed humanlike entities associated with UFOs are none other than the creatures of Dr. Crick's theory. Such creatures may have traveled to earth *personally* and have created Man and other lifeforms in their own genetic image. This proposition is but one step up the ladder from Crick's hypothesis that the seeding may have been accomplished by unmanned space probes.

Evidence other than what has been previously discussed may be reflected in a variety of anomalous events reported by Charles Fort [1874–1932] and his modern day counterparts. They have meticulously recorded hundreds of instances where living and dead animals have fallen from the sky. Most falls consisted of snails, worms, reptiles, fish, crabs, frogs, toads, and insects. These lower lifeforms have high reproductive rates, simple living habits, and require a minimum of attention to raise. Morris K. Jessup, University of Michigan astronomer and author of four books on UFOs, advanced a highly speculative theory in *The Case for the UFO* [Citadel Press and Bantam Books, 1955]. He envisioned alien scientists studying such lifeforms on UFOs. He speculated that the *falls* of lower lifeforms could have originated with dumps from hydroponic tanks in UFOs such as the fish that Betty witnessed being emptied from a tank on an alien craft.

Charles Fort's documentary efforts (over 40,000 notes) included hundreds of unknown flying object reports and anomalous celestial events. His study of such events caused him to propose explanations that were way ahead of his time. One of his hypotheses draws a striking parallel to the *Message*.

> Unbeknown to us, like a farmer's pigs, geese or cattle [which lack the sophistication to understand they are *owned*] man with his own limited perceptions, does not realize that aliens have long ago quarreled over, and eventually divided up, the cosmos, and that our world is the property of some victorious extraterrestrial civilization, which occasionally checks on us, chasing away all unauthorized intruders.[7]

William R. Corliss is the Charles Fort of today. His *Sourcebook Project* and the efforts of the Fortean Society continue to add anomalous events to the collected works of Fort. Such events are further signs that mankind may really be the *wards* of *The Watchers*!

Other physical evidence that may support alien genetic engineering of earth lifeforms concerns unexplainable *animal mutilations*. A brief overview of this controversial subject is in order.

During the last few months of 1974, the now defunct National Investigations Committee on Aerial Phenomena was suddenly inundated with phone calls and letters. They were in reference to strange mutilations of hogs, sheep, horses, and cattle which seemed to originate and spread out from Meeker County, Minnesota. Since then the mutilations have continued in this country and abroad.

A government report attempted to quell the rising concern of worried ranchers who were losing numbers of cattle to perpetrators that no one could catch. The report, written by a former FBI agent, attempted to explain the mutilations away as being mostly caused by predators.

Investigative reporter and TV show producer Linda M. Howe produced an award-winning documentary entitled *Strange Harvest*. It strongly demonstrated that the mutilations were truly anomalous. In spite of government denials, respected and experienced law enforcement officers and seasoned no-nonsense cattle ranchers have linked over two decades of yearly mutilations with UFO sightings.

Typically, the animals are found with selected parts, such as eyes, tongue, sexual organs, udders, and pieces of skin missing. The cuts are made with surgical precision with an unknown instrument that burns. Sometimes all blood is drained. Predators avoid the carcasses. No tracks of the mutilators are found even when the ground is soft or covered with snow. Some animals are found miles from their pastures, apparently dumped from the air. Some have been found on top of hard-to-access mountainous terrain!

Now that the groundwork has been laid, we can proceed to study the final aspect of the anatomy of the UFO abduction phenomenon. This will involve an analysis of the actual genetic procedures being carried out by aliens during abductions. Please bear in mind that descriptions of several human modern medical techniques were not in existence during the time frame of many early abduction cases. This is highly significant because such techniques roughly parallel those used by the aliens decades ago.

At this juncture, I will be quoting somewhat extensively from the results of a detailed study of abduction reports written by the MUFON consultant for UFO physiological and psychological effects. Richard Neal, Jr., M.D., has been involved with UFOs since the early 1960s. He is co-founder of the Southern California UFO Research and Abductee Support Group. His training and expertise are especially suited to the subject at hand. First, a bit of personal background information from Dr. Neal himself.

> My medical specialty is obstetrics-gynecology, a practice that correlates very well with the wealth of recent information being unearthed by researchers Budd Hopkins and David Jacobs, particularly as it relates to medical injuries affecting female abductees.
>
> What we as researchers are beginning to see is that generations of families are having similar experiences of alien abduction.
>
> It is extremely difficult for me to accept that abductees are fabricating a type of hoax or are psychologically unstable. The areas of evidence or injury that I feel are most compelling, from a physician's point of view, are physiological symptoms manifested by individuals, and more importantly, an overwhelming number of permanent/residual scars on the bodies of these abductees.
>
> My focus and interest in UFO experiences has been centered from the beginning on the physiological/injury evidence from a medical standpoint. I have wanted to find out why and how close exposure to UFOs and their occupants has caused individuals to have such a wide variety of problems and symptoms.
>
> When I started my investigations into the physiological aspects in 1978—not only looking into close encounters, but abduction cases as well—I was initially frustrated. Although I knew there were a good amount of fragmented medical injury reports, none

had been placed into the proper perspective so the experience could be studied closely.

I tried to correspond with investigators during case investigations, but received little or no followup medical injury reports to augment my studies to see if some specific pattern was developing.

When it comes to researching the UFO problem, I am always reminded of the state of Missouri—particularly as a physician examining medical injuries and seeking out evidence to substantiate the validity of known physical evidence/injuries in abduction cases. I make the proverbial Missourian demand, "show me."

For approximately two years, whenever I could take time off from my practice, I travelled to nearly every contactee/abductee conference being given. Eventually, I was able to interview and perform personal physical examinations, related to physiological and personal injuries, on about 75 individuals.[8]

Now that we have established the credentials of Dr. Neal, let us examine his findings based upon his composite study of the overall UFO abduction phenomenon. The first segment of the study concerns the most common areas of examination by aliens.

The nasal cavity, ears, eyes and genitalia appear to be the physical areas of greatest interest to abducting aliens. The umbilical region (navel) is as well, but in females only.

Many abductees have described a thin probe with a tiny ball on its end being inserted into the nostril—usually on the right side. They are able to hear a "crushing" type sound as the bone in this area is apparently being penetrated. Many will have nosebleeds following these examinations.

As a precautionary note, I recommend that known abductees who are parents watch their children for any evidence of recurrent nosebleeds that can't be explained. I recommend immediately taking the child to a pediatrician to discover the nature of the nosebleeds. Many researchers believe that alien technology is being used to insert an implant into this area for future tracking of the individual. It is interesting to note that many of the individuals subjected to nasal probing now have a history of chronic sinusitis.

Documented evidence has also shown that some abductees have been probed in their eyes and ears with a similar instrument. With eyes being involved, abductees may experience temporary blindness, blurred vision, swollen, watery and painful eyes (photophtalmia), acute conjunctivitis (red and irritated, inflamed eyes called "pink eye" in lay terms). There's also some questionable history of these individuals developing cataracts. [9]

Physical examination of abductees by Budd Hopkins and Dr. Neal reveal a consistent pattern relative to *scars* left behind in the wake of alien operations on their bodies. The most common areas of the body where residual scars are found are noted as follows.

Scars have been observed on the calf (including just over tibia or shin bone), thigh, hip, shoulder, knee, spinal column and on the right sides of the back and forehead. [10]

Topographically, the mysterious scars fall into two basic groups.

A. A thin, straight, hairline cut, linear, and about 1–3 inches long, and
B. A circular or scoop-like depression, about ⅛-inch to ¾-inch in diameter and maybe as much as ¼-inch deep. [11]

Other physiological effects on UFO abductees concern rashes, burns, and temporary paralysis. Dr. Neal writes that:

In succeeding generations of family exposure to recurrent abduction, we are observing areas of the human body that are consistently and quite visibly affected. This evidence is related to the skin (dermatology) and muscle (musculo-skeletal system).

During their experiences, many abductees/witnesses will feel a tingling, prickling, or static/electric-shock (paresthesia) sensation over the skin, followed by paralysis (involving the musculo-skeletal system) of the entire body, with the exception of an individual's heart and lungs, where minor or no effects may be found.

The bodily marks may remain permanently or become transitory in nature over a short duration, healing or disappearing altogether. Rashes are seen on the body, most appearing on the upper thorax (chest area) and lower extremities (thighs and legs). Many are geometrical in shape, triangular or circular. Other rashes, similar to chronic inflammations such as localized psoriasis, may be found on other body areas. First and second-degree burns have been sustained in a number of cases, and in some cases questionable tumors (lipomas) have been noticed just beneath the skin.[12]

In a large number of UFO abduction cases, biological specimens and samples are taken from the abductees. Dr. Neal states that:

> Aliens have taken blood, oocytes (ova) from females and sperma-tozoa from males, and tissue scrapings from their subjects' ears, eyes, noses, calfs, thighs and hips. When abductees/witnesses are asleep—or possibly under some form of alien anesthetic—there is also some circumstantial evidence to suggest that specimens might have been taken from saliva, aqueous-vitreous humor (eye fluids), cerebrospinal fluid, urine, stool, hair and nails.[13]

Based upon his detailed study of many abduction cases, Dr. Neal had composed a scenario of *how* a typical abduction is accomplished by the aliens. The scenario is divided up into four segments. First there is the *preparation of abductees prior to physical examination.*

> All abductees are given some type of preparation prior to their examination. Some witnesses have reported receiving *oral liquid* medication, others an application of a liquid solution similar to a pre-operative *prep* over various parts of their bodies; some report a tranquilizing effect *telepathically* transmitted from the acting alien examiner, and/or application of an instrument to the head which renders deep relaxation or unconsciousness.[14]

Dr. Neal calls the next segment of the abduction, the *pre-operative stage* which involves the abductees being subjected to some type of *anesthesia* prior to being operated on by the aliens.

> Abductees are subjected to some type of twilight sleep state, where they're in a definite trance or daze; this could result from the liquid application over the body, specific subconscious sug-gestions by the aliens, aliens using some form of our hormones or enzymes to stimulate a neurochemical response, or some type of unknown technology. One odd note in connection with this stage that begs a lot of questions: why is it that so few abductees remember removing their clothes?[15]

During what Dr. Neal calls the *operative procedures* segment of the abduction experience:

Physical examinations take place: probing, insertion, exploration of the body, taking of biopsies, blood or skin samples. During this phase, the abductee may be semi-conscious as the procedures are carried out. Some actually experience pain. Despite objections, the aliens appear to be indifferent to their victims' pain and suffering; on the other hand, some abductees at this stage are given heavier sedation to quiet their fears and apprehension and do not recall any pain with these procedures.[16]

The last segment of the abduction deals with the *post-operative effects* on the percipients in the wake of their harrowing interface with alien operations.

Afterwards, the abductees/witnesses say their bodies feel sore or exhausted as if having been involved in strenuous activity; some explain that it feels they've been tossed around or hit by a Mack truck. This is similar to the known effects of curare, a drug originating in South America that induces therapeutic muscular paralysis.[17]

Some of the medical techniques employed by the aliens roughly coincide with some of our recent medical developments in the art of artificial insemination. Dr. Neal elaborates on these significant parallels between alien and human technology.

Several documented physical traces of the abductee experience correlate fairly well with some of our recognized medical procedures. Most outstanding is one called *laparoscopy*. A cylindrical, tube-like instrument with special optic attachments is placed through a female's umbilical (navel) region for exploration of female organs. With this particular instrument, a physician is able to observe all female organs to determine if any abnormalities are present, as well as obtain ova—eggs—from the ovaries.[18]

A similar technique was described by Betty Hill who was abducted with her husband Barney during the early morning hours of September 19, 1961. This event took place years before man's use of laparoscopy. Betty Andreasson also described the same technique. It is interesting to compare their experiences as relived under hypnosis. Pertinent excerpts are as follows.

Betty Hill The examiner has a long needle. . . . He said he wants to put it in my navel, it's just a simple test. . . . And I'm telling him, "It's hurting, it's hurting, take it out, take it out." And the leader comes over and he puts his hand, rubs his hand in front of my eyes, and he says it will be all right. I won't feel it. . . . He said it was a *pregnancy* test. I said, "That was no pregnancy test here."[19]

Betty Hill was dead right. The medical technology in 1961 had nothing comparable to this procedure nor did it in 1967 when Betty Andreasson was subjected to the same kind of test by alien *beings*.

> *Betty Andreasson* Oh! And he's going to put that in my navel! Oh-h-h-h! Feels like he's going around my stuff inside—feeling it— with that needle.

Like Betty Hill, Betty Andreasson's pain was relieved by the alien leader laying his hand near and on her head. He also told Betty that the procedure was to measure her for *procreation*!

In addition to the similarity between *laparoscopy* and alien technique, Dr. Neal reveals other correlations.

> Correlating with the laparoscopy procedure is a new treatment for infertility called GIFT (Gamete Intra-Fallopian Transfer), which treats infertility by placing sperm and oocytes directly into the infertile woman's fallopian tubes for *in vivo* fertilization. In contrast with *in vitro* fertilization (IVF), GIFT facilitates natural physiological processes to achieve pregnancy.[20]

Male abductees also have reported alien interest in their genitals. Again, this interest shows up in the earliest documented case of this kind. Barney Hill reported that a circular instrument had been placed over his genitals. This resulted in the appearance of a near-perfect circle of warts around his groin. Although removed by surgery, they psychosomatically reappeared in 1964 after he had relived the experience under hypnosis! Dr. Neal comments on this procedure.

> Male abductees report having a cup-like device attached to the penis, which causes ejaculation for sperm sampling; this is highly uncomfortable to the individual. Most have said they sustain transitory small lesions that disappear shortly afterwards. Others claimed to have experienced direct sexual intercourse with an

alien/hybrid female, ostensibly for the purpose of sperm retrieval as well.[21]

It is very disconcerting to realize that abductions and such operations as have been discussed can be carried out on any person at any time or place at will. Their supernaturallike ability to coexist in more than one plane of existence has camouflaged their operation for centuries. Their ability to snatch humans away either in or out of the body is beyond our ken. The very idea that Man can coexist in different space/time locales raises an impenetrable curtain of mystery around their operations. Betty and others have merely caught a glimpse of imponderables heretofore relegated to religion and mysticism.

Physically, mankind is just barely entering the new science of genetics with all of its implications and ethical considerations. It is now entirely conceivable that much of our technological advances along the way have been telepathically spoon-fed to us by the aliens themselves.

As I bring this chapter to a close, there is yet one aspect of alien methodology that must receive further emphasis. *The Watchers* have not randomly selected individuals for their genetics program. Data strongly suggests that specific *families* have been targeted over many generations. MUFON consultant Dr. Neal has attempted to follow the footprints of their procedural methods through his own studies and his training in obstetrics-gynecology. He writes that:

> In focusing on the gynecological and reproductive procedures that have been performed on abductees, I have come to firmly believe there is some type of ongoing genetic manipulation that is occurring within various *family generations* [italics mine]. For purposes of clarification, it is essential for me to use some medical terminology to explain specific facts.
>
> The key to genetic manipulation lies within the DNA (deoxyribonucleic acid) molecules of the human gene cells. These genes control the reproduction and day-to-day functions of *all cells*. It has been estimated that there are probably 30,000–100,000 essential genes in the human cells, assembled in lengthy linear arrays that together with certain proteins form rod-shaped structures known as *chromosomes*.
>
> Chromosomes from certain individuals, through certain culturing techniques, form a customary arrangement or "standardized format" known as a *karyotype*.[22]

Dr. Neal then goes on to say that he believes that the aliens are analyzing selected human gene sequences in order to identify mutant genes that can be used to alter the genetic pool of future generations through selective breeding. But, *why* are they doing this? He explains that:

> Mutation patterns would allow them to re-arrange the genetic coding on certain *loci* (in genetic terminology, the specific site of a gene in a chromosome).
>
> In this manner, they would be able to experiment with a multitude of loci in the various chromosomes, thus bringing about new genotypic individuals in proceeding generations. Perhaps each succeeding generation of *families* [italics mine] is subjected to a different or comparable type of experimentation by the aliens.[23]

I specifically left this characteristic of alien methodology as the closing item for discussion. It has a direct bearing on the subject matter of the next three chapters. They involve UFO skeletons in my family closet including physical evidence of my own abduction experiences.

Chapter Eleven - Notes

1. MUFON, 103 Oldtowne Road, Seguin, TX 78155.
2. Michael D. Swords, "Ufonauts: Homo sapiens of the Future?" *MUFON UFO Journal*, February 1985, p. 8.
3. *Ibid.*, p. 10.
4. *Ibid.*
5. *Ibid.*
6. Travis Walton, *The Walton Experience* (New York: Berkeley Publishing Corporation, 1978), p. 120.
7. Ronald D. Story, *The Encyclopedia of UFOs*, "Fort, Charles," (New York: Doubleday & Company, Inc., 1980), p. 138.
8. Richard Neal, M.D., "Generations of Abductions—A Medical Casebook," *UFO*, Vol. 3, No. 2, 1988, p. 21. (Credit: *UFO Magazine*, 1800 S. Robertson Blvd., Box 355, L.A., CA 90035)
9. *Ibid.*, p. 22.
10. *Ibid.*

11. *Ibid.*

12. *Ibid.*, pp. 21–2.

13. *Ibid.*, p. 22.

14. *Ibid.*

15. *Ibid.*, p. 23.

16. *Ibid.*

17. *Ibid.*

18. *Ibid.*

19. John G. Fuller, *The Interrupted Journey* (New York: The Dial Press, 1966), pp. 164–65.

20. Neal, *op cit.*, p. 24.

21. *Ibid.*

22. *Ibid.*, p. 24.

23. *Ibid.*, p. 25.

CHAPTER

T w e l v e

Branded

I come to this chapter with mixed emotions. Over the past twenty-five years I have built up a solid reputation as a thorough, objective, and skilled UFO investigator. The high-strangeness and speculative nature of this book and the probing of possible *personal* abduction experiences will undoubtedly affect what some would call a well-earned image. This, however, is a minor concern when compared with the impact this might have on the reputation of my family in their respective communities. I can now truly appreciate the courage of past possible UFO abductees to make the decision to go public with their skeletons in the closet.

From early childhood I have had an almost overwhelming fascination with the stars, planets, and the prospects of space travel. In 1947, when UFOs first became national news, I immediately became thoroughly obsessed with them. After a four-year stint with the Air Force and earning a college degree, I became an avid investigator of this strange phenomenon. Over the years I authored five books on the subject. This is the sixth.

A parallel interest in astronomy became so great that I constructed both a planetarium and observatory on my property in 1970. After early retirement from a managerial position within the defense industry, I began teaching children's and adult courses on both astronomy and UFOs at local community colleges. Why this near fanaticism on my part? My intense activities in these areas have often sparked this question from many others. In the past, I would merely respond that I had always been interested in such things. I did not give this persistent question a second thought. But now I do.

I first became acutely aware of something deeply innate in my life that may have instigated these interests in the spring of 1980. This came in the form of memory flashbacks, which occurred when I listened to Betty relive her childhood UFO experiences under hypnosis.

At this time, vague childhood memories heretofore dismissed as nightmares popped into my conscious mind. It was as if someone had flicked them on with a switch. They involved nighttime visitations of strange entities to my bedroom. At the same time I seriously began to ponder about a number of UFO and possibly related paranormal incidents experienced by myself and other members of my family. I began to wonder if such events were isolated or part of a dimly perceived pattern.

As I worked on the contents of this book, I was continually subjected to such flashbacks and also to a number of fantastic synchronisms. Concurrent in my mind was an overwhelming urge to explore my memories under hypnosis. This compulsion coincided with my listening to a specific statement made to Betty by her captors. They had told her that it was now time to present the rest of their message to mankind. After serious thought, I decided that I would undergo hypnosis.

The Massachusetts chapter of MUFON was currently without the services of a professional hypnotist. I contacted a number of prospects in the local area. Within a few weeks I recruited a certified consultant in hypnosis. His name is Anthony [Tony] Constantino.

Tony has an impressive background with years of valuable experience in his field. He directs a Hypnosis Center in Beverly, Massachusetts. Although he had no experience with the UFO phenomenon, he nonetheless was curious and willing to aid MUFON.

My next step was to contact a trusted associate named David Webb. Dave has served as co-chairman of the MUFON Humanoid Study Group. He is an acknowledged expert on abduction cases and is a solar physicist by profession. His prior involvement as a primary investigator of the Phase One and Two inquiries would make his service invaluable.

Dave heartily agreed to be my confidante and observer at any hypnosis sessions. Our appointment with Tony Constantino was arranged for the evening of July 21, 1988. David asked me to reconstruct from memory a chronological summary of personal UFO and paranormal events for him to study prior to the session. I have included it next for the benefit of the reader as well.

Ray Fowler (1933–   )

Age 5/6

I was in the first grade and living in Danvers, Massachusetts at the end of an unpaved street named Dodge Court. I slept by myself in a bedroom that faced a tiny hall that connected four rooms including the bathroom. My parents put a tiny night-light in the bare socket which hung from the ceiling of the little hall so that people could see to use the bathroom at night. My nightmares would begin with a strange electriclike tingling sensation. I would sit straight up in bed and find myself staring at a dark figure outlined in front of the lighted little hall. I would try to scream to my parents but found that I could not talk or move a muscle. The figure would come closer and closer. I would be frightened beyond measure.

This dream occurred more than once and when I again felt the tingling sensation, I knew I could do nothing. Even as a little child, I just let whatever was going to happen take place.

Age 6, 7, or 8

This incident came back to me while writing this book. Briefly, I was alone and sick in bed. The family was downstairs eating supper. My mother brought me up a bowl of a custardlike pudding called *junket*. I consciously remember a small bright light jump from in front of me into the closet and being frightened. I called my mother who finally came upstairs to see what was wrong. She told me that it was my imagination. At the time, I shared a bedroom with my brother Fred. It faced a hallway which we called the big hall alongside the stairs.

Age 8 or 9

When my brother Johnny left the crib downstairs to make way for the arrival of my brother Richard, he moved upstairs into the room with my brother Fred. I moved out into the big hall to sleep by myself on a couch beside a window and some stairs that led to the attic. It was in this room that I had an extremely vivid dream.

I woke up in the night to see light shining through the window. An entity somehow came into the room *through* the window. I have a vague memory of going to the window and seeing this person approaching it on a beam of light. The beam stretched from the window to a mass of lights over the large open court in front of our house. However, I may have got mixed up with my looking out the window later when *we left together*. [Figure 44]

On the following morning, I woke up every excited with the visitation still fresh in my mind. The ecstatic feeling that I experienced during the visit still lingered. I tried to tell my mother about it but she would not listen until later on in the morning. By that time I had forgotten most of what happened. She told me that it was a dream.

Age 13

My first known UFO sighting took place around July 4 or 5 in 1947. I was working on a local farm in Danvers at the time. The owner did not consider Independence Day an excuse for not working the land. I was weeding or thinning parsnips or carrots. Other workers were way behind me. I looked up at the sky. There, descending with a rocking motion, was a white object clearly outlined against the blue sky. It looked like a parachute canopy but there were no shroud lines or person attached to it. Its apparent size was perhaps one quarter the size of a full moon. I yelled back to the others about the object but they couldn't hear and didn't know what I was talking about. I last saw it disappear behind trees. On Monday, July 7, the Salem evening news headlined a number of sightings in the towns adjoining Danvers and Wrest Farm where I had sighted the strange object. Later on that year, I observed a cloudlike, cigar-shaped object hovering high over my neighborhood for hours.

Age 14 or 15

As a teenager and avid sportsman, I used to spend many hours fishing and hunting after school hours. One of my favorite haunts was the Burley Woods in Danvers. Recently, I had a flashback

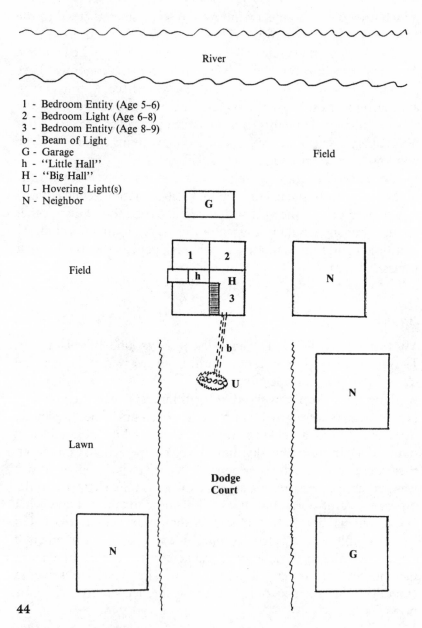

River

1 - Bedroom Entity (Age 5–6)
2 - Bedroom Light (Age 6–8)
3 - Bedroom Entity (Age 8–9)
b - Beam of Light
G - Garage
h - "Little Hall"
H - "Big Hall"
U - Hovering Light(s)
N - Neighbor

Field

G

Field

1 2

h H

3

N

b

U

Lawn

N

Dodge
Court

N

G

44

which, if of a real event, may be significant to this discussion. One afternoon while out in the Burley Woods, I was surprised to find that dusk was setting in. I couldn't figure out how the time had passed so quickly and hurried home to find that my mother was clearing the table from supper. I was scolded for coming home so late. It seemed as if I had started home while it was still light but suddenly it was dusk. This flashback came to me while writing this book and thinking about the typical *missing time* component in so many UFO abduction reports.

Age 32

At this time, I lived in Wenham where I presently reside. On the evening of April 22, 1966, I received a phone call from the Beverly Police about the many reports they had received of a flaming green object streaking across the sky. When I arrived at the area of town where the reports had originated, my car radio announced that a huge meteor had been reported all along the eastern seaboard.

Disgusted, I headed home to work on a huge backlog of UFO reports. As I drove, I noticed an orange light in the sky moving toward me. I kept glancing up, fully expecting to see the conventional running lights of an aircraft. When it drew closer, however, I saw that the whole craft seemed to be glowing. There were no identification lights. It crossed the highway very slowly, and I immediately exited onto a minor road to give chase.

In no time at all, I got ahead of it and parked in a dark field. As it approached, I jumped out of the car and listened intently. A faint purring sound emanated from the glowing thing as it passed almost directly over my head. It continued on into the distance, then swung quickly downward in a graceful arc like half a pendulum swing, and vanished behind distant trees. Unknown to me at the time, my sighting coincided with a spectacular close encounter over the Beverly High School on that same evening sighted by both police and citizens at very close range. Later, the Air Force-sponsored Colorado UFO Project would conclude after their investigation that if the testimony of the witnesses were taken at full face value that what they saw would fit *no other explanation* than that of an *alien vehicle*. Did I see the same object at a distance or one of the similar objects also reported in the area on that night?

Age 35

During a visit to England in July of 1969, I was in a car being driven by my father-in-law. We were on the way to the seacoast and were in the country amidst rolling green fields in all directions. Suddenly, a disk-shaped object descended out of the sky in an arc headed right for the ground. It came down so fast that it seemed impossible for it to stop before crashing. It disappeared behind a distant cluster of trees. No one else in the car saw it. They were busy talking. I can't see how my father-in-law missed seeing it. He was not at all interested in diverting from our route to look for it.

On our trip home, my daughter Sharon and other passengers sighted two silver rectangular UFOs pull up and fly beside the aircraft on their side. Due to the pilot's order to remain seatbelted, I was unable to see them. However, several minutes later, I did see two bright reflections behind us which I photographed. There is no way of knowing whether or not they were the strange objects.

Age 45/46

My fellow investigators will wonder why on earth I did not record the date of this incident. However, as with many of the other experiences, I tended to dismiss them for some reason. Many of them seemingly just could not have happened and I felt embarrassed that they should be happening to me. People would snicker and think that my being so engrossed in the subject had affected my mind! I hope that this is not true! In any event, one afternoon, after backing into my driveway, I went around to the rear of my station wagon to get something that I had placed in the back. I lifted up the rear door, grabbed the item and closed the door. I then turned around to walk away and instinctively ducked as I came face-to-face with a barely visible black cube wobbling like a running-down gyroscope in midair. After ducking under it and quickly stepping to one side, I glanced back to see nothing but open space. I just shook my head and figured that I must have seen some kind of an afterimage or something. I mentioned it to my wife and she agreed, so I just let it go at that. But what if what I had seen was real? It looked real!

Like Betty and others who have witnessed UFOs at close hand, I have experienced a number of paranormal events in my life. Whether or not these are any way related to UFOs is, of course, an open question. But they happened! For the record, I will mention several that perturb me to no end!

Age 16?

One autumn afternoon, probably in 1949, I remember coming home from Danvers Holten High School and going to my bedroom to change out of my school clothes. I kept a magnetic compass on my bureau. When I walked over to the bureau to get something I was shocked to see the needle slowly spinning in complete circles. Almost as soon as I noticed this, it abruptly stopped spinning. It was such a transient thing that I promptly forgot about it until recently while preparing this book.

Age 24?

On a foggy night, probably in 1957, I was driving very slowly through Danvers Port. It was terribly foggy and one could only see clearly directly in front of the car. Suddenly, an old woman glided, not walked, right in front of the car. It happened so fast that I didn't even have time to brake. She appeared to my left, passed within feet of my hood and promptly disappeared to my right into the fog. It did not seem natural to me then or now how an old person could move so fast and in such a strange manner.

Age 46?

In 1980, just after returning from *The Andreasson Affair* publicity tour, I had occasion to enter our cellar from the outside. As I entered the half cellar and glanced to the full cellar ahead, I was taken aback by the presence of a figure. It had dark pants and a white shirt. My vantage point did not allow me to see the head and face. It moved toward me from behind the furnace and turned toward the internal cellar stairs. The figure passed my field of view in plain sight. I entered the full cellar and called upstairs to my wife thinking that it must have been her. She yelled down that she hadn't been down in the cellar. She also was not wearing dark pants and a white shirt! We dubbed this new addition to our family *Maximillian* but Max never appeared again. It was just as well. My wife was not too happy about his appearance!

Age 47?

I have forgotten whether this event took place just before or after the publication of *The Andreasson Affair*. In either case, it was winter and my daughter Sharon was visiting. We thought it would be nice to go skiing up on the golf course at the end of our dead-end street like we used to do when she was a youngster. The weather was clear with excellent visibility. The snow was deep and relatively untouched by others. On the way back home as we moved along a level section of the golf course, we both saw a man standing under a tree ahead of us and to our right. His presence puzzled us for two reasons. He was dressed in a long black overcoat and had on a tall black brimmed hat. He was also standing in deep snow which was very hard to walk on. We headed toward the tree because it was near our normal route home. We glanced up several times and commented about him. But, when we glanced up again, he was nowhere to be seen. This seemed impossible because there was a wide open area all around the tree. No one could have moved that fast. Curious, we skiied over to the tree. There were no footprints where he had stood. The snow lay pristine around the tree except for marks caused by melted snow falling from the tree! Both of us felt very strange about the matter. Personally, I was glad that she had seen him too!

Later on during this same year, which I believe to have been 1981, our family spent two weeks vacationing by Lake Wallace in Canaan, Vermont. One evening, at dusk, my wife and I decided to walk down to the public landing on the lake. Our route took us along a country road that led to a sparsely populated area. On our way back to the cottage, I saw a short stout woman shuffling down our side of the road towards us. A heavy shawl was pulled up around her head like a huge kerchief and she carried a large wicker basket. She approached and passed us within several feet and I wondered where on earth she could be going as it was getting dark. I commented about this to my wife. She gave me a puzzled look and asked, "What lady?" I was shocked that she had not seen her and equally shocked that the old lady was nowhere in sight behind us!

Age 48?

One Sunday morning, in the early 1980s, I attended the North Shore Community Baptist Church at Beverly Farms, Massachusetts. I had another weird experience. On that Sunday, a group of retarded children in Scout uniforms had visited the church. Church members were greeting them in the foyer and trying to make them feel at home with us. I stood watching and one of the little girls came up to me. She looked up, smiled, and puckered her lips making a kissing sound. Obviously, she wanted me to bend over and kiss her. As I stood smiling down at her, wondering if I should, two strong hands grasped each of my shoulders from behind. They applied a firm downward pressure. I thought it was her Scout leader encouraging me to kiss her.

I bent down with the hands still pressing my shoulders and kissed her cheek. When I straightened up and turned to see who had touched me, there was no one there. My back had been about a foot from a wall. No one could have stood behind me!

A number of uncanny synchronistic events occurred to me when I wrote the first two books on *The Andreasson Affair*. It was no different during the preparation of this book. In fact one such unsettling event has provided the basis for the title of this chapter. Renowned psychologist, Dr. Carl G. Jung, defines such happenings as an "acausal meaningful coincidence."[1] In his classic study of the UFO phenomenon, Jung writes that:

> The psychic situation of mankind and the UFO phenomenon . . . seem to coincide in a meaningful manner. . . . Such reflections are not idle speculations; they are forced on us in any serious psychological investigation of the UFO phenomenon.[2]

No one knows for sure what such synchronisms mean or whether they mean anything at all. They may be products of chance. They may hint at a mysterious connection which is part of Man's collective consciousness. I'll mention several prime examples that have occurred over the past several weeks. These happenings fascinate me to the point of almost wondering if something or someone outside of the world of my everyday life is trying to tell me something.

The Oz Factor

When I was working on the chapter entitled *Return from Oz* which, of course, alluded to Dorothy's adventures with little people in a far-away land called Oz, I received a phone call. It was from an abductee whose last name was *Baum*. Frank *Baum* was the author of *The Wizard of Oz*.

A Timely Letter

When I was working on the chapter entitled *UFOs and OBEs* which concerned the paraphysical nature of UFOs, I received a first-time letter from someone in Australia. It was from Riley Crabbe who long ago pioneered the concept of the paraphysical nature of UFOs. In his letter, he encouraged me not to overlook the paraphysical connection!

A Red Letter Day [September 12, 1988]

In the morning, I called my former company to check on a question relating to my retirement insurance. A person who had recently been transferred from another location answered the phone in the personnel office. She was an *abductee* whom I had interviewed years ago!

That afternoon another interesting coincidence took place. I was visited by a person who had lived a mile from me during the mid-1970s. Later, she had been a close associate of Dr. J. Allen Hynek and had been employed by him at the Center for UFO Studies. She had come to confide in me about something that had happened to her in November of 1974. I was shocked to hear her tell me how she was abducted from her automobile while taking a shortcut by fields along a lonely dirt road. The particular road and landing site is five minutes away from my house and is one of our family's favorite spots to walk and ski!

In the evening my wife asked me to take her to see a movie. The movie was playing in the *same* theater that I had imagined being in while under hypnosis! It is called the *Cabot* theater. As she looked up the telephone number to check on the showing time, she came across the name Laurie *Cabot*. Laurie has been proclaimed the official Salem witch by Massachusetts Governor Michael Dukakis and is often a guest on radio and TV shows. When she mentioned Laurie's name, I laughed and said something like: "That's all I need now after what's been going on today—a telephone call from the Salem Witch!" About a half hour later we received a phone call. It was Laurie *Cabot* who had called to tell me about a UFO sighting! I had not talked to Laurie for about a decade.

A Kindred Spirit

On September 18, 1988, while in the midst of typing the description of my childhood encounter with a *being of light* for Chapter 13 of this book, I received an amazing phone call. It was from a school teacher. He was my age and, like me, nurtured an inordinate interest in astronomy from an early age. He had just finished reading *The Andreasson Affair* and felt he must call to tell me about two strange experiences. One involved a UFO sighting in 1964. He had just finished observing with his telescope from the rooftop of his apartment in Boston. Dawn was just breaking when suddenly a huge domed disk-shaped object appeared and hovered momentarily over the nearby John Hancock Insurance building before accelerating away at great speed. A few years later he woke up to see a *beam of light* entering his bedroom. It contained an entity with long blond hair. Like myself, he could not tell whether it was male or female. Like myself, he was filled with an indescribable feeling of love. After he told me his story, I shared *my* experience with him. He felt relieved that someone would listen to him but felt that he did not want to pursue it further. He was curious to remember what else happened but was reluctant to undergo hypnosis. In essence, he felt that he had done his part to just call and tell me about his experience!

The Blond

My mother-in-law and other relatives arrived from England for a three-week visit. This interrupted my work on the book but it was very much on my mind. I was specifically pondering the role of the reported tall blue-eyed beings who have from time to time been seen with the gray dwarflike beings. They seemed to be human beings. In particular, I was interested in the tall man that Travis Walton had encountered during his abduction. Travis had described the humanlike individual as having long blond hair and wearing a transparent helmet. He was dressed in a one-piece jump suit. When Travis attempted to talk with him, he received no response. The tall blond man merely smiled kindly at him in a sort of tolerant manner. For some reason, this scenario stuck in my mind.

On October 2, 1988, while driving my wife and her mother along a country road to church, I may have found out *why* it was on my mind. As I slowed and took a sharp right turn onto a minor road, I gasped in amazement at the personified synchronism that confronted us. An exceptionally tall, very fair-complexioned man stepped out from the side of the road to seemingly thumb for a ride. He had flowing, thick blond hair that extended to just above his shoulders. He was wearing a strange, baggy one-piece jump suit! For a moment, time seemed to stand still as he stared in the window at me with a kind, almost childlike smile. Neither my wife nor her mother had any inkling of what was going on in my mind.

The synchronicity was incredible and I instinctively sped up with the afterimage of that strange smile still imbedded in my mind's eye. I casually remarked to my passengers that the man looked completely out of place in that strange outfit. It reminded me of a NASA flight suit. I am not suggesting that the man was an extraterrestrial but mention the incident as just another of a series of incredible coincidences. The smile still haunts me and I wonder what kind of an outfit he had on. It was too heavy for jogging. Perhaps it was some kind of mechanic's coverall but it was grayish and spotless. I even wondered if someone was playing a practical joke on me.

The surprise encounter reminded me of another incident that occurred when I worked at GTE. Each day I drove the same route to work along a three-lane highway. One morning, as I approached a field on my right, I noticed something silver glittering in the rising sun. To my utter amazement, a man's hand extended from some bushes and released a flat silver balloon in front of my oncoming car. It floated up in front of me and across the highway looking astonishingly like a fat flying disk!

Was this covert release of the balloon in front of *my* car a coincidence? Was it released intentionally for me to misinterpret as a flying disk? Tens of thousands travel this highway to work at numerous defense contractors. If this release were intentional, it had to be someone who knew my schedule and car intimately. If it were not intentional, it was just another one of those thought-provoking *synchronisms* that are part and parcel of my involvement with UFOs.

UFO-related coincidences continued when I brought my visitors up to New Hampshire's White Mountains several days after seeing the blond man. When I purchased a ticket for a ride to the top of Mount Washington, the ticket lady recognized me. She had attended one of my UFO lectures years ago! When we checked into an inn, the innkeeper's son recognized me. He had read *The Andreasson Affair*. Amazingly, he turned out to be my nephew's best friend.

At the inn, my wife and I were escorted upstairs to our room. As I set down our suitcases to open the door, I came face to face with a sign that read *The Blueroom*. I laughed and mused to myself—"When is this going to end?" UFO buffs will recognize that this is the alleged name of the area where UFO artifacts and dead

UFO occupants from UFO crashes are preserved at Wright-Patterson Air Force Base! A classic and well-documented example of a UFO crash in July 1947 can be found in a book entitled *The Roswell Incident.*[3]

Later, while chatting about UFOs to several persons in the inn's lounge, someone inadvertently switched channels on a nearby TV. The program was about some UFO reports originating from Gulfbreeze, Florida.

Upon returning home from vacation, I placed two films with the local Fotomat for processing. When I picked up the developed films later, all the pictures of people, places, and autumn foliage came out beautifully. However, a number of photos that I took of certain physical evidence related to the investigation were completely *blank*. That very same day, Betty phoned to tell me that she had just received back a roll of developed film. All but four photographs on it had come out perfectly. Four exposures taken of a black unmarked helicopter maneuvering near her trailer were blank!

The synchronisms continue. For example, just several minutes after I typed up the sentence describing my trip to Fotomat, my telephone rang. I got up and answered it. It was the local Fotomat calling to inform my wife that her prints were ready!

These anecdotes represent most but certainly not all of the strange coincidences that plagued me while writing *The Watchers*. I have purposely saved the most significant and bizarre synchronism until last. It provided physical evidence of my lifetime association with alien beings. This synchronistic bombshell happened shortly after my first hypnosis session. But first, let us move on to the hypnotic regression session itself.

As I drove to meet with Tony and Dave, it was with mixed emotions. I had left my wife in a turmoil. She did not understand hypnosis. To her it was a form of mind control. To make matters worse, family members convinced her that its use was contrary to our Christian faith. I was unable to convince her otherwise.

On the other hand, my lack of fear and apprehension utterly amazed me. Equally bewildering, in retrospect, is that my compulsion overrode my usual desire to please my wife. For some reason, I really felt that it was the most natural thing to be doing.

In addition, I had a creepy feeling that I was supposed to do it now at this very time. Somehow my usual logical, ultraobjective mind-set had taken a back seat to an overpowering sense of intuition. It was certainly not like me. I wondered silently to myself just what was going on.

I arrived at Tony's home early in order to discuss his new relationship with MUFON. It was a pleasure to know him. His unobtrusive, quiet, and gentle manner put one immediately at ease in his presence. When David arrived, introductions were in order and after a short time of mutual pleasantries, we got down to business.

I briefed Tony on the salient points of my childhood experiences. David, as mentioned, had already been briefed in detail, but Tony needed basic information in order to plan his questions. He wisely suggested that the less he knew about it the better. Leading questions might contaminate information obtained through hypnosis.

A tape recorder was set up and tested for David to operate. Tony gave us both a brief overview about hypnosis and conducted some simple tests to see if I were a good subject. It turned out that I was a good candidate for hypnosis. I still felt no apprehension. It was time to get underway. We had decided to concentrate on the *big hall* incident. I handed Tony written instructions that stated:

1. When regressed to a given event:
   a. Have me describe it from start to stop without any unnecessary interruptions.
   b. No leading questions are to be asked.
2. In some way, demonstrate to David Webb that I am really under what is called hypnosis.

Tony then asked me to sit down in an easy chair in front of him. He turned on some soft music and asked me to place my feet flat on the floor, the palms of my hands on my knees and to close my eyes. I did as he instructed and the process of hypnosis began. Pertinent excerpts are as follows:

Tony You can start out by taking a deep breath which is kind of relaxing. Just hold it a second and let it all out. That's good. And, as you do that, just feel yourself relaxing in the chair. Yeah, that's good. Another deep breath please. Hold it for a second. Let it out. That's good. One more deep breath please. Hold it and let it all out and just really, really sink into that chair and just relax.

As Tony's voice droned softly against the soft music, I could feel my muscles slowly but surely relax. It felt good.

Tony I'm going to ask you, if you can, to visualize the individual colors in their abstract. And I'll mention to you a few objects that will help you to see these colors. For example, I'll start with the color *red* and just feel yourself relaxing. See if you can visualize that color red. Such a vibrant color. Some people find it easy to recall the color of an apple which is red. Some people recall that the divided draperies in this room are red. And sense that peace and relaxation wash over you like a gentle rain and relax.

Tony continued through the colors of the rainbow: *Orange* . . . think of Jack o' lanterns . . . pumpkins . . . squash. . . . *Yellow* . . . canary . . . banana. As I concentrated on each color and visualized each object I felt my hands start to relax and slide along my knees and my body sink deeper and deeper into the chair. My breathing became slow and deliberate just as if I were fast asleep. By the time he reached *Indigo* and *Purple*, I felt my head and body slump into a state of deep relaxation but my mind became sharp and clear. I felt as if there were two mes! One part of me was sleeping in the chair. I could feel it there. But another part of me seemed disassociated from that part of me and yet I was still one person. When I reached this state, Tony again went back through each color and my relaxed body became more relaxed and my subconscious became more disassociated from my body. I could hear and sense everything going on in the room. Street noise from the outside could be heard with perfect clarity and yet my subconscious mind was not distracted. It concentrated on Tony's voice like an auditory homing device. When I had reached this stage, Tony began to question me.

Tony Let's go, let's go back at Dodge Court, Dodge Court, Danvers. The Big Hall . . . the big hall . . . I'd like to take you *before the event* you described. Your grandmother had passed away. Your father came up the stairs. I want you to *begin* at that point. It's okay for you to speak to me.

Tony was referring to another traumatic event that had occurred when I was using the big hall as a bedroom. I had used this event to ascertain *when* I had slept in that part of the house. It must have been in the 1941 to 1942 timeframe.

Ray He came upstairs and yelled to my mother and said, "Henrietta, your mother has passed on. [Family members called my

mother by her middle name instead of Doris.] There was a lot of
excitement. [*pause*] I was told to go to bed. The next morning I
didn't understand what it was all about. My sister Dorothy was really upset with me because I didn't seem to show any remorse and I
didn't really understand what it was all about. She kept saying to
me, "Don't you know what's happening? Do you understand?" I
just, just didn't really want to understand. It was so upsetting to
everyone. I didn't want to be upset.

Then, without warning, Tony homed in on the big hall visitation
incident.

Tony What point was the entity at the window?

Ray [*No answer—I felt myself tense up a bit.*]

Tony That's okay. David's here. I'm here. Go ahead and tell us what
happened. Just relax.

Ray [*slow and deliberately*] I remember—[*pause*]—I think I was only
eight. [*Long pause. A rising feeling of elation—happiness*]

Tony That's all right. You can tell us. David's here. I'm here.

Ray I'm trying to remember. I remember feeling very, very good.

Tony Who was the entity?

Ray I don't know. Years later, I somehow connected the lady with
[*pause*] a lady named Amelia Earhart but that seems ridiculous. I
just have the vaguest remembrance of mentioning that name to my
father after the incident and him saying that she had died. I can't be
sure of that. It's hard to remember. I'm trying my best to remember. I can remember *lights*. I can remember a feeling of [*sudden swell
of emotion causes me to choke up*] *love* and something about maybe
going and sitting down with this person. For some reason or other,
I think of my sister's *Book of Knowledge* that I used to look at an
awful lot. There used to be [*sigh*] a picture of the solar system there
and had an airplane and showed how many days it would take to
get to each planet. It seemed so impossible that we'd ever get to all
the planets.

Tony What did you and the entity talk about?

When Tony asked me this question, the emotions that I had been
restraining suddenly burst upon me. I tried to answer. I couldn't at
first. I began to breathe heavily and then began to sob. This was so

unlike me. I very rarely show my emotions and hadn't cried like this since I was a child.

> *Tony* That's all right, that's all right. We're here.

Finally I was able to answer, but with great difficulty, as the emotions that I was feeling made it almost impossible to talk.

> *Ray* Something *good* is going to happen. [*sobbing*]
>
> *Tony* And did something good happen?
>
> *Ray* It's gonna happen. [*sobbing*]
>
> *Tony* And were you aware when it did happen?
>
> *Ray* It hasn't happened.
>
> *Tony* Will it happen in the foreseeable future?
>
> *Ray* I don't know. It will make me feel very good then. And I'm somehow going to be helping people. [*sobbing and sniffling*]
>
> *Tony* That's okay. We're right here. Everything is going to be all right. Can you sense love from this entity?
>
> *Ray* Wonderful! [*pause*] I could still feel it the next morning and that's why I remembered and told my mother.
>
> *Tony* Let's go back to that night before. Let's see if you can describe the entity, what you felt, what you learned.

I was still trying to control powerful emotions and found it very hard to answer. Also, part of me was already starting to protest that such a thing could really happen to me.

> *Ray* I can't remember what *she* looked like. I can remember—[*pause*]—seemed to be light, just light and *the lights*. I can remember something like a ladder and somehow I remember lights over Dodge Court but I can't be sure what those lights looked like. [*sniff*] I tried—

At this point the tape on my recorder had to be reversed.

> *Tony* Is there anything else you would like to tell us about the entity? Anything else about appearance?
>
> *Ray* Things that I think I've imagined. Things like seeing a black and white picture of *Saturn* and its rings in my book—in my sister's

Book of Knowledge and then seeing, [*sniff*] seeing a modern color photograph and saying, saying, it seems like I've seen that somewhere before and, and also when going back to the *Book of Knowledge* and looking at that planet again and seeing it in black and white—just having the feeling that—[*pause*] "That's all wrong!"

At this time, my mind was rebelling at what I was thinking. In retrospect it seems as if my conscious and subconscious were at odds with each other.

Ray It doesn't really look like that but the—I [*sniff*] think to myself, I must be, I must be imagining these things and building on [*sniff*] a dream or something. I try to remember—so many years—that, I imagine these things and that they—[*sniff*] I just really don't really know if they happened or not.

Before proceeding, a bit of explaining is in order. Briefly, sometime shortly after this childhood experience, I opened my sister's book and saw a black and white drawing of Saturn and had the innate feeling that it really did not look like that. Years later, in 1979, when I saw the first colored photos of Saturn taken by Pioneer 11, I vaguely remember a memory flashback to looking at that black and white sketch. Even under hypnosis, the implication that seemed to be unfolding seemed too ridiculous to believe.

Tony Would you like me to give you a way to discover whether they happened or not?

Ray Yes.

Tony Okay . . . If you want these insights, they will come to you. It's like a name on the tip of your tongue. Sometimes the harder we try to remember the name, the more difficulty we have. Sometime what we must do is just relax. We have to let go and go with the flow and then things are made clear to us. How did the entity enter the room, for example?

By this time, I had stopped crying. The double-edged mental struggle had replaced the strong emotions that I had experienced. I began to talk in a matter-of-fact way.

Ray There's no way *she* could have entered the room except through the—[*pause*] I think *through* the window!

Tony And the window was closed?

Ray The window was closed. It may have been the *screen*—I don't think the window was open. I think the window was closed.

Tony And left the same way?

At this point I began feeling strange emotions beginning to stir within me again.

Ray I think so, I, I just have this feeling that *I went with her.*

Tony You have this feeling? You?

Ray Feeling that I went with her. I have, [*sniff*] I again have these vague remembrances of some kind of *beam of light* between— [*beginning to choke up again*] the window [*sniff*] and the *lights*—and like a *ladder.*

For some reason, I pushed my mind away from this segment of the experience and switched my thoughts to the next day.

Ray And then, the next day, thinking I could find the person by just [*sniff*] climbing the attic stairs, she'd be there. Again, I think I may be imagining these things.

The mental struggle between conscious and subconscious had started once again. My conscious did not want to accept what my subconscious was remembering!

Tony Any idea where the ladder took you? Where this *lady* took you?

Again, the same strange emotions started stirring deep within and I found it difficult to answer Tony.

Ray [*Did not answer. Begins sniffling and crying.*]

Tony The slightest hint?

Ray Just—for some reason—the planet *Saturn*—Just seeing it *as it was.* [*sniff*]

Tony In color?

Ray Um.

Tony But you'd never seen it in color before?

Again the emotions within me became overwhelming. I became very agitated. In parallel with the emotions, the struggle within my mind began once again.

> *Ray* No. [*very agitated*] I can't say that! I can't be sure that that really happened!
>
> *Tony* I understand.
>
> *Ray* [*crying hard*] It could be something that I could just be thinking of and—[*Crying. Could not continue.*]

Tony let me cry for a while and then continued his questioning.

> *Tony* Would you like to relax a little bit now from the questions?
>
> *Ray* [*calming down*] I want to know more if I can. I want to be *sure* that what I remember is *not imaginary*, not a *dream* but if it's *real*!
>
> *Tony* Do you see a beam of light?
>
> *Ray* Vaguely.
>
> *Tony* Is the entity with you?
>
> *Ray* It's more of a feeling than seeing. [*sniff*] I try to see and I can't. I, I just imagine what it might have looked like and I'm not sure that that's the way it really looked like. [*sniff*] It might be a dream. It might be just things I'm imagining and I don't want to *imagine* things! I want to really *know* what happened.
>
> *Tony* I understand, I understand. . . . Would you like me to ask you a few more questions?
>
> *Ray* If it will help me to remember, yes. [*sniff*]
>
> *Tony* Okay, between the time you ascended the light, the beam, the ladder—The time you woke up the next morning—Tell me again what you think you dreamed of.
>
> *Ray* Just *light* [*sniff*] Like a *lady* of light, maybe. [*sniff*] I think it was a lady. Very kind. Very loving. [*sniff*] She was telling me—[*pause*]

Again strong emotions overwhelmed me. It was like something tried to block my answer. I had to struggle mentally to say anything.

> *Ray* I can't be sure of that!
>
> *Tony* That's all right. Say it!

Ray [*struggling to get words out*] That way in time [*sniff*] somehow [*burst out crying*] will help people. [*sniff*]

Tony She would help people?

Ray I will! [*crying uncontrollably*]

Tony That's all right. Take your time. Who will help people?

Again, the mental struggle began. Part of me did not want to accept what the other part of me was saying.

Ray I would. But [*pause*] I've heard this before. [*sniff*] And, I'm wondering if I just be [*sniff*] superimposing what I've heard before on myself. [*sniff*] And, just imagining these things.

Tony And where have you heard it before? And where would you be superimposing it?

Ray [*sniff*] I've heard other people under hypnosis who—[*pause*] feel they've been contacted by aliens who told them that [*pause*] somehow that they were going to be able to help people that— [*pause*] understand what was going to be coming here. And it could be that I'm just [*pause*] taking what these people have heard and then just superimposing it on my own, although I have this *feeling* [*sniff*] that I can't grasp, that something like that *did happen* but I can't remember exactly what it was. It just made me feel very, very good and [*sigh*] for several days after, I wondered *when* this was going to happen. How it was this was going to happen [*sniff*] and [*sniff*] then just forgot about it until recently. [*long pause*]

Tony Just relax.

Ray When I [*pause*] was writing the book, *The Andreasson Affair* [*sniff*] and listening to Betty Andreasson and Bob Luca under hypnosis—listening to their childhood experiences—All of a sudden pops up this dream that I had so many years ago when I had just about completely forgotten about it. Once and awhile I may have remembered it, but didn't—I think that I maybe remembered it when I saw the [*pause*] *Wizard of Oz*. The lady—

Again, for some reason, I began to cry. I could not control myself and could barely make myself talk.

Ray [*gasps*] That wasn't real! Just reminded me of it.

Then I found part of me presenting a very illogical explanation for my experience. For some reason, part of me was desperate to explain it away. In the past, I reasoned that it was a dream triggered by my seeing *The Wizard of Oz*.

Ray Could be that—[*sniff*] It could be that I saw, that I saw that picture of *The Wizard of Oz* and *lady of light*. There was a program on about a lady too that—A radio program that I used to listen to about the *Singing Lady* [*sniff*]. Maybe, maybe because I listened to the program, the *Singing Lady*, this lady with a beautiful voice, who also, I think, was the same lady who played the part, or sang the part—played the part *and* sang the part in *The Wizard of Oz* and listened to the *Singing Lady*—Maybe that caused this dream. Maybe it's just a dream. I think, I think, I think I even thought that at one time after I—even as a little child—I think I thought that when I saw *The Wizard of Oz*.

The problem with my logic was that seeing the movie for the *first* time reminded me of the incident. I was putting the proverbial cart before the horse. *The Wizard of Oz* was released by Metro-Goldwyn-Mayer in 1939. In actuality, I *did not see* it *before* the experience. My first movie was *Snow White*. I saw this with my mother when I was in the first grade. Seeing the wicked witch scared me so much that my mother had to take me out of the theater. My next movie, as best I can remember, was *Bambi*. I fared better at that one. I didn't see *The Wizard of Oz* until much later and it was at that time it *reminded* me of the *lady* who visited me.

Tony When you think of the lady, the entity—Was she human? Was she strange? Was she different in any way?

Ray She was more—[*pause*] You know, I'm not even sure that it was a lady. It was very gentle, so gentle, an ah, just leaving me with this wonderful feeling of love, that I've—I think I've only experienced only several other times in my life. One of which I can't even tell about. But it's just a wonderful feeling that lasted for several days. I think, I guess it was a dream. My mother told me, and then I forgot until recently—Until writing *The Andreasson Affair*. It all came back again. [*becoming emotionally agitated again*] I said, well, it's possible that maybe—[*pause*] I had *other things happen* in my childhood. Maybe, just maybe some of those things happened to me too, but [*sigh*] when I talked to my wife about them—[*pause*] she gets very upset. She didn't want me to be here tonight. She was very upset. And over the years, I have—[*pause*] I said, well, most likely they were just dreams anyhow and I've been involved in this subject for so long that—[*pause*] So many things I've been doing. It's silly. I—Even if something came out under hypnosis, if I go under hypnosis, how could you ever *prove* it was *real*. Maybe I don't even *want* to know! Suppose something did come out and then, ha, you never could prove it. It would be on my mind all the time. And, if you told people about it, they would say: "Ha, ha you've been in this subject for such a long time, it's really finally got to ya!" And I just thought I'd just put this off. But, recently, I was doing *The Andreasson Affair—Phase Three* and the entities told Betty—[*long pause*]

Instantly, deep emotions flared up from within the recesses of my innermost being. I choked up and coughed each time I tried to continue, I literally had to force the next several words out of my mouth.

Ray [*cough*] Now [*cough*] *Now is the time* this is coming together. It's [*now sobbing*] going to—be—revealed! I felt that if things happened in my life, that *now is the time I should look into it*! And I didn't even tell my wife about this until recently. And I felt as I was coming here tonight—"Why am I not nervous?" I was nervous about hypnosis before. I didn't want to be hypnotized. . . . I didn't want to get [*sniff*] involved. And all of a sudden [*sniff*] I felt that *now is the time* and I felt that coming here was the most natural thing in the world to do!

Tony Let me ask you a question. You don't have to answer it out loud if you don't want to. Given the intensity of the emotions that you felt for this entity—is it possible to have the intensity of these emotions with a dream?

Ray I've had dreams before.

Tony Did you have that intensity that has lasted in excess of forty years?

Ray No. Maybe the next day I would feel good about a dream and—[*pause*] I dream about seeing someone who died and alive again and it was a nice feeling to see that person was alive again or something like that. Sometimes you have a dream and you wake up and the dream is so good that you want to go back and you want to continue the dream. Sometimes the dreams are very, very bad and you don't want to—You don't want to go back and dream them.

Tony I'm going to ask you to just relax. I'm going to count from 20 to 1. Just relax, just relax.

Tony began to bring me out of the hypnotic state bit by bit. During the countdown, I felt my two selves slowly moving toward each other, notch by notch as Tony counted. I felt my body slowly but surely straighten up out of the slumped position that it had assumed. I was still under hypnosis when Tony reached the number 1. He kept me slightly under for a purpose unknown to me. Suddenly, he told me that he was going to count to 10 and that when he reached the number 10, I would not remember his name. For some reason, my conscious mind took this as a challenge. As he counted to 10 very slowly, I started to audibly repeat his name. I started as a whisper and increased the loudness of my voice at each count. By the number 8, I was practically shouting *Tony Constantio!* But then it happened.

Tony Nine!

Ray Tony Constanzio!

Tony Ten!

Ray Tony Constanino! Constantio? Tony Constantio?

Tony When I count to three, you'll say it right. One, two, three! Say it!

Ray Tony Constantino!

Tony That's it! Exactly.

I sat quietly in the hypnotist's chair running over in my mind what had happened during this first session. The tape recorder was still running and recording—so were the tears still on my face. Tony had aptly demonstrated that I was under hypnosis!

Dave Here, want a Kleenex?

Tony I, I didn't dare leave and get Kleenex. I'm sorry.

Ray That's all right, that's all right. I didn't expect to be crying tonight. I haven't cried for I don't know how long. I'm not the type of person who cries. I—I'm known as *Spock*—No emotions.

Dave That's right. Well, that proves we were getting somewhere.

Perhaps we were. Deep within I felt as if I had just begun to rouse a sleeping giant. Part of me cautioned that it might be best to let him sleep. Another part of me burned with curiosity and urged me to continue to rattle his cage!

My wife was still upset when I returned home. She did not want to know what had happened and hoped that I would not continue the sessions. I told her that I would think about it during our upcoming vacation but that what was happening was very important to me.

Both of us tried to put our disagreement behind us as we enjoyed the distractions of our vacation during the first few weeks of August. However, this temporary break from the implications posed by the hypnosis session was the proverbial calm before the storm. What was going to happen next would shake off any lingering doubts that I had about the reality of the UFO abduction phenomenon.

It occurred shortly after we had returned from our vacation on Sunday, August 14, 1988. On Monday, the following day, I received a phone call from Betty. She sounded nervous. Some mysterious scars had appeared on her arms. I asked her what they looked like. She described three marks in a triangular pattern and said they were just like the one on her leg.

I had completely forgotten her ever mentioning a scar on the leg. Later, I found a letter from her dated June 1, 1987. She had written that she had found: "And old half-inch scar" on the calf of her left leg like one pictured in Budd Hopkins's book.

At that time, I'm afraid that I took her letter with a grain of salt. Betty and Bob had so many strange experiences that it boggled my mind. I put her latest call in the same category. I felt that the scars probably had a natural explanation and that she was letting imagination get the best of her. But, I told her to photograph both the old and new scars. I instructed her to send copies of the photos to both myself and Dr. Richard Neal for our evaluation and continued working on the book.

The rest of Monday and Tuesday passed without incident. Most of the daytime was spent weeding and harvesting my huge vegetable garden, neglected for the previous two weeks. Even so, the results of the hypnosis session weighed heavily on my mind. Was I really visited by a strange entity as a child? Did I walk through my bedroom window out onto a solid beam of light? Was that cluster of lights hovering over Dodge Court a UFO?

I also wondered what might be revealed if I continued the hypnosis sessions. Suppose I relived an abduction. How could I ever really know that it wasn't a byproduct of my UFO-cluttered mind? Nonetheless, I wanted desperately to know the truth. How could I ever know for sure?

On Wednesday morning, August 17, I received an incredible answer to my questions. It was totally unexpected. It was difficult to accept. But, there it was. I could see it. I could touch it. It was *real*.

I had spent most of that morning typing up pages of this book. Shortly before eleven o'clock, I reluctantly shut off the typewriter. It was time to get ready to go out to lunch with my wife and father. I quickly shaved and hopped into the shower. I followed my usual step-by-step methodical cleansing of the body. As I leaned over to wash my right foot, my soap-filled hand froze in its tracks!

I stared at the side of my lower leg in astonishment. A disquieting aura of disbelief and denial crept over my transfixed wet body. There, just as plain as could be, was a freshly cut scoop mark. I shut off the shower and felt the perfectly round indentation. There was no pain and no signs of bleeding. It looked like a miniature cookie cutter had removed a perfectly round piece of flesh.

For some reason, I laughed incredulously. This whole UFO subject was insane. How did that get there? I knew that I had seen such marks before. Both Dr. Neal's papers and Budd Hopkins's latest book *Intruders* contained photographs of such scoops. I got out of the shower and took Hopkins's book from my library and compared its photograph with the scar on my leg. They were the same.

My mind was on the scar throughout the day. I tried to retain my composure during lunch. Upon returning home I again read Dr. Neal's paper concerning physiological effects on UFO abductees. One of the typical effects was a circular scooplike depression about one-eighth inch to three-fourth inch in diameter and up to one-fourth inch deep. One of the typical locations of such scars was in the area of the *tibia* between the knee and ankle. My scar matched this description perfectly. Not only that, it was so fresh, too prominent not to have been noticed when I had showered the previous day.

Dr. Neal also described a second typical scar left on abductees as a thin, straight hairline cut. My mind then flashed back to several times when I had woken up with a strange hairline cut on the back of my neck. In those days, I did not have the benefit of knowing the results of researchers like Neal and Hopkins. I had dismissed them as self-inflicted scratches made during the night. Now, looking back, I realize that it would have been very difficult to have made such marks with my fingernails. Again I lifted up my pant leg and stared. It was there. It was *real*, whatever it was!

In the evening I set up my camera stand and took a photograph on the last remaining exposure on the slide film in my Canon A-1 35mm camera. While getting ready for bed, I casually asked my wife, who was on the other side of the bed, "What do you think could have caused this?" She glanced over briefly with little interest and simply answered, "I don't know."

I sighed with relief. I felt that I should show it to her but did not want to discuss its possible connection with the UFO abduction phenomenon. She was already very upset and I did not want to further aggravate her condition.

On the following day, I bought some ASA 400 color print film and took a series of photographs of the scar at various angles and with different lenses. I put them in for processing and sent copies to Dr. Neal. Several days later, I received a thick envelope from Betty and Bob. I ripped it open and found a set of photographs. Again, an unsettling chill trickled through my body as I saw the same unmistakable scoop marks on Betty's arm and leg!

The older one that I had foolishly not inquired further about back in 1987, was cut from the back of the calf on her left leg. The three scoop marks on her right arm formed a triangle. The synchronicity of the joint appearance of our scars within the same general timeframe was almost as incredible as the scars themselves. In addition, they appeared when I was strongly desiring some kind of physical proof of our relived experiences. This all reminded me of a not-so-funny incident now, although I had laughed it off then. It had occurred late at night while I was making the long trip home from one of the Phase Two hypnosis sessions in Connecticut. At that time, it was difficult to believe what was coming out of the sessions. At one point along some road that looked across a wide expanse I jokingly said out loud something like, "If you're really doing these things, give me a *sign!*" Instantly, the whole horizon and the sky all around me lit up for a brief microsecond and dissipated. I laughed to myself nervously and half-kiddingly shouted, "Do that again!" Nothing happened and I just laughed this coincidence off. Now, I wonder if it was more than coincidence. I never could explain what caused the bright flash of light.

The next obvious question, of course, was *how* and *when* our scoop marks were made. I had no previous mark, sore, or cut on my skin. I did not inflict the weird depression and I feel certain that Betty didn't either. It seemed to have been done with precision without cutting deep enough to bleed but still cut below the hair line on my leg. Dr. Neal's response to my letter and photographs raised this same question.

August 29, 1988

Ray Fowler
13 Friend Court,
Wenham, Mass. 01984

Dear Ray:

Thank you very much for the photographs. They are indeed among some of the better photographs of scooped out scars I have ever seen. However, what is surprising to me is that you had just noticed this scar—It is quite prominent.

I would like to ask you a few questions:
1) Do you recall anything unusual happening to you on your vacation?
2) Had you noticed any discoloration in the area in the past?
3) Does this area cause you any discomfort, tenderness, tingling, itching sensation?

Dr. Neal then suggested several other things for me to do that I was to keep confidential. However, in answer to his questions, I had to reply *no* to each of them. I did do several things that were outside my normal living pattern. I found it easier to sleep by myself out on a screened porch while on vacation. I also was up in the early morning hours by myself looking at celestial objects with a telescope. However, I cannot remember anything out of the ordinary happening. Since I only first noticed the scar on Wednesday, August 17, I thought immediately of what I had done on the prior evening. Again, there was nothing unusual. I had given an astronomy lecture at the Manchester Beach and Tennis Club. I returned home without mishap or missing time, had some hot chocolate with my wife, and retired to bed.

Betty could not remember anything unusual happening that could account for her older or more recent scars. However, it is most interesting to note that the older scar appeared just before she started having memory flashbacks of *the woman*.

Dr. Neal suggested that we could go to a dermatologist but doubted whether such a specialist would be able to explain these marks. Neither Betty nor I felt comfortable with his suggestion. We felt that it might invite ridicule. I did not want to upset my wife further by placing any more emphasis on the unexplained mark. I would feel obligated to tell her about such a proposed examination. The very idea of aliens touching me either in the past or in the present caused near hysteria on her part. However, I did take my two sons, two of my brothers, and Dave Webb into my confidence. I felt it important to have others see the unexplained mark while it was still fresh. Tony Constantino would also be privy to it for I knew now that I had to attend another hypnosis session. I also decided to ask my personal physician what he thought it might be if the mark was still visible during my next physical examination.

On March 10, 1989, I wended my way to the Beverly Hospital grounds where my personal physician, Philip D. Herrick, M.D. had his practice at the Medical Center. I brought along several photos of the *scar* which I had taken every few months for comparison. During my exam, I showed him both the still-visible scar and the photos and told him that it had suddenly appeared overnight. He looked very puzzled and said that it was *weird* and that I ought to have a dermatologist look at it. Later, when I had dressed and met with him in his office to receive the results of the exam, he again reiterated how strange the scar was. He then wrote out the names of several dermatologists on a slip of paper and suggested that I see one of them.

I was pleasantly surprised that my wife's reaction to Dr. Herrick's suggestion was positive. She urged me to go and find out what it was. She also said that she wanted to know exactly what the dermatologist said no matter what it was. I agreed and immediately made an appointment with W.A. Flanagan, M.D., a dermatologist who had his office in Danvers.

I must admit that I had been nervous and hesitant to bring the *scar* to Dr. Herrick's attention. But I was literally sweating from nervousness when I walked into Dr. Flanagan's office on March 21, 1989. I hoped with all my might that he would not ask any questions about it that would put me on the spot. I do not lie and did not know how I would answer him if he interrogated me too deeply about it. I did not want him to know of my suspicions regarding its UFO-related origin. It would have been terribly embarrassing. I'm sure that either he or Dr. Herrick would have considered such an idea as ludicrous.

In any event, after a long wait I was ushered into an examination room and was examined by Dr. Flanagan. He looked at the photos and peered at the scar under magnification. He pushed around it and asked if there was any tenderness or pain. He looked surprised when I told him that it had suddenly appeared overnight and that I never felt any tenderness or pain. He then asked if I were in good health. I told him that I had just been pronounced perfectly healthy by my physician. He explained to me that some diseases such as diabetes can cause deterioration of tissue causing various sizes of cavities on the body. He said that sometimes there is no apparent explanation for such marks which were labeled with the general term *atrophoderma*.

I pushed my pant leg down and took the photos from Dr. Flanagan who assured me that the mark was nothing to worry about. He did express some surprise that it was healing. I assumed that this was not characteristic of *atrophoderma*. As he started to leave he turned around and said something that sent shivers up and down my spine. It was something like this: "You know, if you had told me that you had been to a Dr. so-and-so for a biopsy, I would have told you that what you have there is a *punch biopsy*. It looks just like one." I was taken aback and blurted out—"But how could it have been done without leaving blood behind!" He looked at me quizzically and said, "I didn't say it *was* a *punch biopsy*, I said it *looked like* a *punch biopsy*." Obviously, if I hadn't had such an operation by a doctor, it could not be what it looked like. I immediately backed off and asked him if such a biopsy would be painful. He said that it would be very painful and that it actually would entail having the wound wrapped in an icepack and bandages.

Dr. Flanagan excused himself and I walked out of the building in such a daze that I forgot to do planned shopping on the way home. His words—"It looks just like a *punch biopsy*" kept going through my mind. Why this was exactly what Dr. Neal thought such marks represented. Not only that, but it was located in what he felt was an optimum place for alien experimentation. I thought back over what he had postulated as I drove home.

> A circular or scoop-like depression, about one-eighth inch to three-fourths inch in diameter, and maybe as much as one-fourth inch deep. . . . Many scars are found over the shin bone. . . . (A) common area for obtaining bone marrow samples /aspirations.[4]

My *scar* was located "over the shin bone." It was a "circular or scooplike depression." It measured about one-fourth inch in diameter and originally was almost one-fourth inch deep. And now a professional dermatologist had just told me that it looked exactly like a *punch biopsy*. It was no wonder that my wife expected the worst when she saw the concerned look on my face as I walked in the door. Needless to say she was very upset about the implications of all this.

I sat down and re-read portions of Dr. Neal's paper about such scars. He pointed out that bone marrow produces the red blood in our bodies and further stated that:

> It is significant, in my opinion, that it is through a human's bone marrow and blood that it is possible to study their chromosomal patterns.[5]

Bizarre as it would seem, both Betty and I had been nearly simultaneously *branded* by unique scars that have been attributed to an alien genetics engineering program. Betty, thus far, chose not to explore their origin under hypnosis. But I wanted desperately to know when and how that circular chunk of flesh was removed from my body no matter what the consequences.

Chapter Twelve—Notes

1. Carl G. Jung, *Flying Saucers* (New York: The New American Library, 1959), p. 17.
2. *Ibid.*, pp. 112, 118.
3. Charles Berlitz and William L. Moore, *The Roswell Incident* (New York: Grosset and Dunlap, 1980).
4. Richard Neal, M.D., "Generations of Abductions—A Medical Casebook," *UFO*, Vol. 3, No. 2, 1988, pp. 21, 25 (Credit: *UFO Magazine*, 1800 S. Robertson Blvd., Box 355, L.A., CA 90035)
5. *Ibid.*, p. 25.

CHAPTER

Thirteen

The Family Closet

It would be almost two months before I could get together for another hypnosis session with Tony and Dave. During this time I continued to work on the book. I decided that it was time to seriously consider the inordinate number of UFO-related events that were hidden in my family closet. Up until now I had chosen to ignore them. But now, in light of the mysterious appearance of my scar and the implications of my recall under hypnosis, I decided to open the closet door.

In retrospect, I felt embarrassed about my family's experiences. I feared that their public disclosure would tarnish my reputation as an objective UFO researcher. In the early days of ufology people who had repeated sightings were always suspect. The repetitive nature of the abduction phenomenon has proven this notion wrong. The aliens' ongoing interest in specific individuals and families of individuals appears to be the norm and not the exception.

It is hard to believe that I could have been so proud and blind to what, on statistical grounds alone, was extraordinary. There was an unmistakable pattern of UFO and anomalous events stretching back to at least three generations in my family. They may be just the tip of the iceberg.

It was time to construct a chronology of family events. Perhaps in doing so, further clues might be discovered that would throw some light on my own experiences including the origin of the scar. I will start the chronology with my mother's family.

Doris H. Fowler/Mother (1904–1987)

Age 12–13

My mother's first UFO experience was so traumatic that she could still visualize the event clearly in her mind's eye. It took place in 1916 or 1917. At that time, her hometown of Bar Harbor, Maine was a summer resort for some of the wealthiest people in the United States. Ornate mansions, huge yachts, and horse-drawn carriages reflected the lifestyles of the Rockefellers, Pulitzers, Astors, Morgans, and McCleans. Automobiles were few and the sighting of an airplane was a rare event.

Mom lived on the other side of the tracks from the rich. My grandparents and their neighbors resided in simple woodframe houses that formed the tiny year-round population of the island. It was a cool, clear autumn evening. Most of the summer folk had returned home. The island had returned to normal and its people braced themselves for a lonely winter. My mother and her friends bounded out of the Episcopal Church into the cool night air. Their club meeting had ended late so they decided to take a short cut home across some fields. Mom said that they had just entered a large field when suddenly bright-colored flashing lights erupted from the sky above them. Brilliant hues of reds, blues, greens, and yellows reflected off the frightened faces of her friends as they froze in their tracks momentarily and looked up. There, directly above them, was a huge dark object encircled with bright flashing colored light. Mom said that one girl began crying hysterically and they all ran home as fast as they could. She said that their parents made light of the incident but discouraged them from talking about it to anyone.

Age 26

Two years before I was born, my parents were renting a bungalow in Beverly, Massachusetts that nestled up against cow pastures which stretched upward to the top of what is called Folly Hill. Mom was not well. It was June 18, 1931. She had just miscarried a premature baby girl on June 14 and was recuperating. During the late hours of the night, the lonely, silent house suddenly became filled with a loud, vibrating, humming sound.

My mother was frightened and the vibrations caused her physical discomfort. Dad got out of bed, put on his slippers and bathrobe and went outside. The weird throbbing noise seemed to come from all directions but he could not see its source. Then, while he gazed upward and around, the noise ceased just as abruptly as it had begun.

I mention this incident for two reasons. First, it coincided within days of the premature birth and secondly, the description of the sound was identical to the sound described by witnesses to some of the UFO sightings that I have investigated. There may be no connection with either of these things but I felt that the event was worthy of mention.

Age 40–41

In the summer of 1945–46, my parents lived in their home in Danvers, Massachusetts. They had bought the house in 1932 using the proceeds from a winning sweepstakes ticket. Mom said that she was out riding alone on her bicycle when an oval, gray object descended out of a cloud, stopped, and then backed up into the cloud. She felt that it was not an illusion. Other than fair weather clouds, the sky was relatively clear.

Age 61

My parents now had retired to Surrey, Maine near my mother's birthplace at Bar Harbor. On the night of March 23, 1966, she was being driven home by a neighbor from Ellsworth. The route to Surrey passed by a peninsula called Newbury Neck which jutted out into a large bay. As they were looking out over the neck they were startled to see a big, round, glowing orange object hovering low over it. They stopped to look. Its apparent size was as large as a full moon. As they watched, an identical orange globe sailed silently out of the northeast and abruptly pulled up and stopped beside the hovering object. Mom wanted to stay to see what happened next but her friend became agitated and drove off for home. She was so frightened that she would not leave my mother's house until she saw her husband come home.

Age 72

Hard winters and advancing age forced my parents to leave Surrey and move southward to South Berwick, Maine, where they could be closer to other members of the family.

This event took place sometime in 1976. In the middle of the night, my mother was attracted by a light shining through the window. Going to the window, she saw a round globe of light the size of the full moon slowly floating above a railroad bed in the field behind the house. As it approached a nearby highway it just blinked out like someone turning off a light bulb.

Age 70s

Sometime in the late 1970s, my mother was in a car driving by Pease Air Force Base. Directly above the base, she sighted a disk-shaped object descend from and re-enter a cloud. It was similar to what she had witnessed so long ago in Danvers.

Margaret/Aunt (1897–1942)

"They took my baby! They took my baby!" These words from an abductee recorded in Budd Hopkins's book, *Intruders,* snapped into my mind as I sat listening to my father reminisce about his courting days with Mom. Budd, an expert in UFO abduction research, was reporting on some rather bizarre findings. Several abductees had mysteriously become pregnant without sexual intercourse. Later, further tests revealed that they were no longer pregnant! Under hypnosis, they relived an experience that mirrored what Betty had witnessed in person. Aliens had abducted and removed the fetus that they were carrying!

Dad rambled on about how he met my mother and then stopped and turned to me and said, "You know? I might have had second thoughts about marrying your mother if I had known about her sister Margaret." I asked what he meant by this. He told me that Margaret had some kind of mental problem which had to be treated by the Mental Institute at Bangor, Maine. He thought it might have been related to an obsession about a baby being stolen from her. [My check with medical records indicates that she was admitted because of a fear of being left alone when her husband went to work. Both may be UFO-related phobias.] He went on and said that if he had known this, he might not have married Mom because Margaret's illness might have been hereditary. One time she actually grabbed a baby from a mother's baby carriage and made off with it. I was suddenly reminded of what a woman named Kathie had related to Budd Hopkins. Her pregnancy had been confirmed by both urinalysis and a blood test. Several months later she had a completely normal menstrual period. Worried, she immediately went to a doctor.

> I had a normal period, not even as heavy as I sometimes have. I *knew* I'd lost the baby. My mom said that sometimes you do have a light period or spotting or whatever and can still be pregnant, but I *knew* I wasn't. . . . I went in to have the test but knew what it would show. [showed negative] I couldn't stop crying. I kept saying, "They took my baby. They took my baby," and I cried so hard they didn't know what to do with me. But I *knew* somebody took my baby.[1]

Under hypnosis, Kathie relived a traumatic UFO abduction experience during which alien entities removed the fetus from her body.

My aunt Margaret [mother's sister] never did have any children. Dad did not know if she had experienced any miscarriages. She died of a heart attack in her mid-forties. Was her obsession instigated by her childless marriage? I don't know, but again I felt strongly that her story should be one of the many skeletons in my closet.

Priscilla/Aunt (1906–1978)

Age 70

In April of 1966, my mother's sisters, Priscilla and Lois, along with my great-aunt Emma, lived in the city of Cambridge, Massachusetts. A large window faced a busy street called Broadway. Emma was watching television and her attention was suddenly attracted by bright lights from outside. She glanced out and remarked to my aunts that—"There's one of those flying things that they talk about!" Priscilla told me that they all went to the window and saw an oval object with flashing colored lights hovering near the top of an adjoining building. It remained for a few moments and then sped away. Unknown to them, I had been logging reports of such objects from all over the area. Several years later, Aunt Priscilla was to have yet another strange experience.

After my parents had moved from Surrey to South Berwick, Maine, Aunt Priscilla decided to go there for a visit. My parents slept upstairs and Priscilla slept downstairs in the small den on a sofabed. Sometime in the early morning hours, bright orange light flooded through the two side windows and the front window. It was so brilliant that it woke her up with a start. She sat up and gaped at the reddish orange glow streaming in from outside. Her first thought was that the house was on fire but for some reason she did not get out of bed to sound the alarm. From that point on she could not remember anything except waking up in the morning and wondering what on earth she had seen. Since this same phenomenon has been reported before in conjunction with UFO activity, I have included it here.

Raymond F. Fowler/Father (1901–)

Age 22

My father is a very unusual man. On the surface, one would never guess that this quiet, retired executive has been privy to a multitude of mystical experiences. These have included the sighting of UFOs, out-of-the-body experiences, precognitive dreams, and apparitions of people long ago dead.

The beginning of these reported paranormal experiences can be traced to a specific near-death event in his life that could possibly have involved what we now call UFOs. Prior to this event, Dad had no interest or personal experience with such phenomena. Orphaned at an early age, he had joined the Navy and became one of the pioneers in a new technology called radio.

Because of the sheer number of experiences he has mentioned or recorded, it would be impossible to mention them all here. Suffice it to say that most of them are in the order of very high strangeness. Although some are analogous to some aspects of Betty and Bob's OBEs, most seem to fall outside the norm of the UFO phenomenon. For the purpose of this chapter, it will be more than sufficient to record in his own words how it all began near Bar Harbor, Maine, where he met and married my mother.

> In 1923, at the age of 22, I was a radioman in charge of a U.S. Naval Radio Compass Station atop Otter Cliffs on the beautiful island of Mount Desert, in Maine. My watch was from 4:00 P.M. to 4:00 A.M.

One late autumn day, a violent electrical storm was in
progress when I reached the station to relieve the day man. He left
for the main transatlantic station a quarter of a mile away wishing
me luck. I would need it, for static was terrific. The storm winds
were near hurricane strength and had spread out over the North
Atlantic shipping lanes. The ships were constantly calling in for
bearings. At 11:00 P.M., the S.S. *George Washington* started
testing for bearings. A violent lightning bolt hit the cable outside
the building. In seeking a ground, it went through the transmit-
ting key, jumped through the air space and landed right inside my
abdomen! It lodged behind my solar plexus where it remained
and revolved like a fiery sun inside of me! Amazed, I sat in the
operator's chair transfixed. I could only watch it wonderingly as it
whirled inside of me. It was eight inches in diameter. By this time
I should be dead, I thought. It was pulsating resonantly with my
heartbeat in a slow and steady rhythm. When I looked up, I was
more amazed than ever. There was a soft light that went *through*
the compass station roof, through the storm and darkness of the
night, up to what appeared to be a radiant star. I tried to
move—to get out of my chair—but found that I could not move
even an eyelid. However, I was conscious of a pulsating in the ray
that was turning that ball of fire within me in perfect time with
my heartbeat.

I looked down and saw that the ray went *through* the floor of
the compass station deep into the rocks that formed Otter Cliffs.
I sat calmly in an eternity of silence, the peace of which was
beyond description. It seemed that in these rays of light that
neither time nor space existed.

Suddenly, the rays expanded about seven feet in all directions.
Three distinct flashes of light unfolded into three majestic-looking
smiling men in shining robes of light. Although they did not
speak, my thoughts and theirs were in perfect attunement making
verbal speech unnecessary. My thoughts formed many questions
concerning them: the light rays; the electronic fire inside of me;
and what manner of star it was that projected such rays. But the
thought-questions went unanswered.

These three beings were fine-featured and had light cream-
textured complexions. Their eyes were so bright it was difficult to
see the color but I thought they were blue. The brilliant aura
surrounding them made it impossible for me to determine the
color of their hair for they wore strange velvety-looking hats
which were like three tiers of rolls upon their heads. Like their

robes, the headdresses were rich blue in color. They wore soft doeskinlike form fitting boots.

Next began the strangest ball game anyone has ever witnessed. The being on my left pointed his finger at the ball of fire still revolving within me. In a flash of light, it leaped into his open hand. He held it for an instant during which the ball was reduced to six inches in diameter. Then he tossed it to the open hand of the one in front of me. He held it for an instant reducing it to four inches or thereabouts. Whereupon, he threw it to the one on my right who held it and reduced it to two inches. He then threw it to the one on my left who tossed it into the copper mesh screening of the station where it disappeared in a shower of sparks. All three smiled, bowed, and disappeared in three flashes of light.

After this experience abruptly terminated, Dad was able to move about. Upon checking the equipment he found burned out transformers and pools of melted insulation all over the operating table. The power cables and their internal solenoids were burned out. He was covered with some kind of oil residue with a smell so fragrant that when he breathed he could taste it.

Dad, like Betty Andreasson, interpreted this close brush with death and its related experience within the context of his religious beliefs. He had no other paradigm within his experience for comparison. But, all interpretations aside, one cannot even prove the reality of such an experience in and of itself. I can assure the reader, however, that he thoroughly believes that this and his other experiences are real. I can only vouch for the reality of two. Both were precognitive in nature.

The first involved one of his strange lifelike dreams which he related to both my wife and me who were living with my parents at the time. He dreamed of entering a huge empty theater and sitting down. The lights dimmed, curtains moved back to reveal a large white screen, trumpets blew, and the screen lit up. A date appeared in bold letters accompanied by a thunderous voice that roared: "On this day the Cosmic Age will be ushered in!" Then, the screen darkened, the curtains closed, the lights in the theater came on, and Dad walked out.

My wife and I rolled our eyes at each other and mentally sighed, "Here we go again!" But I did write the date on a scrap of paper and placed it on my bureau. By the time the date arrived, the slip of paper lay long forgotten collecting dust. I suddenly remembered it amidst all of the excitement that gripped the world on that date. Newspapers headlined the once in a lifetime event. Russia had orbited the first artificial satellite and had thus ushered in the Space Age! As Sputnik whirled around the Earth, I rushed to my father with the scrap of paper. The date which I had scribbled on it read: October 4, 1957! Dad had completely forgotten about his dream and its prediction.

The other precognitive event that I can vouch for involved a UFO and my wife.

Margaret/Wife (1934–   )

I met and married my wife in 1955 during a tour of duty with the Air Force Security Service in England. Little did she know that when she uttered the words to take me for "better or for worse" that UFOs would come along with her American bridegroom!

My situation and location necessarily kept my interest in UFOs at a low profile. Margaret's worldview did not and does not include them. Today her attitude has moved from disassociated skepticism to sheer fear of the subject.

Her first experience took place in 1961 after my Dad had predicted that we both would see a UFO within two weeks. His prophecy was only 50 percent correct but that was not his fault.

Age 27

On June 24, 1961, my wife and I were driving through the countryside on the way to Salem, New Hampshire, where I was a church youth director. It was raining lightly and distant thunder rumbled as the sun began to filter through dissipating clouds. As we passed a large field in Haverhill, Massachusetts, Margaret cried out in alarm: "Ray! What is that thing over the field?" Since she often teased me about flying saucers, I refused to look and quipped: "You can't fool me, it will just be the sun coming out from behind the clouds!" Then she grabbed my by the shoulders and shouted, "Look now before you miss it! I'm not kidding."

It was too late. The field was now behind us and by the time I turned around and rushed back, the object was nowhere to be seen. Margaret described it as having been cylindrical in shape but with a fat midsection. It was silver and facing sideways to the road as it hovered over the field at treetop level. A short, stubby, swept-back wing jutted out from its side. It had no rudder or vertical stabilizer. We reported it to the Air Force. I am still mentally kicking myself for not looking.

Age 30s?

Other than nightmares about alien beings, Margaret has had only one extremely vivid lifelike dream that may be related to UFOs. I have no date for the incident, which occurred sometime in the 1970s. All I have is a sketch of what she saw drawn on the back of a discarded envelope.

One night in the early morning hours, something caused my wife to wake up. When she did, she saw a sharply defined beam of light, a foot or two in diameter, shining *through* the ceiling onto my head. Within the beam there were wavering rays like heat waves at times and streams of beads-of-light at other times. Thinking that she must be having a nightmare, she leaned over cautiously and put out her hand to touch the beam of light. When it illuminated her hand, she snatched it back in fright and pulled the bedcovers over her head. That was all she could remember when she awakened in the morning to excitedly relate to me what she had seen or dreamed. I asked her to draw what she had seen and stuffed her sketch away in my file to be forgotten for some time.

Margaret's mother, father, and brother have never sighted a UFO. I have three brothers and a deceased sister. Two of my brothers have had personal UFO sightings.

Frederick/Brother (1936–   )

Age 11

Sometime in the fall of 1947, Ricky, as he was nicknamed, ran breathlessly into the house yelling for me to come outside and see a flight of strange objects in the sky. I ran outdoors with him and up onto nearby Day's Hill where he had sighted them. The sky was empty. He said that he saw a formation of several cigarette-shaped objects gliding along in the sky. (That same year, my mother, sister, brothers, and I observed a cigar-shaped cloud hover high above the house for hours on a clear, windless day. It disapeared while we went inside for lunch.)

Richard/Brother (1941–   )

Age 23

On October 1, 1964, my brother Dick sighted a flying disk in broad daylight. The UFO flew over the research facility in Danvers where he was employed as an engineer. He carefully noted its elevation, angular size, and speed. It passed under a cloud. A check was made with the U.S. Weather Service to ascertain the height of the cloud base. Using simple trigonometry, Dick estimated that the object was about twenty-five feet in diameter and flying three hundred miles per hour at an altitude of 2,000 feet.

Age 27

In August of 1968, Dick left the night shift at the research facility in Danvers and began walking to his apartment about a mile or so away. As he crossed the parking lot, something caused him to glance up. He sighted a red light descending out of the sky. As he stood watching he experienced a very strong feeling that he was being watched. It descended behind trees toward a river. He last saw it as a cluster of red lights gliding low over the river. The same night I received an anonymous call from a person who was sitting on a porch overlooking the river and saw a silent dark object carrying red lights fly by them along the river.

Dick has also had some striking paranormal experiences in the form of detailed precognitive dreams that were quite frightening when they played out later in real life in exact detail.

My wife and I have four children. Two have had striking UFO sightings in broad daylight.

Sharon/Daughter (1958–   )

Age 11

On July 29, 1969, our family was flying back to the United States after vacationing with my wife's parents in England. While over the Atlantic, Sharon shouted across the aisle that two silver objects had just pulled up beside the plane. Both she and the woman passenger beside her described them as rectangular in shape. The woman was extremely nervous. As I handed my sleeping son to my wife and reached for my camera to rush across the aisle to take a picture, the pilot's voice sounded over the intercom: "Ladies and gentlemen. Please return to your seats and fasten your safety belts. We are expecting strong turbulence." I sat and watched in complete frustration as passengers on the other side of the plane watched the objects until they disappeared under the aircraft. Years later, a commercial airline pilot told me that when UFOs were sighted near an airliner, having passengers fasten their safety belts was a standard operating procedure in the event evasive action had to be taken.

David/Son (1968–   )

Age 8

In the summer of 1976, a Goodyear blimp had swung in very low over a golf course at Wenham, Massachusetts. David and his friends chased excitedly below it as it nosed down to land at nearby Beverly airport.

Later on in August, our family vacationed at Canaan, Vermont. Our cottage was set up on a hill overlooking Wallace Lake and the Canadian border. Because of a steep embankment, I had to be very careful when I backed out of a driveway to make the descent to the road below. It was a nice sunny day when David and I backed out of the driveway for a trip to a favorite fishing spot. David was looking out of the back window to help guide me as I edged out slowly toward the embankment. Suddenly he shouted, "Look, Dad. It's the Goodyear blimp!" I didn't know what he was talking about and told him to watch the driveway for me. I told him that the Goodyear blimp didn't fly way up here. As I backed safely around and headed down the hill, David was still peering out the window and asked, "Where did it go?" I stopped the car and looked out over the lake and asked him what he was talking about. He described a typical domed disk. I sank back in my seat feeling jinxed. As in the case of my wife's sighting, all I had to have done was to look. When I got David back in the house, I asked him to draw the Goodyear blimp for me. He carefully sketched an oval object with a *bump* on top. The bump was a dome.

I then asked Dave to draw how the object moved. He carefully traced an upward steplike line. "It was like it was going up stairs," he said. Then he drew wiggly lines around the object and said, "It stopped and wiggled all over and then it was gone."

My heart sank. The typical domed disk—the typical zig-zag movement—the typical wobbling on the axis before changing direction or darting away. There was no way that young David could have concocted such a story. He did not call the object a UFO. To him, it was the Goodyear blimp. Was someone watching our family? Why?

The answer to this question seems to have been discovered by researchers such as Dr. Neal. As mentioned, his studies indicate "there is some type of ongoing genetic manipulation that is occurring within various family generations." He theorized that such experiments would bring about "new genotypic individuals in proceeding generations." Dr. Neal further conjectured that "each succeeding generation of families is subjected to a different or comparable type of experimentation by the aliens."

In light of all of this, the reason for the scoop mark on my leg becomes obvious. The scar is the result of a *biopsy* taken as part of the aliens' ongoing genetic research within families of human beings. Why was it taken from this part of my body? Again, Dr. Neal thinks that he might have the answer.

> Many scars are found over the shin bone (tibia) and hip bone (iliae crest), which are common areas for obtaining bone marrow samples/aspirations. Simply speaking, bone marrow produces the red blood cells in our bodies. . . . It is significant . . . that it is through a human's bone marrow and blood that it is possible to study their individual chromosomal pattern.[2]

Dr. Neal also points out that abductee age may be a determining factor to where on the body such biopsies are taken.

> The marrow of the long bones, except for the proximal portions of the humeri [upper arm bones] and tibia [shin bone], becomes quite fatty and produces no more red cells after the age of 20.[3]

Both Betty and myself passed age twenty decades ago. This being the case, the scoop marks on her upper arm area and mine on my upper shin area provide strong circumstantial evidence for the validity of Dr. Neal's hypothesis.

All of these factors made me just that more anxious to proceed with the hypnosis sessions. Amidst further family protests, I found myself again driving to Tony's house to keep yet another appointment to unlock the secrets of my subconscious.

Chapter Thirteen—Notes

1. Budd Hopkins, *Intruders* (New York: Random House, 1987), pp. 117, 118.
2. Richard Neal, M.D., "Genetic Code under Seige," *UFO,* Vol. 3, No. 2, 1988, p. 25. (Credit: *UFO Magazine,* 1800 S. Robertson Blvd., Box 355, L. A., CA 90035).
3. *Ibid.*

CHAPTER

F o u r t e e n

Rekindled Memories

I arrived at Tony's home at 7:00 P.M. sharp on September 7. I discussed MUFON business until David arrived and then I broke the news to Tony about the scar. David had already seen photographs of it and knew of the circumstances surrounding its sudden appearance. Tony, on the other hand, knew nothing about it and its probable connection to the UFO abduction phenomenon. From the expression on his face when he and Dave examined it, I could see that it came as a shock to him. He probably wondered what on earth he was getting involved in.

Tony had planned to continue his probe of the *big hall* and *little hall* incidents. He was determined to get behind the mental block that prevented full disclosure of what I had experienced as a child. His game plan was to use a certain procedure that he had found successful in the past.

David and I now had a primary interest in when and how the scoop mark on my leg took place. Dave insisted that this be covered in the present session. Because of my family pressure, none of us could be sure if there would be further sessions. Meanwhile, our discussion of these matters had taken up precious time. We had less than an hour left of the session. A compromise was struck. Sometime during the hypnotic probe, Tony would address the question of the scar.

Tony decided to use a technique that would help me to be an *observer* rather than a *participant* of any relived experiences because of my emotional reaction at the last session. After putting me into a deep state of relaxation, he had me imagine myself entering a movie theater. In my mind's eye I found myself going into the local Cabot Cinema in Beverly. I passed the ticket booth, refreshment stand, and walked through the lobby and sat down in the theater.

Tony then brought me back in time to the big hall incident. He told me that I could watch what happened on the screen. I tried to see it on the screen but could not hold the scenes together. I found myself actually looking at the *big hall* as if I were there.

> *Ray* I'm beginning to see myself lying on the couch. I can't make out my features too well. . . . It's very hard for me to, to retain a picture on a movie screen in my mind. It just keeps on slipping away.
>
> *Tony* That's okay. Go ahead.
>
> *Ray* I'm looking under the—I don't know what you call it—The thing where the attic stairs go up and you can see on the outside. There's a wall and you can sorta get under there. I looked under there first.

This was the first place that I looked for the *lady* when I woke up in the morning.

> *Ray* And then I, I did crawl up the stairs and I looked up the attic stairs. I don't think I, I don't think, I don't think I went up at first. I think later on in the morning I actually went up the [attic] stairs . . . to find this person, whoever it was and for some reason I think that she's up there. I don't know why except—[*pause*] except, ah [*pause*] except [*pause—begins to breathe heavily*] It reminds me of something. [*trying to quell emotions*] It reminds me of something. Reminds me of something like a *ladder*. [*pause*] I think if I go *up* then I'll find her again.
>
> *Tony* Can you see the *light* at this point?
>
> *Ray* No, this is the next morning that we're talking about. I'm looking for the lady.
>
> *Tony* Climb the stairs, climb the stairs.
>
> *Ray* I climbed the first three steps and I think that I looked up and I then went down looking for my mother. I tried to tell her but she

didn't want to listen to me at all. She was busy. "Later on." [she said]

Tony What did you want to tell your mother?

Ray I wanted to tell her something before I forgot it. It was just so great and wonderful. I—She wouldn't listen to me.

Tony Can you listen to yourself talking to her?

Ray Just vaguely. She's working and I, I don't understand why she doesn't want to listen to me and—[*I'm at the point of tears.*]

Tony That's okay.

Ray It's—I want to tell her and it's *going* [i.e., from my memory] and I'm trying to remember it and she doesn't want to listen and she doesn't listen until later on in the morning.

As I just typed these last few words, I received one of the flashbacks that Tony predicted might happen. I remembered going to my mother and bursting into tears. She asked me why I was crying and I told her that it was because she wouldn't listen to me. She stopped and smiled and let me tell her what I could remember of what happened.

Ray And then she tells me it's a dream and by that time it's all gone practically. It, I just can't remember anything but when I first got up it was wonderful and I could remember a lot and I wanted to tell her about it but she wouldn't, she wouldn't listen to me.

Tony Let's go back. Let's go back to when you first got up. You approach your mother.

Ray Um.

Tony You tell her that you have something wonderful to tell her.

Ray I don't think I told her that. I forgot what I told her. I just told her someone came to me at night.

Tony Okay, but this time have her say, hear her say—"Tell me all about it?" How would you explain it?

Ray [*long pause*] That someone came to me, woke me up, sat down with me and talked. [*pause*]

Tony Was it a dream?

Ray I don't know. It seemed so real. I, I think I showed her my—I think I showed her my—First I showed her my, my heavy big Bible story book. I think I showed her that and I think I showed her my sister's *Book of Knowledge*.

Tony How did she react?

Ray [*long pause*] I can just remember showing her the pictures of the different planets and there's an airplane attached to a dotted line that goes to each planet. It says how many days or years it takes to get to these planets that we can do it.

Tony How does she react?

Ray I'm trying to remember. I can't remember.

Tony again asked me why I thought the entity was a *lady* and if the experience was a *dream*.

Ray I—just reminds me of a lady because of—just gentleness, love and gentleness-like. Seems real—Seems real—Seems real—Seems real.

Then, for some reason my voice lowered to a whisper.

Ray I can remember vaguely going to the window with her or whatever and seeing a beam of light from the window. [*I gasp!*] I think I *went out* but I can't be sure. It's very, very hard to hold it all together. I just—It's like it's there and it's there, it's there and it's gone.

Each time I started to get the slightest glimpse of what lay outside the window, a mental shade would be pulled down to block my view.

Ray And I think that's—

Almost without warning, the same unnatural emotions that I had experienced at the last session welled up within me. A terrific mental battle between my will and the mental shade ensued. I exerted tremendous willpower as I tried to look out the window.

Ray —why I thought that, ah, that *thing that we walked on* was, ah, the thing that we walked on was, ah, the thing that we walked on, that thing that—

I was engaged in a giant mental tug-of-war with I don't know what. My mind went blank and my words kept repeating themselves as if suddenly my memory was like a phonograph needle stuck in the groove of a spinning record. I began gasping for breath and found it difficult to breathe!

Tony That's okay, just relax! Just relax!

I was determined to force out my words to describe what kept blinking off and on at the window.

Ray was—like—a—*ladder*! [*panting heavily*]

Then, whatever it was temporarily completely overpowered and shattered whatever willpower I had left.

Ray I can't see anything! I can't see anything! I can't see anything!

I continued to pant heavily. I was crying and my voice was reduced to a whisper.

Tony That's okay. Relax.

I again exerted all the willpower that I could muster and attempted to look out the window once more.

Ray I can't see anything [*gasp*]—I can't see anything [*gasp*]—I can't see anything [*gasp*] *I can see the beam*!

Again, for a fleeting second, I saw the beam of light directed to my window presumably from the cluster of lights that I had seen before. But, again, the mental shade slammed down. I knew that it was a losing fight. Whoever, whatever had won!

Ray [*panting and shivering*] I can't see anything! I can't see anything!

Tony stepped in and calmed me down, relatively speaking, and asked me an intriguing question.

Tony Are you programmed to forget?
Ray I don't know. [*panting*] I don't know! I don't know!

Tony again spent time calming me and then tried an interesting experiment. He told me that my *subconscious*, not my *conscious* mind, would answer a series of questions that would demand a *yes* or *no* answer. I was not to answer these questions audibly but would answer yes by raising my right index finger and no by raising my left index finger. I heard him leave his seat and come over to me. He tapped my index fingers back and forth repeating yes, no, yes, no and then began asking questions.

Tony Is something being blocked? Is your subconscious blocking it?

I could feel tension developing between my two index fingers but neither moved upward. I answered verbally.

Ray I don't know. [*begin gasping again*]

Tony Are *you* blocking it?

Ray I don't know. [*breathlessly*]

Tony Don't answer! Allow your fingers to! This is yes [*taps right index finger*], this is no [*taps left index finger*]. This is yes, this is no, this is yes, this is no. [etc.] I want *you* to be disassociated! *You do not move those fingers!* Try to visualize. Are *you* blocking the information?

Ray [*Now panting very heavily.* I felt my left finger go up automatically for *no*.]

Tony Okay, that's fine. Relax, relax. Just relax. HAVE YOU BEEN PROGRAMMED TO FORGET?

I moved from heavy panting to violent spasmatic breathing. There was tremendous tension building up between my two fingers. I could feel both of them quivering and then, my right index finger moved quickly up and down for YES!

Tony Just relax, just relax. I'll have you open your eyes in just a few seconds. Just relax. Just relax. Just relax.

I could feel my breathing pace slowly coming back towards normal as I periodically quivered and sniffled in the chair. Tony, continuing the ploy of having me review the episode in a movie theater, calmed me down even more as his gentle voice echoed in my ears.

Tony What you can do if you feel that you want to is just get up out of that chair and walk to the front lobby and get a cold drink, a glass of lemonade or orange juice. . . . You must remember that in this room is care and love and concern. There is camaraderie. Just relax, just relax.

After Tony had restored me to a normal emotional state, he had me re-enter the theater and again take my seat. He proceeded to ask me about another childhood experience. It concerned a recurring nightmare of a dark figure approaching me in another bedroom at Dodge Court in Danvers.

> *Tony* Tell us what happened.
>
> *Ray* I wake up and sit up and—[*pause*] and [*long pause*]

I was there. I was back in my bed sitting up and staring in sheer horror at the figure outlined in front of the little hall door that entered my room. The little hall connected with the big hall to my left, an adjoining bedroom directly across and the bathroom to my right. A long cord with a bare light socket hung from the ceiling. A little nightlight barely lit the hallway for late night trips to the bathroom. The figure was small, perhaps four feet tall. His clothes looked dark and it looked like some sort of a cloak draped around him. On his head was a weird brimmed hat or headgear. It was so strange that hard as I try, I cannot visualize it. I could not see his face but innately I knew that it was scary.

> *Tony* Is it a dream?
>
> *Ray* I don't think so! [*starting to breathe heavily*]
>
> *Tony* Tell us what you saw.
>
> *Ray* [*breathing heavily—voice trembling*] I s-s-seeee a dark figure standing in the hall! [*sniff*]
>
> *Tony* Is it friendly?
>
> *Ray* [*trembling voice*] No, I don't think so. It's scary! It's scary! It's still in the little hall! [*I begin coughing uncontrollably.*]

Tony interrupted to help me out of the situation but it was too late. I was there and locked into the most terrifying experience in my lifetime!

> *Tony* You can back away from this!

I tried but it was impossible. I was there sitting up in bed. My back was pressing between the bed headrail into the wall. I felt a strange *tingling* sensation. I could not move. I tried to call out. Tony and Dave watched alarmed as my back pressed deeply into the back of the chair and I became hysterical.

> *Ray* I can't. I'm leaning against the wall and my pillow. [*crying and panting*] I can't move, can't move. I CAN'T MOVE!
>
> *Tony* Just relax! Just relax! Back away from it!
>
> *Ray* I can't move! I can't move! I CAN'T! He's there and I can't move! [*gasping and gulping for air.*]
>
> *Tony* Okay! You can press the *button* on that seat and the screen will become dark. You can just relax!

I began blowing out excess air and began to breathe heavily before finally settling down. But, again, without warning, the horrifying scene reappeared.

> *Ray* He's there again! [*breathing heavily again*]
>
> *Tony* Just let it fade away. Let him fade away. Press that *button.*

Tony was referring to a chair button that would make the screen fade away. Believe me, my finger was pressing down and indenting the hypnotist's chair at that point!

> *Tony* Allow that screen to become blank and allow the lights to come on in the theater. Just relax. Just allow relaxation, peace, and calm to wash over you.
>
> *Ray* [*blowing out air to control breathlessness*]
>
> *Tony* Just relax. . . . You can leave that theater now. Just get up and walk out through the lobby—by the concession stand— through the glass doors. Just walk right out. You're back out on the street—on the sidewalk.

My body literally shuddered all over with relief as I walked out of the theater into the fresh night air.

> *Tony* It's a beautiful day, really beautiful day. . . . The sun is shining.
>
> *Ray* It's night! . . . It's nice though—summer sounds.

Several times my mind shot back to the horror that I had experienced in the theater. Each time, Tony was right on top of the situation and calmed me down. But then he suddenly interrupted with a firm stern voice. He said he would name colors. He commanded me to name the first thing that came into my mind that reminded me of each color. Our conversation proceeded in a rapid fire succession: ". . . Red . . . Apple . . . Orange . . . An orange . . . Yellow . . . A canary." Then Tony jolted me with an unexpected command.

> *Tony* Very, very quickly, tell me something about the scar on your right foot! Your right leg!
>
> *Ray* It looks like a, had, a blob, blob taken out. Ha! I first noticed it in the shower. I thought—"This is crazy! Ha, ha, ha, ha. The Andreasson's, the Lucas's just told me about scars. Where does this thing come from? Ha, ha, ha. This is crazy. Ha, ha,"—I thought to myself.
>
> *Tony* Is this the first time you noticed it?
>
> *Ray* [*ignoring his question*] Where did this come from? I, this thing is getting so crazy. Ha, ha, ha. [*I begin coughing.*]

Tony quickly left his chair and came to me. He started the index finger routine again, tapping each finger as he spoke.

> *Tony* This is yes and this is no. This is yes and this is no. [etc.]
>
> *Ray* [*only half listening*] Yes and No? Yeah, all right. Okay, Yes, No. Right. [*still looking at scar in my mind's eye*] Crazy, crazy, crazy. This whole subject's crazy.
>
> *Tony* When you saw the scar, was it more than five days old?
>
> *Ray* [*left index finger shot up signifying no*]
>
> *Tony* Was it more than four days old?
>
> *Ray* [*again, left index finger quickly raises no*]
>
> *Tony* Was this scar at least three days old?

A strange feeling of tension suddenly gripped me. I began to breathe heavily in short pants.

> *Ray* I'm trying to make my fingers work but I'm thinking of the whole thing. I can't! I can't! It's hard to! It's—the tension between my fingers and my mind. [*sniff*] I, I can't. My fingers want to go but my mind wants to overpower my fingers!

Tony I understand. Don't try. Just relax. Just relax. Just relax. If I mention the color *green*, what do you see?

Ray [*laugh*] The first thing that comes to my mind is a *green button* at the Registry of Motor Vehicles during a color-blind test. [*laughing*]

Tony Give me a yes or no answer quickly! Were you programmed to forget about this scar?

Instantaneously, I felt the now familiar grip of something interfering with my thought processes. I felt rigid and began to pant again, first slowly, then faster and faster until I was literally gulping for air. The tension between my fingers and my mind became so intense that I could feel myself shivering all over. The feelings running through me were the same as when I earlier had tried to see out the *big hall* window. I exerted as much willpower as I could muster against whatever was affecting me and I felt my trembling right index finger slowly rise, signifying *yes*, before instantly snapping back down.

Tony immediately stepped in at that point and very slowly brought me back to normal consciousness. I opened my eyes and didn't say a word as I tried to collect my senses.

Dave Are you all right?

Ray Whew!

Tony Are you all right now?

Since the tape recorder was left running momentarily, I'll transcribe my initial reactions to what seemed to be a tremendous mental block.

Ray [*ignoring their questions*] There's something there I don't want to remember. I want to remember but I don't want to remember! Both at the same time! This is really crazy. Half of me wants to and the other half doesn't. It's like a fight going on. It makes me mad. It makes me really mad! I was really mad at something!

Dave [*to Tony*] Why did you stop?

Tony I didn't want to subject Ray to anymore of that. The conflict was tremendous. When, when you have the entire body trembling like, ah, that, ah then it's just time to calm down!

Dave Yeah.

Ray [*still ignoring their comments*] *They* have no right to do that. They've no right to *make* me forget. And, I don't know, but—ha—I was really mad. No matter what I did I couldn't get through it.

Dave Do you feel for the first time that there's something there preventing you?

Ray I don't know if it's me, because I don't want to know, or, I don't know if it's something else. It's, it's part of me that don't, doesn't want to remember and there's part of me that does, or, there's something out there that, that doesn't want me to. And somehow it's taking *my* will, no matter what I *want* to do! It's not letting me do it and that's not right!

Dave This all could have been in the past? That some, perhaps *external* force might have programmed you?

Ray I don't know. I don't know *when*. But, every, but every time I got to that *window* [big hall] and I started talking about that beam of light going out to those lights, [*sigh*] I'd get really upset and the very emotions, and the upset—being upset—would just *block* everything, anything, that was there. I just couldn't get through it. It just makes me mad. The same thing with that *scar*. When we got to *three days*, [*pause*] my fingers and my mind were in conflict with each other. I couldn't, I—My fingers wanted to say something but my mind wouldn't let them say it. Then, if my fingers—vice-versa— It was like a big struggle between my fingers and my mind and I was trying to come in as sort of a *victor* over whatever it was but I couldn't do it. I just couldn't do it!

In Tony's report to me regarding the sessions, he made the following comments based upon his longtime experience using the art of hypnotic regression.

Regarding the "Big Hall" incident: you were visibly agitated, distressed, frustrated as evidenced by your facial demeanor, body contortions, tone of voice. There was an obvious conflict between wanting to remember and not being able to remember what occurred when the "light"/presence took you to your bedroom window. . . . Your *finger responses* indicated you were not intentionally (consciously or unconsciously) forgetting what occurred then, but that you had been *programmed* to forget what had occurred then.

   Regarding the "Small Hall" incident: you were visibly frightened and quite panicked as evidenced by your body contortions and trembling as well as your facial demeanor and tone of voice—all this, plus your pushing back against the chair, indicated you were reliving the same emotions Wednesday evening that you experienced when the incident originally occurred. Bringing you out of the theater did return you to a pre-induction state of calm, although there was a flash or two of panic even then, as you apparently remembered what you had just then experienced in the theater.

When probing for the origin of the strange scar, Tony believed that I had been programmed to forget what had happened. Concerning my reactions, he wrote that:

> Because of your overall frustration, fright, panic, I felt then [as I do now] that it was physically, emotionally, spiritually, ethically and morally prudent to end the session by bringing you back to the "normal" state of consciousness. It was an emotionally exhausting experience for me although more for you.

Indeed, Tony had told Dave and me after the session he had performed many age regressions in his time. But he had never seen such a violent reaction before.

Tony warned me not to listen to the tape of this session until several days had passed. He also mentioned the possibility that the hypnotic probe may unleash further memory flashbacks and to be on guard for them. Unfortunately for me, my curiosity got the better of me. On the following evening I began transcribing the tape. It was a mistake. I tried to listen dispassionately as an unattached person. But, as I listened, I had to fight off the *déjà vu*-like emotions that rose up from deep within me. The more I tried, the more tense I became. My stomach developed severe cramps. Frustrated, I shut off the recorder and went outside into a beautiful starlit night to get some fresh air. The cramps persisted.

To get my mind off these incredible things, I decided to go down to my backyard observatory and spend some time observing the sky. As I opened the shutters in the observatory dome, I saw a brilliant meteor come out of the west and go by at a tremendous speed. "What a wonderful treat!" I thought. It was so unusual and looked as if it would go from horizon to horizon before burning out. I trained the fourteen-inch Schmidt-Cassegrain telescope on Saturn which hung low in the southwestern sky and wondered.

A shout from my son up at the house shattered my mental

reverie. I had a telephone call. It was a young lady from Connect-icut who had reported a UFO to Bradley Field. They relayed her call to me. I told her that the flashing object she was seeing near the Big Dipper was the bright star Capella. She had also seen the meteor burning out in the eastern sky and was very excited about it. But, all of these diversions did nothing to quell my stomach cramps. The emotions I had again reawakened were persistent and Tony was not there to calm them down!

I hurried back to my observatory and shut it up for the night. I barely made it back to the house before beginning a long bout with an upset stomach. The emotion-packed recording and think-ing about that wretched mark on my leg had caused this violent psychosomatic reaction.

I do not have a heart condition. But because of the tremendous strain that I was experiencing, I seriously thought about putting further hypnosis sessions on hold. The mental block encountered during the two sessions was powerful. Even under hypnosis I had a strange realization that I was fighting a losing fight. But then two incidents changed my mind completely. They came in the form of two amazing flashbacks of memory.

Both flashbacks erupted just two weeks after the second hypnosis session. The first took place on the night of September 22 as I lay talking to my wife in bed. My recall was instigated by a simple remark that she made to me: "You can always fall to sleep at the drop of a hat." Instantly two forgotten events burst forth from the recesses of my mind.

The first memory concerned the night of August 16. How could I have forgotten that eerie sleepless night? Up until this point, I remembered only coming home from an astronomy lecture that I had given to a nearby club. What I had forgotten was that I was kept awake into the wee hours of the morning by a strange up-tight electriclike feeling. On the following morning of August 17, I had discovered the scar!

My second flashback was of a dream that I had just had the night before my wife had made her innocent remark about my sleeping ability on September 22. During the night of September 21, I had a frightening nightmare. It was peculiar. One usually visualizes things in a dream. In this instance, I dreamed that I could not see. I felt myself being moved somewhere. When I opened my eyes to see what was happening, all that I could see was black. Somehow I knew that I was dreaming and tried to wake up but I could not. Finally, when I did wake up I almost blurted out loud—"They are operating on my leg!"

As I lay there recuperating from this nightmare, it dawned on me that perhaps it had something to do with my scar. I wondered if what had happened back in August had leaked out of my subconscious in the form of this nightmare. I told myself that I must remember this dream. I started to reach for the Kleenex box to put on my bureau to remind me in the morning. I started to reach for it but that was the last thing I remembered.

I tried to keep my composure as my wife continued chatting away to me. It was frustrating not to be able to share with her what her cryptic remark had done for me. Perhaps, I thought, these recalled memories could be further enhanced by hypnosis.

Almost two months passed before I tried once more to pry open my Pandora's box of hidden memories. I say "once more," because I promised my wife that it would be the last session. She was severely depressed and needed breathing room. My promise was her light at the end of the tunnel.

CHAPTER

Fifteen

Forbidden Fruit

I arrived at Tony's home for my last session shortly before 2:00 P.M. on October 29, 1988. David arrived several minutes later. The session would be several hours long. It was decided to divide it into two equal parts. The first segment would be a broad-brush attempt to discover how many UFO encounters I had experienced. The plan was not to dwell on any one potential experience but to proceed with a chronological summary of such events. Then, after establishing a baseline, one or more encounters would be selected for a detailed interrogation during the second segment of the session. Another attempt to elicit information about the scar would also be covered during this timeframe. In the event that nothing new surfaced, both David and Tony had a list of all the events that I could consciously remember for their review under hypnosis.

The actual hypnosis regression lasted almost two hours without a break. It would take more pages than this chapter to record everything said. Much would be repetitious or related to hypnotic procedures. The outline that follows will adhere to the chronological sequence of the subjects covered during the session.

The Little Hall Incident

Tony Tell me the circumstances of your first encounter.

Ray I remember waking up at night—[*pause and begins breathing heavily*]—wa-a-a-king up.

At this point I choked up with fear and could not talk.

> *Tony* Just relax, just relax.
>
> *Ray* Se-e-e-ing [*pause*] a figure in black at the *little hall* doorway [*pause*] outlined. A little light from the ceiling hanging there. [*long pause and deep breathing*] I can't remember anything before that. I don't think so.
>
> *Tony* Do you remember seeing the *being* before that?
>
> *Ray* My mind is blank before that, I—It seems to be the first.
>
> *Tony* Could you see the features of that being?

At this juncture, I merely repeated that the entity was dressed in black, perhaps had a cloak and was wearing a strange hat. I again related the strange prickling feeling and paralysis that prevented me from yelling for help or moving. When the visitor returned on one or more subsequent nights, I, for some reason, felt that it was no use to struggle but to just let happen what was going to happen. New material retrieved had to do with the facial features of the entity:

> *Ray* It was awful when he got close. When he got close, *it* was awful strange looking, like—[*mental block*] I've tried to remember. I've tried to draw pictures of the hat. I've tried to remember the face and all I can say is it's so strange and so weird that, ah, I can't even draw the hat right. I've tried and tried and tried. Just weird.
>
> *Tony* Can you describe it to us now?
>
> *Ray* [*no answer and breathing heavily*]

Tony finally got me to try to describe the hat and as I described it, I began to see some vague facial features of the face under it.

> *Ray* I see something like a round face and very strange eyes.
>
> *Tony* What shape eyes?
>
> *Ray* [*I start sobbing.*]
>
> *Tony* Just relax, just relax.
>
> *Ray* I think they're round. I'm not sure. [*I lose the brief mental picture.*]
>
> *Tony* Are they round like human eyes?
>
> *Ray* No! No!

Tony What is above the eyes?

Ray [*tries to recapture the image*] I don't think he had any eyebrows. Just, just plain, strange pastel-white face. [*now breathing heavily in short pants*]

Tony What did you see below the eyes?

Ray I can't see. I'm not even sure about the eyes. [*begins to pant more heavily*] I can't see! I'm trying to see. I can't see! I can't see! I can't! I can't even see if he has ears.

Tony Look at the floor and tell me what you see. Look at the floor.

Ray [*breathlessly*] I can't see the floor. I see—the bed's in the way.

Tony Look further down his body. What do you see?

Ray [*still panting*] I think he's, he's got black, he's got black clothes on. It's dark. The only light I can see is in the hall and he's not in there. He's so close that I can't do anything! I just can't do anything!

Tony How long was he there?

Ray [*panting*] I don't know. The next thing I remember is I wake up. [*breathing heavily*] I just wake up and it's all gone. It's all gone. It's just a dream. It's just a dream. Ha! Just a dream. [*lets out long sigh*] Just a dream.

Dave and Tony continued their interrogation. Much of what was retrieved was repetitious. However, a question from Dave brought an interesting answer.

Dave Did this dream only occur when you were around six or seven? Anytime after that?

Ray No, I remember seeing something like this on the golf course [Wenham Country Club] with my daughter Sharon but he seemed to be taller than, than what I saw in the bedroom. But that, that wasn't a dream. We both saw that.

Tony Could you see his features on the golf course?

Ray No. We were skiing along and in the deep snow and we saw this fellow and it looked like an old-fashioned, black overcoat or something and, strange black hat and he was standing beside a tree looking at us. And I says to my daughter, Sharon, I says, "I wonder who that is over there?" And she looked over and says, "I don't know."

And I says, "It's rather strange to have somebody out here like that." We skiied along some more and we kept glancing at him. He's still there and we talked some more and got closer and we looked up and he *wasn't there!* And there's no—

Tony Did you see his eyes or any of his features?

Ray No. It's too far away and couldn't figure out where he went because there's golf course all around there. Even if he ran, he couldn't have got away. So, we were so curious, we went over to the the, the tree. And there were *no tracks* there and—no tracks!

Tony You said that in the little hall incident, that you knew that *being* would be there because you would get a *feeling.* . . . Did you get that aura on the golf course?

Ray No, no, it just looked like a—somebody dressed out of fashion. We may have got a strange eerie feeling after we saw there were no footprints there. But that was just because, you know, how on earth? We must have been seeing things or something. . . .

Dave Why do you connect that figure with the figure that you just talked about?

Ray Because he seemed to have dark clothes on and a strange hat that people wouldn't—I don't think people wear a hat like that. Maybe no connection at all. . . . It didn't remind me of it then. It only reminded me of it after we had these hypnotic regression sessions. And, we, ah, you had me *draw* that—[*feels fear*] that, that, thing [*fear grips me so strongly that I can hardly speak*] that, they—

I started sobbing violently as I again was mentally in my bedroom staring at the small dark figure in the *little hall.*

Tony Just relax, just relax.

Ray That th-h-h-ing in the doorway. [*I force these words out and begin breathing heavily and literally blowing out air!*]

Tony Just relax, relax.

Ray [*hysterically*] I don't want to think about that thing in the doorway! I don't want to think about that thing in the doorway! I don't want to think about that thing in the doorway!

Tony Just relax, just relax.

Ray [*whisper*] I don't want to think about that thing in the doorway.

Tony Just relax. Just jump ahead in time. Just let go of that thing in the doorway. Just let go of that thing in the *drawing.*

Ray [*gasping for breath and crying*]

Tony Just take a deep breath—Let it out. Let your mind just search forward to the *next* encounter and a different entity.

As I transcribed this particular segment of the session from the tape, I had several *seeming* flashbacks of memory.

1. Equating the *little-hall* visitor with [in kid's language] a *China man*.
2. Being *in* the lighted *little hall* and seeing a pale white face that looked Chinese.

Armed with this new visual input, I found a drawing in Budd Hopkins's book, *Intruders*, that *reminds* me of the little-hall entity's face. I have attempted to sketch my fleeting memory of this face [Figure 45] but cannot be sure of its accuracy. It is merely my impression and may have been influenced by my close association with UFO research.

The Big Hall Incident

When Tony asked me to move forward in time to my next encounter, my mind immediately jumped to the *big hall* experience. Again, Tony and Dave tried unsuccessfully to get me to remember

45   "Little Hall" Entity?

what the entity looked like and what happened when the entity brought me to the window. Essentially, I just rehearsed the salient points that I had recounted and relived during the prior sessions. One additional interesting sidelight was my remembering that I showed the entity my *Children's Bible Story Book*. Amazingly, I came home after the session and accidentally found this well-worn book! I had thought that it had been thrown out years ago but there it was in my bookcase along with a number of different versions of the Bible! Another interesting synchronism.

I am sure that it had been there all along. I just must have put it there and forgotten it. In any event, it helped to date the big hall incident further. It was inscribed:

> Raymond Eveleth Fowler
> Xmas 1939
> From Mother & Daddy

My birthday was November 11, 1933. I would have been six years old in 1939. I started school early in September 1939. I was in the big hall when my grandmother died on August 1, 1942. Thus, I was between eight and nine when this experience took place. It must have taken place during the school summer vacation or on a weekend because I did not go to school on the day of the incident.

The *new* information about the big hall incident came out during this third hypnotic session just after I mentioned seeing *lights* out the window as I approached it with the entity.

Tony Did you go through the window with *her*?

Ray [*I gasp and begin shivering violently.*]

Tony Just relax, just relax.

Ray [*breathing heavily and fearful voice*] I think so!

Tony Just relax. It's okay.

For some reason, I found myself literally terrified about the prospect of talking about going out the window with the entity.

Tony Just relax, it's okay.

Ray I think I went through. I'm not sure.

Tony You're doing very well. Just relax.

Tony then proceeded to take some time calming me down before coming back to the subject at hand. But I immediately reacted violently when again confronted with going out the window.

> *Ray* [*shivering all over and gasping for breath*] When I try to remember that, I just, I just—
>
> *Tony* Don't try, that's all—
>
> *Ray* But when I try to remember that, it, everything wells up within me and I just—It just overpowers me. I can't—I don't know why. It's, this, this, my whole being just fills with something and I just—I [*pause to try to catch breath*] Maybe *I'm not supposed to remember this.* I want to remember.

This latter statement may be very significant as we shall see further on in this chapter. It came out quite unexpectedly. Tony decided to probe once more.

> *Tony* Do you feel that you left the house?
>
> *Ray* Yes.
>
> *Tony* When you left the house, did you go alone?
>
> *Ray* No. [*starts gasping and breathing heavily*] No. I went w-w-with this person but [*pause*] I think we're up high! I think we're up high! I think we're up high! I think—It's, it's so high—I, I don't want to look down. [*terrified and crying*]
>
> *Tony* That's all right. Don't look down!
>
> *Ray* [*becoming hysterical*] I don't want to look down! It's high! It's high! I'm gonna fall! I'm gonna fall! I'm gonna fall!

Even as I type these words, I feel the emotions trying to surface again.

> *Tony* Just relax. Just relax your body.
>
> *Ray* Uh! uh! uh! I'm gonna fall!

Tony's voice sounded very concerned on the tape at this point and he did his best to get me out of the terrifying situation that I now found myself in.

> *Tony* Go back to your bedroom. Go back to your bedroom.
>
> *Ray* I'm gonna fall, I—

Tony Go back to your bedroom. Go back to your bedroom!

Ray I'm goon fall!

Tony You won't fall. You're here!

Ray [*still shouting*] I don't want to fall!

Tony You're here with David and with me.

Ray Don't want to fall! Don't want to fall!

Tony You're here with David and with me.

Ray We're *on that beam*, I think! Don't want to fall!

Tony Just relax, just relax.

Ray Don't want to fall! It's high up! It's high up! I—How do we do this?

Tony Come back to your bedroom. Come back to your bedroom.

Ray Yeah! Yeah!

Tony Sitting on the bed. And just relax.

Ray Yeah!

Tony And just relax.

Ray Yeah! Yeah! I am, I'm trying! I'm trying!

Tony What is the next thing you remember? Do you remember waking up in the morning?

Ray Yeah, I remember waking up in the morning. Feeling wonderful. [*Calmed down now*]

I then again recounted how I tried to tell my mother and how later, when seeing the movie, *The Wizard of Oz*, being reminded of the dream. Tony tried unsuccessfully to find out how long I was gone with the entity and how I returned. I could only remember waking up the next morning.

I recorded these details of my reaction to demonstrate how terrified I was when I presumably left the house through the window. Of particular interest is my very real impression of being up high and moving along the beam. Consciously, I have a vague remembrance of this beam connecting the window with the blurred mass of lights hovering over Dodge Court. Another vague memory is being encouraged or comforted by the entity as we moved along on the beam.

During the debriefing [non-hypnotic] after this session, I tried to describe what I was feeling and why I felt so frightened.

Dave When you were up high—Do you mean that you were, ah, completely open? There was nothing around you? You're just looking down at the ground?

Ray That's, that's the impression I got. Whether it's true or not, I don't know. It's like—You *know* if you're walking on a bridge, you've got *something under you*. But, if you have *nothing under you*—I mean, I'm not saying this is it—But, if you have *nothing under you*, it isn't supposed to happen. And, you think you're going to fall because there's *nothing* there. And that's, that's the impression I got. But, I don't know whether I'm reading into it or not. I don't know.

If such an event really happened and somehow I was made to forget it, I have something perhaps significant to report. Again, it is an impression. Whatever blocked my memory could somehow short-circuit my *visual* memory but it could not block the *emotions* and other sensory impressions such as being up high and the fear of falling. I got this impression all along. The *visual* part of my experience was almost completely blocked but the accompanying emotions were still there. I felt no such strong emotions when consciously remembering them as flashbacks. But, when under hypnosis and reliving the events, the emotions were terribly real and strong.

After asking many questions about the big hall experience, Tony decided to move on. He asked me to recall my next encounter. The first thing that came to mind was a memory flashback that I had experienced consciously several days before the session. I do want to say at this point that I am not really sure of the chronology of this event. I am doing research with members of my family, old photographs, and input from the town historian for Danvers, Massachusetts in an attempt to firmly date each event at least within a particular year. Under hypnosis, I seem to be following the chronology of when I *remembered* each event. Time will tell.

The Jumping Light Incident

Ray [*very long pause*] The next thing that comes to mind is being sick in bed but not in the big hall. But in the room that faces the big hall and being sick. And my mother had brought me up some junket to eat. And I'm eating my junket. [*pause*] There's something there that frightens me and I call for my mother. And she finally starts coming up the stairs. And I see this bright sparklike light jump out from in front of me and go into the closet. She comes into the room and I told her about it. She said, "You're just imagining things." And I said, "It went in the closet!" And she, she went over and looked in the closet and she said, "There's nothing in the closet. It's all your imagination." But I don't remember, I, I, I don't even remember, I don't even remember what it was before the light jumped into the closet that made me call for her. The light was frightening because it was small and bright and it just jumped. It didn't float. It just jumped right into the closet.

Tony Jumped from where to the closet?

Ray It must, it must have been in front of me when I was eating my junket. I can't remember that part. All I can remember is just as she's coming up the stairs, all of a sudden this light jumps from in front of me—just jumps so fast that it f-f-f-frightens me. It, ah—

Tony Just slow down your mind so that you can describe the light. Slow it down a bit.

Ray It's like a light when you take—You used to have these round candies [NECCO wafers]. And there were different colors. And the white color, if you, in the dark, took it and broke it, you'd get a bright flash of light. That's what it reminded me of.

As best as I can remember, the light was about the size of a dime but it had no discernible shape because of its brightness. The closet door was ajar. It did not go *through* the closet door. It was a yellowish-white but more white than yellow. That is my impression. [See Figure 44, page 244]

The Wrest Farm Incident

Dave Were there any other subsequent encounters that you recall?

Ray [*long pause*] I remember seeing a, I remember seeing a—what I thought was a parachute when I was working on a farm. [*pause*] But it wasn't a parachute because there was no one hanging from it. It was just like the top of a parachute. And, ah, it was coming down strangely. It was coming down—one end going up and one end went down. It was like rocking back and forth, back and forth.

Tony How old were you when you saw it?

Ray I think I was twelve or thirteen. I was working on a farm and I watched it for just a few seconds and 'til I was sure that it wasn't a parachute and then just turned around and called for, for people who were way behind me, weeding, to look at it. And they couldn't hear me. They didn't know what I was talking about. And so I turned back just in time to see it go down behind trees. And I thought, "It has to be a parachute," so I looked in the papers, ah, *Salem News*, I think it was, to see if a plane had crashed. I asked—I told my mother and father that I thought I saw a parachute coming down. Nothing . . . There was an article in the *Salem News* several days later that said *flying disks* were seen in Wenham and Beverly and I've always wondered whether or not that was what I saw.

I have taken a photograph of the *Salem News* front page headline about flying disks. It is dated Monday, July 7, 1947. I estimate that I saw the object on Friday, July 4 or Saturday, July 5. Wrest Farm, if I remember correctly, did not consider the Fourth a holiday for its workers in those days. Since I avoided working Saturdays, it was probably on Friday. Interestingly enough, the *Salem News* story states that a single disk was seen at Magnolia that same afternoon (10 airmiles away).

During the hypnosis session I estimated the disk to have been several miles away. It was hard to tell because I did not know its real size. Its apparent size was about one quarter the angular size of a full moon. It was a dull white color and it reflected some sunlight. I believe I saw it sometime during the afternoon hours.

I had given Tony a list of consciously remembered interesting incidents that I wanted to examine under hypnosis. Since time was of the essence, Tony decided to begin asking me about some of these experiences. The first involved a flashback that occurred while writing this book. It was a vague remembrance of *missing time*.

The Burley Woods Incident

Tony Would you like to discuss Burley Woods, Danvers?

Ray Oh yeah, that's where I used to go hunting. And I used to go there everytime I could after school with my gun and spend the afternoons out there. I just loved to be out in the woods and go wading in the brooks and just loved to be out there all by myself.

Tony Would you like to tell us about the *missing time?*

Ray Oh, that's probably nothing. I had a flashback when we were doing the hypnotic session and I was doing the book. Sometimes when I was thinking about these other things that came out under hypnosis—things that I remembered when *The Andreasson Affair* was being written—that these *other things* would flash back in my mind—like a *spinning compass* on my bureau, for example. Sometimes I wonder if that really happened. But it's—[I got sidetracked temporarily from the Burley Woods.] I remember how strange it was, coming home, just, ah getting my clothes off and getting changed into my play clothes and going to the bureau and just seeing that compass *spin*. That's strange. The Burley Woods? Yeah, I can remember a time that, ah, that I went out as usual. I can't remember exactly where I went or what I did. But, I remember going into the woods as usual and all of a sudden it became *dark* all of a sudden, almost dark. And, I couldn't figure out why it was so dark and thinking, "Boy!" I didn't have a watch. And by the time I got home it was just about dark. . . . I came into the kitchen and my mother says, "Where have you been?" She says, "Supper is just about all over. We've been worried about you? Where have you been?" I said, "I went to the woods and I thought I set back in good time." She said, "Well it's awfully late." And I said, I didn't have any explanation except I must have been so interested in what I was doing out there that all of a sudden, it was dark and I came home.

Tony Can you see yourself when you first went into the woods?

Ray I used to always follow the same old route. I used to go over Day's Hill and through the barbed wire fence and over the railroad bridge that Mr. Friend built for his model railroads. I used to go around the point with the Danvers River there and I used to come out near the Danvers, old Danvers High School and cross the road in front of the high school and come to the brook. And there used to be a place there you can barely cross on stones. And, over the stones, and then, there's a short cut if you climbed a tree and just let the tree branch bend, you could get over the brook on that side. And I'd walk across the field, ah, some bushes, through the field to the icehouse. The icehouse, they used to call it Third Pond. That's the path I used to always follow. And I used to just wander around and see the wildlife.

Tony Okay, let's go back to the beginning of that, that little trip in the woods. . . . See if you can tell at what point you stopped seeing the familiar landmarks. Just relax.

Ray I can't remember where I was when I thought it was getting awfully dark, awfully fast. I can't remember exactly where that was.

I think it was near the icehouse but I'm not sure. I thought, "Boy! I better get out of here—get going fast!" I remember I was—I, I think I remember—I think I was really going fast. I was! I didn't care what was in my way! I was—didn't want to get stuck there in the woods at dark. I was plowing my way through the brush. Just—Get out of there! Get out of there! Get out of there! Get out of there! Because it's getting dark—Yeah.

Tony What was the other reason?

Ray I don't know.

Tony Do you see any other reason why you wanted to get out of the woods?

Ray I don't know. I—ha!—I wondered if there was another reason. When I had this flashback to that [*incident*], I thought to myself— "Missing time? Why haven't I remembered this before?" This thing just sort of popped into my mind now. What happened then? Was this my imagination or did this really happen or am I trying to make more out of something?

Tony Okay, let's go back to the icehouse? Can you see it there?

Ray Yeah, it was really a nice little pond.

Tony And on that day, just go back a minute before you get to the icehouse. Where are you?

Ray I most likely came along that road [a dirt road that bordered two sides of the pond]. I can't remember if I did at that time or not. Really, all I can remember is just looking at the sky and seeing how dark it was . . . and I just really lit off for home as fast as I could because—ha—I couldn't figure out why it was so dark.

Tony and Dave tried over and over again unsuccessfully to get me to remember what had happened prior to my suddenly noticing that it was dark. I just kept repeating the same scenario and ending up being very late for supper. Their attempts and my response were repetitious and I only will include a few more highlights.

Dave Do you often, ah, lose track of time in the woods?

Ray No, I don't . . . I knew what time I should be home. I—it just got dark so suddenly. I mean, you know, usually it *starts* to get dark and you say, "The sun's down there." You *know* where the sun is and you *know* it's about time to start heading home *now*. But, all I can remember is that all of a sudden, it was all of a sudden dark.

It wasn't gra-a-a-dually getting darker and darker. It was like being shocked that—"How did it get so dark?"

When I played back and transcribed this portion of the taped hypnosis session, several things stood out as perhaps significant. I also had another flashback of what might be a real memory.

First, during one portion of this segment, I again recounted how I arrived late for supper and how I tried to explain to my cross mother why I got home late.

Ray I tried to explain to them that, "Hey, I *thought it was time to leave* and I just, I just, I don't know, I just," [*pause*]—She wasn't too happy about it.

It appears to me that at a certain time that I *knew* that it was time to leave and started to wend my way home in plenty of time and then all of a sudden it was dark. During another portion of the session, another interesting comment caused me to have the aforementioned memory flashback.

Tony When you, when you realized it had *suddenly* become dark— Just see yourself *standing* there and perhaps looking up. What do you feel?

Ray [*pause*] It was just like something *totally unexpected* that's happened—jolted or shocked—and all of a sudden you realize . . . you're out in the woods and it's getting dark and you've got to get home, and just going as fast as I could.

When I was transcribing the above words, my mind suddenly formed a mental picture as I pencilled out the words?

Just see yourself *standing* there

and:

What do you *feel*?

It may all be my imagination but I saw myself *lying* not *standing* and *feeling* sharp stones or sticks digging into my body. I saw myself in a flannel shirt jump up, wonder what was going on, seeing how dark it was and taking off for home. Again, I cannot be sure that this scenario is real or imagined. I do know that my reaction was one of *fear* when Tony then asked me why I had said the words—*something totally unexpected that's happened.* Up to this point while recounting this incident, I had shown little emotion except that of curiosity and some excitement as I ran home through the woods. However, when Tony queried me about my cryptic remark, I felt the same *fear* that I had experienced during other incidents, suddenly well up within me.

> *Tony* Your choice of words is interesting. Something *totally unexpected* had happened. What was the *reason* you chose these words?

When Tony sternly asked me that question, a sudden feeling came over me. It was the same kind of feeling that one would have if caught red-handed stealing or doing something wrong. The feeling left as quickly as it had come as I snapped back an answer to Tony's question.

> *Ray* I didn't expect it to get dark!

Then, momentarily I felt something within me collapse as if I had been covering something up and had slipped up somehow.

> *Ray* I was [*I let out a loud gasp and start breathing heavily.*]

I literally had to force out my next words. I could hardly talk because of the strange emotions welling up from within me.

> *Ray* It just got—All of a sudden it was dark! Darker than it was supposed to be.

I'm afraid that this is as much as we could retrieve from the Burley Woods incident. I cannot explain why my later flashback of *lying* on the dirt road and *feeling* the uneven ground digging into my body did not come out while I was under hypnosis. I have found, however, that some of my memory flashbacks have been instigated by word association.

The North Sea Incident

> *Tony* Would you like to discuss . . . something about a disk in England?

Tony was referring to my frustrating sighting of a disk descending and landing while vacationing with my wife's parents in England during July of 1969. It was July 21 or 23.

Ray Oh yeah, ah, just driving, driving to the North Sea with Mr. and Mrs. Pike and Sharon and Beth and Raymond and Margaret. They were all in the back seat and I was in the front seat with Mr. Pike driving along open countryside and sort of a hill to our left and some trees. All of a sudden, this, this disk-shaped object came down so fast. And it didn't come down straight. It came down in this weird *arc*. And it came down so fast. And it went down behind the trees. I thought it was gonna—I was just waiting for an explosion or something. Nothing happened and I asked my father-in-law, "Did you see that?" He said, "I didn't see anything." And I told him what *we* [don't know why I used plural] had seen and I guess, ah, my wife sort of gave me a hard time in the back seat. I wanted to see if we could go over there and see what it was. And no way was he going to go anywhere. Just going to right to the North Sea to the beach with the kids. I thought to myself, "Boy, if I had this car by myself I would certainly go over there and look!" And that was a perfectly clear sky and that just came down so fast. I don't know why it just didn't—

Tony Was this in the daytime?

Ray Yeah, it was in the daytime. It was a beautiful day. Clear sky and the thing just came down sort of like—[*I demonstrated an arc with my hands. My eyes were closed.*]—and so fast. I couldn't see how it could have stopped before just crashing in the ground.

Dave Who else saw this?

Ray I can't understand why my father-in-law didn't see it. Maybe because he was just paying attention to driving and I was just sort of looking around the countryside. It happened so fast that you could have almost blinked your eye and it would have been gone. So, I can see why he, why he *probably* didn't see it. If he did see it, he wasn't saying anything.

Dave So, you were the only one who saw it?

Ray Um, but it *was* there. And it couldn't have been a bird. It couldn't have been a balloon. And it went so fast and in this perfect arc. Ah, it couldn't have been a reflection. I mean, it was just too tangible and too real.

The Mid-Atlantic Encounter

Ray And then, on the way back [from England]—On the way back flying along—We were in a plane, July '69 [July 29, 1969] coming home. And, I had my son Raymond, ah, sound asleep. It took a long time for him to get to sleep. And my wife insisted it was my turn to have him on my lap. And, ah, so she could move around. And I just got him asleep. And, just across the aisle there, everybody was excited, looking out the window. And I asked, what was going on over there and Sharon said, "There're two *things* out here, Daddy!" And I says, "What do you mean?" And she says, "There's two *things* flying out here." And I said, "Well, what do they look like?" And she said, "like box kites." And, I saw other people looking and I said, "Margaret, take the baby!" And she says, "No." She didn't want to take the baby. "Don't be silly. It's probably nothing." And, I had to give her the baby and I grabbed my camera and I started to undo my safety belt. And the pilot came in [on the intercom] and said, ah, everybody get back to their seats and fasten their safety belts. They expect turbulence. [*worried voice*] And, [*sighed*] I was completely frustrated. I asked my daughter what they were doing now, next? And she said that they're going under the aircraft. And I grabbed my camera and I set it up and I pressed my eyes against my porthole on my side and I looked and looked and I couldn't see anything. And and the pilot didn't come back on. Everybody just stayed seat-belted. And, finally I saw some *blobs* out the window reflecting sunlight and I thought to myself, "That's probably not what they saw but I'd better take a picture." So, I took a picture of—that's what I got on the film—just blobs, two little blobs of something reflecting sunlight and a brighter blob. It was—I didn't see the brighter blob but I just took a picture of the two smaller blobs. But, when the film came out, there was a brighter one as well. And years later, when I was doing a talk show, a pilot called in . . . and said that . . . they were told that when a UFO approached the craft that the first thing they do is ask everybody to fasten their safety belts, that they expect turbulence. I thought to myself, "The pilots must have seen those things too."

The Black Box

Tony continued to scan my list of incidents that I wanted to address while under hypnosis.

> *Tony* You have something about 1980s, ah, you turned around after leaving your car and saw a *black box* hovering and gyrating. [At 13 Friend Court, Wenham, MA]
>
> *Ray* I backed in the driveway and, ah, I had something in the back of my station wagon. I've forgotten what it was.

Interestingly enough, as I was transcribing this section of the tape, I remembered what it was. It was a TV stand for a black-and-white TV that we purchased in 1979. Thus, the incident happened in 1979, not the 1980s as I had guessed earlier.

> *Ray* I opened the station wagon door—you pull it open, I believe—I got it and I closed it and I turned around to walk in the, the front door and right in front of me seemed to be a hazy, blackish box about six, maybe eight inches in diameter. It reminded me of a run down—a running down gyroscope. One of those things— just wobbling. And I was walking fast. I turned around and was walking fast and it was right at my head level and I ducked under it. And when I got up on the other side of it and turned around, it was gone. I went in and told my wife and I says, "You know, you won't believe this." And she didn't believe it. She said I must have been seeing things. And I thought to myself, "It was so real that I had to duck to get under it." And why? It was really weird. I thought to myself, "All these things that happen, there's just enough there to think there's something there. But, when you really think about it, you can explain each one of these things away by saying, 'Oh well, you know, it was just an afterimage or something.'" But, it was so real. It was!
>
> *Tony* Did it make any noise?
>
> *Ray* No, it was—It wasn't ghostly because it was solid. But, it seemed to have a sort of haziness about it. It was just sort of like a gyroscope, sort of winding down. It was, it was spinning fast enough so I think it was square but it was sort of blurry as well. So, you couldn't really absolutely tell whether—I tried to think about it afterward and it just reminded me of a black box. Ah, and I said, "I better not tell too many people about this, ah, my wife's reaction, ah, but ah—"
>
> *Tony* When you first saw it—Was it at head level?
>
> *Ray* Yeah. If I had—I was walking very fast and I was just about to—I must have been about two, maybe three, maybe two feet away. And it was staring me right in the face and I just had a, sort a, duck! And I got up and I swung around and I said, "What on earth was that? It's gone, it's gone!" And I went in.
>
> *Tony* You remember? It was gone?
>
> *Ray* It was gone. And I thought to myself, "Am I seeing things?" And I just went in the house and I said, "You won't believe what I

just saw!" And, of course she didn't believe me. [*laugh*] I don't
know. It's just another strange, strange thing. There's a string of
these strange things that's just *almost something there* but you can't
really prove it. It's really strange, strange.

Our predetermined schedule dictated that it was time for Tony
to try what he later described as being an *ideomotor* procedure.
He played soft music as he talked me gently into an even deeper
state of relaxation. He then used a methodology that he had
employed during the last session. I was asked to raise my *right*
index finger to answer *yes* and my *left* index finger to answer *no*.
The theory was that my subconscious mind, rather than my
conscious mind would respond automatically to questions demanding a yes or no answer.

In order to further distract my conscious mind, Tony had me
systematically subtract seven from numbers starting with number
200. He told me that he might cut in and ask me what number I
was at and then ask me to start adding numbers. To make sure that
I could do this accurately, I literally began whispering out my
arithmetic. While I did this, Tony continually touched my right
index finger and said, "This is yes," and then my left index finger
and said, "This is no." I soon found myself paying very little
attention to him as I tried my best to subtract accurately. Rather
than transcribe all of this data, I will list the questions that Tony
asked and how I responded to each enquiry.

Tony Were you programmed to forget the *big hall* incident? [Yes]

When Tony asked me this question I instantaneously found myself
in an emotional turmoil. I began breathing violently and became
nearly traumatized as my *right* index finger quickly popped up and
down. Tony calmed me down quickly and continued to probe my
mind.

Tony Is there a time that you will remember the *big hall* incident?
[Yes]

Again I experienced the same violent reaction as my right finger
snapped up. But this time, I could not be calmed down easily. Tony
finally accomplished this by getting my mind back on counting and
I began adding by twos.

Tony Do you know *when* you will remember? [Yes]

My reaction was even more violent as my right finger flew up. Tony rushed over to my side and rubbed my shoulder and back. He assured me that I would be all right and that he and Dave were right there with me. He then asked the next question.

Tony Was your visitor from another world? [Yes]

I began shivering all over and was breathing so hard that I had to start blowing the excess air out. Again Tony intervened with words of assurance and restored relative calmness.

Tony Later, can you write or draw a description of that vessel? [No]

I again experienced great difficulty in breathing as my left index finger hesitantly began shaking and then popped up. Later, when reviewing the tape, I could not and still do not understand why I answered *no*. Perhaps I never saw the outside of the vessel. I only remember a blur of lights over Dodge Court.

Tony then asked me if I remembered what happened [separate questions] 1,2,3, and 4 minutes after I reached the window of the *big hall* with the entity. Again I became very upset but in each case signified *yes*.

Tony . . . Four minutes after you reach the window? [Yes]

Ray Don't want to remember! Don't want to remember!

Tony Just relax. David and I are here. David and I are here.

Ray Don't want to remember! Don't want to remember! Don't want to remember!

Tony That's okay, that's okay.

The Night before the Scar

At this point, Tony decided right in the middle of my traumatic reaction to ask me the proverbial sixty-four thousand dollar question.

Tony Do you know what caused the *scar* on your right leg? Do you know? [*In a demanding tone*] Tell me quickly! [Yes]

I suddenly felt confronted by something totally alien and began literally pushing the heavy chair that I was sitting on backwards toward the wall! My right finger moved up and down as I pushed the chair back in sheer terror. Tony again came over to me and began rubbing my right shoulder trying to comfort me.

Tony You're in the room now with David and me! You're right here with David and me!

Ray I don't want to remember! I don't want to remember!

Tony You're right here with David and me.

Ray I don't want to remember! I don't want to remember! I don't want to remember! Don't want to remember! Don't want to remember!

Tony decided to continue to probe using the list of questions that he had put together without my knowledge.

Tony Did that *big hall* incident have anything to do with *The Wizard of Oz*? [No]

Tony Just relax, just relax, just relax. Just relax, just relax. All right. David and I are here. It's okay, I'm going to play some more music. It's very calming. I'm just going to turn the tape. . . . Just continue to subtract those numbers.

Tony reinforced the *ideomotor* procedure and then without warning snapped a question at me.

Tony Was the scar on your right leg caused by a physical exam? Answer quickly! [Yes]

As soon as I heard his question, I began literally shivering all over and once again was in an emotional turmoil.

Tony Just relax, just relax, just relax because the music will start in just a few seconds.

Ray Yes. [*deep sigh and heavy breathing*]

Tony Do you remember *how* that scar was caused? Quickly! Yes or no? [No]

A struggle between my fingers ensued and finally my left finger signified *No*. Later statements may have revealed why I could not remember. I may have not been allowed to *see*.

> *Tony* You said that you *can't* remember. But you can *try* to remember. If we could do a movie, could you pretend to remember? Just relax.

My breathing became even heavier and I found myself taking in great gulps of air.

> *Ray* I don't think I'd better! I don't think I'd better! I don't think I'd better!
>
> *Tony* Just relax. That's okay. *Why* do you think that you shouldn't?
>
> *Ray* I shouldn't remember!
>
> *Tony* You should not remember?
>
> *Ray* No!
>
> *Tony* Is it *time*?
>
> *Ray* No! I don't remember! I shouldn't remember! I don't know why I don't want to remember. I want to remember but I don't want to remember.
>
> *Tony* Will you be allowed to remember later?
>
> *Ray* [*I did not answer—breathing very heavily.*]
>
> *Tony* Will *they* allow you to remember this?
>
> *Ray* [*I did not answer—breathing heavily.*]
>
> *Tony* Just relax, just relax. You're doing very, very well.
>
> *Ray* Someday I'll know all, I'll know it all, I'll know it all!
>
> *Tony* How do you know that you'll know someday?
>
> *Ray* I don't know but someday I will.
>
> *Tony* Is this not the *time* to remember?

At this point I retorted with something that may be very significant. It seemed that Tony broke through my amnesia by using the term *they* which helped trigger my response.

> *Ray* *They* told me not to remember.
>
> *Tony* Say that again!

Again, I reacted violently. Something deep within my mind did not want me to go any further.

> *Ray* [*Barely can utter words*] They don't, the, *they* told me not to remember!
>
> *Tony* Who told you not to remember?
>
> *Ray* [*My mind evaded the question.*] Whoever. I don't know. I wanted to see them but I can't see them. They wouldn't let me.

Tony tried to no avail to elicit further information about *who* told me not to remember. He also tried unsuccessfully to discover the date on which the *scar* was inflicted. He was successful in having me relive a flashback that I had received regarding the night I may have received the *scar*. Again, it was such an emotional experience that sometimes I could hardly articulate.

> *Ray* I remember a night. . . . And I wondered if that was the night that, ah, before I noticed the *scar* on my leg. [*Fast, panicky voice*] The night I've been trying to remember for such a long time but couldn't! And I *remembered* [*whispered*] . . . I came back from vacation [August 14, 1988] and on Monday [August 15] and Tuesday [August 16] I, ah, really worked hard trying to bring that garden back into shape 'cause it was all full of weeds and I had to harvest and [*took a deep breath—getting harder to talk*] I had to go out that night [August 16] to talk about astronomy to [*breathlessly*] the Manchester Beach and Tennis Club. And, I went, and, ah, [*taking deep gulps of air now*] I went ah,—Everything went all right. I came back and, ah—I came back and, ah—Margaret was waiting for me and, ah, asked me if I wanted a cup of cocoa before I went to bed, you know? And, [*took a deep breath*] I thought, "Boy, am I going to sleep well tonight." I had just about had it. [*gulped down another deep breath*] And, ah— [*paused and voice lowered*] I went to bed and, ah— [*paused and began whispering*] And I had this, ah, real up-tight feeling and I thought—[*paused and let out deep breath*] "Don't tell me I'm not going to be able to sleep. I'm so tired. Why can't I sleep?" . . . And just a strange electriclike prickling up-tight feeling! [*voice gets louder*] Like something that's just about to happen but isn't going to happen. And I thought, "This is silly, I've got to get to sleep!" And I just tossed and turned. [*deep breath*] I looked at the clock and the clock was after 11 o'clock and I [*deep breath*] said, says, "I've got to get to sleep. Maybe if I got up and went some-

where else I could get to sleep." [*voiced lowered again*] And then, [*deep breath*] I remembered another night like that, that I couldn't get to sleep and I went out into the, ah, the den [downstairs livingroom] and I, all by myself, I brought my pillow and I went to sleep. And, ah, so maybe that's what I've got to do. I said, "No, this is silly—[*deep breath*]—I don't want to go out there—[*deep breath*]—in the [upstairs] den and sleep!" And midnight came and, ah, still couldn't sleep. [*breathing faster and voice panicky*] And I couldn't get to sleep. I couldn't understand it.

Dave Are you in the den now, Ray?

Ray No, I'm in my own—sleep.

Dave In your bed?

Ray And I—In my own bed and I thought . . . this reminds me of, ah, [*deep breath*] this *feeling* I felt when I relived those [little hall] episodes under hypnosis. "I wonder if they're going to come for me tonight?" I started even to laugh to myself. I says, "This is crazy! Don't start thinking like that."

My voice literally sounded drowsy as I continued to relive the eventful night.

Ray And one o'clock came and two o'clock came. And, I, ah said— "If you guys are really gonna come and get me, I wish you'd come and get me now cause I want to get to sleep. Come and get this over with!" And, ah, [*pause*] I must have gone to sleep because I don't remember three o'clock or four o'clock. I—don't remember— this—thing. [*whispering*] Just didn't remember it.

In fact, as mentioned, I did not remember this nor the dream about a *leg operation* until the flashbacks instigated by my wife's remark about sleep.

Tony Is it true that you don't know how it [the scar] got there? Yes or no?

I immediately choked up and could hardly force the answer out of my mouth to Tony.

Ray I, I think I know. That dream—That dream I had.

Tony What dream? Tell us about that dream. Just relax.

Ray The dream I had, you know? I, something was being done to me. I wanted to wake up. I wanted to see what was going on. I couldn't feel anything being done to me but I *knew* something was being done to me.

Tony Tell us about the dream.

Ray That *was* the dream! It was a crazy dream. Usually you dream that you *see* things. My dream was about I *couldn't see* things. But, I wanted to see things. And I tried to open my eyes and all I— [*pause*] I feel as if I'm being moved around, and—

Tony How were you moving around?

Ray I don't know. I feel as if I'm being moved around and I, I, I think I even opened my eyes but I—[*pause*] What's going on here? I can't move! I, I opened my eyes and I see *black!* I say, "What's going on?" And I wanta wake up! I wanta wake up! I wanta see what's going on! And I can't do that. And all of a sudden I wake up—[*pause*]—And the first thing that comes to my mind is— "THEY'RE OPERATING ON MY LEG!" And I say, "I *must* remember this!"

Tony *Why* did that come to your mind?

Ray [*with panicky voice*] I thought, "I *must* remember this because I might be dreaming about what happened when *they* put that— [*pause*]—*scar* on my leg. Maybe, maybe it was blocked from my mind but—Maybe I'm reliving this in the dream and I *must* remember! What can I do? Shall I put the Kleenex, shall I put the Kleenex box on the bureau? And then, when I ask myself in the morning, 'What's the Kleenex box doing on my bureau?' I'll say, the *dream*! I gotta write this down!

Tony How were they moving you around? What was your sensation? Were you carried? Were you being wheeled? Were you walking? Were you floating?

Ray [*panicky voice*] I don't know. I just felt something was happening to me and I, I got to know. "What's going on here? Why am I not *feeling* anything?" I mean, I *know* that something's being done but—And I want to know and, I—"I'll open my eyes and see!" And I opened my eyes but all I could see was *black!* It was a terrible nightmare 'cause I kept on struggling and struggling, trying to find out what was going on to—with me, and I—[*took deep breath*] I couldn't find out what was going on. And then, I, I wake up! And I, I, almost said out loud—"they're, they're operating, operating on my leg! I *must* remember, I *must* remember, I *must* remember! I've got to remember tomorrow morning. I've got to tell Dave, I've got to, I, I . . . Maybe I dreamed what happened that night! And I've *got* to remember this!" But the crazy thing is that, ah, I didn't remember the next morning.

Tony stepped in and using the *ideomotor* response procedure shot a quick question at me which took whatever was blocking my subconscious by surprise.

Tony Does your subconscious remember? Quickly! Yes or No?

My *right* index finger shot up and down and I was immediately filled with raw panic and began sobbing uncontrollably. Tony rushed over to me and caressed my shoulder and gently instructed me to relax but it didn't make any difference. I literally became hysterical.

Ray [*sobbing*] I don't want to remember! I don't want to remember! I can't remember!

Tony That's all right, just relax.

Ray [*sobbing*] I don't want to remember! I don't! Don't! Don't! [*now shouting*] Don't make me remember! Please don't!

Tony No, no. We won't.

Ray [*hysterically*] *Please* don't make me remember Don't, Don't! I don't want to remember!

It took Tony some time to calm me. He brought my mind's eye to a family vacation spot in New Hampshire and had me describe all the nice times we had experienced there. Slowly but surely I began to unwind.

Ray [*now whispering*] I don't want to remember. I don't want to remember.

As my voice began to trail off, it seems as if the *truth* of the matter may have leaked out inadvertently!

Ray I don't want to remember. I don't want to remember *much*. *Not supposed to remember.* [*pause*] Not supposed to remember. Not supposed to remember.

These last enigmatic words seemed to reflect my earlier statements that I had been *programmed* to forget these traumatic experiences!

Tony slowly but surely brought me out of hypnosis and back to my everyday world. My fingers were asleep. I rubbed them and stretched. I was amazed when he told me that I had been under hypnosis for about two hours! It took me a few minutes to join in the debriefing discussion. I just stared into space trying to remember and comprehend what I had just experienced. One lingering mental afterimage dominated all others. There were some things that I was not supposed to remember. For the time being, perhaps for good reasons, these memories were *forbidden* fruit.

I asked Dave Webb to write up his estimate of the situation based on his vast experience in this area. Although frustrated that the hypnosis sessions could not continue, he nonetheless complied.

> My experience tells me that you probably did have contacts possibly throughout your life, and that others in your family may have also. Normally, I would not reveal my ideas so early in an investigation. But clearly we are not conducting a normal investigation here and I see my role as advisor and confidant.

I respect David's opinion very much as do his peers in the field of UFO research. If I did have such contacts, I believe that I may have some kind of linkage with *The Andreasson Affair*. The entity that I encountered in the big hall at Dodge Court indicated that I had been chosen to do something significant for mankind. When Betty stood before the fiery Phoenix she was told that she had been chosen to show the world. Could it be possible that I have been chosen to record their message for mankind?

CHAPTER

Sixteen

The Message

As I came to this chapter, I feel totally inadequate to do it complete justice. Alien claims, technology, and operations are all part of their revelation to mankind. Such require analysis by a number of academic disciplines. These would include physical sciences, psychology, psychiatry, philosophy, sociology, anthropology, and even theology. I am merely a UFO investigator reporting on the results of my ten-year inquiry into this fascinating case. Thus I find it quite impossible to fully grasp and present resultant data and their implications except in a broad summarized fashion.

The original and complete relived and recorded accounts are lengthy, internally consistent, and logical unlike a dream. Many facets are consistent with other abductee experiences. No talented actress would be able to do what Betty does. Her unscripted descriptions flow out naturally and effortlessly. Betty is actually reliving in her mind's eye events that she really believes happened.

The following pages contain synopses based on these original hypnosis sessions taped between April 3, 1977 and May 24, 1988. They contain Betty's descriptions of encounters that took place between 1944 and 1988. Her experiences did not take place in a vacuum. They occurred against the backdrop of a number of interrelated events. A correlation will be made with these events as we now trace the evolution of *The Message* from its inception to its grand finale.

Part I—The Message

Betty Aho—Age 7

It has to be more than just coincidence that *both* Betty and Bob Luca were *selected* by *The Watchers* in the late 1930s or early 1940s. Research has shown that it was this period that the acceleration of the aliens' genetic program may have begun. Both had been *watched* prior to their first contact with the *beings*. Both were contacted during the summer months of 1944 and twenty-three years later both were abducted in 1967. Furthermore, their mutual abduction experience would be the common denominator that led to acquaintance and then marriage.

Bob was only five years old in 1944. Two aliens in a glowing domed disk-shaped object delivered their message to him as he sat paralyzed on a swing behind his house at Meriden, Connecticut.

> They say my name . . . inside my head. They say first that I shouldn't be afraid. . . . They told me that I can't remember. . . . It's not time. . . . When I'm older it will be time. They'll decide when. . . . It's for later . . . when I'm older. . . . These people are doing something that is going to be good for everybody. . . . That kind of *light* [UFO] has come to a lot of people . . . They visit other and they're going to visit other people . . . not just me. . . . They *know about your life when you get big*. . . . Some will *meet each other*. . . . They will have something in common. They will see something like I see now. It will be part of caring for what is to be. Many people would see this thing and in time they will meet each other. . . . In time the people in the light will be back and the people that have seen them before *will not be afraid* when they come back.

Little Betty Aho was innocently playing in a small hut when the buzzing marble-sized glowing ball entered and affixed itself between her eyes. She too received a message.

> They're calling my name. It sounds as if somebody jumped in my head. . . . I said, "Where are you?" And they said, "Right here." I said, "But I can't see you." And they said, "That's all right, we see you." They're like all talking together . . . saying the same thing [i.e., in unison] . . . "Wee little child." They said they've been watching me grow. . . . They are going to take me someplace but

not yet . . . something about five years or so. . . . It's coming to a time that I will know the *One*. . . . They said I'm coming along fine . . . that they're making certain things ready. . . . They're going to show me something . . . that everybody will be happy about . . . that everybody will learn something from. And they said people will understand . . . people that I tell . . . what they're going to show me. . . . They just want to look me over *from the inside*. . . . They tell me I'm going to be very happy soon . . . that I'm going to find the *One*. I will know the *One*. . . . I will feel the *One*. . . . I feel a little squiggly in my head . . . and they say . . . I would not remember for a long time. They said, "Just remember the *bee*." [Betty initially thought the glowing ball was a bee.]

Thus, the initial composite message given to Betty and Bob as children was only to be remembered later on in their adulthood. It was that the aliens, who know our future, had been selecting many people in the early 1940s for some unknown purpose. Those who were contacted would be used in some way in the future to help people understand that the aliens were doing something beneficial for mankind and to help people not to be afraid of the coming of the aliens. Betty was especially chosen to see the *One*. A hint of their genetics program is found in their cryptic comment that they wanted to look Betty over *from the inside*! Dr. Richard Neal, on the basis of his detailed studies of abduction cases, states that:

Initial blood samples, bone marrow aspirations and tissue samples are taken between ages 5 and 20. This would be the time frame for specific and early genetic studies on the chromosomes of abductees as a follow-up from another generation, with studies performed to see if a certain pattern is consistent within the particular family.[1]

At this point, one can only speculate as to *why* the aliens decided to both begin conditioning mankind and accelerating their longterm genetics engineering operations at this point in time. But what was happening on planet Earth in 1944 might have triggered these unearthly events.

In 1944, World War II was in full swing. Thousands of bombers, fighters, and rockets filled the skies of the European and Far Eastern war theaters. Wholesale destruction and the loss of millions of human lives must have presented a terrible sight to those who said they were the caretakers of all lifeforms on the earth.

During these terrible times, two highly significant events were occurring. One was taking place in Earth's air space and the other on its surface. I feel sure that each had an important bearing upon each other. The December 25, 1944 issue of *Newsweek* heralded the event in our skies by leaking the bare details of the appearance of unexplainable happenings to the American public.

The Silver Sphere Puzzle

Dispatches heavily censored by Supreme Headquarters revealed that American pilots have recently encountered a new phenomenon over Germany: silver-colored spheres resembling huge glittering Christmas tree ornaments . . . sometimes translucent, floating singly or in clusters.

These mysterious spheres, also witnessed by Betty during her encounters with the aliens were the so-called *foofighters*. As these alien devices monitored the war in the skies, the very *thoughts and intentions* of a highly classified operation by our scientists was also being monitored by the technology of *The Watchers*. It was called the *Manhattan Project* and was headed by top scientist, Dr. Vannevar Bush. He directed the efforts of a select group of scientists from many Allied countries in a race against time with the Germans to develop the Atomic Bomb. Ironically, Dr. Bush would soon be chosen to head the most highly classified operation in history. It was reportedly administered by an elite group selected by the President of the United States. The subject studied would be UFOs!

Thus, the first waves of modern UFO sightings began with the development, testing, and usage of the atomic bomb. For the first time in man's history, the awesome forces of atomic energy were to be unleashed. Man now would have the power to destroy not only himself but all lifeforms on the earth. The aliens' response was swift and well organized.

First, their monitoring operation was dramatically expanded. Waves of UFO sightings followed World War II. One of the aliens' specific interests was in the area of atomic weaponry. Documents released via the Freedom of Information Act reveal the grave concern of our military as the aerial objects showed up over sensitive installations such as the Los Alamos Atomic Energy

Commission Project. In January 1949, Eustis L. Poland, Colonel, US Army Intelligence (G-2) sent a memo on behalf of the Commanding General of the Fourth Army at Houston, Texas, to the Director of Army Intelligence at the Pentagon:

> Agencies in New Mexico are greatly concerned over these phenomena. . . . It is felt these incidents are of such great importance, especially as they are occurring in the vicinity of sensitive installations, that a scientific board be sent to this locality to study the situation with a view of arriving at a solution of this extraordinary phenomena with the least practicable delay.[2]

Second, the aliens began an accelerated program that centered on the reproductive processes of Man and his fellow lifeforms on earth. *Why?*

Betty Aho—Age 12

Five years later in 1949, the aliens, true to their word, contacted Betty by the same means. By this time the huge UFO waves of 1946 and 1947 had come and gone. The crash of a UFO and its dead occupants at Roswell, New Mexico in July of 1947 had instigated the formation of the aforementioned group headed by Dr. Vannevar Bush. The Air Force's Projects *Sign* and *Grudge* simultaneously collected UFO sighting data for this group and supporting agencies while at the same time debunking the subject to the public to avoid panic and to protect national security. But in the woods of Westminster, Massachusetts, a little girl had communion with the very forces that the major governments of the world were trying desperately to deal with!

> There is someone speaking in my head. . . . It's the same voice . . . said the time has come and just be still. . . . They're checking and they're saying *another year.* . . . They said, "She's got another year." . . . They said I will learn about the *One.* . . . They said they are preparing things for me to see. . . . They are all saying the same thing [i.e., in unison]. Then after, they tell me to stand up and I won't remember. And they're telling me to go up by the hole [where she had set an animal trap] and bend over and to look in and that I won't remember for a long time yet.

What did the aliens mean when they told Betty Aho that they were *checking her* and that she *had another year* to wait before they would take her with them? As mentioned, Betty was twelve years of age. In retrospect, it is now obvious that their reason for waiting longer was *sexual* in nature. Betty had not quite begun an important event in her life—*puberty*!

> During infancy and childhood the immature egg cells exist as primary *oocytes* numbering 2 million at birth, but reduced by age 21 to 300,000. The ripening of the primary oocytes begins at puberty, usually between ages 9 and 17 (the average is 12.5 years). Like the male, at puberty the female child becomes an adolescent. . . . The first menstrual flow, or period, marks the *beginning of a female's reproductive life.*[3]

Betty Aho—Age 13

By 1950, both the United States and Russia had accumulated large stockpiles of nuclear weapons. Aboveground and atmospheric tests of increasingly powerful atomic bombs were routine occurrences. The Korean War broke out and the fear that some incident or accident might upset the precarious balance of power between the Soviets and the United States had become a dominant factor in world affairs. Both the United States and Russia were racing each other to produce an even more fearsome atomic weapon—the *hydrogen bomb*! *The Watchers* continued their complex programs of surveillance and genetics.

During 1950, Betty Aho was thirteen years old and a real young lady in the fullest sense of the word. She was now *physically* ready for her first abduction by the aliens. During this abduction Betty was given a specific *object lesson* for mankind prior to her mysterious visit to the *One*. She was shown a number of glass or icelike exact representations of animals and plants which momentarily *became alive* when she was allowed to touch them.

> And I'm reaching out to touch a butterfly and when I did, it's fantastic! It's beautiful! There's all color coming into the butterfly now, and it's flying around and around. When I touched it, it got color and lived and it's flying.

Then, something just as fantastic occurred as Betty watched the butterfly flutter about in amazement.

Oh, it's stopped. Its color is going and it's fading into a tiny speck of light, like a tiny speck of light. Then it goes back into the ice-form of that butterfly. That was amazing!

The very same thing happened when she touched a model of a flower. I specifically have mentioned this particular incident because of what the aliens said to Betty about it.

I asked him—"What's happening?" He says, "This is for you to remember so *mankind will understand.*" And I said, "But why did it turn color and fly away when I touched it?" He told me that I will see when I get *home.* He said, "*Home* is where the *One* is."

What can we make of this incredible object lesson? Through it, the aliens might be telling us that they were capable of both designing and giving life to the forms of life that they were responsible to maintain on earth.

After Betty returned from seeing the *One* in the world of light, she experienced yet another facet of what Dr. Neal calls the *Teenage Phase*.

During this time, some kind of implant is inserted so that the individual can be followed at a future date—after further analysis of samples obtained by the alien researchers.[4]

Betty's teenage abduction was true to form. As mentioned, the aliens removed Betty's eye. They then inserted what appeared to be a glass pea-sized object and one or more tiny glasslike slivers into her head cavity with two long, glowing needles. She could feel the needles moving around inside. After her eye was replaced, Betty was then subjected to what seemed to be an *acceptance test* of the implanted devices. The aliens also performed a number of operations on Betty's body with needlelike probes. Suffice it to say, these instruments were most likely used to obtain further samples from Betty's body including *ova*! This was not recognized during our investigation in 1980. Now, in retrospect, we see that step-by-step Betty was being used to show us how, and later why, the aliens were carrying out their genetic operations. Concerning the *Pre-Adolescent* and *Teenage Phases,* Dr. Neal writes that:

Some of the individuals may be abducted again, possibly due to a failed implant or for re-confirmation of certain genetic information.[5]

As we know, Betty was indeed abducted again in 1967 at age thirty but before that event she had a 1961 encounter with an alien being in the woods behind her house at Westminster, Massachusetts. Again, the alien communicated with Betty and through Betty, added yet another dimension to their slowly evolving message to mankind.

The *being* seemed to make a direct connection between the aliens' intervention in earthly affairs and Betty's Christian faith. This has disturbed both reader and researcher alike. It has been suggested that either the aliens were accommodating Betty's faith to make them acceptable to her or that Betty's subconscious somehow was superimposing her belief system upon her UFO experiences. The other alternative, of course, is that there is a *real connection*. I must leave that to the reader to decide but have no choice except to include what the alien reportedly told Betty during this intriguing encounter.

Betty Andreasson—Age 24

Betty, if you will recall, was doing housework and heard a strange sound that drew her out of the house to climb an adjoining wooded hill. There, she came face to face with one of the typical dwarf-sized alien beings who told her the following.

> He has been sent and I am not to fear. The Lord is with me and not to be afraid. . . . They are pleased because I have accepted [Christianity] on my own. . . . I am to go through many things and that love will show me the answers because I have given my heart over to love the Son. . . . Many things shall be revealed to me. Things that I have not seen . . . ears have not heard. . . . I shall suffer many things . . . but will overcome them through the Son. . . . I have been *watched* since my beginning. I shall grow naturally and my faith in the Light will bring many others to the Light and Salvation because many will understand and see. . . . The *negative voices* don't like it. . . . [They] are against man . . . bad angels that wanted to devour man . . . hurt man . . . destroy man . . . because they are jealous . . . of the love that is upon man. . . . Telling me strange things . . . I don't know what they're about. . . . That for every place there is an existence. . . . That every thing has been formed to unite. . . . [He says] Jesus is with me . . . that I will understand as time goes by . . . for me

not to be anxious. . . . They want me to grow and live
naturally . . . that I am blessed and that I will forget and I am
now to go back to my house and I will not remember. . . . He
says, "Peace be with you as it is."

Needless to say, these are astounding and thought-provoking words
if this event actually took place exactly as reported. Yet stranger
things were in store for Betty when she was abducted by the aliens
from her home in South Ashburnham six years later.

Betty Andreasson—Age 30

The year 1967 was significant in the history of ufology. A huge
UFO wave, public reaction, and Congressional UFO Hearings in
1966 sparked by then-Congressman Gerald Ford, had resulted and
government taking drastic measures to curb public interest and
alarm. The hearings resulted in the Air Force contracting the
University of Colorado to perform an *alleged* independent study of
UFOs to assuage public and congressional outcry. I served as an
Early Warning Coordinator, relaying and co-investigating Massachusetts UFO reports, for this project, which was headed by
well-known physicist Dr. Edward U. Condon. However, the
so-called Condon Study turned out to be a double ploy to collect
additional UFO data from the public on the one hand and to
whitewash the reality of UFOs on the other. The Condon Study
was in full swing in 1967.

Reportedly, Dr. Condon helped the government put the kiss of
death on civilian interest in UFOs in exchange for his past record
being cleared from national security problems he had incurred with
the House Un-American Activities Committee during the McCarthy and Nixon witch-hunts that had begun in 1947. The so-called
Condon Report's marriage with government UFO policy was
exposed by *Look* magazine[6] and the book *UFOs—Yes![7]* authored by
Condon's co-principal investigator, Dr. David R. Saunders, professor of psychology at the University of Colorado. Civilian scientists
studying the problem were outraged. Of interest is the violent and
emotional outrage of my correspondent, Greece's most respected
scientist, Dr. Paul Santorini. Santorini, a colleague of Einstein and
one who had been officially involved in Greek UFO investigations,
wrote the following to me when Dr. Condon died in 1974:

UFOs are a scientific certainty, but it is a pity that many
authorities and most of the official "scientists" are too stupid to

admit facts that they are not in a position to interpret otherwise.

My age allows me not to be ashamed to express my sincere satisfaction at the news of Dr. Condon's death: it is a pity that an eminent scientist of his level blindly executed orders to back with his name a "Report" that constitutes a scientific shame. But, I understand, this was done to please some authorities unhappy with his "securities" affairs.[8]

I mention the Condon Report and its background at this juncture to give the reader some perspective as to what lengths the government was willing to go in order to keep the truth about UFOs from the public eye. This report was just one facet of the government's disinformation policy which was enhanced by the CIA's Psychological Strategy Board in the early 1950s.

In a document released to UFO researchers via the Freedom of Information Act, a memorandum to Walter Bedell Smith, the Director of the CIA, from H. Marshall Chadwell, the Assistant Director of its Office of Scientific Intelligence, stated that:

> "Flying Saucers" pose two elements of danger which have national security implications. The first involves mass psychological considerations and the second concerns the vulnerability of the United States to air attack.[9]

The memorandum recommended:

> That the Director of Central Intelligence advise the National Security Council of the implications of the "Flying Saucer" problem. . . . That the Director, Central Intelligence Agency discuss this subject with the Psychological Strategy Board. . . . That Central Intelligence Agency with the cooperation of the Psychological Strategy Board develop and recommend for adoption by the National Security Council a policy of public information which *will minimize concern and possible panic resulting from the numerous sightings of unidentified flying objects.*[10]

I feel reasonably sure that in 1952, world governments did not have an inkling of the *real mission* of the powers behind the UFOs. Their main concern was the intrusion of sovereign airspace by unknown vehicles which took an inordinate interest in our development of atomic energy and the location of stored and deployed atomic weapons. However, by 1967 the major world governments must have known about the abductions and genetic operations upon their citizenry.

The Condon Report may have dismissed UFOs but the UFOs were not listening. The year 1967 brought scores of unexplained reports to my attention as Massachusetts Director of a Subcommittee for the National Investigations Committee on Aerial Phenomena (NICAP). At that time I did not have the vaguest notion of Betty's abduction from her home at South Ashburnham. However, there were many sightings all around the perimeter of her hometown. Many of the domed disks and cylindrical objects observed at close range caused electrical interference with automobile ignition systems, radios, and television, and even area power failures. A former Coast Guard pilot and owner of a small airport, awakened by a humming sound, went outside to be confronted by a domed disk manned by two small humanoid figures. Towns all around Betty's hometown reported oval objects hovering over freshwater ponds in the area. In the adjoining town of Leominster, a wife watched helplessly as a hovering oval object paralyzed and pinned her husband to the outside frame of their car. Just one week before this occurred, Betty Andreasson was abducted from the adjoining town of South Ashburnham.

Part of Betty's 1967 abduction experience falls into the category that Dr. Neal has labeled the *Adult Stage*. He writes that:

> The pattern we are seeing at the present seems to reveal abductees undergoing some form of ongoing genetic exploitation, implementation or manipulation, such as genetic coding. This is where we see the most consistent, most documented procedures of the abduction phenomenon, such as artificial insemination techniques—continued on some abductees throughout their reproductive years.[11]

Indeed, during Betty's first *adult* abduction, a long needle was pushed into her navel. She was specifically told that she was being *measured for procreation*.

> I can feel them moving that thing around in my stomach. . . . They've stopped. [*very heavy breathing*] And he's putting his hand on my head. [*sighs, heavy breathing*] Now he's talking with them about something—about something missing, missing . . . missing parts or something, I think he's saying. Oh! He's pushing that needle again . . . around, feeling things. . . . "I don't like this!"

They're looking at me. They're saying something about some kind
of test. "I don't want any more tests! Get this thing out of me!"

I recently questioned Betty about this segment of her 1967
experience in light of what we now know about the aliens' genetics
program. She informed me that several months after her seventh
and last child [Cindy] was born, on December 9, 1963, she became
pregnant again. During her gynecological exam, a Pap test indicated that she probably had cancer of the cervix. She was told that
unless drastic measures were taken, the cancer could spread fast.
Under the advice of her physician, Betty tearfully allowed the fetus
to be aborted and she had a *hysterectomy*. Is it any wonder that the
aliens talked about "missing parts?"

During the 1967 abduction, the aliens subjected Betty to other
tests and removed a tiny BB-sized implant through her nose.
However, throughout all of her UFO experiences, Betty was much
more to the aliens than a test subject or depository of genetic
material. From the onset, she was being spoon-fed information—a
message—to "show mankind." After the examinations, Betty was
taken by the spacecraft to an unknown world to what would be the
apex of her experience.

After being placed in a tank of liquid to protect her from
harmful effects during transit, the spacecraft landed and abutted
itself to a cavelike entrance hewn out of solid rock. Passing through
this entrance, Betty, floating along between two alien entities,
entered a huge unearthly place. The trio floated above a trestlelike
track high in the sky. Below, Betty saw distant domelike buildings,
water, vegetation, and a strange flying craft. She also passed over a
pyramidlike structure with a sculptured head affixed to its apex.

It looked sort of like an Egyptian head, and it had like a, you
know, how they wear those hats?

I am digressing for a moment to mention this because Betty sees a
striking similarity between the *pyramid* and *head* and some anomalous formations discovered on the surface of Mars reported at a
July 7, 1988, Washington, D.C. press conference. Ex-astronaut
Brian O'Leary told reporters that the origin of what appears to be
a Martian *face* is sufficiently indeterminate to warrant a closer look.
Computer enhancement of the photographs taken during NASA's
1976 Viking mission indicate that the structures may be *artificial*.

Further information about these formations can be found in the May 16, 1988 copy of the prestigious journal, *Applied Optics* and in a recent book entitled *The Monuments of Mars*.[12] But, let's get back to Betty.

As Betty traveled between her two abductors along the high trestle, she entered a beautiful crystalline structure to witness a holographiclike presentation of the death and rebirth of the *Phoenix*. After this astonishing object lesson, Betty heard a thundering chorus of voices blended together as one mighty voice which addressed her by name and asked her a question.

> *Voice* You have seen and you have heard. Do you understand?
>
> *Betty* No, I don't understand what this is all about, why I'm even here.
>
> *Voice* I have *chosen* you.
>
> *Betty* For what have you chosen me?
>
> *Voice* I have chosen you *to show the world*.

The *voice*, like the alien of the 1961 encounter, seemed to be intimately familiar with Betty's Christian faith and identified itself with it. The investigators, including myself, looked at each other incredulously as Betty relived this segment of her 1967 abduction. The 1961 message with its religious connotation was unknown to us during the Phase I investigation so this was our first confrontation with the seemingly *spiritual* side of the aliens' message. None of us knew just what to make of it. The Phoenix experience was perhaps the most traumatic facet of Betty's 1967 abduction experience. I have seen men with no strong religious background come to the point of tears when listening to a playback of the tape recording of this particular aspect of *The Andreasson Affair*.

After the literally overpowering Phoenix experience, Betty was returned to the spaceship and returned home. Just before disembarking, the alien in charge gave Betty a debriefing which again added to the overall message being given to mankind through Betty.

> And he says, "Child, you must forget for awhile.". . . He says my
> race won't believe me until much time has passed, our
> time. . . . They say they love the human race. They have come to
> help the human race. . . . And unless man will not accept, he will
> not be saved. He will not live. All things have been planned. Love

is the greatest of all. They do not want to hurt anybody. But, because of great love . . . they cannot let man continue in the footsteps that he is going. It is better to lose some than all. They have technology man can use. It is through the spirit but men will not search out that portion. . . . Man is not made of just flesh and blood. . . . He keeps telling me of different things. Of what is going to take place, what is going to happen. They are going to come to the earth. Man is going to fear because of it. . . . He says that he had had others here and many others have locked within their minds, secrets. And he is locking within my mind certain secrets. *And they will be revealed only when the time is right.*

As I write this book, it has been over twenty-one years since Quazgaa uttered these words. Apparently *now* the time is *right* for all the secrets hidden in Betty's mind over the Years are rushing through the floodgates of her subconscious mind as she is finally being allowed to remember her post-1967 UFO encounters and abductions!

Betty Andreasson—Age 36

The year 1973 brought the largest UFO wave in recorded history. In addition, there were more reports of humanoid creatures seen with UFOs than in any other period since a similar wave in 1954. To UFO researchers, 1973 has become known as *The Year of the Humanoids*. Most probably, what witnesses were observing was the conscious tip of a huge number of abductions that now lay buried deep within the subconscious minds of abductees. This sudden step-up in the aliens' operations coincided with their decision to finally tell Betty *why* they needed to perform genetic operations on human beings. Their reason lay dormant in Betty's mind until the *appointed time* fourteen years later.

If you will remember, during the first segment of Betty's 1973 abduction, she had been shocked at the sight of two *fetuses* being taken from *the woman*. She had watched in horror as the aliens pushed long needles into one of the fetuses' head and ears prior to plunging it into a tank of liquid connected to strange apparatus. Let's go back and listen in on the conversation that erupted at that time.

> *Betty* Ohhhhh! They're telling me they *have* to do this. And I'm saying—"*Why* do you have to do such a terrible thing?" And one of

them is saying—"We *have* to because as time goes by, *Mankind will become sterile*. They will not be able to produce because of the pollutions of the lands and the waters and the air [*sighs deeply*] and the bacteria and the terrible things that are on the earth!

All along the aliens had been telling Betty that they were preparing something *good* for mankind. This was certainly the dark side of the *message* of *The Watchers*. What was the bright side? I sat down and carefully reviewed all that the aliens had told Betty since their first known encounter in 1944 right up through her more recent experiences in the 1970s and '80s. Then it struck me. The message had been there all along but had not become obvious to me at all until it was juxtaposed against the stark background of the impending *extinction of Man*! Betty's next abduction experiences would be the last in a series of powerful object lessons designed to proclaim the bright side of the aliens' message. In not recognizing it, I was guilty of something that *The Watcher* called Quazgaa had told Betty during her debriefing in 1967, namely—*It is through the spirit but Man will not seek out that portion*!

More about this later, but first, let us continue our chronological survey of Betty's encounters and the unfolding *message* of the aliens.

Betty Andreasson—Age 38

The year of Betty's next encounter with the alien entitities, 1975, also brought intensified UFO interest in areas where atomic weapons were stored and deployed. Alien interest in atomic energy development can be traced back to the early years of modern UFO history. I believe that their interest is directly tied to their concern about the survival of mankind on this planet. A formerly classified SECRET document, dated January 2, 1952 addressed to General Samford, Director of Air Force Intelligence, describes the

> . . . *persistent* [italics mine] reports of unusual flying objects over parts of the United States, particularly the East and West coast, *and in the vicinity of atomic energy production and testing facilities*. [italics mine][13]

In 1966, while working within the Minuteman Program Office at GTE, I was able to find out, in part, what was going on at

Minuteman sites during UFO visitations. I met active and former Minuteman Launch Control Officers and Site Technicians who told me that Minuteman launch control equipment was being disrupted during the UFO sightings over the missile sites on Strategic Command Bases. GTE had designed, produced, and installed this equipment. It was designed to operate under nuclear attack. However, no one told the UFOs this and they could disable the capability of Minuteman Launch Control facilities with ease. There was no defense. Russian sites, I'm sure, were experiencing the same frustrations.

Although these "events," as they were surreptitiously called, were known among a few researchers with inside information, they did not get media attention. However, when I leaked data to the respected newspaper the *Christian Science Monitor,* all hell let loose at the Pentagon's public information office on UFOs. The *Christian Science Monitor* had investigated my claims and published a front page story worldwide. GTE was phoned by both the Strategic Air Command and the Pentagon. I received orders from GTE via the Pentagon to cease and desist releasing such information or the Air Force would send an official letter of displeasure to GTE about the incident. It could have meant losing my security clearance and/or my position so I behaved myself for the time being!

However, in October and November 1975, UFO sightings around Strategic Air Command Base Atomic Weapons Storage Areas and atomic-weapon tipped Minuteman missiles became so plentiful that leaks to the press came from every direction. It was national news. On some nights, a number of bases were visited simultaneously. Documents retrieved through the FOIA give a running commentary of the radar visual sightings and the futile attempts of ground strike teams, light aircraft, and F-106 jet interceptors to down the celestial intruders! The books *Clear Intent*[14] and *Above Top Secret*[15] provide excellent documentation of these and many other events.

It was against this background of significant UFO events that Betty Andreasson had her next encounter with *The Watchers.* The nighttime bedroom visitation was brief but it too was significant. In essence, Betty was told:

> It is *now time.* . . . They're telling me . . . very soon, I will *begin* to remember. . . . They're setting things in motion.

Betty also received portents of tragedy concerning what turned out to be marital problems, a divorce, and the death of two sons. But

1975 was the pivotal point of her hitherto forgotten experiences. Things *were* set in motion which resulted in the Phase I and II investigations and the writing and publication of *The Andreasson Affair* and its sequel *The Andreasson Affair—Phase Two*!

Betty Andreasson—Age 39

Betty's brief encounter with one of *The Watchers* in 1976 as she was in the process of dressing for an anniversary party was also brief. The message was personal. Simply, she was told that she had gone through enough, things were going to change and there would be hardship in it. As we know now, her problem-husband walked out of her life that very night as things were probably even then being set in motion for her to meet and later marry abductee Bob Luca. But there is a message to us as well in these last two brief encounters. It is that *The Watchers*, true to their name, are able to know and control both humans and their destinies to some extent. This, of course, is very disconcerting. However, their abilities do have limitations as we learned from Betty's next encounter with *The Watchers*.

Betty Andreasson—Age 40

Betty had two brief but traumatic encounters in 1977. The first occurred in the form of an interruption of a telephone call with Bob Luca, who had just been interrogated by my investigators about his conscious UFO sighting in 1967. Both Betty and Bob heard the angry foreign language which sounded like a mad buzzing hornet. Betty believed she understood telepathically that the voice or voices said something like "it is finished" or "it is done." The voices sounded very angry. Later on that night, Betty and her children were literally bombarded by loud noises and balls of light just after Betty was confronted once again by one of *The Watchers* who told her that her two sons were about to be killed and that they could not intercede. She was assured that it would turn out all right and that her faith would see them all through the terrible ordeal. Betty could not consciously remember the visitation part of the event and the terrible message about her sons until recently under hypnosis, but her subconscious memory filled her with a great dread of something terrible about to happen. As mentioned, she visited and shared her fears with me just prior to her sons' deaths in an automobile accident. From this experience we learn that although the aliens have some ability to control time and foresee some future events, they are not allowed to intercede in some matters. The whole question of time and time travel is a philosophical quagmire of paradoxes which cannot be covered in this book. Suffice it to say that *The Watchers* claim that our time is *localized* and they are not bound by such a limitation. To them, the past, present, and future are *now*!

Bob and Betty experienced a number of poltergeist and other anomalous events from time to time. In March of 1978, Betty, Bob, and Betty's daughter, Cindy, sighted three triangular and one spherical craft from their car while driving along Route 86 in Connecticut. However, seven months later, both Betty and Bob would share a new kind of abduction experience that would shed further light on the *bright* side of *The Watchers'* message to mankind.

Betty Andreasson—Age 41

In 1978, Betty and Bob saw themselves *leave their bodies behind* at their home in Meridan, Connecticut just after being startled by a dull whirring sound over the rooftop of their bedroom. Their shared OBE was designed to strengthen past object lessons already experienced by Betty and which served to undergird the aliens' revelation that—*"Man is not made of just flesh and blood."* If we go all the way back to *The Watchers'* first communications to Betty, we can see the genesis of this part of their message when they told this little child that she was being prepared to meet the *One*. Their *physical* interest in Betty always seemed to be a secondary matter. The chief reason for teenager Betty Aho's abduction was for her to enter the *Great Door* to meet the *One*. In order to do this, she had to undergo an OBE. In this state, although obviously located in another plane of existence, she retained a bodily appearance identical to the one she left behind. Although she was not allowed to verbally describe her visit, a detailed study of Near Death Experiences (NDEs) seem to indicate that her visit *home* to the *world of light* was identical to the accounts given by persons who have had an NDE. Thus, from the very beginning, the very message content of the aliens was *paraphysical* in nature.

Glimpses of this concept are also seen in the religious or spiritual content of Betty's contact with the alien in the woods in

1961. When we come to Betty's first abduction as an adult in 1967, we also find that the *physical* interest in Betty, although obviously important, was not the primary reason for her abduction. The climax of her experience was the Phoenix. During this incredible confrontation, Betty was told in no uncertain terms by a thundering chorus of voices that she had been *chosen to show the world*. But the fiery death and rebirth of the Phoenix accomplished something else. It portrayed an overpowering object lesson of immortality. Betty's teenage visit to what *The Watchers* referred to as *home* implies that this indescribable *world of light* was the place of her origin. That she could not enter it in her *physical* body obviously tells us that *home* exists on another plane of existence. Betty was told that *home* was going to be experienced by everybody and that the *Great Door* ultimately would be available to all. Thus, Betty's visit to the *One*, its striking similarity to NDEs, and the *Phoenix* symbol of immortality combine to give us the bright side of the *message* to mankind. *The Watchers* seem to be telling us that Man's true essence can coexist in more than one plane, not only in this life but in the next. Their message also implies that Man, in some form, may have preexisted in the *world of light* prior to being born into the plane of existence which we call *life*. The place called *home* is both the origin and destination of Man's true essence: *"Man is not made of just flesh and blood!"*

Betty and Bob's 1978 abduction accentuated and added to the bright side of *The Watchers'* message. Both were taken out of their bodies. Their physical bodies were left behind but at first, their *other selves* looked identical to the inanimate shells they had vacated. They could see each other, feel each other, and even cling to each other as they were swept upwards by technology or power beyond our ken! They were just as real in this interim plane of existence as they had been back on earth. But, the plaster, wooden beams, and shingles of their house at Meridan were like some ghostly mirage as their *other bodies* passed through them as if they did not exist! But this state of coexistence with and recognition of two existences did not last long. Another amazing transformation of their so-called bodies took place.

Betty and Bob were engulfed by a swirling multicolored mist. Concurrently their bodily features began to lose their natural color. Both first became like whitish-gray ghosts of themselves and then it happened. Betty described the awesome sight as she watched the unbelievable unfold as a hypnotized *observer* watching a pretend *television set*.

And she's [i.e., Betty] starting to come into golden color, and as she does, *all her features are disappearing* and her whole body looks like it's becoming *light*!

Immediately upon this transformation, Betty was greeted by similar human *forms of golden light*. The huge circular domed construction she found herself in was also filled with a golden aura. She had lost track of Bob but she concurrently observed both the small gray-skinned *Watchers* and three family members being operated upon on tables on a lower floor. Wherever she was and whatever form she was in, she still was able to see both *The Watchers* and human beings. All three were able to coexist in this huge round craft or area with sections that rotated in opposite directions.

As soon as Betty's glowing body of gold light merged with others of similar description, she completely lost track of herself. One would think that at this point that the high strangeness factor of her experience had peaked but even more unimaginable happenings were about to unfold.

Betty watched in amazement as the group of human light forms seemed to participate in what appeared to be a joyful game or highly animated ritual. During this activity, now forgetful that she was a member of the group she was observing, she watched as the light-beings floated about a giant glowing coil of circular bars of light that seemed to energize their bodies on contact. Then, another inconceivable transfiguration of the human light forms took place before Betty's wondering eyes. The human light forms floated up to and leaned back against square metallic plates which were connected to long straps of light.

Oh my word! Is that weird! On my word! . . . Those beings just seem to roll into a *ball* of bright light and roll over that strap! Just rolled and *consumed* the strap as it went down and came down to the floor there. And there's a *ball of light* just sitting there!

This was another one of *The Watchers'* series of object lessons for mankind through Betty to demonstrate Man's paraphysical nature. Betty's warm living complex body of flesh and blood was left behind in the comfort of her home. She was put through an ongoing metamorphosis during an OBE that reduced her consciousness to a small glowing ball of light energy! It is quite conceivable that each one of these balls of vibrant light energy represent the ultimate essence of Man—his *Soul*!

In a moment, the ball of light changed back into the human forms of light again. They then engaged in a seemingly illogical ritual that involved a number of geometrically shaped objects before lining up and parading through a *door.* As they passed through the door, each took on ghostlike human features once again. Betty, watching on the hypnotically produced *television set,* was shocked to realize that she had been one of the light forms in this celestial charade. Perhaps it is of significance that her companions were multiracial in appearance. *The Watchers'* message was for *all!*

We don't know how Betty and Bob were returned to their so-called *physical* bodies at their home in Meriden, Connecticut, because at that moment, the experience was so traumatic that Betty slipped from a participant to an observer. Bob stepped in and brought her out of hypnosis to prevent undue stress and anxiety. However, just prior to his doing this Betty was met and escorted to the exit of the huge revolving ship by several enigmatic entities that she had met before after her visit to the *One.* At that time they had escorted her back through the *Great Door* to her *physical* body which stood at its entrance. I refer, of course, to those whom Betty describes as: *"men in white robes with white hair!"*

Who are these strange entities with human bodies who also are capable of interplane travel? They have been seen on earth accompanied by *The Watchers* and they have been reported by witnesses who have been returned to their *physical* bodies after an NDE.

Suffice it to say that *The Watchers* seem to have used this particular experience to underscore their determination to show Man that there is a paraphysical or spiritual side of life that he has basically ignored. It was an amplified echo of what Quazgaa had told Betty just prior to leaving the UFO during her 1967 abduction experience.

> They have technology that Man could use. . . . It is through the spirit. . . . If Man will just study nature itself, he will find many of the answers. . . . Man will find them through the spirit. Man is not made of just flesh and blood.

If Betty's experiences are truly grounded in reality, then Man's body of flesh and blood now existing in what *The Watchers* call localized time, is vastly more complex than anyone could ever have imagined. Our bodies of intricate living protoplasm would be a mere shadow of our true natures and abilities. Just as incredible would be the fact that *The Watchers* have the supernaturallike power to transform it at will by a technology that is paraphysical in nature.

This would become even more apparent during Betty's next abduction. Although Betty has vague memories of bedroom encounters in 1981, 1982, and 1984 [see Appendix A], the next abduction took place in 1986 from her trailer at Higganum, Connecticut.

Betty (Andreasson) Luca—Age 49

This particular encounter, if you will recall, took place while Betty was reading her Bible on the sofa. Again, the same dull whirring sound was heard that had preceded her dual OBE and abduction with Bob. Instantly, she became paralyzed from head to foot as a *Watcher* materialized by the sofa. When he placed a small box by her on the couch, she immediately was out of her body looking at herself lying there. When she hesitantly reached out her hand to touch her physical body, she gasped in amazement when her hand passed right through it! The OBE seemed to be instigated by the box. Their transportation also seemed to be initiated by an instrument that *The Watcher* removed from his belt which caused a shower of sparkly light to engulf both of them. Betty next found herself floating above an area with an utterly strange landscape that had no counterpart in reality. She then floated over a vast area with a horizon that stretched to infinity. It was carpeted with crystal spheres as far as the eye could see.

Suddenly the shadow of a huge flying bird whisked along the ground below. A shower of specks of light prefaced a rumbling sound. The spheres on the ground began to move as if they had come to life. Concurrently, a loud thunderous voice called to Betty. It reassured her guilty conscience about the abortion of her eighth child for medical reasons.

Her abductors again told her that they were caretakers of the forms that life had taken on our planet. They assured her that their abductions of men and women were for good reasons. It was being done to monitor environmental effects on the body and to achieve the restoration of the human form. Again they stressed, perhaps for the very last time, that the balance of nature on earth was in jeopardy.

The Watchers have delivered their Message to mankind through Betty. Betty has apparently fulfilled her part of an intricate plan to condition Man for what is coming upon the earth. What can we make of all of this? I will give my personal thoughts on the matter in the epilogue. But as far as the basic meaning of the Message goes, it is provocative, yet straightforward.

Betty's mentors have told us that they have always coexisted with Man and are genetically related. They have identified themselves as caretakers of the forms of life that have developed on earth. Over their existence, they have conducted a longterm genetics program to prolong and improve life on this planet. Their female sex have developed gynecological deficiencies requiring the use of human surrogate mothers for the reproduction of hybrid offspring.

The reason given for the sudden acceleration of their genetics program was that Man was going to become sterile. His many-faceted pollution of the environment was out of control. It would lead to the death of life on this planet. Therefore, steps were being taken to collect and preserve earth's lifeforms for existence elsewhere.

One of the most awe-inspiring aspects of their message was a demonstration of their paraphysical nature and its accommodation in their technology. Concurrently, they also demonstrated that Man too is more than flesh and blood. Death and physical extinction was not the end. His true essence would continue to live on in places beyond his limited comprehension.

Several mysteries, however, still remain unexplained. Who are the mysterious tall, robed, human-appearing figures that are involved in UFO and Near Death Experiences? Are they our original ancestors from somewhere else in this vast universe? What is the complete meaning behind the *Great Door* being opened and available to all of Mankind? When will all abductees meet with each other? When will they be used to help people not to be afraid when *The Watchers* appear overtly to mankind.

Apparently, the answers to these provocative questions are not meant to be known at this time. But, whatever the future may hold, *The Watchers* have promised that it will be a happy occasion—Something that will be *good for mankind*.

Chapter Sixteen—Notes

1. Richard Neal, M.D., "The Alien Agenda—Genetic Code Under Seige," *UFO*, Vol. 3, No. 2, 1988, p. 25. (Credit: *UFO Magazine*, 1800 S. Robertson Blvd., Box 355, L.A., CA 90035).

2. FOIA Release/Personal Files.

3. Irwin W. Sherman and Vilia G. Sherman, *Biology—A Human Approach* (New York: Oxford University Press, 1979), p. 178.

4. Neal, *op. cit.,* p. 25.

5. *Ibid.*

6. John G. Fuller, "Flying Saucer Fiasco," *Look,* May 14, 1968, p. 60.

7. David R. Saunders and R. Roger Harkins, *UFOs?—Yes!* (New York and Cleveland: The World Publishing Company, 1969).

8. Personal files.

9. FOIA Release/Personal Files.

10. *Ibid.*

11. Neal, *op. cit.,* p. 25.

12. Richard C. Hoagland, *The Monuments of Mars* (Berkeley, CA: North Atlantic Books, 1987).

13. FOIA Release/Personal Files.

14. Lawrence Fawcett and Barry J. Greenwood, *Clear Intent* (Englewood Cliffs, NJ: Prentice-Hall, Inc., 1984).

15. Timothy Good, *Above Top Secret* (New York: William Morrow and Company, 1988).

E p i l o g u e

Final Comments

We now reach that stage in the book where I will provide personal reaction on its overall content. As mentioned in the introduction, I elected to take the content of Betty's hypnotic recall at full face value. I wanted to see for myself where it would take us. The result of this venture was a scenario of ultra-high strangeness. In addition, quite unexpectedly and dramatically, I too found myself a communicant of the abduction phenomenon.

Throughout this enquiry, I have honestly endeavored not to let my background influence either conscious testimony or recalled memories. I have tried my very best to accomplish my objectives. These included experiencing the effects of hypnosis and exploring curious childhood memories. Having done both, I believe that it will be easier to deal with prospective hypnosis subjects. I can now tell them that I have been there. This has also helped me to appreciate better the trauma that abductees experience during abductions. I soon will share their vulnerability to reactions from the public and media.

In a real sense, I feel like a medical researcher who has inoculated himself in order to experience and treat a disease under study. I believe this to have been the honest and objective thing to do. Many others have put their reputations on the line. They sincerely believe that their experiences and resultant implications affect all of mankind. Could I do less?

As I bring *The Watchers* to a close, I would like to provide final comments on the following subjects in this order: The UFO

Abduction Phenomenon, The Andreasson Affair, The Message, and my own Abduction Experience.

The Abduction Phenomenon

What have I concluded about reported UFO abductions? What kind of a rationale can be presented for their reality? These are honest questions demanding an answer for the reader. One should be informed what the author believes about his subject and *why*.

First, I have no doubt whatsoever that UFO reports of landings with occupants have been made by credible witnesses. Such documented reports exist as pure unadulterated fact. Most observers of these events are not abductees. They merely sighted both UFO and occupants as a real-time happening.

The following letter was published in the prestigious journal *Science*. It was written by astronomer and former USAF UFO investigator, Dr. William T. Powers. It certainly bears out my contention.

> In 1954, over 200 reports over the whole world concerned landings of objects, many with *occupants* [italics mine]. Of these about 51 percent were observed by more than one person. In fact, in all these sightings at least 624 persons were involved, and only 98 of these people were alone. In 18 multiple witness cases, some witnesses were not aware that anyone else had seen the same thing at the same time and place. In 13 cases, there were more than 10 witnesses.[1]

The reader should bear in mind that these two hundred reports are statistics for just one lone year. One should also realize that had these same witnesses observed earthly crimes, their testimony could have put criminals behind bars.

Secondly, UFO occupants, like UFOs, fall into widely reported specific categories. Thus, no doubt exists that UFO reports contain typical descriptions of humanoid alien beings. Again, people who describe the aliens are not necessarily abductees.

Thirdly, reports exist from credible, sane persons who claim to have been abducted by creatures described by nonabductee witnesses. Many elements within their abduction accounts have a commonality. Some of these elements have had little or no public exposure. In some cases similar physical marks are left on the abductees' bodies. All of these elements provide strong circumstantial evidence that abductions are grounded in reality. Finally, proposed alternative hypotheses for abductions fall short of explaining them in earthly terms.

These facts, and now my own probable abduction experience, leave me with little reason to doubt the reality of this phenomenon except for cultural prejudices. Our minds have been trained from childhood to reject that which does not conform to the collective norm. UFO abductions obviously fall into that category.

We can theorize, critique, and speculate. But when all is said and done, we are always led back to the fundamental question. Is the abduction experience an incredible product of the *inner* space of mind or of aliens from *outer* space? To again quote *Pogo* - "Either way, it's a mighty sobern' thought!"

The Andreasson Affair

What can be said about the reality of Betty [Andreasson] Luca's longterm series of UFO experiences? This is a crucial question. Upon it rests the validity of most of the information presented in this book.

Personally, I find it extremely difficult not to believe that Betty has actually had these UFO experiences. Her credibility as a witness is unassailable. Never before have I or fellow investigators scrutinized the overall background of a witness so thoroughly. Character-reference checks, a lie detector test, psychiatric interviews, and my ongoing close relationship for over a decade have produced no flaw in her mentality or credibility.

Under hypnosis, Betty not only recounts but *relives* her UFO encounters. She does this in intricate detail with corresponding emotion, trauma, and body movements. She is able to provide detailed drawings that tally exactly with her verbal testimony. Weeks, months, and even years later she is able to relive selected segments of her experience upon demand by a hypnotist.

I have found very few people, who after listening to taped transcripts of her hypnosis sessions, go away unbelieving that the experiences are real. There is little doubt in their minds that Betty is actually mentally seeing and reliving events that are real to her. Those who have heard and commented upon the tapes have represented a broad spectrum of society. Some have been seasoned scientific investigators of UFOs such as the late Dr. J. Allen Hynek.

Dr. Hynek was an astronomer and professor of astronomy at Northwestern University. He directed both the Dearborn Observatory and Lindheimer Astronomical Institute. Earlier, he had served as associate director of the Smithsonian Astrophysical Observatory. When the Russians launched *Sputnik*, it was Dr. Hynek who was given the task to set up and operate an installation to track its movements. More pertinent to our subject, Dr. Hynek was chief scientific consultant for our government's UFO projects. His evaluation of *The Andreasson Affair* is found in the foreword that he graciously provided for the book.

> In the area of UFOs, deeper acquaintance reveals a subject that has not only potentially important scientific aspects but sociological, psychological, and even theological aspects as well. The Andreasson Case involves all these aspects. . . . It is not nonsense. . . . Neither is there the slightest evidence of hoax or contrivance. . . . More and more of these high-strangeness cases are surfacing. Like the Andreasson Case, they outrage our common sense and . . . constitute a challenge to our present belief systems.[2]

Such statements based upon the results of thorough inquiry are extremely important. Scientific evaluation is the only litmus test that we have for the authenticity of the aliens' message.

The Message

The Message of *The Watchers* has gone a long way in explaining many heretofore mysterious aspects of the UFO phenomenon. Since the early 1940s researchers have wondered why UFOs were appearing in our skies in large numbers. Questions were raised relating to the lack of official contact, government secrecy, and the growing number of *missing time* UFO encounters. Over the years, slowly but surely, it became apparent that such amnesic experiences were directly related to reported UFO abductions. The genetic content of abductions presented yet another mystery.

All of these mysteries find an answer in the message. The acceleration of UFO activity is directly related to Man's increasing destruction of earth's life-supporting environment. In response, *The Watchers* have stepped up a genetics program that stretches back to the beginning of Man himself.

"Man is going to become sterile"—"they are the same substance as Man"—"the fetuses become them"—Who could ever have imagined such things? Their very improbability adds to the probability of their truth. Why? They provide logical answers to the key questions of the UFO phenomenon. In other words they fit the missing pieces of the puzzle.

Some of these missing pieces relate to other questions posed by people of all ages. The paraphysical side of the message addresses the paraphysical nature of Man. Since Man became Man he has always had an innate belief in life continuing after death. This universal intuition has been expressed in the ageless revelations of mystics, prophets, and religions. Now the subtle hints engendered by the experiments of parapsychologists and the hypotheses posed by quantum theory take on new meaning. The true meaning of OBEs and NDEs has become clear. Man really is *more than flesh and blood*.

The revelation that Man is going to become sterile and extinct on this planet is inconceivable. But signs are all about us that attest to its authenticity. This is the dark side of the Message.

However, the other side of the Message concerns Man's transition after physical death. His current existence in *localized time* is preparatory in nature. It may be just one of many steps behind and before him during his evolving being. *The Watchers* have already been allowed to experience these steps.

During the abduction of patrolman Herbert Schirmer, one of his captors pointed to the starry sky. What he then said may indicate what awaits us after our brief stay on Earth: *You yourself will see the universe as I have seen it.* Perhaps this is what our limited concept of Heaven is all about. This is the bright side of the Message of *The Watchers*. It is an exhilarating and exciting prospect!

My Own Abduction Experience

It would be remiss of me not to make some final comments about the results of my own hypnosis sessions and my anomalous scar. Not many years ago, I would never have seriously entertained the prospect of personal UFO abductions. Even as I write now, the idea is so utterly foreign that the logical side of me dismisses it outright. But there is another part of me, an intuitive part. It inwardly witnesses to the reality of things buried deep within my subconscious which began to be uncovered by hypnosis.

Which should I believe? I don't really know. My conscious childhood memories, now confirmed by hypnotic recall, intrigue me. My family's extraordinary association with UFOs seems more than coincidental. Then there is my scar. It has started to fade but it is still there. Its paradigm is completely consistent with the shape and location of typical physiological effects upon UFO abductees. All of this seems to provide minute, teasing glimpses of something incredible occurring in parallel with my otherwise normal life.

To be objective, I must attempt to provide some personal critique to what I have previously related about my experiences. Both the *leg operation* nightmare and flashback of my sleepless night occurred a month after the scar appeared. Obviously, the question of its origin was on my mind. Thus a question certainly has to be raised about the connection. Was the nightmare a dream reflecting subconscious memory of a real abduction? Conversely, was it just a dream influenced by my concern about the scar?

Another question that should be discussed has to do with my memory. I desperately tried to remember whether something unusual had occurred during the night before the scar appeared. I failed to remember anything unusual even when asked this question under hypnosis. All that I could consciously remember was coming back from an astronomy lecture and going to bed.

The sleepless night and the experience of a continual prickly, electriclike feeling were real events. Sleepless nights are a rarity with me. The prickling sensation was weird and extraordinary. Why couldn't I remember this the next day? Why couldn't I remember this while under hypnosis? It took an innocent remark by my wife and word association to snap this back into my conscious memory.

I now can equate that prickling feeling with the sensation that I felt as a child just prior to encounters with a strange entity in my bedroom. Was my forgetfulness a natural slip of memory or was I *programmed* to forget? Similar types of recall by dream and association are historical and typical facets of the UFO abduction phenomenon.

I do believe that I, along with Betty and a host of others, have really had abduction experiences. I am also convinced that the synchronistic appearance of similar scars on both Betty and myself indicate our mutual linkage to *The Watchers* and their operations on our planet. But I must admit that for the present time, I am hiding behind that word *experience*.

In the prologue, under the caption *alternative hypotheses*, we saw that experiences may have a variety of catalysts other than physical events. This may seem cowardly to some but I need this option to continue living a normal life.

I feel that I have taken on a weighty responsibility in writing this book. I had no idea that the Phase Three inquiry would lead to such startling revelations. A definitive solution to the UFO phenomenon with linkage to the extinction of Man was infinitely more than I had bargained for.

What does one do with such provocative information? It could be one of the greatest revelations in Man's history but it could also herald his demise. For some reason, *The Watchers* want Man to know both about his plight and about the nature of their operations. Thus, I feel obligated to reveal this information and the circumstances surrounding it.

One wonders why *The Watchers* have used this method to inform us of these things. Why haven't they informed world governments? One can only imagine the results of such an act. Official contact and release of their message by world leaders would cause chaos. Alien methodology all along has been a slow conditioning of mankind to both their presence and operations. This information, like leaven, is permeating society in a way that will produce the least cultural shock.

I continually wonder who will believe the contents of this book. Simultaneously, I then realize that neither belief nor disbelief will change the circumstances if they are true. What if they are not true? What if some logical explanation can be found that will negate the reality of the UFO abduction phenomenon and its life-threatening implications? I do not believe that this will be the case. But if it were, at the very least I will have called attention to the terrible damage mankind is inflicting on this planet.

Whichever the case might be, one important fact remains. Man must engage in an immediate all-inclusive program to repair and protect the environment. If he does not, the Message of *The Watchers* might become a reality. Life on earth would become extinct. Dare we wait to find out?

Epilogue Notes

1. William T. Powers, Ph.D, "Analysis of UFO Reports," *Science*, Vol. 156, 7 April 1967, p. 11.

2. Raymond E. Fowler, *The Andreasson Affair*, (Englewood Cliffs, N.J.: Prentice-Hall, Inc., 1979) pp. 8, 9.

Appendix A

Chronological Summary of Known Encounters

A–1 Betty [Andreasson] Luca

Year	Age	Inside	Outside	Day	Night	Synopsis	Date of Hypnosis Session
1944	7	X		X		*Playhouse Incident*: Ball of light lands between Betty's eyes. Hears voices.	1980: 4/1
1949	12		X	X		*Woods Encounter I*: Meets alien. Ball of light lands between eyes. Hears voices.	1980: 4/7, 21
1950	13		X	X		*Abducted from Field*: Taken to underground area. Examined/Eye removed. Meets the *One*.	1980: 4/21, 25, 28; 5/10, 15, 22, 29; 6/11 1988: 7/10
1955	18	X			X	*Anomalous Voice*: Hears her name called.	1980: 6/11
1961	24		X	X		*Woods Encounter II*: Drawn by impulse to nearby woods. Meets alien with message.	1980: 6/11
1967	30	X	X		X	*Abducted from House*: Examined. Visited alien place. Phoenix. Chosen to show world.	1977: 4/3, 9, 23, 30; 5/7, 14, 21; 6/4, 18, 23, 25; 7/16, 23, 28
1973	36	X	X		X	*Bedroom Encounter*: Abducted. Witnesses birth of fetus and alien technology.	1980: 6/11 [mental block] 1987: 11/16, 19; 12/8, 28 1988: 1/23; 2/7; 2/10

A–1 Betty [Andreasson] Luca

Year	Age	Inside	Outside	Day	Night	Synopsis	Date of Hypnosis Session
1975	38	X			X	*Bedroom Encounter*: Alien reveals that "It is now time." She will begin to remember.	1988: 2/16
1976	39	X		X		*Bedroom Encounter*: Alien predicts marital difficulties to end. Hardship will come.	1988: 2/16
1977	40	X			X	*Bedroom Encounter*: An alien warns Betty of the impending death of two of her sons.	1988: 2/16
1978	41	X	X		X	*UFO Sightings/Shared OBE*: Sights 4 UFOs from car. Abducted with Bob via an OBE.	1988: 5/13, 22, 24
1981	44	X			X	*Bedroom Encounter*: Shadowy figure.	1988:5/13
1982	45	X			X	*Bedroom Encounter*: White-suited alien.	1988: 5/13
1984	47	X			X	*Living room Encounter*: Shadowy figures seen in kitchen while watching TV. Paralysis. Blindness. Feels something penetrate head.	1988: 5/13
1986	49	X	X	X		*OBE Abduction*: Alien appears in trailer and instigates OBE. Takes her to strange place.	1988: 5/13; 7/9
1987	50	?	?		X	*Anomalous Scar*: A scooplike mark appeared on calf of right leg.	None

A–1 Betty [Andreasson] Luca

Year	Age	Inside	Outside	Day	Night	Synopsis	Date of Hypnosis Session
1988	51	X			X	*Anomalous Scars:* Three scooplike marks forming a triangle appeared on right arm.	None

*Some memory of experience prior to hypnosis.

A–2 Bob Luca

Year	Age	Inside	Outside	Day	Night	Synopsis	Date of Hypnosis Session
1944	5		X	X		*The Swing Incident:* Domed disk with two aliens communicate by mental telepathy.	**1980**: 3/17, 24
1967	29		X	X		*Abducted from Car:* Disk descends from large cylindrical object and lands behind trees near road. Examined physically by aliens.	1977: 12/03 **1980**: 4/1
1978	41	X	X		X	*Shared OBE:* Betty reported that he was abducted with her via an OBE and taken to a large round-shaped facility. [craft?]	Bob to date does not want to undergo hypnosis.

*some memory of experience prior to hypnosis.

A–3 Ray Fowler

Year	Age	Inside	Outside	Day	Night	Synopsis	Date of Hypnosis Session
1938–1939	5–6	X	?		X	*Bedroom Encounter:* Visitations by entity in dark clothing. Remembered leaving bedroom with entity with pale face and slanted eyes.	**1988:** 7/21, 9/7, 10/29
1939–1941	6–8	X			X	*Bedroom Encounter:* Tiny glowing light hovers and jumps into closet.	**1988:** 10/29
1941–1942	8–9	X	X		X	*Bedroom Encounter:* Abducted by entity on beam of light through window to hovering lighted object.	**1988:** 7/21, 9/7, 10/29
1947	13		X	X		*Daylight Disk:* Observed disk descending with falling-leaf motion behind trees while working on a farm. Observed cigar-shaped object.	**1988:** 10/29
1947–1948	14–15		X		X	*Missing Time:* Walking in woods in bright daylight when suddenly it got dark and the sun was setting. Found self lying on ground.	**1988:** 10/29
1966	32		X		X	*Nocturnal Light:* Sighted droning, glowing object on same evening as local close encounter was reported.	None
1969	35		X	X		*Daylight Disk:* Sighted disk descending to the ground behind trees in England.	**1988:** 10/29

A–3 Ray Fowler

Year	Age	Inside	Outside	Day	Night	Synopsis	Date of Hypnosis Session
1979	45–46		X	X		*Daylight Disk: Gyrating small black box-shaped object hovered several feet from me at head level.	**1988:** 10/29
1988	54	?	?		X	*Anomalous Scar: Scoop mark appeared above shinbone overnight.	**1988:** 9/7, 10/29

*Some memory of experience prior to hypnosis.

Appendix B

The following paper prepared by Massachusetts MUFON Investigator Joseph Nyman provides the reader with a typical profile of a person who unknowingly has experienced an abduction by aliens. Readers who believe that they may have experienced such an abduction may write the author or Betty and Bob Luca at the following addresses. A self-addressed, stamped envelope must be provided to assure a reply.

Raymond E. Fowler
13 Friend Court
Wenham, MA 01984

Betty and Bob Luca
P.O. Box 125
Rockfall, CT 06481

The Latent Encounter Experience—
A Composite Model
by Joseph Nyman

Introduction

As a principal or secondary participant in the investigation of more than thirty close-encounter claims, the author has heard a number of recurring themes in encounter relations that seem to indicate a consistent pattern.

It is the purpose of this paper to use these consistencies in the establishment of a model experience to be called the *Latent Encounter Experience* (more commonly known as an *abduction*) and to elaborate on its stages. The model (Table I) will be heuristic in the sense that it will suggest certain tests that may serve to modify the model itself.

First, a word about terminology—the word *abduction* has, in the writer's opinion, become distended and misshapen after so many months of nurture at the bosoms of the media. Indeed, one debunker with no apparent understanding of the claims or claimants, has focused on the point that these *abductions*, having not been reported to the FBI, can't be taken seriously. Totally ignored is the fact that the vast majority of percipients have little or no immediate recollection of their experience, and have enormous difficulties in later articulation (see the Table III summary of difficulties that typically must be overcome, in part or in total, by the percipient).

Abduction, of course, carries the notion of unwillingness, and by implication, the notion of complete postevent memory. The writer's study of encounter claims, images, and memories, indicates that the *former* is not always the case and the *latter* hardly ever the case. Use of the term *latent encounter*, while having the disadvantage of implying an experience, has the advantage of being neutral enough to deter the sensationally inclined and sidestep meaningless arguments.

To be most objective, since indisputable verification is lacking, an even more neutral term would probably be better—on the order of latent encounter *imagery*. This implies something hidden, something met, and mental associations linking the two. For convenience, the author will use *Latent Encounter*, or LE.

Although some of the information used to prepare this model has come from the percipient's conscious memory, most has been collected as the result of having claimants attempt to relive an unresolved experience. The setting used has been one in which the concerned individuals have been initially given suggestions causing them to relax, focus their attention and memory on the unresolved experiences, and then form a chain of associations to the unresolved experience which might contribute to its resolution.

After ten years of work with individuals whose statements have been incorporated into this model, the writer has gained some insight into their motivations and willingness to expose themselves and their lives to scrutiny and possible ridicule. In all cases but one (almost certainly a hoax) their major motives were judged to be:

1. fear for their own sanity, although the great majority were functioning well in life.
2. need to have an unresolved, puzzling experience explained.

Table II supplies an indication to the reader of how a number of percipients have reached the point of active investigation.

With the above in mind, let us move forward to the proposed model and its stages. Table I is a summary representation of the eight *stages* of the model. Associated with each stage number is a short descriptive characteristic.

Table I

THE LATENT ENCOUNTER CYCLE
CHARACTERIZED BY MEMORY OR IMAGE

Stage 1 Anxious anticipation of something unknown, fore-warning.

Stage 2 Transition of consciousness from normal awake state. The transition is mostly from fear and terror to immediate calmness and acquiescence.

Stage 3 Psycho-physical imposition and interaction.

Stage 4 Overlay of positive feelings, reassurance. A sense of source and purpose given.

Stage 5 Transition of consciousness to normal waking. An aftersense of fear/pleasure/happiness, lingers.

Stage 6 Rapid forgetfulness of most or all memory of experience.

Stage 7 *Marker* stage: what little is remembered is remembered as an incongruity, with unresolved conscious memories, repetitive dreams.

Stage 8 Cycle repetition at very specific ages.

Let's now amplify each of these *stages* based on the author's investigations.

Stage 1

The percipient experiences a subtle urge or prompting, as if originating from within, to:

1. be at a required place at a certain time.

2. expect something strangely familiar but yet unknown.

This forewarning is usually accompanied by anxiety with no apparent source.

Stage 2

At the required place and time, the percipient experiences an unusual phenomenon followed by a transition in awareness such that the individual proceeds from a state of normal wakefulness with its concomitant functions of volition, emotion, and memory to a state characterized by calmness, acquiescence, and limited mobility (what the author calls the CA state). There are consistent physical and mental effects described by a number of percipients in this stage that the author will not elaborate on here.

Stage 3

This is the stage about which books are written and movies made. Rich with bizarre imagery, and emotion filled, this stage is the most difficult for the percipient to relive. It is replete with images of mental communication and involuntary submission to physical procedures.

This is the stage of the *table*, the *scar*, the *needle*, the *machine*, the *probe*, etc. This is the stage of the *ova*, and the *sperm*, and the *baby*!

Stage 4

The physical procedures have been completed. The percipient is ready to return, but not before a positive bias is mentally imposed to be the lasting emotional remnant of the experience. The *veneering* can be a multipart process involving *recognition*, *explanation*, and *understanding*. It can also include the projection of *love*, the guided *tour*, and the *life review*. It is conducted by that entity who has the *special relationship* with the percipient. The nature of that relationship is beyond the scope of this paper.

Stage 5

In the case of an LE intersecting normal waking activity, the transition from CA state to normal can be, to use Budd Hopkins's perfectly descriptive term, seamless. It seems as if there has been no intervening experience. Yet there remains an afterimage resulting from the emotional veneer imposed in *Stage* 4, a cover story to explain anything unusual or inconsistent resulting from the encounter itself. The afterimage includes a feeling of prohibition against discussing or remembering any aspect of the experience. This last extends to members of groups that have just *shared* an experience. The result; no exchange, no discussion, *no happening*.

LE's proceeding from bedroom intrusions end by returning the awakened sleeper to a state of sleep. The resulting morning memory is one of unease or nightmare.

Stage 6

Within minutes of the *Stage* 5 waking transition, most, if not all, conscious memory of the encounter has become latent in memory. As fleeting as a dream trace, the LE imagery is locked away and superceded by routine or sleep. Generally, the CA state leads back into the percipient's pre-encounter situation.

Stage 7

In most cases, and despite the positive veneering, an anxiety-provoking fragment remains. Sometimes it is painted by memory to conform to an image the percipient finds more portable and less threatening. Other times, it is a nameless fear or feeling of something unresolved, an experience that the mind returns to over and over again without conscious resolution. More generally, this signal in conscious memory, or *marker* memory, as the author likes to call it, is an incongruous image, accompanied by a nameless anxiety that appears to have no conscious resolution and which forces itself to mind repetitively. This is the point from which *investigations begin*.

Stage 8

Continuing work has now made it clear that the individual LE is only one of a *sequence* of such experiences that takes place at specific intervals in an individual's life. It is far from a random process! What has come very sharply into focus is that at least a portion of these specific intervals occur at ages that can be directly related to the formation and maturation of the human sexual function! At this time it is probably not wise to publish these ages as a check to further case work.

The interval between LEs is punctuated by claims of two types of exotic phenomena, one of which manifests objectively, but rarely, and the other of which is purely subjective and seemingly continuous. The *objective* phenomenon manifests mostly in *telekinetic* effects, while the purely *subjective* can be described as *consciousness monitoring* in which the percipients feel themselves to be *observed* and *directed*. The latter subjective awareness is often characterized by shifts in interest and life direction.

The author feels that, initially, *Stage 7* provides the suggestion for an interesting test. Two groups, one of which is identified as having *marker* memories, the other of which is identified as having none, can be subject to identical association-inducing procedures. The *marker* memory group would be expected to have significantly more images relating to this model than the *nonmarker* memory group. The design of an experiment with this end in mind is planned shortly.

A study proposal is now in preparation by a well-known psychologist to survey percipient transformative effects. This is expected to reflect directly on *Stage 8* concepts. The author would be pleased to hear from others suggesting other tests and experiments.

Joseph Nyman
19 Longmeadow Road
Medfield, MA 02052

Table II

INDICATIONS OF THE LE CYCLE IN THE PERCIPIENT

1. *Puzzlement*: The percipient has been puzzled or upset by his/her *marker* experiences(s) for months or years.
2. *Puzzle-Solving Action*: The percipient has attempted to resolve the incongruity without success.
3. *Decision*: The percipient has reached the point of needing to resolve the incongruity.
4. *Readiness*: The percipient is willing to come forward to find out what happened.

Table III

DIFFICULTIES IN BRINGING THE LE TO MEMORY

1. The percipient feels that if one admits to the experience it is an admission of one's own insanity.
2. If the percipient has enough conviction and strength of character to know that one is not insane, there is always the feeling that others may not be so kind.
3. The percipient wants to repress the trauma and helplessness of the experience.
4. The percipient has difficulty in remembering something that took place in another state of awareness, much like the difficulty in remembering dreams.
5. The percipient has a feeling of prohibition—*one should not remember*!

A p p e n d i x C

A Letter to Betty

13 Friend Court,
Wenham, MA 01984
October 25, 1988

P.O. Box 125
Rockfall, CT 06481

Dear Betty:

You asked me to include my own comments upon your belief that the aliens are *angels* and that UFOs are connected with the Judeo-Christian tradition. This is a precarious task with many pitfalls. First, this is not a religious book per se. It is a documented account of your abduction experiences told against a backdrop of UFO abduction research and its findings.

However, since your abductors reportedly equated themselves with Biblical events, I feel justified in responding to your request in this section of the book. This does not mean that I necessarily accept this aspect of their reported message. Some say that you have superimposed your own belief-system over the abduction experience in order to retain your faith. On the other hand, the Biblical connection may be an authentic part of your reported experience.

In order for me to respond to your request objectively and without prejudice to those outside of Judaism and the Christian faith, I must set firm ground rules.

1. The Bible and related literature will be used as literary source data without recourse to its religious content.

2. For argument's sake, the historicity and accuracy of the selected data will be taken at face value.

3. Anomalous clouds, lights, and objects in the air or on the ground will be called *UFOs.*

4. Nonearthly entities described as gods, sons of God, archangels, angels, seraphim, cherubim, watchers, holy ones, mighty ones, etc. will be called *aliens.*

When we employ these ground rules, I find events in the source data that would certainly be reported as UFOs if they were observed in modern times. These recorded events also reflect the same *Types* of UFO experiences reported today, namely:

NL   Nocturnal Lights.
DD   Daylight disks [or other shapes].
CE   UFO within 500 feet of observer.
CE1   UFO only.
CE2   UFO with physical effects.
CE3   UFO with occupants.
CE4   UFO abduction.

Here are a few examples for your review:

NL   Exodus 13:21,22—Matthew 2:9.
DD   Exodus 13:21,22—Isaiah 60:8—Acts 22:6.
CE1   Genesis 15:17—Protevangelion* 14:10–12—1 Infancy* 1:10.
CE2   Exodus 14:19–29.
CE3   Exodus 3:1–5 and 33:9,10—Ezekiel 1:1–28—Matthew 28:2,3—Mark 9:4,7,8—Luke 2:8,9.
CE4   II Kings 2:11—Acts 1:9–11—II Corinthians 12:2–4.

Again, I would stress that the above events, if reported by modern witnesses, would be called UFO experiences. One must also assume that if ancient witnesses did indeed observe UFOs that they would describe them in nontechnological terms as extraordinary clouds, lights, wheels, etc.

I would also call to your attention that some of the physical and psychic effects associated with modern UFO experiences also are alluded to in our data source. Here are several examples for your review.

Physical Effects
    Artifacts: Exodus 16:4 and Psalm 78:25.
    Blindness: Genesis 19:11.
    Fog: Exodus 14:19.
    Heat: Genesis 19:1,13, 24–38.
    Levitation: Exodus 14:22,29—Ezekiel 3:14,16.
    Luminescence: Exodus 34:29,30—Matthew 17:2.
    Paralysis: Daniel 8:15–18 and 10:4–9—Matthew 28:
    2–4—Revelation 1:12–17.
    Suspended animation: Protevangelion* 13:1–10.

Paraphysical Effects
    OBE: 2 Corinthians 12:2–4.
    Transfiguration: Matthew 17:1–9—Mark 9:1–8.

Genetics
    Hybrid births: Genesis 6:2–4.
    Anomalous births: Genesis 18:2,9–10 and 21:2—Luke
    1:7,11–13,24,57 and 1:26–34.

There you have it, Betty. All of these references presuppose that *aliens are angels*. However, this is a highly speculative presupposition. Few members of the Judeo-Christian faiths would accept such an idea. It would be totally abhorrent to many.

You ask me what I personally think about the idea from my own perspective as a Christian UFO researcher with formal Biblical training? If we take the Biblical events referenced at face value, I would not separate the religious message from the events. If there is a true UFO/Bible connection then I would assume the angels/messengers were extraterrestrial missionaries to this planet. Strangely enough, Carl Sagan in his book entitled *Intelligent Life in the Universe* asks—"Can we exclude the possibility of extraterrestrial evangelism?"—when discussing motivations for alien visitation to earth.

Whether a UFO/Bible event connection exists or does not exist, the very fact that UFOs exist presents a formidable challenge to any religion that has not allowed for extraterrestrial life in their theology. Theologians should have begun long ago to expand geocentric religious concepts that should have disappeared with the Copernican revolution.

---

*Non-canonical apocryphal legends about the nativity. [See Notes 1 & 2]

The important thing to remember, Betty, is that throughout history, both theology and scientific theories have had to be expanded over and over again in the light of new knowledge. Not too many years ago, theologians believed that the earth was created in 4004 B.C. and scientists believed that our Milky Way galaxy was the whole universe! Sometimes changes in traditional thought are distasteful and alarming to the generation in which they occur. However, they in no way changed the basic message of the Christian Gospel in which you have faith. Don't be afraid of truth. Truth, like good medicine, might taste bitter but in the end it promotes intellectual and spiritual health. I'm sure that's what the Creator would like all of us to have. Keep the faith!

Sincerely yours,

Ray Fowler

Note 1—Joseph reportedly saw both people and animals in a state of suspended animation around the cave in which Mary lay in labor just prior to the birth of Jesus according to the *Protevange-lion of James*. This same document describes a *bright cloud* over the cave and a *bright light* in the cave when Jesus was born.

Note 2—*1 Infancy* also records the legend that the cave in which Jesus was born was—"filled with lights, greater than the light of lamps and candles, and greater than the light of the sun itself."

S E L E C T E D

Bibliography

The Thompson Chain-Reference Bible, *New International Version*. Grand Rapids: Zonderman Bible Publishers, 1983.

Carpenter, Donald G., Major, USAF, ed., *Introductory Space Science*, Volume II. USAF Academy, 1968.

Clarke, Arthur C., *1984: Spring—A Choice of Futures*. New York: Ballantine Books, 1984.

Condon, E.U., *Scientific Study of UFOs*. New York: E.P. Dutton & Co., Inc., 1969.

Coxe, A. Cleveland, D.D., *The Ante-Nicene Fathers*. 10 vols. Grand Rapids: William B. Eerdmans Publishing Company, 1951.

Davies, Paul, *Other Worlds*. New York: Simon & Schuster, 1980.

Davis, William O., "Communication with Extraterrestrial Intelligence." *IEEE Spectrum* (March 1966) 161, 162.

de Chardin, Pierre Teilhard, *The Phenomenon of Man*. New York: Harper & Row, 1959.

de Chardin, Pierre Teilhard, *The Appearance of Man*. New York: Harper & Row, 1965.

Druffel, Ann and D. Scott Rogo, *The Tujunga Canyon Contacts*. Englewood Cliffs, NJ: Prentice-Hall, Inc., 1980.

Fawcett, Lawrence and Barry Greenwood, *Clear Intent*. Englewood Cliffs, NJ: Prentice-Hall, Inc., 1984.

Fowler, Raymond E., *The Andreasson Affair*. Englewood Cliffs, NJ: Prentice-Hall, Inc., 1979 and New York: Bantam Books, 1980, 1988.

Fowler, Raymond E., *Casebook of a UFO Investigator*. Englewood Cliffs, NJ: Prentice-Hall, Inc., 1981.

Fowler, Raymond E., *The Melchizedek Connection*. St. Paul: Trinity Publishing House, 1981. (Copies available from author)

Fowler, Raymond E., *The Andreasson Affair—Phase Two*. Englewood Cliffs, NJ: Prentice-Hall, Inc., 1982.

Fuller, John G., *The Interrupted Journey*. New York: The Dial Press, 1966.

Fuller, John G., "Flying Saucer Fiasco," *Look*, Vol. 32, No. 10 (1968), 58–63.

Good, Timothy, *Above Top Secret*. New York: William Morrow and Company, 1988.

Graham, Billy, *Angels—God's Secret Agents*. New York: Doubleday & Company, Inc., 1975.

Hoaglund, Richard C., *The Monuments of Mars*. Berkeley: North Atlantic Books, 1987.

Hopkins, Budd, "The Extraterrestrial—Paraphysical Controversy." *MUFON UFO Journal*, No. 153 (1980), 3–5.

Hopkins, Budd, *Intruders*. New York: Random House, 1987.

Keel, John A., *UFOs: Operation Trojan Horse*. New York: G.P. Putnam's Sons, 1970.

Lipp, J.F., *Project Sign Technical Report No. F-TR-2274-IA*, Appendix "D." February 1949.

Mead, Margaret, "UFOs—Visitors from Outer Space?" *Redbook*, Volume 145, No. 5 (1974), 57–59.

Monroe, Robert A., *Journeys Out of the Body*. New York: Anchor Press/Doubleday, 1973.

Moody, Raymond A., Jr., M.D., *Reflections on Life after Life*. New York: Bantam Books, Inc., 1977.

Neal, Richard, M.D., "Generations of Abductions—A Medical Case-book," and "The Alien Agenda," *UFO Magazine*, Vol. 3, No. 2, (1988), pp. 21, 25.

Nyman, Joseph, "The Latent Encounter Experience—A Composite Model," *MUFON UFO JOURNAL*, No. 242 (1988), 10–12.

Oberg, James, "Terraforming." *Astronomy*, Vol. 6, No. 5 (1978), 6–25.

Powers, William T., "Letters," *Science*, Vol. CLVI (1967), p. 11.

Sabom, Michael B., M.D., *Recollections of Death—A Medical Investigation*. New York: Harper & Row, 1982.

Sagan, Carl and I.S. Shklovskii, *Intelligent Life in the Universe*. San Francisco: Holden-Day, Inc., 1966.

Saunders, David R. and R. Roger Harkins, *UFOs?—Yes!* New York and Cleveland: The World Publishing Co., 1969.

Sherman, Irwin W. and Vilia G. Sherman, *Biology—A Human Approach*. New York: Oxford University Press, 1979.

Story, Ronald D. "Fort, Charles." *The Encyclopedia of UFOs* (1980), 138.

Strieber, Whitley, *Communion*. New York: William Morrow, 1987.

Sullivan, Walter, *We Are Not Alone*. New York: McGraw-Hill Book Co., 1964.

Swords, Michael D., "Ufonauts: Homo Sapiens of the Future?" *MUFON UFO Journal*, No. 202 (1985), 8.

Temple, Robert R.G., *The Sirius Mystery*. London: Sidgwick & Jackson Limited, 1976 and Futura Publications Limited, 1979.

U.S. Congress, House of Representatives Committee on Science and Astronautics, *Proposed Studies on the Implications of Peaceful Space Activities for Human Affairs*, 87th Congress, First Session, Report No. 242, Washington: Government Printing Office, 1961.

Vallee, Jacques, *Passport to Magonia*. Chicago: Henry Regnery Co., 1969.

Walton, Travis, *The Walton Experience*. New York: Berkeley Publishing Corporation, 1978.

Zeidman, Jennie, *A Helicopter–UFO Encounter over Ohio*. Chicago: J. Allen Hynek Center for UFO Studies, 1979.

Index

Above Top Secret, 342, 350, 376
Adam, 206
Adapa, 206
Agrest, M.M., 205
Aho, Betty (*See* Luca, Betty)
Aho, Eva, 3
Aho, Waino, x, 3, 132
Air Force (*See* United States Air
  Force)
Air Force Academy (*See* United
  States Air Force)
Air Force Cambridge Research
  Laboratory (*See* United States
  Air Force)
alternative hypotheses, xvii, xx,
  353, 356
American Association for the Ad-
  vancement of Science
  (AAAS), 193
American Psychological Associa-
  tion, xxiv
Andreasson Affair, The, xix, 1, 3, 5,
  14, 17, 31, 35, 38, 86, 124,
  128, 134, 141, 144, 147, 153,
  163, 198, 199, 208, 247, 249,
  251, 252, 262, 311, 326, 339,
  343, 352, 354, 357, 375
Andreasson Affair—Phase Two, 1,
  16, 86, 191, 200, 215, 343,
  376
Andreasson, Betty (*See* Luca,
  Betty)

Andreasson, Bonnie, 35, 37, 131,
  138
Andreasson, Cindy, 131, 138,
  338, 344
Andreasson, James, Jr., 129, 140
Andreasson, James, Sr., 3, 35, 38,
  46, 129–133
Andreasson, Rebecca (Becky), 4,
  5, 13, 136–138
Andreasson, Todd, 136, 140
Andrus, Walter H., xiv
Angels, 4, 153, 211, 334, 371,
  372
Angels—God's Secret Agents, 376
Ante-Nicene Fathers, The, 375
Apparitions, 241, 246, 247
Appearance of Man, The, 203, 215,
  375
Applied Optics (journal), 339
Argentina, 71
Ashburnham, MA, 2, 38, 52, 53,
  96, 111, 117, 127, 135, 138,
  202
Astronomy (magazine), 215
atomic energy, 26, 330
atomic weapons, 330, 332, 336,
  341
Australia, 249

Babylonia, 26, 206, 214
Bach, Gitto, 209, 210
Bar Harbor, ME, 273, 274, 277

Beverly, MA, 241, 245, 248, 273, 287, 310
Bible, The Holy, 172–174, 180, 205, 211, 305, 348, 372, 373
Biology, A Human Approach, 350, 377
biopsy, punch, 270, 271, 284
blond entities, 224, 228, 229
Bolk, Louis, 222
Bradley Field, CT, 298
Brazil, 212
Brookings Institution, 197
Buenos Aires, Argentina, 71
Bush, Vannevar, 186, 330, 331

Cabot, Laurie, 250
Cabot Cinema, Beverly, MA, 250, 287
California, 135, 221
Cambridge, MA, 276
Canaan, VT, 248, 283
Canada, 72
Cantania, Italy, 151
Capella (star), 298
Carpenter, Donald G., 214, 375
Casebook of a UFO Investigator, 375
cattle mutilation (*See* mutilations, animal)
Center for UFO Studies, 250
Central Intelligence Agency (CIA), 188, 336
Chadwell, H. Marshall, 336
Chaldea (*See* Babylonia)
changelings, 208
Chiapas, Mexico, 209
Chile, 210
chimpanzee(s), 222, 223
Chinese, xiii, 209, 304
Christianity (*See* Religion and UFOs)
Christian Science Monitor, 342
Clark, E. E., 208
Clarke, Arthur C., 196, 203, 215, 375
Clear Intent, 342, 350, 375

Cohen, David, xviii
Communion, xi, 86, 109, 377
Condon, Edward U., xxv, 335–337, 375
Congress, U.S., 335, 377
Connecticut, 35, 134, 135, 267, 344
Constantino, Anthony O., xiv, 241, 253–264, 269, 272, 284, 286–296, 300–326
Corliss, William R., 230
Coxe, A. Cleveland, 375
Crabbe, Riley, 249
Crick, Francis, 228, 229

Danvers, MA, 242, 243, 246–247, 255, 269, 274, 275, 282, 292, 308, 310
Davies, Paul, 185, 191, 375
Davis, William O., 199, 200, 215, 375
de Chardin, Pierre Teilhard, 203, 204, 215, 375
doppelgänger, 175, 215
Druffel, Ann, xiv, 215, 375

Earhart, Amelia, 256
Eden, 206
Elat, Eitan, xviii
Ellsworth, ME, 274
Encyclopedia of UFOs, The, 238, 377
England, 245, 251, 282, 314, 315
Eridu, 205, 206
Eveleth, Doris H., 255, 256, 273, 274
Eveleth, Margaret, 275, 276
Eveleth, Priscilla, 276, 277
Extraterrestrial Intelligence (ETI), 375
Eyton, B. J., 72

Fargo, ND, 70
Fawcett, Lawrence, 198, 350, 375
Federal Bureau of Investigation (FBI), 230, 365

fetus(es), xii, xxii, 22, 24, 27–30, 46–51, 56, 60, 76, 202, 213, 222–228, 275, 340, 355
Fitchburg, MA, 3, 134, 140
Flanagan, W. A., M.D., 269, 270
Florida, 5, 20, 31, 55, 57, 86, 109, 133, 135
folklore, 207–209, 212
Fontes, Olava, 211
foofighters, 69, 71, 330
Fort, Charles, 229, 230, 238, 377
Fowler, Bethany (*See* Plante, Bethany),
Fowler, David, 283, 284
Fowler, Doris, 255, 256, 273, 274
Fowler, Dorothy, 256
Fowler, Frederick A., 242, 281
Fowler, John, 242
Fowler, Margaret E., xiv, 280, 281, 315, 316, 322
Fowler, Raymond E. (author), ix, x, xii, xiii–xiv, xix, 16, 17, 58, 67, 84, 86, 110, 124, 133, 134, 139–140, 176, 191, 201, 215, 238, 240–264, 286–296, 300–326, 335, 351–353, 355–357, 364, 371–374, 375
paranormal experiences (*See* apparitions)
Phase One investigation, xvi, 32, 126, 133, 145, 209, 241, 339, 343
Phase Two investigation, xvi, 2, 5, 7, 9, 14, 19, 32, 35, 126, 127, 137, 138, 142, 143, 145, 150, 198, 209, 241, 267, 343
Phase Three investigation, xvi, 15, 31, 33, 263, 357
synchronistic experiences (*See* synchronisms)
UFO experiences, 124, 255–264, 286–296, 300–326
Fowler, Raymond E., Jr., 315
Fowler, Raymond F., 277

Fowler, Richard A., 242, 282
Fowler, Sharon M. (*See* Gamble, Sharon M.)
Freedom of Information Act (FOIA), 17, 70, 330, 336, 342, 349
Fuller, John G., xiv, xxv, 239, 350, 376

Gamble, Sharon M., 246, 247, 282, 302, 315, 316
General Telephone and Electronics Company (GTE), 252, 341
Genesis (The Holy Bible), 206, 211, 216, 372, 373
Good, Timothy, 350
Gorman, George, 70
Graham, Billy, 376
Grant, Margaret (*See* Eveleth, Margaret)
Great Door, the, 144, 145, 146, 147, 148, 150, 151, 345, 347, 349
Greenwood, Barry J., xiv, 350, 375
Gulf Breeze, FL, 253

Harkins, R. Roger, 350, 376
Hartland, Edwin S., 207, 208, 209, 212
Healey, John, 189
helicopter(s), xii, 35, 188
Helicopter–UFO Encounter over Ohio, A, 191, 377
Herrick, Philip D., M.D., 269
Higganum, CT, 172, 173, 176, 348
Hill, Barney, 235, 236
Hill, Betty, 235, 236, 237
Hilliard, OH, 67
Hoaglund, Richard C., 350, 376
Homo sapiens, 204, 221–224
Hopkins, Budd, xiv, 51–52, 197, 212, 215, 231, 233, 265–266, 275–276, 285, 304, 367, 376

Howe, Linda, 230
Hynek, J. Allen, 4, 128, 188, 250, 353–354
hypnosis, x, xv, xvii, xviii, xix, xx, 1, 6, 7, 10, 12, 17, 18–19, 31–34, 42, 51–52, 55, 57, 87–109, 111–132, 137–139, 142–145, 147, 150, 153–180, 181, 199, 201, 235, 236, 241, 250, 251, 253, 254, 258–264, 265, 272, 275, 276, 286–296, 298, 300–326, 327, 343, 347, 351, 353, 355–356

IEEE Spectrum (magazine), 215, 375
ideomotor procedure, 318, 320, 325
ihk'al, the, 209, 214
implant, 5, 9, 11, 12, 23, 45, 55, 106, 232, 333, 338
incubi, 211, 214
Indian, American, 208
Intelligent Life in the Universe, 205, 215, 373, 376
Interrupted Journey, The, xxv, 239

Jastrow, Robert, 197
Jesus, xiii, 39, 137, 138, 183, 203, 334, 374
Journeys Out of the Body, 190, 376
Judaism (*See* Religion and UFOs)
Jung, Carl Gustav, xxii, xxiii, 249, 271

Keel, John A., xiv, 208, 209, 215, 376
Kentucky, 210

laparoscopy, 235, 236
Latent Encounter Experience, A Composite Model, 364–370
Leominster, MA, 3, 7, 143, 337
Liberty, KY, 210
lie detector, 5, 33, 353

lightning, 58, 78, 79, 278
Lipp, J. F., 214, 376
Look (magazine), 335, 350, 376
Luca, Betty, ix, x, xi, xiii, xiv, xv, xix, xxi, xxii, 1, 5–14, 16, 17, 20, 32–33, 35, 37, 38, 57, 74, 83–86, 110, 133–135, 139, 152–153, 183–184, 192, 198, 200–201, 206, 209, 213, 221, 225–226, 235, 241, 246, 253, 263, 265, 267, 269, 275, 277, 284, 326, 327, 364, 371–374
1944 encounter (age 7), 1, 2, 7, 143, 328, 329, 341
1949 encounter (age 12), 1, 2, 8, 9, 143, 331
1950 encounter (age 13), 1, 2, 9, 13, 142, 143, 332
1955 encounter (age 18), 1, 2, 13
1961 encounter (age 24), 1, 2, 13, 125, 334, 339
1967 encounter (age 30), 1, 2, 3, 4, 11, 14, 18, 42, 69, 182, 201, 328, 334–335, 337, 339, 345
1973 encounter (age 36), 30, 35–51, 87–109, 111–125, 129, 133, 202, 203, 207, 241, 279, 340
1975 encounter (age 38), 126–132, 341–342
1976 encounter (age 39), 130, 131, 132, 133, 137–139, 343
1977 encounter (age 40), 135, 343
1978 encounter (age 41), 152, 153, 154–171, 344–346
1981 encounter (age 44), 153, 348
1982 encounter (age 45), 153, 348
1984 encounter (age 47), 153, 348

1986 encounter (age 49), 152, 153, 172–176, 181, 348
Luca, Bob, xiv, xv, xix, 5, 6, 20, 32, 33, 35, 38, 42, 57, 58, 74, 83, 86, 110, 134, 135, 136, 139, 152, 153, 200, 265, 267, 277, 343, 364
  1944 encounter (age 5), 6, 328, 329
  1967 encounter (age 29), 6, 7, 127, 128, 134, 328
  1978 encounter (age 40), 344–346
  as hypnotist, 20, 31, 58–65, 74–84, 87–109, 111–125, 126–132, 137–139, 144–145, 153, 154–180, 202, 203

MacNeil, Roderick, 207
Manchester, MA, 268, 322
Manhattan Project, 330
Mars (planet), 196, 338
Massachusetts, 3, 241
Massachusetts Institute of Technology (M.I.T.), 187, 188
Max, Fred, xiv, 6, 52, 53, 55, 57, 58, 127, 142, 174
  as hypnotist, 1, 2, 6–14, 17, 18–34, 38–51, 52–55, 143, 144, 173, 213
McCarthy, Eugene, 335
Mead, Margaret, 192, 193, 194, 214, 376
Melchizedek Connection, The, 376
Meriden, CT, 6, 153, 156, 172, 328, 344–345
Mexico, 209
Minnesota, 230
Minutemen (missile), 341, 342
molecular displacement, 184
Monroe, Robert A., 141–142, 190, 376
Monuments of Mars, The, 339, 350, 376

Moody, Raymond A., 152, 191, 376
Mount Desert Island, ME, 277
MUFON UFO Journal, 151, 215, 238, 376, 377
mutilations, animal, 230, 231
Mutual UFO Network (MUFON), ix, 41, 84, 95, 120, 151, 221, 231, 237, 238, 241, 286, 364

National Aeronautics and Space Administration (NASA), 187, 188, 190, 196, 197, 252, 338
National Investigations Committee on Aerial Phenomena (NICAP), 67, 230, 337
National Opinion Research Council (NORC), 183
Neal, Richard M., xiv, 221, 231, 232, 233, 234, 235, 236, 237, 238, 265, 266, 267, 268, 270, 271, 284, 285, 329, 333, 337, 349, 350, 376
Near Death Experience (NDE), 148, 149, 150, 151, 152, 344–345, 347, 349, 355
neoteny, 222, 223, 225, 227
New Haven, CT, 135
New Mexico, 331
nephilum, the, 211, 214
New Scientists, The (magazine), xviii
Newsweek (magazine), 330
1984: Spring—A Choice of Futures, 215, 375
Nixon, Richard, 335
Nobel prize, 228
Nyman, Joseph, xiv, 364–370, 376

Oberg, James, 196, 215, 376
obstetrics-gynecology, 51, 52, 231, 237
Odom, Charles, 70
Ohio, 67, 188
Olavarria, Argentina, 71, 72
O'Leary, Brian, 338

One, the, 10, 11, 110, 143–150, 329, 331–333, 344, 345, 346

Other Worlds, 191, 375

Out-of-the-Body Experience (OBE), xxiii, 11, 16, 115, 116, 141–143, 147, 148, 149, 150, 151, 152, 153, 154, 155, 171, 172, 174, 183, 190, 198, 210, 249, 277, 344, 346, 348, 355

ozone, 54

Passport to Magonia, 207, 215, 377

Pease Air Force Base, 275

Pentagon, the, 188–190, 331, 342

Peru, 71, 210

Phenomenon of Man, The, 203, 215, 375

Phoenix, the, 5, 18, 178, 181, 326, 339, 345

Pioneer 11 (Space Mission), 258

Plante, Bethany, 315

Police, 133, 134, 245

Powers, William T., 352, 357, 376

Project *Grudge*, 331

Project *Magnet*, 185

Project *Sign*, 194, 214, 331

Psychiatry and UFO abductees, xx, xxi, xxii, 5, 17, 335, 336, 353, 366

Quazgaa, 19, 201, 340, 341, 347

Rahn, Peter, 208

Recollections of Death—A Medical Investigation, 190, 376

Redbook (magazine), 214, 376

Reflections on Life after Life, 191, 376

religion and UFOs, xiii, xiv, 14, 206, 207, 279, 334, 339, 344, 371–374

Rhine, Mark W., xix, xxi

Rio de Janeiro, Brazil, 212

Rip Van Winkle, 209

robed entities, 151, 152, 226, 228, 229, 278, 279, 347, 349

Rogo, D. Scott, xiv, 203, 204, 215, 375

Sabom, Michael B., 151, 152, 190, 376

Sagan, Carl, 205, 206, 215, 373, 376

Salem Evening News, Salem, MA, 310

Salem, MA, 244, 250, 310

Salem, NH, 280

Samford, Major General, 341

Santorini, Paul, 335

Saturn (planet), 257–259, 297

Saunders, David R., 335, 350, 376

Science (journal), 352, 357, 376

Scientific Study of Unidentified Flying Objects, xxv, 375

Second Coming of Christ (*See* Religion and UFOs)

Sentinel and Enterprise, Fitchburg—Leominster, MA, 134

Sherman, Irwin W., 350, 377

Sherman, Vilia G., 350, 377

Shklovskii, Iosef S., 205, 215, 376

Sirius Mystery, The, 205, 215, 377

Smith, Wilbert B., 185

Snow White, 262

Sourcebook Project, 230

South Ashburnham, MA, 3, 14, 18, 19, 67, 69, 127, 147, 182, 201, 335, 337

South Berwick, ME, 275, 277

Sprinkle, Leo, xxi, 210

Sputnik, 280, 354

Stafford, Mona, 210

static electricity, 62, 69, 78, 79, 88, 233

Steep Rock, Ontario, Canada, 72

Steep Rock Echo, The, Ontario, Canada, 72–74

Story, Ronald, 238, 377

Strange Harvest (TV Documentary), 230
Strategic Air Command (*See* United States Air Force)
Strieber, Whitley, ix–xiv, 86, 109, 377
Stross, Brian, 209
succubi, 211, 212, 214
Sullivan, Walter, 377
Sumer, 205, 206, 214
Surrey, ME, 274, 277
Swords, Michael D., xiv, 221–225, 238, 377
synchronisms, 135, 241, 249, 251–253, 267, 305, 356

telepathy, xvii, 5, 6, 14, 22, 81, 118, 119, 121, 127, 131, 152, 184, 198, 200, 225, 226, 234
Temple, Robert R. G., 215, 377
Terraforming, 196, 215, 376
Texas, 70
Thomas, Elaine, 210
Tujunga Canyon Contacts, The, 215, 375
Tzeltal Indians, 209

UFO (magazine), 238, 271, 285, 349, 376
UFOs,
  associated *alien instruments*, xvii, xxiv, 5, 10, 12, 230, 232, 235, 333, 337, 340, 367
  associated *amnesia*, xvii, xviii, xx, 5, 6, 7, 14, 125, 128, 130, 132, 138, 180, 201, 207, 234, 235, 260, 291, 295, 296, 306, 321, 331, 335, 339, 356, 370
  associated *effects*, xxii, xxiv, xxv, 54, 68, 89, 95, 96, 97–100, 102, 103, 116, 120, 233, 265–268, 295–297, 298, 310, 319, 320, 322, 323, 324, 326, 346, 352, 355–356, 367
  associated *flight characteristics*, 73–79, 135, 245
  associated *genetics operations*, 26, 47, 48, 198, 213, 227, 329, 333, 337–338, 340, 354, 373
  associated *message*, xvi, 25, 52, 200–201, 326–327, 338–339, 341, 345, 347–349, 352, 354–355, 357
  associated *mind control*, xvii, xviii, 3, 5, 10, 11, 13, 14, 19, 212, 286, 296, 310–313, 325–326, 331, 339, 342
  associated *noise*, 54, 58, 74, 245, 273, 274
  associated *smells*, 54
UFOs: Operation Trojan Horse, 215, 376
UFOs?—Yes!, 335, 350, 376
Union Pacific (movie), 134
United States Air Force (USAF), xix, 4, 68, 95, 128, 187, 188, 190, 193, 194, 197, 199, 240, 245, 280–281, 335, 341, 342, 352
United States Army (USA), 331
United States Coast Guard (USCG), 337
United States House of Representatives (*See* Congress, U.S.)
University of Colorado UFO Study, xix, 335
University of Wyoming, xxi, 210

Valdes, Armando, 210
Vallee, Jacques, xiv, 207–208, 209, 212, 215–216, 377
Vermont, 248
Villa-Boas, Antonio, 211, 212
vivarium, 96, 101, 111, 112, 227

Walton, Travis, 226, 227, 238, 251, 377

Walton Experience, The, 238, 388
Washington, DC, 197
Watson, James, 228
We Are Not Alone, 377
Webb, David, xiv, 241, 253–256,
264, 269, 272, 286, 295–297,
300–326
Wenham, MA, 245, 268, 283, 302,
310, 316, 364
Wentz, Walter, 207, 211

Westminster, MA, 3, 8, 13, 45,
125, 140, 141, 143, 331, 334
Wizard of Oz, The, 110, 249, 261,
262, 307, 320
Wooster, Harold, 199

Zeidman, Jennie, 188, 189, 191,
377